WORD/INFORMATION PROCESSING CONCEPTS

WORD/INFORMATION PROCESSING CONCEPTS

Careers, Technology, And Applications

Marly Bergerud
Cypress College

Jean Gonzalez
Cypress College

John Wiley & Sons
New York   Chichester   Brisbane   Toronto

Cover photographs courtesy of Radio Shack, Division of Tandy Corporation and the National Aeronautics and Space Administration.

Library of Congress Cataloging in Publication Data:

Bergerud, Marly, 1942-
   Word/information processing concepts.

   Includes index.
   1. Word processing (Office practice)
2. Word processing (Office practice) — Case
studies. 3. Word processing equipment.
I. Gonzalez, Jean, 1945-   II. Title.
HF5547.5.B44   651.7   80-22328
ISBN 0-471-08499-9

Printed in the United States of America

10 9 8 7 6 5 4 3 2 1

To my son, Christen, and my dearest friend, Don

To my mother, Bo

Preface

The automated office of the future could exist today. The obstacle to progress lies not in the lack of technology, but in the costs involved in obtaining the technology, reorganizing the office, and getting people to accept change. The only constant in today's office is change. Changes in technology continue to transform and broaden the definition of word processing, so we have used the term "word/information processing" to describe the word processing industry while it is in transition from word processing to information processing. The professional organization International Word Processing Association changed its name in 1981 to International Information/Word Processing Association to reflect this transition.

Often people with expertise in using word/information processing technology are promoted to operative levels of management, with little or no management training. It is not within the scope of this book to provide management training, but Chapters 8 through 11 discuss the concepts that are necessary in managing the change to word/information processing. If employees are to be productive using the new technology, they need to work in an environment planned for their physical and psychological well-being. Also, people who work in this environment need to develop new skills and new attitudes toward their work. We therefore felt it necessary to include a discussion of both the technological and human elements in word/information processing.

A study of the word/information processing industry would not be complete without an insight into actual case studies. Through the cooperation of many organizations, we have been able to provide this insight. These case studies appear in Chapter 12.

As educators, we can do little about technological costs, but we can be instrumental in preparing people for changes that are inevitable in the office. As office technologies develop, these changes must be reflected in office education curricula.

Although the acquisition of equipment is desirable for training people in the area of word processing, it need not prevent the introduction of word/information processing concepts. Concepts can be taught in industry seminars or through existing business education courses such as machine transcription, advanced typing, secretarial procedures, office procedures, business communications, office management, or any other business-related course. With this in mind, we designed our textbook for both the educators who are fortunate enough to be able to restructure their office education curricula to include a course in introduction to word processing and for those who must use the text within existing courses. It can also be used by people in industry who want to gain insight into the total concept of word/information processing. Each chapter is a complete study unit and lends versatility to the way in which the text might be used. The study unit consists of behavioral objectives, a readable text with clearly defined terms, study guide questions, questions on concepts, and a case to check the reader's understanding.

The resource manual contains a detailed lecture outline for instructional use, transparencies, activity questions, cases, additional chapter tests, a final examination, and supplementary instructional aids.

We hope that you will find this text readily adaptable to your needs and an enjoyable reading experience.

Marly Bergerud
Jean Gonzalez

Acknowledgments

Space would not permit us to thank individually all of our colleagues, friends, and family who encouraged and supported us during the writing and preparation of this book. After much deliberation as to whether it would be wise to attempt to single out individual names, we decided to mention some of the people whose contributions most stood out in our memories.

For reviewing our manuscript and contributing excellent critiques or suggestions: Glen L. Boyer, Brigham Young University; Donald Busche, Saddleback College (Main Campus); Eleanor Flanigan, County College of Morris; Cathy Fothergill, Kilgore College; Dr. Leonard Kruk, John Wiley and Sons, Inc.; Joy LeCompte, Cypress College; Marilyn K. Popyk, Henry Ford Community College; Shirley Propes, West Valley Occupational Center; Doris E. Sadovy, San Jose City College; Dorothy Sandburg, First Bank Systems, Inc.; Dr. Harold Smith, Brigham Young University; Marguerite (Mimi) Will, Foothill College; and Shirley Nagg, Rochester Business Institute.

For preparing the manuscript and help in meeting our deadlines: Anita Rogers, who provided the original keyboarding; Gary North, who spent hundreds of hours in revision work; and Patti Claffey, Beverly Lampson, Terri Granados, John Parkson, Linda Parotto, Carol Woodward, Ginger Boles, Barbara Horton, Abel Soto, and Brian Young, who also contributed their time.

For their invaluable information: Dr. Bill Baker, Brigham Young University; Dan Cahil, Interstate Electronics Corporation, a Subsidiary of A-T-O Incorporated; John Connell, Office Research Technology Group; Dan Fink, Interstate Electronics Corporation, a Subsidiary of A-T-O Incorporated; Herbert Kaplan, Dictaphone Corporation; Hugh Tucker, Interstate Electronics Corporation, a Subsidiary of A-T-O Incorporated; Fred Oehlert, Dictaphone Corporation; Joan Rilje, California Vision Service Plan; Bob Rosek, Stenograph Corporation; Tom Vandermeyden, Automatic Word Processors.

The following people provided original material that appears in the text:
For writing and contributing Chapter 11, Don Hucker, Professor at Cypress College and management consultant.
For applications: Frances Ashbaugh, Information Systems Center, Rockwell International; Gary North, Automatic Word Processors; and Vivian Oldfield, Energy Systems Group, Rockwell International.
For industry case studies: Stephanie Ferguson, Institute for Medical Research; Jane Hruska and Peggy J. Rogers, Arent, Fox, Kintner, Plotkin, and Kahn; Sally L. Kwasigroch, MONY, The Mutual Life Insurance Company of New York; Sally Lyons and Deb Prikl, Sambo's Restaurants, Incorporated; Frank Malone,

United States Nuclear Regulatory Commission; Doreen Nolan, Sierra Research Corporation; Dana R. Oliver, Hanes Knitwear; John Preston, Olivetti Corporation, Marlene Riggs, Lincoln General Hospital; Barbara Rochette, Kwasha Lipton Consulting Actuaries and Employee Benefit Services; Phillip Russell, Sundstrand Corporation; and Dorothy Swegal, CoverGirl Temporary Office Personnel, Incorporated.

We would like to extend a special thanks to Gary North, whose technical knowledge, editing in the many revisions of the manuscript, and constant assistance was invaluable.

I, Marly Bergerud, want to thank my family, Connie and John Friel, Sharon and Stan Schuricht, and my parents, Florence and Winnie Balsukot, for the interest they showed in my work. I particularly want to thank Don Hucker for his constant encouragement, guidance, contribution to the text, and assistance in editing. And Christen Erik Bergerud, my son, I thank for his patience and I hope that someday he will realize the importance of this endeavor and the enrichment that it has brought to my life.

I, Jean Gonzalez, want to thank my family, Augustus Pethrosavage, my father; Vicki and Bob Cunningham, Mary and Chris Pfeiffer, and Jacqueline Dippel for their enthusiasm and interest; and my friends David Kennedy, Carolee Freer, and Charlene Schick for their understanding.

To anyone we might have missed and to anyone along the way who made our task a little easier, we offer our sincere thanks.

M.B.
J.G.

Contents

Chapter 12   Industry Case Studies   324

Glossary   357

Answers to Chapter Study Guide Questions   380

Index   384

WORD/INFORMATION PROCESSING CONCEPTS

PART 1

INTRODUCTION TO WORD/INFORMATION PROCESSING

When you read a newspaper today, you can easily get the impression that there are worldwide shortages of nearly everything. You read about an energy crisis, a food crisis, a water crisis, or a housing crisis, all caused by vanishing resources. A resource that is creating a very different type of crisis is information. Businesses need to acquire information for a variety of reasons. Organizations acquire and generate hundreds of documents to meet various government regulations and so that management can assess progress in meeting customers' demands, determine their competitive position, help develop new products or areas of service, and for numerous other reasons. Where information is concerned, there has been uncontrolled growth rather than a shortage. Nearly 75% of all the information available to humankind has been created since the early 1960s. Millions of pieces of information are recorded daily, and the total amount is doubling nearly every six years.[1]

Uncontrolled growth in information

The problem faced during any crisis is one of management. As our supplies of fuel and water decrease, we have to learn how to make the most of what remains. As our supplies of information increase, we have to learn to organize it to get the best use from an overabundant supply.

Organizations receive billions of new pieces of information daily. They have to gather it, change it, send it, store it, and find it when they need it. To keep from being overwhelmed by information, some organizations use word processing: a way in which people make better use of information through improved procedures and modern equipment. Word processing enables us to store recorded information so that we can retrieve it at a later date.

Word processing to organize information

Part I describes the industry of word processing and how it fits into the total picture of moving and handling information. Part I also details new careers created by the growth of word processing and the changes it has created in the office, resulting in improved efficiency and productivity.

[1]John J. Connell, "Office of the 80s," *Business Week*, February 15, 1980, p. 20.

CHAPTER 1

Word and Information Processing: Development, Careers, and Technologies

The objectives of this chapter are to:

1. Define information and information processing.

2. List the steps in the document cycle.

3. Define word processing and explain its origins.

4. Contrast the traditional office with today's office.

5. List some of the reasons why more efficient office procedures and updated equipment are needed in today's office.

6. List the major parts of a word processing system.

7. List the main reasons for the growing utilization of word processing.

8. Summarize the benefits of word processing for the secretary, the manager, and the organization.

9. Describe how several industries use automated equipment.

10. Identify a number of career opportunities available as a result of information processing.

11. Identify the new technologies associated with the steps of the document cycle.

Automation has been used for years in such areas as agriculture and industry; today, automation is being used in the office. The technology that made the first impact on office productivity was word processing. This chapter describes what word processing is and how it has affected office operations. It also describes how other new technologies are gaining acceptance. The term "word processing" only applies to a small segment of the total picture of information processing. Since many offices are in a transitional stage—some using word processing equipment and some using equipment with greater capabilities—the term **word/information processing** more appropriately encompasses the new technologies available today. This chapter describes the history of word processing and the move toward information processing.

For many decades, equipment has been used to increase productivity. Using equipment for this purpose is known as **automation.** In the past, automation was limited to agriculture and industry. Farmers used tractors to increase their crop production; automation contributed in great measure to the agricultural revolution. Factory workers using automated equipment were able to produce more goods; automation applied to factory work helped create an industrial revolution.

Agricultural and industrial revolution

Today, many observers point out that each farm worker is supported by $70,000 worth of equipment and each factory worker by $35,000 worth of equipment, yet office workers until recently have been supported by only $2,000 to $4,000.[2] The reason organizations spent so little money on office automation is that they have considered the office as a service center not directly related to producing goods for profit. Therefore, management has found it very difficult to justify spending money for equipment to increase office productivity. Older types of office equipment such as electric typewriters, early calculators, and dictation equipment have had little effect on automating the office. Only since the early 1960s have managers recognized the importance of new office automation technology and begun to automate the office.

The office is a service center

The highest labor costs in business today are found in the office. Office salaries are rising 12% to 15% per year and will double over the next six years.[3] Approximately 75% of office costs are related to labor, and every new wage increase and fringe benefit program for workers increases labor costs.[4] The need to increase productivity and reduce office costs has become more and more important to management. In response to this need, automation in the office is creating a revolution in the way in which we handle and process information.

Office labor costs are high

What Is Information?

Information is words, symbols, or numbers — in written or unwritten form — that are used to express an idea. **Information processing** is the movement of these words, symbols, or numbers from the origination of an idea to its final destination. Everyone moves information in one way or another whether that person is a student, a housewife, a scientist, or a business executive.

Information processing

You can probably remember the last time you prepared a report. First, you researched several articles, extracted the information you needed, and made a few pages of notes in longhand. Later, you gathered your notes, typed the final copy, and made a copy for yourself. The next day, you delivered the original (Figure 1.1). Preparing your report was a type of information processing that could have been greatly speeded up and simplified through the use of automation. Your report is only one of a number of types of paperwork referred to as **documents.** Other types of documents are letters, forms, proposals, and invoices. As you wrote this report, you were moving information through a number of steps in what is called the **document cycle**: origination, production,

The document cycle

[2]Ibid. p. 24.
[3]Ibid, p. 19.
[4]Ibid. p. 22.

4

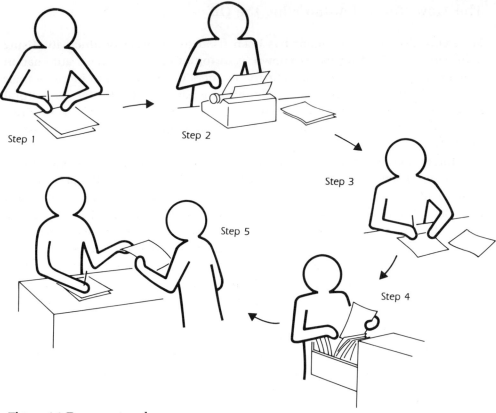

Figure 1.1 Document cycle.

reproduction, filing, storage and retrieval, and distribution. You *originated* the document, *produced* the document, *reproduced* a copy of it, *filed* a copy for later use, and *distributed* the original copy.

What Word Processing Is All About

Preparing your own report

Don't you wish that producing a report were as easy as we made it sound? It was probably far more complicated and time-consuming. You set out to prepare your report by researching several articles. You jotted down a few pages of long-hand notes, gathered your ideas, typed a rough draft, made revisions, retyped your rough draft several times, and finally got your ideas together.

Type

Next, you started on your final copy. You put a clean sheet of paper in your typewriter and began. Two lines down the page, you made an error, so you put in a new sheet of paper and started again. The second time you forgot to come down enough lines, so you ripped out that sheet and started over. Finally, you were off and typing 60 words a minute—until you made a mistake. Then you carefully corrected your error and once again began to type, but more slowly, so you could determine where to place your footnotes. Ten hours later, you were finished. Too exhausted to proofread your final copy, you asked a friend to do it for you. Your friend found two spelling errors right in the middle of page 3. What did you do then? You retyped that page. Sound familiar? (See Figure 1.2)

Retype

Retype again

Wouldn't it be great to be able to make a rough draft of your entire paper,

You set out to do your ~~first~~ ~~last~~ report by researching several articles. You then took a few pages of longhand notes, gathered your ideas typed your rough draft, made revisions, ~~corrected~~ retyped your rough draft many times ~~before you~~ and finally got your ideas together.

Rough draft

Next, it was time to start your final copy. You quickely

Final: First attempt

The second time you forgot to come down enough spaces, so you ripped out that sheet and started over. Finally you were off and typing 60 words a minute and going well until you made a mistake. Then you carefully corrected your mistake and once again began to type, but this time slower so that you could determine where to place your footnotes.

Final: Second attempt

Ten hours later, you finished. Too exhausted to proofread your final copy, you asked someone to do it for you. That person found (spelligerrors) right in the (middel) of page 3. What did you do then? You typed page 3 over. Sound familiar?

You thought you
were finished

Figure 1.2 Wouldn't it be great to be able to rough-draft your entire paper and retype only your changes?

What Word Processing Is All About

retyping only the changes (insertions or deletions) you make instead of retyping each page many times? Developments in modern dictation and typing equipment have made this possible. Today's equipment helps to create a faster, more efficient, more economical method of document production. Through the use of word processing, the document cycle remains the same but new equipment changes the way the document is handled. If you make errors or revisions, the entire document does not have to be retyped.

The steps you took to produce your report are similar to the steps that occur in producing a document in a traditional office. In such an office, the people involved are usually referred to as the boss and the secretary. In the traditional office, the following steps are taken to produce a document.

Steps to produce a document

Step 1. The boss originates correspondence.
Step 2. The secretary types the correspondence and returns it for the boss's signature or for revisions.
Step 3. The secretary makes a copy for the file.
Step 4. The secretary files a copy for future reference.
Step 5. The secretary sends out the original copy.

These steps are referred to as the **workflow** of the document.

Workflow

Using proper methods and procedures to move the document through the various stages of workflow is an important consideration in word processing (see Chapter 9). Now, however, let's look at step 2, production of the document. This step in the document cycle was the first to be affected by word processing, and has changed tremendously over the centuries.

The Origins of Word Processing

Capturing the word

Throughout the centuries, people have used various tools to help us process information. What has changed is the methods and tools used to handle the information. In early Babylonian days, information was recorded on clay tablets. Later, the quill pen was used to write words on paper and was a big improvement over chisels used to cut letters into stone. Word processing began with the first attempts at providing a record of our words. Today, highly sophisticated equipment is used to record ideas in printed form.

Attempts at producing words in recorded form resulted in inventions that brought about easier ways of recording ideas. One attempt succeeded in recording the spoken word; other attempts produced such inventions as the printing press and the typewriter. All of these made recording ideas in printed form much easier.

Form letters

The typewriter can produce original documents one at a time, but offices sometimes need to produce hundreds of original-looking documents daily. To meet this need, businesses have had to resort to **form letters.** In a form letter, the body of the letter is printed but the secretary types in the name and address; often such a letter does not look professional. For example, the secretary might type the name and address in a different type style than that which was used to type the letter (Figure 1.3). If the paper is not inserted correctly when

Patti-Ruth Originals

378 CAROLET LANE, ORANGE, CA. 92669
TELEPHONE: (714) 639-7991

April 11, 1980

Mrs. James Cornell
3434 Clybourn Avenue
North Hollywood, CA 91607

Amount Due $150.00
Date Due April 26, 1980

Dear Friend:

We are writing because our good customers like you
generally like to be reminded if they have overlooked
a payment.

Your account is overdue, but you can easily take
care of this matter by sending your check in the
envelope we have enclosed.

Sincerely yours,

Collection Department

Figure 1.3 Form letter.

typing the name and address, the margins are uneven.

In the early 1900s, equipment manufacturers looked at the volume of letters that organizations sent out and developed a typewriter that could type out many original letters after a master had been typed once. This typewriter was

Figure 1.4 Magnetic Tape Selectric Typewriter (MT/ST). *Courtesy of International Business Machines Corporation.)*

Recording typewritten letters

able to mechanically "play back" a number of letters in the same way that a player piano could play a tune. But the technology did not end there. In 1964, International Business Machines (IBM) introduced the Magnetic Tape Selectric Typewriter (MT/ST), adding another dimension to what a typewriter could do. This machine, called a "text editor" by some, allowed the secretary to not only play back documents repetitively but also to edit documents by adding or deleting paragraphs and rearranging margins. (See Figure 1.4.) The magnetic tape, similar to that used in a home tape recorder, captures keystrokes the way that tape captures your voice. The magnetic tape on the MT/ST makes it possible not only to record a document and play it back but to make changes in the document.

Type only revisions

Using an MT/ST or a similar text-editing typewriter, you could have recorded the entire rough draft of your report as you typed it. After you proofread your copy, you could have played back the tape and made revisions or corrections without retyping the entire document.

How The Term "Word Processing" Originated

The MT/ST helped in preparing reports and other documents, but organizations that obtained the equipment often did not have trained persons to operate it or the know-how to apply the capabilities of the equipment properly. Consequently, this expensive piece of equipment often sat, unused, in a remote corner. Furthermore, the typical office setup, utilizing clerical workers in an unspecialized way, was not always the most efficient way of organizing people.

The manufacturer of the MT/ST soon realized the problem and introduced the concept of work specialization. The tasks of the traditional secretary were divided into typing functions and nontyping functions. The people who performed the typing could then be trained as specialists who would understand the capabilities of the machine and apply those capabilities to best serve the organization.

Administrative secretary

The persons trained to use the equipment came to be known as **correspondence secretaries.** The persons trained in nontyping or administrative duties became known as **administrative secretaries** (Figure 1.5). They were taught to assist with management reports, file documents, plan itineraries, compose letters, etc. When IBM started promoting the concept of work specialization to organizations using the MT/ST, it noted that the automated typewriter was doing for words and numbers in office paperwork what data processing was doing for the accumulation of numeric data. Therefore, the concept was called "word processing."

The office, however, was still in a state of chaos. People did their jobs with few guidelines. To change this, standard procedures had to be developed. Equipment could be used more efficiently when standard procedures were followed. For example, if all letters are typed in full-block form with all lines beginning at the left margin, secretaries can type letters faster and all correspondence looks uniform (see Figure 1.6).

Correspondence secretary

Standard procedures alone were not sufficient to end the chaos in the office. Office functions were viewed as a whole to determine how to increase efficiency. The origination, production, reproduction, filing, storage, retrieval, and final disposal of files were considered along with the resources that were available: people, information, equipment, and procedures. Viewing these parts to see how they can interact for the good of the whole is called the **systems approach.** As a result of utilizing the systems approach, the word processing concept expanded into a managed system of handling equipment, procedures, and people.

Figure 1.5 The tasks of the traditional secretary were divided into administrative and correspondence functions.

The Core of a System

All systems have certain identifiable parts. They include:

Input. What the system works with—the source of information.
Processing. Changes the input undergoes that result in the final product.
Output. What the system produces—the final product or end result.
Control. Standardization of work and measurement of results.
Feedback. Information that tells whether the expected results have been obtained.

Parts of a system

In the **word processing system** (Figure 1.7), the **input** is the information going into the system. For example, a manager answers a letter responding to a

Input

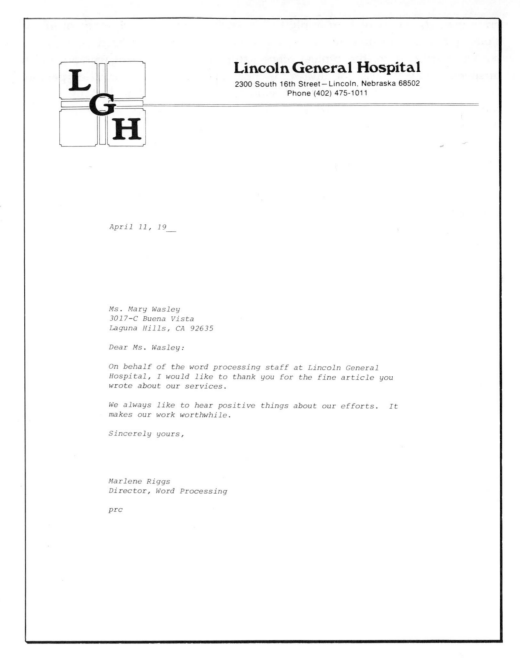

Lincoln General Hospital
2300 South 16th Street — Lincoln, Nebraska 68502
Phone (402) 475-1011

April 11, 19__

Ms. Mary Wasley
3017-C Buena Vista
Laguna Hills, CA 92635

Dear Ms. Wasley:

On behalf of the word processing staff at Lincoln General
Hospital, I would like to thank you for the fine article you
wrote about our services.

We always like to hear positive things about our efforts. It
makes our work worthwhile.

Sincerely yours,

Marlene Riggs
Director, Word Processing

prc

Figure 1.6 Standard formats are used for efficiency.

customer's request. The words used in the response become the input to the word processing system. (Chapter 2 describes the word processing equipment that made it easier and more economical to input words.)

The **processing** of information occurs on automated equipment. For example, when the secretary types the response made by the manager to the customer's request, the processing occurs as the secretary types. The secretary is transforming information into a typewritten form. The **output** is the finalized document. (Chapter 4 describes the various types of automated equipment that caused the volume and quality of paperwork to increase significantly.)

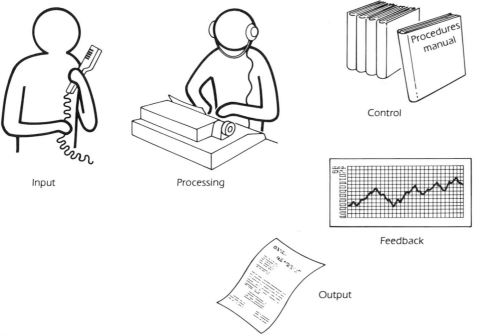

Figure 1.7 A systems model.

The last two parts in the word processing system, **control** and **feedback**, caused a considerable change to take place in the office. Offices were not used to controls. These elements were associated with factories and other production areas of the organization, but not the office. Word processing systems introduce controls to the office. Standardizing work is one form of control. The manager, for example, can be assured that all letters sent to customers will be set up in the same manner regardless of who types the letter, if guidelines are established for document appearance. Another form of control is the supervision of all secretarial activities. In offices where secretaries are properly supervised, they receive more even workloads and work that is distributed among many secretaries can be done faster.

Controls in the office

Measuring the amount of work that is produced also is a form of control. Often, work is measured by the number of lines or pages a secretary produces in a day. The production records provide feedback, and the feedback from these records reveals whether the results of word processing are as expected. For example, a manager might plan to be able to produce 150 documents a day using word processing. By keeping production records measuring the work produced, the manager can determine if that goal is being achieved. Such records provide information for future decisions on what new equipment to acquire and how many people to hire.

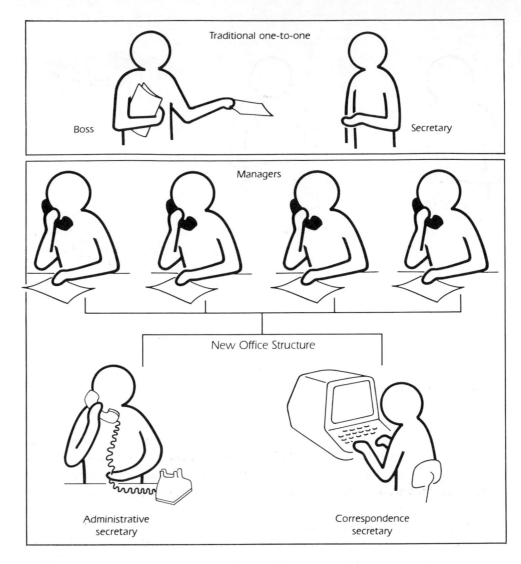

Figure 1.8 Comparison of the traditional office and the new office structure.

How Word Processing Affects the Traditional Office

The systems approach calls for a change in the **traditional office structure.** The standard **one-to-one relationship** (one boss to one secretary) is replaced by another office structure. Secretaries might not do all the typing and nontyping tasks for one boss, but might work for many people (see Figure 1.8). Because the secretary's work comes from several different sources, a supervisory person is needed to distribute the work evenly, to be responsible for the work getting done, and to provide reports to management on how well the system is working. This new position provides secretaries with promotional opportunities (referred to as career paths) that were previously nonexistent.

Reorganization changes tasks and creates career paths

Also, with this reorganization, the secretary now has a job with clearly defined responsibilities, knows what tasks the job entails, and has a career path to follow in the organization. Since the secretary no longer works for one boss, the secretary's loyalty is to the organization instead of to one person.

The reorganization of staff also results in a change in the physical appearance of the office. Since a secretary no longer works for one person, there is no reason to be stationed outside the boss's door and secretaries are often grouped together in open areas. Equipment and decor have changed to adapt to the open office atmosphere.

When word processing systems were first created, the emphasis was upon establishing totally **centralized services.** Most word processing administrative (nontyping) tasks and correspondence (typing) tasks were grouped together in one area called a **center** (Figure 1.9). The emphasis was on producing great volumes of clerical work such as letters, memos, reports, and proposals.

Centralized services

The use of automated typing equipment in the centers greatly increased output, but the need for a more efficient method of input was soon recognized. Dictation equipment, therefore, came into use.

Meanwhile, the entire centralized approach came under scrutiny. Although the center worked out very well in some cases, the totally centralized concept was not the best method for all organizations so several alternative systems developed. The varied systems provide organizations with the opportunity to design a system to fit their particular needs. The systems in existence today range from totally centralized administrative and correspondence centers to small clusters of office workers called **work groups.**

Alternative systems

The early focus of word processing was on the equipment and the increased production of office documents so as to free secretaries from repetitious

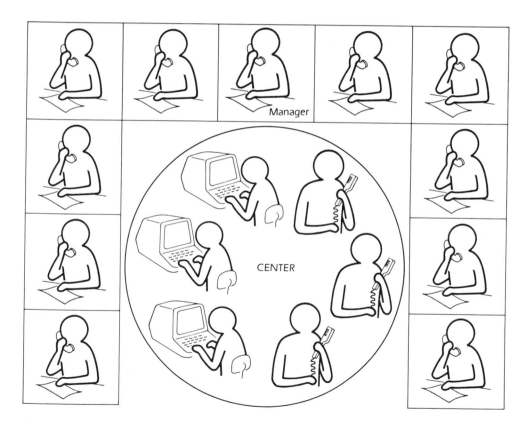

Figure 1.9 A word processing center.

tasks and allow them to assume more managerial responsibilities. Secretaries who were relieved of typing responsibilities could do some of the tasks formerly done by their bosses. They could compile reports, prepare audio-visuals for presentations, and compose letters and memos. The concern in word processing gradually began to shift to finding better and faster means of distributing the processed information. You will see in Chapters 3 through 7 how technology brought about new developments in storage, retrieval, and distribution of processed information to take advantage of the savings in time and money caused by word processing.

New developments

Who Benefits from Word Processing

Career benefits

Secretaries. Clearly, the secretary gains some important career opportunities from an office reorganization. The secretary with good skills and abilities has more opportunity for advancement. No longer should the success or failure, status or lack of status of a manager determine his or her secretary's position. New positions created by office reorganization turn a dead-end job with little or no potential for career advancement into one with a career path leading toward management.

Immediate benefits for the secretary

The immediate benefits for the secretary result from using the word processing equipment to reduce some of the daily annoyances that secretaries face. Secretaries spend their days trying to produce error-free copies while typing at an even pace. Often they type a letter straight through, only to find a word omitted in the second paragraph. Frequently they complete a letter and are asked to revise one of the paragraphs because the boss was misinformed about certain statistics or wants to add a paragraph. They spend hours retyping a long monthly statistical report when only a few minor changes from the previous month are needed. Much of their work becomes monotonous; they may type the same letter to different people so many times that they memorize it.

Word processing equipment relieves the boredom of repetitive typing, thus making the production of such documents less tedious. It makes the job of correcting and revising long documents easier and less time-consuming. Word processing equipment frees secretaries to do other, more creative, work within the organization.

Immediate benefits for the manager

Managers. The immediate benefit for managers is that the new office reorganization not only speeds up their paperwork process, but also provides them with an administrative assistant to ease some of the burden of their administrative responsibilities. Many administrative assistants handle much of the detail work for managers. It also helps to relieve some of the daily annoyances they experience. For example, managers often need administrative support help in areas other than typing. They would like to delegate additional responsibilities, but their secretaries are often too busy with their typing workload to be able to accept them. Managers are often forced to hire temporary help to get large volumes of typing done in short periods of time. At other times, employee vacations or illnesses have forced managers to look for temporary help. Much of their time is spent having to wait for needed documents and end-of-the-month

Figure 1.10 Word processing benefits secretaries, managers, and the organization. The IBM 5520 Administrative System is an aid to the office. *(Courtesy of International Business Machines Corporation, General Systems Division.)*

reports simply because the daily workload keeps their secretaries busy. Managers often wait to dictate an important letter because their secretaries are on vacation, attending seminars, busy with other work, or absent.

Word processing equipment enables the managers to use their time more efficiently to become more productive. It provides them with additional administrative support if they need it. Word processing equipment enables managers to carry on during rush periods, employee turnover, absences, and vacations. It provides managers with high-quality professional clerical work.

The Organization. Organizations must face the tremendous problem of dealing with increased paperwork and the cost of additional personnel necessary to handle the expanded workload. Clerical costs represent approximately 27% of total office costs and the remaining 73% represents the costs of managers, professionals, and other workers.[5] As these figures continue to rise, they add to the cost of producing paperwork.

Word processing checks office costs

Word processing has helped to check some of these rising costs. It has done this by reorganizing the office and dividing the secretary's job into two separate positions to create specialists. Secretarial services are supervised, so the specialists can be made accountable for the quality of work they do and the amount they produce. The work can be measured and the results given to management to help justify the cost of equipment. Management personnel, whose salaries make up the greatest percentage of office costs, can become more productive because they have better secretarial support. Word processing, therefore, allows the organization to utilize properly its most important resource — people. In addition to cost savings, the organization derives other benefits. By providing people with more creative jobs and the equipment necessary to produce higher quality work, the organization is able to service its customers better, maintain good public relations, and present a good image of the organization to the public (see Figure 1.10).

Who Uses Word Processing?

The most recent labor statistics show that office workers represent the second largest employment group in the United States. These statistics also indicate that clerical employment will increase faster than total employment. The chances are that you will be an office worker included in one of these statistics, but even if you are not, you may still use word processing in your home or in whatever career you pursue.

Office workers second largest employment group

How large might the market for word processors become? International Data Corporation (I.D.C.), an independent consulting firm, estimates the market might reach $4.2 billion in the United States by 1984, up from only $780 million in 1978 — an average annual growth rate of 32%.[6] Much of the excitement and optimism is based on the projected demand for information processing by managers who are eager to boost the productivity of secretaries and typists. Professionals whose jobs require a good deal of writing are anxiously awaiting new devices that will help to more easily perform their jobs.

Customers for the new electronic equipment include law firms, publishing companies, brokerage houses, government agencies, hospitals, and insurance companies — all organizations that turn out a large number of reports and other written material.

[5]Ibid.

[6]"Business Communications Alternatives for the Eighties," International Data Corp., Supplement to *Fortune*, December 14, 1979.

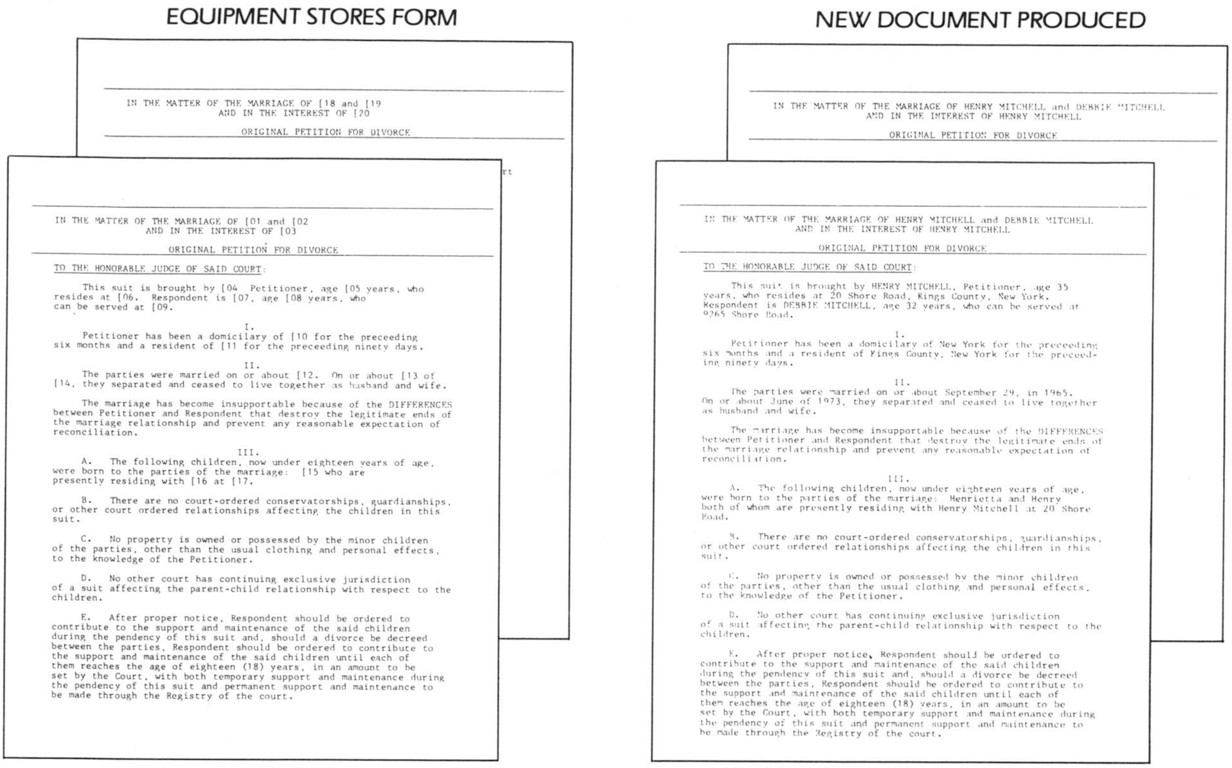

EQUIPMENT STORES FORM

IN THE MATTER OF THE MARRIAGE OF [18 and [19
AND IN THE INTEREST OF [20

ORIGINAL PETITION FOR DIVORCE

IN THE MATTER OF THE MARRIAGE OF [01 and [02
AND IN THE INTEREST OF [03

ORIGINAL PETITION FOR DIVORCE

TO THE HONORABLE JUDGE OF SAID COURT:

This suit is brought by [04 Petitioner, age [05 years, who resides at [06. Respondent is [07, age [08 years, who can be served at [09.

I.

Petitioner has been a domicilary of [10 for the preceeding six months and a resident of [11 for the preceeding ninety days.

II.

The parties were married on or about [12. On or about [13 of [14, they separated and ceased to live together as husband and wife.

The marriage has become insupportable because of the DIFFERENCES between Petitioner and Respondent that destroy the legitimate ends of the marriage relationship and prevent any reasonable expectation of reconciliation.

III.

A. The following children, now under eighteen years of age, were born to the parties of the marriage: [15 who are presently residing with [16 at [17.

B. There are no court-ordered conservatorships, guardianships, or other court ordered relationships affecting the children in this suit.

C. No property is owned or possessed by the minor children of the parties, other than the usual clothing and personal effects, to the knowledge of the Petitioner.

D. No other court has continuing exclusive jurisdiction of a suit affecting the parent-child relationship with respect to the children.

E. After proper notice, Respondent should be ordered to contribute to the support and maintenance of the said children during the pendency of this suit and, should a divorce be decreed between the parties, Respondent should be ordered to contribute to the support and maintenance of the said children until each of them reaches the age of eighteen (18) years, in an amount to be set by the Court, with both temporary support and maintenance during the pendency of this suit and permanent support and maintenance to be made through the Registry of the court.

NEW DOCUMENT PRODUCED

IN THE MATTER OF THE MARRIAGE OF HENRY MITCHELL and DEBBIE MITCHELL
AND IN THE INTEREST OF HENRY MITCHELL

ORIGINAL PETITION FOR DIVORCE

IN THE MATTER OF THE MARRIAGE OF HENRY MITCHELL and DEBBIE MITCHELL
AND IN THE INTEREST OF HENRY MITCHELL

ORIGINAL PETITION FOR DIVORCE

TO THE HONORABLE JUDGE OF SAID COURT:

This suit is brought by HENRY MITCHELL, Petitioner, age 35 years, who resides at 20 Shore Road, Kings County, New York. Respondent is DEBBIE MITCHELL, age 32 years, who can be served at 9265 Shore Road.

I.

Petitioner has been a domicilary of New York for the preceeding six months and a resident of Kings County, New York for the preceeding ninety days.

II.

The parties were married on or about September 29, in 1965. On or about June of 1973, they separated and ceased to live together as husband and wife.

The marriage has become insupportable because of the DIFFERENCES between Petitioner and Respondent that destroy the legitimate ends of the marriage relationship and prevent any reasonable expectation of reconciliation.

III.

A. The following children, now under eighteen years of age, were born to the parties of the marriage: Henrietta and Henry both of whom are presently residing with Henry Mitchell at 20 Shore Road.

B. There are no court-ordered conservatorships, guardianships, or other court ordered relationships affecting the children in this suit.

C. No property is owned or possessed by the minor children of the parties, other than the usual clothing and personal effects, to the knowledge of the Petitioner.

D. No other court has continuing exclusive jurisdiction of a suit affecting the parent-child relationship with respect to the children.

E. After proper notice, Respondent should be ordered to contribute to the support and maintenance of the said children during the pendency of this suit and, should a divorce be decreed between the parties, Respondent should be ordered to contribute to the support and maintenance of the said children until each of them reaches the age of eighteen (18) years, in an amount to be set by the Court, with both temporary support and maintenance during the pendency of this suit and permanent support and maintenance to be made through the Registry of the court.

Figure 1.11 The preparation of legal documents is simplified by word processing.

Industry Applications

Word processing is currently used successfully in organizations such as law firms, hospitals, supply companies, government agencies, hotels, health care facilities, insurance companies, and others. In some cases, the equipment described in the following examples does more than edit or revise text and could more accurately be called information processing equipment. In many organizations, word processing equipment is used until it is realized that the needs of the organization go beyond editing and revision. When this happens, equipment with information processing capabilities is added. The case studies in Chapter 12 provide many such examples.

A Law Firm. One of the earliest and largest users of word processing and its related technologies was the law firm. Words are the backbone of the legal profession. The primary product of any law office is not justice, but paperwork. These paper documents are legal, binding documents that must be perfect. The use of very precise language requires revision after revision until a document is finally correct and ready for distribution.

Legal paperwork must be perfect

Many documents produced by law firms are composed of large sections of text that do not change. For example, some contracts change very little. Only names and dates might be changed when a new contract is written. The parts of a document that remain the same can be stored and revised (see Figure 1.11).

Most text in law firms does not change

A law firm may have a center with one or more pieces of automated equipment in operation 24 hours a day producing only one particular type of document. A center that specializes in one type of document or application is called an *application center*. The remaining paperwork may still be done by secretaries in a traditional boss/secretary setting. The attorney's secretary might handle short correspondence that is nonrepetitive and most likely will not be revised. The application center handles the long repetitive documents.

Maintains master files of clients

Olsen and Schuricht, a law firm in Houston, Texas, uses word processing to balance its case loads. The firm maintains master files in its word processing equipment that reflect the client's name, address, telephone number, type of legal proceeding, the attorney assigned to the case, due dates, and total time spent preparing case information. When the partners are considering a new client, conflict-of-interest lists can be prepared to assist them in determining whether they can represent the client. A list can also be prepared indicating the attorney's name, the case load, the amount of time spent handling each case, and the date the attorney's cases appear on the court calendar.

The types of documents processed by this firm on its word processing equipment include wills, contracts, leases, testimonies, security registrations, and agreements.

Government regulations create paperwork

Word processing aids in revision

A Hospital Supply Company. One reason why hospital supply companies use word processing is because of the huge amount of paperwork required by government regulations that govern the industry (see Figures 1.12 and 1.13). For example, Mid-Valley Supply Company, a hospital supply company in Binghamton, New York, has a department that publishes technical specifications for materials and procedures used in the organization's manufacturing plants. The organization has 30,000 specification documents on file each containing an average of three pages. Over 60% of these documents are constantly undergoing revision that, before word processing, would have required retyping from scratch and several proofreadings, even though many of the revisions were only minor.

Word processing increases number of proposals written

A Government Agency. The California State Department of Education, a government agency, provides funds for many projects, such as second career education proposals under the California Employment Training Act. For every project the agency initiates, it produces a large volume of paperwork. Such projects require plans, funding proposals, and grant requests. Follow-up procedures can include verification of fund expenditures and analysis of program effectiveness. One particular agency has increased the number of funding requests it is able to make by using word processing equipment to prepare these documents. The agency is able to store sections of the proposals that remain the same, such as the background statement, target population, and vita of the grant proposers.

Status of facilities must be kept current

A Hotel. Hotels use word processing because the success of their organization depends upon being able to keep their facilities fully occupied. A hotel must verify the availability of rooms and services and respond quickly to requests for information. The Clarence Parker Hotel in Memphis, Tennessee, is a hotel that has facilities for executive meetings, conferences, banquets, political rallies, and union arbitration meetings. Since its guests frequently inquired about the availability of secretarial services, the hotel decided to provide these services. Now guests are able to pick up their room telephone at any hour of the day or night

Figure 1.12 Hospital supply companies use word processing. *(Courtesy of Ames Color-File Corporation)*

Figure 1.13 Huge amounts of paperwork are created by government regulations. *(Courtesy of Bankers Box/Records Storage Systems)*

Figure 1.14 Hotels use word/information processors such as the Monotype HS/80 hotel reservation and guest accounting system. *(Courtesy of Monotype Communications Limited.)*

and dictate material that will be prepared for them by the hotel's word processing center the following day. The center is often requested to handle minutes, agendas, and material for distribution at meetings.

An important part of the success of this hotel depends upon its ability to keep its facilities occupied at all times, and the word processing center supports the sales staff in this effort. A list of all those who use the facilities is kept up to date. When the hotel expects slack periods, the sales staff sends past customers brochures advertising special rates. The sales staff provides complete and rapid followup with confirmation letters for reservations and proposals concerning requested rooms, seating arrangements, and other accommodations.

A Health Care Facility. Many administrative functions in hospitals are supported by word processing. These functions include appointments, billings, medical records, and communications. A patient's medical, legal, and financial status must be immediately documented and distributed to various locations in the hospital.

Patient's medical status is immediately documented

The documents produced in hospitals require procedures different from those in other industries. The reason for this is that many documents are final as written and become part of a patient's medical file, with revisions by the doctor rarely necessary. In the health care industry, it is difficult to standardize many medical descriptions or examinations. One way this has been accomplished, however, is to store a standardized examination report — called a "normal" — for each medical processing specialty. The doctor then simply dictates any sections of the report needed for an "abnormal" patient condition, and the rest of the document is filled in by the standardized material.

Financial and statistical reports, special projects, public relations brochures, professional papers prepared by the staff, newsletters, press releases, and government and insurance reports are all part of the application of word processing to the health care industry.

Word processing tracks data

In Cunningham Hospital in Grand Forks, North Dakota, a pathologist uses word processing equipment to track data to determine whether there is a relationship between age, sex, or race and a particular disease. Using codes to identify these characteristics, all reports are filed including information on the patient's name, age, race, sex, and history of treatment. This information can then be sorted, selected, and analyzed. This capability of the word processing equipment assists the pathologist in finding trends in illnesses and developing generic classifications.

An Insurance Company. Insurance companies frequently use word processing equipment because of the tremendous amount of paperwork that is exchanged between them and their clients. For example, when a client purchases automobile insurance, he or she must fill out an application. The application is then sent to the underwriting department for approval. In the meantime, the underwriting department issues an insurance binder which serves as a temporary policy until the actual policy is issued. When the company issues the policy, they also send a "new client" letter. Other correspondence between the customer and the company might include letters sent to remind the client to pay insurance premiums and notices to the client of changes in amounts of

High volume of paperwork

Figure 1.15 Master file list of clients.

Figure 1.18 A form letter used to solicit new business.

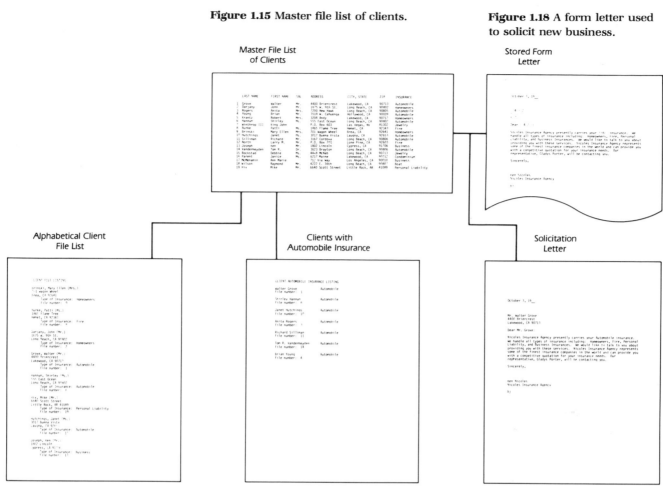

Figure 1.16 Client file listing printed alphabetically.

Figure 1.17 List of clients who have automobile insurance.

Figure 1.19 Form letter (Figure 1.18) combined with the name and address of a client from the master file list (Figure 1.15).

insurance coverage. The company might also send letters to solicit the customer's personal or home insurance business.

The Nicoles Insurance Agency in Long Beach, California, makes a list of the names and addresses of all its clients and the type of insurance its clients carry (see Figure 1.15). The company can then automatically get an alphabetic listing of all its customers. This listing shows a file number to reference each client's file stored in the equipment (see Figure 1.16). The company can also get a listing of only the clients who have a certain type of insurance (see Figure 1.17). A form letter such as the one in Figure 1.18 can be sent to each of the clients who appears on this list. Each client's name and address is combined with the form letter to produce a completed letter such as the one in Figure 1.19 that is sent by the agency to solicit new business.

Career Opportunities

The growth of word processing has created many career opportunities in marketing and equipment sales, training, equipment operation, service, systems analysis, management, quality control, and consulting.

Marketing and Sales of Equipment and Supplies

Meet many types of people

Marketing and equipment sales provides good opportunities for people interested in a sales area that has tremendous growth potential. Salespeople come into contact with all types of people: lawyers, doctors, educators, business executives, realtors, airlines personnel. To prepare for this position, you should take courses in marketing and sales and word processing concepts. In some organizations, an A.A. or B.A. degree in marketing or sales is required.

Training

Since information processing is such a new and rapidly expanding field, there are many opportunities to train equipment purchasers and users.

Seminar Leaders. Professionals in the word processing industry provide seminars for people in education, industry, and the business community throughout the United States and abroad. These professionals usually have B.A. or M.A. degrees in business education, business administration, or office occupations.

In-house Training Instructors. Organizations hire people to do nothing but train people in information processing activities. Such training might include the use of dictation equipment and techniques, the use of automated typing equipment, refresher courses in grammar and English skills, and business communications. Usually people hired for these positions have B.A. degrees in business education.

Training Instructors for Vendors. Most vendors train a limited number of people from an organization when it buys equipment. Instructors work either in their own organization's training facility or go out and train people at their place of work. Some of these instructors are called marketing support representatives (MSRs). A marketing support representative serves as a liaison between the organization and the user of the equipment. Initially, the MSR trains some of the people from the organization and then remains on call to handle questions or problems as they arise, suggest new applications, and keep personnel up to date on new equipment. MSRs usually have B.A. degrees in business education or business administration. Courses in speech, marketing, and sales are helpful in preparing for this position.

Writers of training manuals

Organizations employ people to develop machine manuals, audiovisual aids, and other training materials to accompany their equipment. To prepare for this position, you can take courses in English, creative writing, and word/ information processing concepts.

People are needed to perform the initial keyboarding of information (sometimes referred to as text or data entry). Others specialize in performing text-editing functions that differentiate word processing equipment from ordinary typewriters. The level of skill these people possess makes them invaluable, highly-paid employees. Still others become skilled on the equipment used in the reprographics, micrographics, and records processing areas. Courses in English, typing, equipment operation, transcription, and word processing concepts are helpful in preparing you for these positions.

Keyboarding specialists are needed

Service

Organizations must have good equipment servicing because they stand to lose a great deal of time and money if their equipment does not work properly. Service people are needed to go into the organization and repair equipment when and if it breaks down. Courses in electronics and equipment repair are helpful.

Equipment must be kept in working order

Systems Analysis

Systems analysts are trained to understand both the work the organization does and the new information processing technologies. They keep informed of the organization's changing paperwork needs, and based on their knowledge, they recommend the equipment needed to handle the organization's needs and suggest ways existing equipment can be used to greater advantage. Systems analysts often have A.A. or B.A. degrees in word or data processing. Courses in computer programming, word and data processing concepts, and equipment operation are beneficial.

Understanding organization and technologies

Management

Managers and supervisors are needed to oversee the system. They may start as typists entering text or data into a system, become specialists on equipment, move into system analysts positions, and gradually assume a key management position. Or they can be people who are formally educated in management and learn about information processing on the job. Courses in principles of management, human relations, communications, word/information concepts and management, and speech prepare you for a management position.

People must oversee the system

Quality Control

People are needed who have good English, editing, and writing skills to act as composers, editors, and proofreaders. The quality of the final work is only as

Good English, editing, and writing skills needed

good as the skills of the people who prepare it. Often the people who submit work to be done by the automated equipment are not the best writers. Many organizations employ people to help compose documents, edit, and proofread work for errors. To prepare for these positions, you can take courses in English and creative writing. In many organizations, B.A. degrees in English are required.

Consulting

Organizations bring in people to help them decide what aspects of information processing and equipment they need, help them write procedures, sell management on the idea of word processing, and be available to answer questions. These people work for a period of time with one organization then move on to another. Three nationally-known consulting groups are Office Technology Research Group in California; Booz, Allen and Hamilton in New York; and The Yankee Group in Massachusetts. Consultants often have degrees in business administration, data processing, or word processing, and extensive experience in the field.

Many other opportunities exist for you in related fields. If you are knowledgeable in the area of word processing, you might want to consider the following possibilities.

Secretarial service

1. Open a secretarial service and use word processing equipment to speed the flow of paperwork. An example of an agency that specializes in this service is The Paper Factory in Minneapolis, Minnesota.

Write for trade magazine

2. Work for an office products or other trade magazine as a writer on office automation. Trade magazines that hire such writers include *Administrative Management, Word Processing Report, Word Processing Systems,* and *Modern Office Procedures.*

Research and provide trends

3. Work for an organization doing research that provides users with industry trends and the latest information in equipment and procedures. Such organizations include Datapro Research Corporation, Stanford Research Institute, Office Technology Research Group, and Quantum Science.

Temporary service

4. Work for or provide a temporary help service that provides industry with part-time workers trained on word/information processing equipment. An example of one such organization is Kelly Services.

Chapter 10 provides a further breakdown of specific job categories in word processing. A good starting point for many of the careers listed in this section is a degree in word or information processing offered by many colleges (see Figure 1.20).

The Office of the Future

Gains in office productivity are lost if documents are produced rapidly only to be slowed down in the process of distribution. Documents must be distributed

CYPRESS COLLEGE

ASSOCIATE DEGREE AND
PREPARATION FOR EMPLOYMENT

WORD PROCESSING

This curriculum is designed to prepare students to enter the word processing industry in the areas of administrative support, correspondence support, word processing supervision, or any related area in which word processing skills are needed.

Required Courses

Course Number	Course Title	Units
111	Business Communications	3
55	Business English	3
121	Introduction to Word Processing	2
3	Advanced Typing	3
85AB	Keyboarding for Word Processing	2
112	Effective Dictation Procedures	2
86	Managing the Word Processing Center	2
111	Introduction to Data Processing	3
51	Copy Processing/Office Machines	4
269	Office Management	3
49	Office Procedures	4
50	Information Systems/Model Office	4
266	Human Relations in Business	3
52	Records Administration	2
		40

WP 121 INTRODUCTION TO WORD PROCESSING
This course studies the development of today's modern office through the use of automated equipment and trained personnel. Emphasis is placed on the organization of word processing from imput through distribution, equipment available, and roles of participants in word processing systems. Visits to actual word processing installations provide many opportunities for students to learn of current job openings, and new career paths in the field of word processing for men and women.

WP 85 ABCDEF KEYBOARDING FOR WORD PROCESSING   2-2-2 units
A course designed to provide the basic procedures necessary to operate various standalone and shared-logic systmes. A minimum typing speed of 40 words per minute is required and concurrent enrollment in WP 121 is recommended. Enroll for *only* the one hour lecture per week and then on your first day of class pick out your 3 other lab hours.

Mgmt. 112 EFFECTIVE DICTATION PROCEDURES
*Nine week course
A course designed to provide instruction in the use of modern dictation equipment. Emphasis will be placed on employing effective dictation techniques and composing original documents.

WP 86 MANAGING THE WORD PROCESSING CENTER
*Nine week course
This course will appeal to anyone interested in managing a word processing center and those who are already managers. The subject areas to be studied are organizing, implementing, and managing the center and evaluating word processing equipment. A word processing systems study and work measurement methods will be included. Techniques for maximizing human resources will be developed.

Figure 1.20 Word processing curriculum.

rapidly to take advantage of the time and money saved by using word processing equipment. To do this, new technologies have been developed that allow documents to be sent faster than by using the U. S. Postal Service.

Word processing, therefore, is only one of the new technologies that has been developed for the office. In the future, these new technologies will be linked together to make the office a place for managers to obtain and use the information available in the organization through an information network. An information network is a total information system. This system may include voice processing, word and data processing, reprographics, records processing and micrographics, and telecommunications.

Development of an information network

Voice Processing

Voice processing is the term used to describe a system where the human voice is the method of originating information for an information processing system. Machine dictation is a form of voice processing. Talking to a keyboard that responds by performing a keyboard instruction or by typing the spoken words is another more advanced form. Voice processing is discussed in Chapters 2 and 5.

Origination

Word and Data Processing

Word processing and data processing are the two terms associated with the production of information in an information processing system. Word processing refers to the use of automated equipment to produce such things as letters, reports, and other text material. **Data processing** refers to the use of electronic computers to gather, manipulate, summarize, and report on the numbers, statistics, and other data that flow through an organization. The production of information using word and data processing is discussed in Chapters 4, 6, and 7.

Production

Reprographics

Reprographics is the term associated with newer methods of reproducing or duplicating information that may involve a computer. Much of the information managers need must be put in printed form to produce such things as brochures, reports, and booklets. The older methods of reproducing material required that material be retyped to be put into printed form. Reprographics may eliminate the retyping of documents if a link exists between the original typing and the final output. Reprographics is discussed in Chapter 5.

Reproduction

Records Processing and Micrographics

Records processing and **micrographics** are two terms used to describe how information is stored in ways other than in the traditional file cabinet. With records processing, information may never need to be recorded on paper; it can

Records and Storage

be entered into a computer, filed electronically, and retrieved only if needed. Using micrographics, the information is stored on *film*. Micrographics is discussed in Chapter 6.

Telecommunications

Telecommunications describes the electronic method of moving information utilizing telephone lines. Telecommunications is discussed in Chapter 7.

Distribution

In the past, these technologies were not widespread because of their high cost. Today, technological advancements have lowered costs and made an information processing system a reality in the office. Each technology described above has developed as a separate activity with its own manufacturers, its own techniques, and its own vocabulary. Within organizations, these technologies are usually part of separate departments and the idea of developing a coordinated plan for all office functions has only recently been contemplated.

Manufacturers of the new technologies felt that users of automated equipment who were familiar with data processing might be resistant if newly developed office equipment involved computers. People who had used the services of data processing departments may have had some poor experiences. They might have had to wait for materials for long periods of time, or they might not have been able to get timely reports completed because of data processing equipment failure. Therefore, the manufacturers of the new group of technologies for the office have even coined phrases that intentionally avoid any mention of computers. Instead, they developed "office of the future" terminology around two known elements: the typewriter and the telephone. The new technologies on which the office of the future is based, therefore, are word processing (typewriter technology) and telecommunications (telephone technology). However, even a quick look at either of these two areas shows that computers play a significant part in each of them and in most of the new technologies. What the "Office of the Future" really includes is computer systems with powerful capabilities for handling words and numbers.

Yesterday's office has traditionally pigeon-holed each of the technologies into separate, distinctly different departments. Those departments may duplicate the activities of other departments. For example, the accounting department may produce a report that includes statistics the legal department may need. In both departments, the same material has to be typed. When duplication like this occurs, people, equipment, supplies, and information are used inefficiently.

As managers within organizations become aware of the other technologies used in various departments, they realize a need to work toward some common goal. The goal is to make information and technology available to all groups within the organization that duplicate the activities of other departments. That goal can now be met by using the wide range of information processing technology, reorganizing procedures, and effectively using an organization's most important resource: people.

The term "word/information processing" shows the expansion of technology from the traditional word processing concept to a much broader definition encompassing all of the information processing technologies.

Reprographics

Summary

Office costs are rising

Office costs are rising because of the increase in quantities of information office workers must handle. Approximately 75% of these office costs are labor costs. Office automation was developed to decrease office costs and increase office productivity. This development created a revolution in the way in which we handle or process information.

Information processing

Information is words, symbols, or numbers in written or unwritten form used to express an idea. The movement of that information is called information processing. The document cycle represents the steps involved in the movement of information in the workflow of a document. These steps include origination, production, reproduction, filing and storage, and distribution.

Document cycle

Word processing, one of the information processing technologies, began with the first attempt to provide a record of our words. For centuries, people have used various tools to process information, from marking on clay tablets to the very sophisticated equipment used today. In the early 1960s, equipment manufacturers began developing equipment to assist office workers in handling the information overload and increase their productivity. Manufacturers also encouraged the concept of work specialization as an additional means to increase productivity. Since this new equipment was doing for words in office paperwork what data processing had been doing for data or numbers, this concept was called "word processing."

Word processing

This chapter has described the word processing industry: how word processing as an industry began; how the term came about; what a word processing system is; how word processing has affected the traditional office; and how secretaries, managers, and the organization have benefitted from word processing.

Some industries using word processing include law firms, hospital supply companies, government agencies, hotels, health care facilities, and insurance companies.

Users of word processing

A variety of career opportunities now exist in word processing, in the areas of marketing, sales of equipment, training, equipment operation, service, systems analysis, management, quality control, and consulting.

Careers in word processing

Word processing is only one of the new office technologies. Many other technologies have been developed that handle origination, production, reproduction, filing and storage, and distribution of documents. These new technologies make up the different areas of information processing. They include voice processing, word and data processing, reprographics, micrographics and records processing, and telecommunications.

The new technologies

Key Terms

Word processing
Automation
Information
Information processing
Traditional office structure
Document cycle
Input
Processing
Output
Word processing system
Control
Feedback
Centralized services

Systems approach
Storage and retrieval
Data processing
Reprographics
Records processing
Micrographics
Telecommunications
Word/information
   processing
Administrative secretary
Correspondence secretary
Work groups
Work flow
Voice processing

Study Guide

This study guide provides you with feedback to find out how well you are doing. Use a separate sheet of paper to record your answers. When you have finished check your responses with the answers at the back of the book.

Matching: Choose the answer that best defines the word in the left column.

1. Word processing
2. Input
3. Information processing
4. Voice processing
5. MSR
6. Systems analyst
7. An office
8. Output

a. A person who serves as a liaison between the vendor and the user of equipment.

b. A person who recommends to the organization ways to handle changing paperwork needs.

c. The source of information.

d. A method of originating information for an information processing system.

e. The movement of words, symbols, or numbers from the origination of an idea to its final destination.

f. People make better use of information through improved procedures and modern equipment.

g. The final product or end result in written or unwritten form.

h. A place or many places where managers use the information network of the organization.

Multiple choice: Select the letter or letters that best answer each question.

9. Managers recognized the most important way of decreasing office costs was to:
    a. Hire more people
    b. Purchase more automated equipment.
    c. Increase productivity of office workers through automating the office.
    d. Decrease the number of office employees in the organization.

10. Which of the following steps of the document cycle is out of sequence?
    a. Origination
    b. Reproduction
    c. Production
    d. Filing, storage, and retrieval
    e. Distribution

11. Which of the following is not a description of a job responsibility for the new role of administrative secretary?
    a. Typing of long reports
    b. Preparing itineraries
    c. Filing documents
    d. Composing correspondence

12. Until recently, the primary reason for not using the new technologies in the office was that:
    a. Employees were not trained to operate the new office equipment.
    b. The cost of computer technology for the office was too high.
    c. The equipment took up too much space.
    d. None of the above.

13. Word processing is a simple way in which people make better use of information through:
    a. New equipment.
    b. Better trained people.
    c. Improved procedures.
    d. Improved procedures and modern equipment.

Completion: Write the correct answer on a separate sheet of paper.

14. A word processing system is a managed way of handling _____ , _____ , and _____ .

15. The major parts of any system are _____ , _____ , _____ , and _____ .

16. List three of the new technologies:

   _____ , _____ ,
   and_____ .

17. The steps in the document cycle are: _____
   _____ , _____ ,
   _____ , and _____ .

18. Compiling reports, arranging calendars, and answering
    the phone are examples of functions handled by the
    _____ secretary.

True/False: Write + for True, 0 for False for each question.

19. Word processing equipment enables managers to use
    their time more efficiently and become more productive.

20. Standardization of work and measurement of results are
    two forms of control.

21. Organizations face the problem of dealing with in-
    creased paperwork and the cost of additional personnel
    necessary to handle the expanded workload.

22. The term "telecommunications" is the new technology
    associated with the area of distribution in the document
    cycle.

23. Very few new career opportunities are available as a
    result of word processing.

24. Word processing relieves the boredom of repetitive typ-
    ing and frees the secretary to do other more creative
    work within the organization.

25. Standard procedures are often used in offices that have
    word processing.

26. In the systems approach, the traditional office structure
    of the one-to-one relationship is replaced by another
    office structure.

Questions on Concepts

1. Define information and information processing.
2. List the steps in the document cycle.
3. Define word processing and explain how it began.
4. Contrast the traditional office with today's office.
5. List some of the reasons why more efficient office procedures and updated equipment are needed in today's
   office.
6. List the major parts of a word processing system.
7. List the major reasons for the growing popularity of word
   processing.
8. Summarize the benefits of word processing for the secretary, the manager, and the organization.
9. Describe how several industries use automated equipment.
10. Identify a number of career opportunities available as a
    result of information processing.
11. Identify the new technologies associated with the steps
    of the document cycle.

Case and Activities

The marketing and research firm of Hutching, Inc. is a service
organization that tests the public's reaction to certain manufacturer's products.

   When the organization began ten years ago, the marketing department had one secretary and one manager. Since
the volume of paperwork increased, the department now has
two file clerks, a secretary, and a receptionist. The manager is
responsible for directing the office staff and for hiring and
supervising a number of people who conduct surveys by
interviewing the public in shopping malls and other public
places. The department also surveys the public by sending
out form letters and questionnaires. The quality of the form
letters is not very good because the manager also employs a
high school student five afternoons a week to do nothing but
insert names and addresses on the printed form letters. The
student often makes typographical and spelling errors when
typing them, or starts over if he discovers he has misaligned
the inside address. If the secretary has time to proofread the
student's letters, she is able to have him retype the names and
addresses again on another form letter.

   The manager spends a great deal of time corresponding
with the organizations who use the services of her company.
She writes most correspondence in longhand because the
secretary is too busy typing reports for these organizations
and revising questionnaires. The secretary often gets bored
because many times she retypes the same page over and over
because the same pages appear in reports to several organizations. When her secretary is too busy to tabulate the results
of the surveys, the manager also has to do this. Both file clerks
never seem to get caught up with filing the incoming questionnaires. The receptionist answers the phones and greets
prospective customers and spends the rest of her time trying
to look busy. The receptionist is unable to help with any of the
typing tasks because she doesn't know how to type. She is
very bored with the job, but needs to keep it because she is
attending college at night and hopes to receive her degree in
English in another year.

1. Do you think this organization utilizes its people most
   effectively? Why or why not?
2. Suggest several ways to make this office more productive.
3. How would the use of word processing improve the
   organization's image?
4. Could word processing equipment eliminate some of the
   paperwork? Explain.
5. Might word processing reduce office costs?

Activities

1. Interview people in any of the career categories mentioned in this chapter or consult a career planning center
   to get more information on career opportunities and
   salaries in word processing.
2. Read an article in the most recent literature on each of the
   new technologies and write an abstract of it.
3. Consult the Occupational Outlook Handbook, U. S. Department of Labor, Bureau of Statistics, on the number of
   people involved in white collar or office occupations.
   Summarize your conclusions in a written report from the
   information obtained in this handbook.

Key Terms

Word processing	Systems approach
Automation	Storage and retrieval
Information	Data processing
Information processing	Reprographics
Traditional office structure	Records processing
Document cycle	Micrographics
Input	Telecommunications
Processing	Word/information
Output	processing
Word processing system	Administrative secretary
Control	Correspondence secretary
Feedback	Work groups
Centralized services	Work flow
	Voice processing

Study Guide

This study guide provides you with feedback to find out how well you are doing. Use a separate sheet of paper to record your answers. When you have finished check your responses with the answers at the back of the book.

Matching: Choose the answer that best defines the word in the left column.

1. Word processing   a. A person who serves as a liaison between the vendor and the user of equipment.

2. Input   b. A person who recommends to the organization ways to handle changing paperwork needs.

3. Information processing   c. The source of information.

4. Voice processing   d. A method of originating information for an information processing system.

5. MSR   e. The movement of words, symbols, or numbers from the origination of an idea to its final destination.

6. Systems analyst   f. People make better use of information through improved procedures and modern equipment.

7. An office   g. The final product or end result in written or unwritten form.

8. Output   h. A place or many places where managers use the information network of the organization.

Multiple choice: Select the letter o
each question.

9. Managers recognized the mc
creasing office costs was to:
   a. Hire more people
   b. Purchase more automated
   c. Increase productivity of of
tomating the office.
   d. Decrease the number of c
ganization.

10. Which of the following steps c
of sequence?
   a. Origination
   b. Reproduction
   c. Production
   d. Filing, storage, and retrie'
   e. Distribution

11. Which of the following is
responsibility for the new re
tary?
   a. Typing of long reports
   b. Preparing itineraries
   c. Filing documents
   d. Composing corresponde

12. Until recently, the primary r
technologies in the office w
   a. Employees were not trair
equipment.
   b. The cost of computer te
too high.
   c. The equipment took up
   d. None of the above.

13. Word processing is a simple
better use of information tl
   a. New equipment.
   b. Better trained people.
   c. Improved procedures.
   d. Improved procedures a

Completion: Write the correct a
paper.

14. A word processing system
   _____ , __
   _____ .

15. The major parts of any sys
   _____
   _____ , and

16. Li
ar

17. Th

18. Cc
the

True/F

19. W
the

20. Sta
tw

21. Or
cre
ne

22. Th
ass
cyc

23. Ve
res

24. Wc
ing
wc

25. Sta
wo

26. In t
of
offi

Questi

1. Def
2. List
3. De
4. Coi
5. List
dur
offi
6. List
7. List
pro
8. Sur
tary
9. Des
mei
10. Ider
resu
11. Ider
of th

PART II

TECHNOLOGY

The combinations of equipment in each of the technologies in information processing are often referred to as systems: dictation and voice processing systems, word and data processing systems, reprographics systems, records processing and micrographics systems, and telecommunications systems.

Each system is composed of one or more types of equipment that allow the functions of inputting, processing and storage, outputting, and communications to occur. In the various systems these functions are accomplished in different ways. In Chapters 2 through 7, you will learn how these functions are performed on dictation and word processing equipment systems—two of the major systems in word/information processing.

CHAPTER 2

Input

The objectives of this chapter are to:

1. Identify several ways of originating information.

2. List reasons for using machine dictation over other methods of origination.

3. Identify three categories of dictation equipment.

4. Describe the different components that make up dictation and transcription equipment.

5. Discuss the two types of recording media.

6. Explain some of the special features of portables, desk-top units, and central recording systems.

7. Identify some of the differences between a large and a small central recording system.

8. Describe some future advances that will make using dictation/transcription equipment easier.

The equipment that makes up a dictation system consists of three components that are used to perform inputting, processing and storage, and outputting functions. Inputting to a dictation system refers to the act of dictating words into the system. Processing and storage is the recording of the spoken word. In word processing, after the word is recorded, a person called a **transcriptionist** sits at an automated keyboard, listens to the words, and types them into the system. This procedure refers to both the outputting phase of a dictation system and the inputting phase of a word processing system. Ideas in the form of words, therefore, are considered both input to the dictation system and the input to the entire word processing system.

Ways of Originating Information

In the traditional office, the boss often writes information by hand or dictates it to a secretary. Machine dictation is another method used in today's office. Handwriting, dictation to a secretary, and machine dictation occur in the origination part of the document cycle. Therefore, they are often referred to as ways of originating information. In word processing, the person using these methods is often called a word **originator**. That person may also be called a manager, principal, or author. The word originator may be a manager, an administrative secretary, or anyone who needs to put an idea into typewritten form. For example, many court reporters dictate the notes they take during a court session.

MACHINE DICTATION

Advantages	Disadvantages
1. Machine dictation is a faster method than longhand. It is also an acquired skill. With a little practice, an originator can increase the dictation rate and thus increase office productivity.	1. The initial cost of equipment may discourage many employers from using it.
2. A secretary doesn't need to be present to take notes. The originator is not affected if the secretary is absent, away from the desk, or occupied with other important matters.	2. Dictation is a skill that must be learned. The originator must be trained to dictate properly.
3. Anyone in the office can transcribe the originator's notes. The message is not a jumble of symbols readable by only a few.	3. If the company does not replace its outdated machine dictation units, it might be using older units, which are sometimes inferior.
4. The transcriptionist no longer has to decipher written symbols. Instead, the transcriptionist listens to spoken words and types.	
5. The transcriptionist can transcribe faster from the spoken word than from any other means.	
6. Some equipment even permits the secretary to transcribe while the originator is dictating.	
7. Electronic note-taking is possible. The originator can leave messages for the secretary that aren't intended to be transcribed.	

LONGHAND

Advantages	Disadvantages
1. Only one person is involved.	1. This method is a slower means of transmitting ideas than shorthand or machine dictation.
2. No special skill such as shorthand is required.	2. Transcribing from written notes can be tedious and time-consuming.
3. Only a pad of paper and a pen or pencil are needed.	

SHORTHAND

Advantages	Disadvantages
1. This method is faster than longhand.	1. Much time is wasted during the dictation process because the originator is often interrupted.
2. The transcriptionist transcribes from own notes, not from the originator's.	2. The secretary must be present while the originator is dictating.
3. The secretary can assist the originator in dictation by supplying the right word.	3. The transcriptionist must know some form of shorthand.
	4. The person who takes the notes or someone who knows the same system of shorthand must transcribe the notes.
	5. The secretary must transcribe from written symbols. Therefore, the transcription rate often decreases when symbols are illegible or after long periods of time have elapsed between dictation and transcription.

Figure 2.1 Origination methods: advantages and disadvantages.

Doctors dictate patient histories, postoperative surgical reports, and general pa-tient information.

Machine dictation offers a number of advantages over longhand or shorthand (Figure 2.1). Speaking is by far a faster way of communicating an idea than writing it. You can dictate a letter approximately four times faster than you

Why use dictation equipment?

can handwrite it. People who use machine dictation, therefore, can also make better use of their time. For example, in hospitals, radiologists (doctors who read X rays and determine whether or not patients have suffered any injuries) spend their time examining X rays and reporting on the results. By dictating their diagnoses, they are able to handle many more patients a day than if they had to spend time handwriting all their reports.

In offices, people who are highly paid decision makers can also become more productive by using machine dictation instead of handwriting.

Machine dictation is also more efficient than shorthand because it eliminates the need of a second person to be involved in recording the idea. The spoken word goes directly from the originator to the transcriptionist. The transcriptionist is the person who transcribes dictation.

Dictation provides time and cost savings

Machine dictation saves time for the secretary who no longer has to transcribe from poorly written notes. Secretaries are better able to plan their time since they no longer are interrupted to take dictation when they are in the midst of other activities.

Machine dictation also provides a cost savings. For example, by using machine dictation, police stations have been able to cut down on employee overtime and reduce part-time staff. By dictating their daily reports, police officers can finish their work on time and even become more productive.

Easy to use

The final reason for using machine dictation is that the equipment used for dictating is easy to operate. Prerecorded instructions on some dictation equipment even tell originators how to operate it. Originators simply pick up a phone-like instrument and a recording tells them what to do next. Technological advances (discussed later in this chapter) will continue to improve dictation equipment.

Basic Machine Dictation/Transcription Operations

Where dictation equipment is used

Flying in an airplane at 30,000 feet, a salesperson opens his briefcase, reaches for a small 5"x 7" black case and begins to dictate an outline of a new marketing approach that he will propose when he gets back to his home office.

An executive lifts a microphone from her desk and dictates a memo informing her staff of new federal regulations.

A field manager phones in from a telephone booth a progress report on the work at one of his company's construction sites. All three originators in the previous examples are using **dictation equipment** (see Figure 2.2). On most dictation equipment, originators can do the following:

1. Dictate.

2. Review dictation and regulate the volume and tone while listening to the recording.

3. Make simple corrections without having to redictate the entire letter.

4. Signal the end of dictation or the end of the tape.

5. Give special instructions to the transcriptionist.

Figure 2.2 Dictaphone's Thought Master Series Dictation/Transcription. System 260 has special features for both originator and transcriptionist. It has a built-in telephone answering capability. When fitted with a phone-in adapter, the unit automatically answers and records up to 30 minutes of dictation. *(Courtesy of Dictaphone Corporation.)*

The equipment a transcriptionist uses when listening to dictation (see Figure 2.3) includes standard features that allow the transcriptionist to do the following:

Transcription equipment

1. Locate any special instructions prior to transcription.
2. Control the flow of dictation.
3. Regulate the tone and volume of dictation.

Figure 2.3 Transcriptionist using the System 260. *(Courtesy of Dictaphone Corporation.)*

4. Measure the amount of dictation that has to be transcribed.

Dictation equipment contains both a microphone or handset and a recorder. With some equipment, the microphone and recorder are located in the same unit. With others, the microphone ties in directly to a recorder located on an originator's desk. With still others, only the microphone may be located on the originator's desk and the recorder may be located elsewhere in the organization.

Components of the equipment

The transcriptionist can listen and control the flow of dictation because the **transcription equipment** contains a headset and a footpedal. Some equipment, however, uses a bar at the base of the typewriter instead of the footpedal to control the flow of dictation.

Some dictation/transcription units are combination units that can be used for dictating or transcribing dictation. A single unit can serve both the originator and the transcriptionist. After removing the microphone when the originator finishes dictation, the transcriptionist can transform the unit into a transcription unit by adding a headset and footpedal. Such units reduce the initial cost of purchasing equipment but are not always convenient because they may not be available to the person who needs them.

Both dictation and transcription equipment use media. Media is the material on which the originator's words are recorded.

Types of Recording Media

Discrete media

Dictation equipment is often categorized by the media it uses. The two types of media dictation units use are external or **discrete media** and internal or **endless loop** media; dictation units are often referred to as discrete media equipment or endless loop equipment. External refers to media that is external or outside the equipment. Internal refers to media that is inside the machine. Internal media usually cannot be touched or handled.

External Media

Magnetic or inscribed

Discrete media are media that are small, moveable, external media that are inserted into a dictation unit and used for recording dictation. After dictation, they are removed from the dictation unit, placed in a transcription unit, and removed when the transcriptionist is finished listening to and transcribing the dictation.

Discrete media falls into two categories: **magnetic media** that can be reused, or inscribed media that cannot be erased or reused. For example, **inscribed media** is only used when a permanent, noneraseable record is needed.

If you already have a stereo record player or a cassette tape player, you are already familiar with two types of discrete media used in the entertainment field: records (inscribed media) and tapes (magnetic media). Some discrete dictation media used in offices are tapes in standard, mini, or microcassettes; belts; and discs (described in Figures 2.4 through 2.8).

Figure 2.4 Standard or universal cassettes. *(Courtesy of Memorex Corporation.)*

Figure 2.5 Minicassettes. *(Microcassettes are the same size.) (Courtesy of Norelco.)*

Figure 2.6 Magnetic discs. *(Courtesy of International Business Machines Corporation.)*

Figure 2.7 Disc Cartridges. *(Courtesy of International Business Machines Corporation.)*

Figure 2.8 Magnetic belts. *(Courtesy of Memorex Corporation.)*

Discrete media has several advantages:

1. The recording media can be used in a portable dictation unit and transported anywhere.

2. During rush periods, media can be easily distributed to several transcriptionists for transcribing.

3. Dictation can be stored permanently.

4. Confidential or high-priority dictation can be transcribed separately.

On the other hand, if the originator uses a discrete media machine, some disadvantages are:

1. Someone must always remove the media from the equipment and give it to the transcriptionist.

2. A medium may have to be changed during dictation because it may not be long enough to hold the originator's entire dictation.

3. The transcriptionist has to wait for the originator to finish with the medium before transcribing it.

4. Dictation backlog is hard to determine because it is difficult to know how much is on each separate medium, especially since each side of the medium may contain different amounts of dictation. Newer equipment may overcome this disadvantage.

5. Dictation may be misplaced or damaged from excessive handling.

6. Dictation media are sometimes difficult to identify for filing and storage purposes.

Internal Media

Endless loop media resembles the tape used in the old reel-to-reel tape recorder. Instead of having to rethread or rewind the tape each time the spool runs out, however, the two ends of the tape have been spliced together to form a continuous loop. The tape fits within a case referred to as a **tank** (see Figure 2.9). The tank consists of a record head and a transcribe head (see Figure 2.10). When the originator dictates, the tape that is used up sinks to the center of the tank between the record and transcribe heads. When the transcriptionist begins transcribing, the tape is pulled across the opposite head. The tape that has been transcribed falls to the bottom of the tank and is ready to be reused as the tape moves back to the dictation head.

If the originator is using an endless loop unit, the question of what to do with the media after dictation is no longer a problem. The media is contained in a tank and is not handled by the originator or anyone else. Some advantages of endless loop media are:

1. Since the media is never handled, it cannot be misplaced or mishandled.

2. The media does not usually get filled because it is constantly being erased and reused.

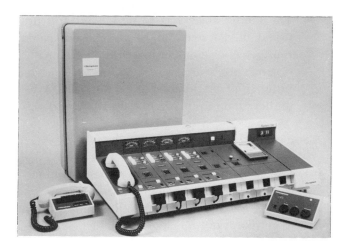

Figure 2.9 Dictaphone Thought Tank System 193. Notice the endless loop tank in the background. *(Courtesy of Dictaphone Corporation.)*

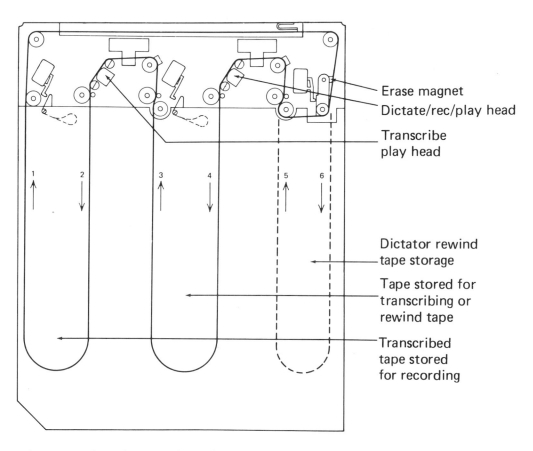

Erase magnet
Dictate/rec/play head

Transcribe
play head

Dictator rewind
tape storage

Tape stored for
transcribing or
rewind tape

Transcribed
tape stored
for recording

Figure 2.10 This schematic shows the inside of a Dictaphone Thought Tank System 193. Notice how the tape drops from the dictate head (4) and is pulled by the opposite transcribe head (3) when transcription takes place. *(Courtesy of Dictaphone Corporation.)*

Types of Recording Media

3. The media never has to be loaded and unloaded, nor does any additional media need to be purchased as the volume of dictation and number of originators increase. Occasionally, however, the volume of an organization's dictation might grow to be too great for the units, or the number of originators might increase. When this happens, additional endless loop units might have to be added.

Some disadvantages of endless loop are:

1. The dictation segment cannot be distributed to several transcriptionists. One transcriptionist might have to transcribe the entire document and, if it were a lengthy rush item, the transcriptionist could not have any help in getting it out quickly.

2. The dictation cannot be filed unless it is transferred to discrete media.

3. The media is not portable and, therefore, the transcriptionists have to be assigned to one area.

4. High-priority dictation may be hard to locate if it is buried within the tape.

The newer endless loop dictation equipment has already addressed some of these concerns. For example, newer equipment provides ways to search and locate high-priority dictation quickly, and some has a means of permitting more than one transcriptionist to work on the same dictation segment.

Media Compatibility

Dictation equipment is versatile enough to fit the needs of originators who must use the equipment for a variety of purposes, and the media helps give the equipment its versatility. For the transcriptionist to be able to transcribe media dictated on one type of dictation equipment, the media the transcriptionist uses must be the same (**compatible**). In many cases, if the media is not compatible, an adapter can be used. For example, a minicassette can be transcribed on a standard cassette transcription unit by adding an adapter to the unit.

Dictation Equipment Commonly Used

The three categories of dictation equipment are: **portable dictation units, desk-top units,** and **central recording systems.**

A Look at Portable Dictation Units

Portable dictation units are usually battery-operated and intended to be used by originators for notetaking when they are away from the office (Figures 2.11 through 2.14). The transcribing is usually done on a unit located in the

Figure 2.11 The Dictaphone Travel Master is a portable that uses standard cassettes. The NiCad power pack recharges in 30 minutes. *(Courtesy of Dictaphone Corporation.)*

Figure 2.12 The Dictaphone Travel Master is a portable dictation unit with an electronic indexing feature. This feature allows the user to superimpose tones or designate instructions to the transcriptionist for ease of transcribing and rapid place finding. *(Courtesy of Dictaphone Corporation.)*

Figure 2.13 The Memocord K77 Mini is a portable that uses minicassettes. It weighs 10 ounces and measures 1″ x 2 7/8″ x 4 1/2″. *(Courtesy of Memocord, USA.)*

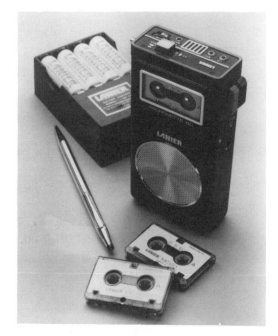

Figure 2.14 The Lanier Microsette 60 is a portable that uses microcassettes. *(Courtesy of Lanier Corporation.)*

Dictation Equipment Commonly Used

office. Because they are inexpensive, portable dictation units make up nearly one-third of all the dictation units sold.

Portable dictation units always use discrete media. Some may use magnetic discs or belts, but they most commonly use tapes in **standard, mini-,** or **microcassettes.** Standard cassettes hold up to 120 minutes of dictation, or 60 minutes on each side. Mini- and microcassettes can now also hold as much as 120 minutes of dictation.

Indexing feature

Most portable dictation units have an **indexing feature** that provides some way for the originator to give special instructions to the transcriptionist. Some portables use an **odometer** (counter) for this purpose. The originator can set the odometer to "0" at the beginning of dictation and write down numbers to let the transcriptionist know at what point dictation ended or at what point a special instruction occurred (see Figure 2.11).

The odometer method has been replaced on many newer portables by an **electronic cueing device.** The originator can press a button and mark the media with an electronic signal. The indexing signals are then stored on the recording media for the transcriptionist to use when transcribing.

Portable dictation units are often used together with other types of dictation units. Some advantages they provide include the following.

Advantages

1. They can be taken off the premises and can be easily carried in an attache case or pocket.

2. They can be used in places where other types of equipment would not be practical, such as in meetings or seminars, on buses, or in planes.

Some disadvantages are:

Disadvantages

1. They can easily be lost, misplaced, or stolen.

2. The batteries may run down while the person is dictating.

Some features to look for when buying portable dictation equipment are:

—Indicators that blink to show that batteries are low.
—An end-of-tape signal to let the originator know how much dictation time is left.
—One-button control for record, review, quick-erase, fast forward, and revise.
—A way for the originator to signal the transcriptionist by using electronic cueing devices.
—Two-way recording capability that allows the originator to tape both persons involved in a phone conversation.
—A charging unit to recharge batteries.

A Look at Desk-Top Units

Desk-top units are so named because they are generally small enough to be located on the originator's desk (Figures 2.15 through 2.17). Desk-top units can

Figure 2.15 Dictaphone's Thought Master Series Dictation/Transcription System 260 is composed of desktop units that use standard cassettes. Each unit has an electronic indexing feature that indicates the number and length of the document. The indexing feature also allows the originator to put in special instructions for the secretary. *(Courtesy of Dictaphone Corporation.)*

Figure 2.17 Norelco's Tracertrack Desktop System 120 is a desk-top dictation system that uses minicassettes. The dictation unit incorporates its recording medium within a cordless microphone. Originators can electronically index dictated material. *(Courtesy of Norelco Corporation.)*

Figure 2.16 Lanier's OMNI is a desk-top dictation/transcription system that uses microcassettes. *(Courtesy of Lanier Corporation.)*

be used specifically for dictation, or they can combine for both dictation and transcription as discussed later in this chapter.

Desk-top units provide flexibility for users because they use discrete media and are not permanently installed. The media they use are **belts, discs,** and **tapes** in standard, mini-, and microcassettes. Desk-top units, like portable dictation units, are sometimes "**dedicated**" or used specifically by one originator or for one type of work. For example, they may be used for the originator who has an exceptionally large dictation load or someone who has a large volume of high-priority dictation.

Dedicated

Desk-top units are popular in offices where one transcriptionist does all the transcribing for one originator. Sometimes originators use desk-top units and have their media transcribed in work groups or word processing centers. In such cases, the desk-top units must be compatible with the units used for transcription.

Desk-top units have standard features that provide the originator with a way to give the transcriptionist special instructions. Some machines use **paper index strips** for this purpose. The originator uses a lever on the machine to mark the end of dictation or give special instructions. The originator gives the index strips to the transcriptionist along with the media. The transcriptionist can then scan the media before transcribing to determine the length of dictation and any special instructions the originator may have dictated. The index strip method has been replaced on many newer desk-top units by an electronic cueing device like the one used on portable dictation units.

LED

Some desk-top units are now equipped with an electronic display (called an **LED—light-emitting diode**) to let the originator see at a glance his or her location on a cassette (Figure 2.15). When the originator makes signals on the tape to indicate the number of dictated documents and any special instructions, the signals appear as dots on the electronic display to let the originator see exactly what is on the tape.

The transcription unit also has an identical display to let the transcriptionist see at a glance the number, location, and length of documents, and any special instructions the originator might have.

Some features desk-top dictation units may have are

Special features

—A two-way recording capability that allows the originator to record both sides of a phone conversation.
—A phone-in capability that allows the originator to call in dictation anytime during the day or night.
—An electronic cueing device that allows the originator to signal the transcriptionist.

Some new desk-top units are also cordless. Such units are similar to portable units in that the originator does not have to remain at a desk while dictating. They are called desk-top units because their cordless microphone rests in a desk-top unit when not being used (Figure 2.17).

Central recording systems usually provide the greatest efficiency and cost savings. Fewer pieces of equipment and fewer secretaries are needed to reach the greatest number of originators.

Central recording systems consist of central recorders that are permanently installed and wired to either handsets or telephones. Central recording systems handle large volumes of dictation using either discrete or endless loop media (Figures 2.18 through 2.21). The discrete media systems, however, have **automatic media changers** that hold a large number of discrete media. The media changers automatically eject the individual discs or cassettes after they become filled or at some predetermined time. For example, Jacobs Transit Company in Louisville, Kentucky, has determined that the average amount of dictation time for each originator is four and one-half minutes. Therefore, their machines are preset to allow for five minutes of dictation time and then automatically eject the cassette and bring into the media changer an unused cassette. Someone, however, must fill the media changer with unused media when all the individual cassettes or discs are filled and must also distribute the media to the transcriptionists. Such systems can be used to get high priority dictation done quickly as many transcriptionists can be working on one project. These systems are also often used because the originator may wish to have the cassette or disc stored for future use. The endless loop media system is a closed system; the media is never handled. The dictation is ready to be transcribed minutes after the originator begins to dictate.

Work distribution

Immediate transcription

Central recording systems are sometimes further categorized into large central recording systems and small central recording systems. **Small central recording systems** use discrete or endless loop media. They are meant for a small group of originators, anywhere from 2 to 25. As they are permanently installed, they are directly wired to the recorders. More than one transcription station can be wired to a single recorder. Each recorder is usually dedicated to a specific type of work.

Large central recording systems also use either discrete or endless loop media. However, they are meant for a large group of originators, anywhere from 25 to 1,000. They, too, are permanently installed and have handsets directly wired to the recorders. Several transcription stations can be wired to a single recorder. Large central recording systems can have full phone-in capabilities. The originators use the numbers located on the telephone to control the recorders. For instance, one number may start the recorder, another stop it, and a third might allow the originator to review the dictation. Another number might also allow the originator to reach someone where the recorders are located.

Both large and small systems can provide a way of managing dictation and transcription referred to as **word management.** Word management is accomplished by equipment that automatically logs in dictation. Large dictation systems can also be equipped with a **supervisor's control monitor** as shown in Figures 2.22 and 2.23, p. 48 and 49. A monitor is usually located at the supervisor's desk and used for obtaining the following information:

—Originator's identification: name, department, and type of work.

—What dictation is in progress, what needs to be typed, what is high-priority, what has been keyboarded.

—How long the job is.

—Who the transcriptionist is.

—What time dictation entered the center.

—What time the work was completed.

Special features

Some special conveniences some central dictation units have include the following:

—VOR (**voice-operated relay**) that prevents the tape from running when the originator is not speaking. The transcriptionist then doesn't have to wait through long periods of silence.

—A means of testing and rejecting tapes if they are broken or incorrectly inserted.

—A recorded voice that asks the user for an I.D. code and tells the originator how to use the system and how much recording time is left on the media.

—**Dual-track system.** The originator is able to insert special instructions or corrections as they occur in the dictation. When a correction or instruction needs to be made, the originator switches to another track. Some vendors call this practice "**writing in the margin**" because it resembles the way corrections are made in the margins of documents. To alert the transcriptionist to switch to another track, a tone will sound where the originator's insertion takes place.

One hospital located in Houston, Texas, uses a small central dictation system with handsets located in eight locations throughout the hospital: two in pathology, two in radiology, and four in places convenient for physicians and assistants. Two transcriptionists located in a center where the recorders are located transcribe all the material from the eight originators involved. The dictation is dedicated exclusively to radiology reports, pathology reports, and discharge summaries. The transcriptionists are highly trained in the specific medical terminology required for these reports.

This hospital also uses a large central recording system. Three hundred fifty doctors can use any of sixteen telephones located throughout the hospital to dictate into the four large recorders located in the same location as the seven small recorders. Four transcriptionists are on duty during the day and two others during the evening to transcribe all of the doctors' general dictation. Doctors are also able to dictate from their homes, using their home phones, at any hour.

Future Advances in Dictation Equipment

Dictation equipment will continue to become more attractive to users. In the future, the originator will be able to insert words within a recording more easily. Now an originator can make changes only by recording over previously recorded material.

Figure 2.18 Sony's Network Model RD-6000 is a central recording system with an automatic cassette changer that uses standard cassettes. Defective cassettes automatically eject. This system provides a recording that tells the originator how to operate it. *(Courtesy of Sony Corporation.)*

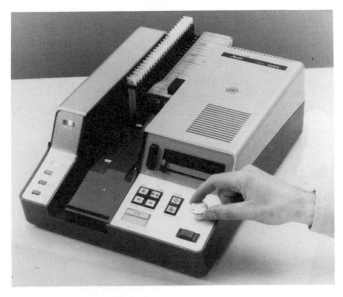

Figure 2.19 Norelco's Automatic Dictation System is a central recording system with an automatic cassette changer that uses minicassettes. *(Courtesy of Norelco Corporation.)*

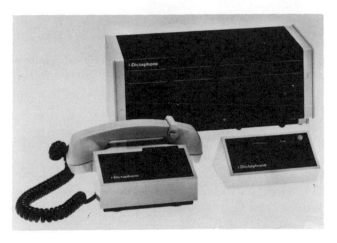

Figure 2.20 Dictaphone Thought Tank System 192 is a central recording system that uses endless loop media. It is designed especially for a small central system. The system's mini word controller console digitally displays in minutes the amount of dictation ready for transcription in each endless loop recorder. *(Courtesy of Dictaphone Corporation.)*

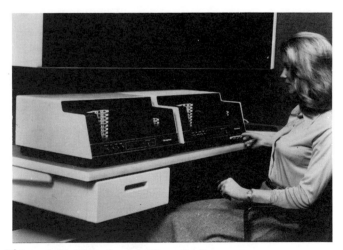

Figure 2.21 Dictaphone's Thought Center System 293 is a central recording system with an automatic media changer that uses standard cassettes. It is designed especially for large central systems. *(Courtesy of Dictaphone Corporation.)*

Figure 2.22 Dictaphone's Thought Tank System 192 — Mark II has a supervisor's control monitor to control work flow through its endless loop media tanks. *(Courtesy of Dictaphone Corporation.)*

Deleting parts of the recording now leaves gaps of silence, but in the future, these gaps will be eliminated and it will be easier to remove information.

Locating points of dictation is sometimes difficult on certain dictation equipment. In the future, the originator will be able to locate a particular spot on the media easily and will be able to find the beginning or end of dictation instantly.

Often the originator would like to hear everything that is on a sixty minute tape but does not want to spend an hour listening to the entire tape. In the future, the originator will be able to fast-review without voice distortion. The originator will be able to use this feature to listen to dictation while proofreading or just listen to the entire dictation in a shorter period of time.

Some of these features will also aid the transcriptionist. The transcriptionist will be able to locate points of dictation easier and scan to the beginning or end of dictation instantly. The fast-review feature will allow the transcriptionist to listen to the dictation and review it while proofreading. Another feature will let the transcriptionist quickly find (access) work out of sequence and locate high-priority dictation easily.

Dictation will play a greater role in the future when the voice is used not only to input information to the dictation system, but also to input information directly into the word processing equipment system. For example, voice processing will be used to give simple commands to equipment and eventually to produce text directly from the spoken word. As a result, more people in the

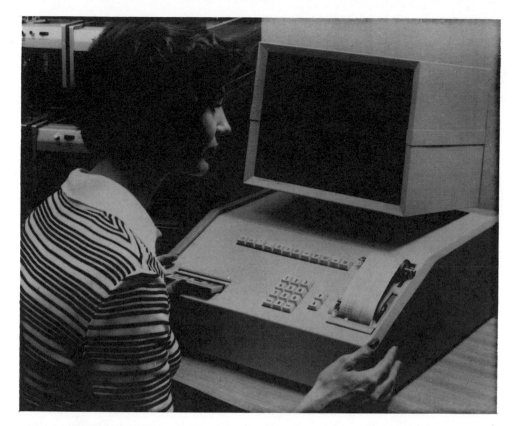

Figure 2.23 Lanier's New Monitor TM is a supervisor's control monitor that allows recorded cassettes from any system recorder to be instantly identified. The CRT screen automatically displays while a printer makes a paper copy identifying the cassette by number and recorder, day and time of input, author identity, and length of dictation. *(Courtesy of Lanier Corporation.)*

word processing environment will need to develop dictation skills. Some of these new systems are discussed in Chapter 5.

What Users Say

The following questions are often asked about discrete and endless loop media. The replies will acquaint you with improvements dictation units have undergone as a result of criticism and suggestions from people who have used the equipment in their organizations.

1. Can you permanently store information on endless loop media?

   No. Although the tapes are extremely long and dictation in the tank may not be erased for quite some time, once the dictation is transcribed, it is removed from the tape. If you have an endless loop system and wish to permanently store dictation, you must use an adapter that will allow you to rerecord onto discrete media.

2. How do you rewind endless loop media in order to reuse it?

   You don't. Some users note that this is one of the time-saving features of endless loop media.

3. Endless loop units function on the principle "**first-in**, **first-out**," meaning that whatever dictation goes into the machine first gets transcribed first. Does that mean that a secretary cannot schedule priority work?

   No. In some of the older units, the ability to "**search**" or to find priority work was difficult. Newer models, however, have excellent search capabilities and make locating rush work easier. Those who use endless loop media systems have commented that because the tanks are emptied quickly by transcriptionists and turnaround time is fast, rush work generally is not a problem.

4. Isn't it advantageous for the transcriptionist to see the media and determine the length of the dictation to be transcribed?

   No. Users find that discrete media allows the secretary, instead of the supervisor, to pace the workload. With discrete media, the secretary can estimate how much transcription time remains by counting the number of pieces of media. On endless loop media the secretary does not know how much dictation time exists.

5. Using discrete media, is it ever possible for the secretary to begin transcribing the document the originator is dictating right after the originator begins to dictate?

   No. This feature is possible only with endless loop dictation systems.

6. Our office has a centralized dictation "**on-line**" system. One manager, however, dictates many lengthy documents and ties up the phone lines for hours at a time. Other people who would like to use the center are often discouraged by these long periods of busy signals. Is there a solution to our problem?

   Yes. A manager who has that type of workload should have either a portable dictation unit or a desk-top unit that is "off-line." Your center would then have to decide whether to rerecord the discrete media onto the endless loop or to purchase an adapter that allows discrete media to play out through the endless loop system. Another solution is to provide one tank set aside (dedicated) for that manager's use.

7. Which system requires the least amount of monitoring, endless loop or discrete media?

   Endless loop. Endless loop requires less monitoring because there is no need to replenish the supply of media. In discrete media systems, someone must always be available to see that a fully loaded medium is removed from the recorder and that a new supply is added.

8. I've heard dictation equipment salespeople mention voice-operated relays, or "VOR." Does VOR mean that a machine begins to record when it hears a voice?

   Yes. VOR means that a voice activates the machine to record. Voice-operated relays are devices that prevent gaps of silence that occur when the originator is organizing dictation or not speaking into the recorder.

9. Must you listen to the entire dictation before beginning to transcribe on endless loop media to know if there are any corrections or changes in the dictated material?

   No. On some endless loop systems there is a device called "writing in the margin." When you reach a point of change or correction in the dictation, an electronic indicator tells you to switch to another track where the correction has been dictated.

10. Does VOR produce "**voice clipping**"?

    Sometimes. Voice clipping occurs in some recorders because it takes time for the recorder to speed up when it is initially activated. When this happens, some of the words may be omitted or clipped. Some machines use a **buffer** method, which is the best VOR method. The buffer consists of a recording machine within a recording machine to prevent clipping.

Summary

Chapter 2 discusses longhand, shorthand, and machine dictation as three methods of originating documents. Machine dictation is preferred in word processing because it is a more efficient method. The three types of dictation equipment are portables, desk-tops, and central recording units. They use either discrete or endless loop media. The person responsible for originating ideas is called the originator. The originator is anyone who wants to put words into actions. In the traditional office, the originator is usually a manager. In the word processing environment, the originator may be a manager or an administrative secretary. The person responsible for deciphering the words of the originator is known as the transcriptionist and is often the correspondence secretary in the word processing system.

Key Terms

Originator
Dictation equipment
Transcriptionist
Transcription equipment
Media
Discrete media
Endless loop media
Magnetic media
Inscribed media
Tank
Compatibility
Portable dictation units
Indexing feature
Standard cassette
Minicassette
Microcassette

Odometer
Electronic cueing device
Desk-top units
Paper index strips
Light-emitting diode (LED)
Central recording system
Automatic media changers
Word management
Supervisor's control monitor
Voice operated relay (VOR)
Dual track tape system
On-line
Dedicated
Voice clipping

Study Guide

This study guide provides you with feedback to find out how well you are doing. Use a separate sheet of paper to record your answers. When you have finished check your responses with the answers at the back of the book.

Matching: Choose the answer that best defines the words in the left column.

1. Originator

    a. media that can be physically handled.

2. Transcriptionist

    b. battery-operated dictation units that can be used by originators when they are away from the office.

3. Portable dictation units

    c. material on which recording is made.

4. Desk-top dictation units

    d. name for the person who needs to put an idea into typewritten, readable form.

5. Central recording systems

    e. individual or combination dictation units small enough to be located on the originator's desk.

6. Media

    f. person who listens to notes and keyboards them.

7. Discrete media

    g. equipment confined to one originator or used for one type of work.

8. Endless loop

    h. units that are capable of serving many word originators and large volumes of dictation, usually having supervisory controls to monitor workloads.

9. Dedicated equipment

    i. recording media that is contained in a tank and cannot be handled.

Multiple Choice: Select the letter or letters that best answer each question.

10. A unit that can be hand carried out into the field is called a:
    a. Central dictation unit.
    b. Handset.
    c. Portable unit.

11. Media that are never handled are called:
    a. Minicassettes.
    b. Endless loops.
    c. Magnetic discs.
    d. Magnetic tapes.

12. Which of the following is considered to be the greatest advantage of using discrete media?
    a. Discrete media dictation units do not take up much space.
    b. Work can be evenly distributed during rush periods.
    c. People can learn to use discrete media dictation equipment faster than endless loop dictation equipment.
    d. Discrete media takes up less storage space.

13. On which media is it possible to permanently store information?
    a. Inscribed.
    b. Endless loop.

14. "First-in, first-out" refers to:
    a. The initial sound that activates a recorder.
    b. The first dictation recorded on an endless loop system, that will be transcribed first.
    c. The first person dictating into a center will have his or her dictation transcribed first.

Completion: Write the correct answer on a separate sheet of paper.

15. A dictation unit used for one purpose or one originator is said to be _____ .

    dedicated

16. Material on which a recording can be made is called _____ .

17. Two types of media used by dictation units are: _____ and _____ .

18. Endless loop media is encased in a _____ .

19. Three ways of providing a transcriptionist with special instructions while using dictation equipment are: _____ , _____ , and _____ _____ .

20. Discrete media can be magnetic or _____ .

21. A _____ is used to prevent periods of silence on the media, which occur when the speaker is not dictating into the recorder.

22. A belt is an example of _____ media.

True/False: Write + for True, 0 for False for each question.

23. With endless loop systems, losing media is never a problem.

24. Longhand is the slowest method of transmitting ideas.

25. The greatest disadvantage of endless loop media is that work distribution may not be possible.

26. The greatest advantage to discrete media is that the transcriptionist may begin to transcribe as soon as the originator begins to dictate.

27. Endless loop systems are used primarily in places where people need to keep their recorded dictation.

Questions on Concepts

1. What are three common ways of originating information?
2. Why is machine dictation often recommended in word processing?
3. How does each of the three categories of dictation equipment differ?
4. Describe the different components that make up dictation and transcription equipment.
5. Discuss some of the special features of portables, desk-tops, and central recording systems.
6. Describe where portables, desk-tops, and central recording systems are most frequently used.
7. Describe some of the future advances in dictation/transcription equipment that will make the originator's and transcriptionist's work easier.

Case and Activities

Barnes and Brown, an electronics firm in Dayton, Ohio, purchased 250 portable cassette dictation units for its salespeople who work in the field. At the end of a year, they had to replace a number of units that were reported missing. They also found that the cost of supplying tapes for their salespeople was quite substantial.

1. What advantages do you think the organization received from supplying their salespeople with dictation equipment? What advantages did its salespeople enjoy?
2. What alternative does Barnes and Brown have to its present dictation system?
3. What are some limitations that discrete media present?

Activities

1. Time a friend while he or she writes a letter in longhand. Then time your friend while he or she dictates the same letter into a machine. Compare the time difference.
2. Compare the cost of two brands of each of the three types of dictation equipment.
3. Interview several managers and ask them if they use machine dictation. Why or why not?

CHAPTER 3

Processing and Storage

The objectives of this chapter are to:

1. Describe the different categories of documents found in an office.

2. Describe some machine features that make the production of various documents easier.

3. Define memory.

4. Explain the difference between internal and external storage media.

5. List three types of external storage media.

6. Compare the storage capabilities of magnetic cards to magnetic diskettes.

7. Explain the difference between sequential and random storage of information.

8. Discuss the differences between software- and firmware-driven equipment.

Equipment used in a word processing system consists of basic components used to perform inputting, processing and storage, outputting, and communicating functions. This chapter covers the processing and storage functions.

Inputting refers to getting information into the word processing system. Keyboarding (typing) is the primary method of inputting and is generally done on an automated typewriter keyboard. It is not the only method of inputting, as you will learn in Chapter 5

Processing refers to the ability of the equipment to change information into some other form. For example, during processing, editing changes are performed. Making these changes is referred to as text editing. Text-editing changes include changing words, adding lines, deleting whole paragraphs, and changing margins. The machine edits text through the use of a central processing unit (**CPU**). A CPU is actually a computer that uses a program or set of instructions to allow the operator to perform editing functions by simply depressing a few keys located on the typewriter keyboard. This chapter describes the various types of editing changes the equipment performs while processing the document, and other capabilities the equipment possesses to handle the various documents an office produces.

Storage refers to the ability of an automated typewriter to remember information that has been keyboarded. The automated typewriter allows information to be stored internally while it is being keyboarded. Most equipment also allows information to be stored externally on media similar to the dictation storage media described in Chapter 2. This chapter discusses the different kinds of storage media and the methods of storing information on external media.

Outputting is generally referred to as the final printing of information after it has been keyboarded, stored, and edited. Other forms of outputting are discussed in Chapter 5.

Communicating is the ability of one automated typewriter to send information to another automated typewriter. Communicating between machines is usually done over telephone lines. Automated typewriters can also communicate with other equipment, as discussed in Chapter 5.

Word Processing Handles Problems in Document Production

Before equipment could be developed to handle the paperwork in an office, manufacturers had to understand the categories of paperwork. These categories include the following.

1. Short documents such as letters and memos that are produced for one-time use (see Figure 3.1).

2. Long textual material as found in reports and proposals (see Figure 3.2).

3. Documents composed of information that is standard and does not change (see Figure 3.3, p. 58).

4. Documents composed of lists of information (see Figure 3.4, p. 58).

Categories of paperwork

Once manufacturers recognized these categories, they could build equipment to automate the production of certain parts of each document. To understand what word processing equipment does, it is helpful to look at the ways these documents were produced prior to word processing and think about what had to be done to help simplify their production.

Short One-Time Documents

In the traditional office, the secretary generally types **short one-time documents** and uses an eraser or some other method (correction fluid or tape) to correct errors that are spotted immediately. Corrections (incorrectly entered characters) and revisions (changes made to the content of the document) needed after the paper is removed from the typewriter are harder to make. They require reinserting the document in the typewriter, aligning the typed line, squeezing in characters, retyping the whole letter, or using correction fluid to blot out unwanted characters.

If you work in an office that primarily produces one-time letters and

Figure 3.1 Short one-time document (letter).

memos, you want equipment that will let you reduce the number of keystrokes you have to make and allow you to make corrections and revisions easily.

The features found on automated typing equipment that reduce the number of keystrokes include the following.

Reduces number of keystrokes

An **automatic carrier return** that returns the carrier to the left margin when you reach a certain point.

An **automatic center** that centers words on a line.

An **automatic tab grid** that sets up tabs at frequent intervals, such as every five spaces. This feature saves you from having to set up individual tabs.

Phrase storage that stores certain phrases you frequently use, such as "Yours truly," your return address, and greetings.

The features for making corrections and revisions include the following.

Features for corrections and revisions

The **backspace key** enables you to make simple corrections because it lifts off the character(s) you mistakenly type.

The **special keys** located at the typewriter keyboard enable you to make minor editing revisions—changes such as deleting characters, words or lines.

After revisions are made, the machine must also close up (merge) the blank spaces left by the words, lines, and paragraphs that have been deleted, adjust the margins where necessary (margin adjust), and allow you to hyphenate words when necessary at the end of a line (hyphenation).

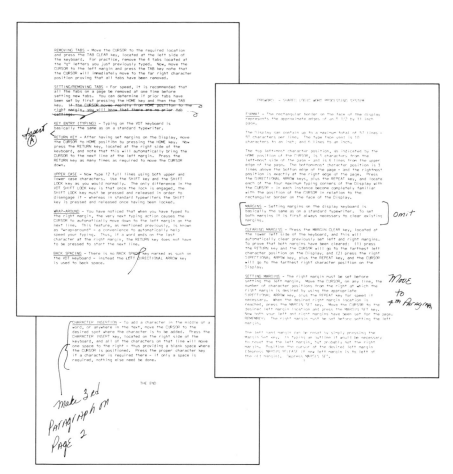

Figure 3.2 Heavy-revision document (report).

An office that has this type of paperwork does not need word processing equipment with capabilities much beyond the ones listed in the preceding paragraphs. Word processing equipment with these limited capabilities include IMB Electronic models 60, and 75; Exxon QYX models 1, 2, and 3; and the Olivetti 401.

Heavy-revision Documents

Long documents such as reports, manuals, minutes, proposals, and job specifications are often created by more than one person. They are usually not typed in final form the first time. Often the originators add, delete, alter, and move around paragraphs and pages. **Heavy-revision documents** are often documents created for one-time use. Sometimes parts of them are retyped from previous reports and sometimes the information in them is information that is retyped in different departments because it is used also in someone else's report. More than one person might be involved in creating the document and in assembling and typing it.

In the traditional office, the secretary types the entire document. When revisions are needed, the secretary usually makes them by retyping whole pages. When whole paragraphs need to be switched around, the secretary might use the cut-and-paste method—cut out the paragraphs, arrange and paste them in the new order, and photocopy them. This method does not work if an original

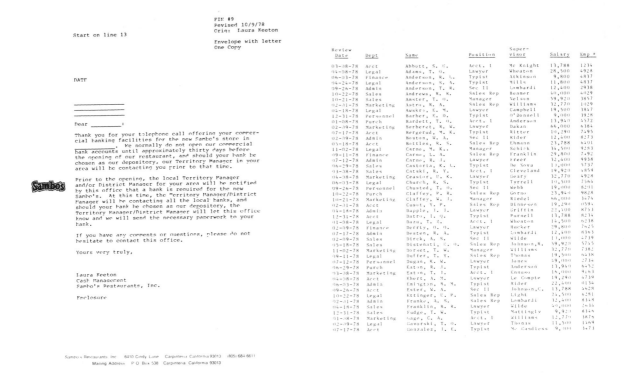

Figure 3.3 Form document for repetitive use (form letter).

Figure 3.4 List.

copy of the document is required.

If you work in an office that produces a large volume of long documents that are produced for one-time use, you need equipment that will let you make massive revisions easily. Making such revisions requires more than the simple editing features described in the previous example; it requires that you be able to move whole paragraphs and pages, and introduces several new problems. For example, if the part of the text that is crossed out in Figure 3.5 were removed, the equipment would have to merge the text together on page one and also move the text from page two to page one. If a paragraph or two were added to page one, creating more information than would fit on the page, the text on page two would have to be moved down to provide room at the top for the additional text (see Figure 3.6).

Keyboarding and revising these long documents also creates other problems for the secretary. For example, often the reports will contain footnotes that must be properly placed and columns of figures that must be typed accurately. The equipment built to handle this category of documents has features to make these heavy revisions possible. Using special keys, you can give the machines several instructions that will make the production of these long documents easier. The following features are found on equipment designed for heavy revision:

Pagination and repagination. Takes a multi-page document and redivides it into pages consisting of a certain number of lines. It may also number or renumber all of the pages of text (Figure 3.7). This feature is known as auto page numbering.

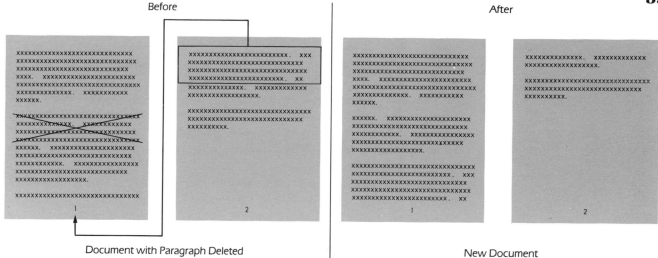

Before — Document with Paragraph Deleted

After — New Document

Figure 3.5 Deleting paragraphs.

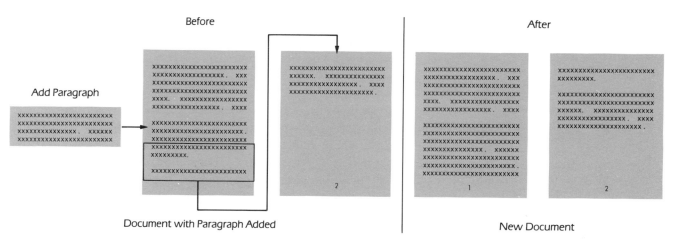

Add Paragraph

Before — Document with Paragraph Added

After — New Document

Figure 3.6 Adding paragraphs.

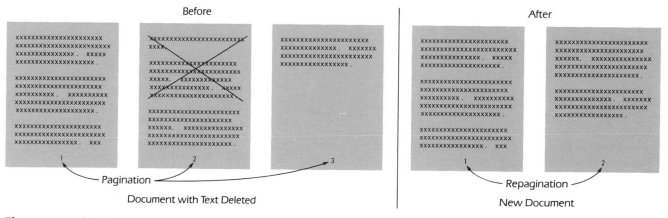

Before — Pagination — Document with Text Deleted

After — Repagination — New Document

Figure 3.7 Pagination.

Word Processing Handles Problems in Document Production

Justified right margins. Lines up all the lines of type at the same point to form a straight rather than ragged-right margin (Figure 3.8).

Columnar interchange. Switches around whole columns of numbers automatically.

Decimal alignment. Lines up decimal points in columns of numbers.

Table of contents update. Updates the table of contents of your report as new sections are added or as the section numbers and titles change.

Superscripts and subscripts. Places numbers slightly above or below the regular line of type where necessary in expressions such as H_2O or 4^2.

Headers and footers. Places uniform information, such as section numbers and title names, on each page.

Footnoting capabilities. Sets the bottom margin to allow space for footnoting.

Math pack and math edits. Adds, subtracts, multiplies, and divides columns of figures or simply verifies the accuracy of column totals.

Dictionary. Checks the spelling of words against a number of frequently used or technical words (Figures 3.9 and 3.10.).

Global search and replace. Searches through a document for words or sets of characters and replaces them with new ones (Figure 3.11).

Block. Takes information that has been keyboarded and saves it for when it is needed. For example, if you keyboard the inside address of a letter, you can block and save it. Then when you are ready to print the envelope, you can recall it.

Most of the equipment that does heavy revision has a television-like screen. A feature on most equipment with screens is called **scrolling**. The scrolling feature allows you to see a different portion of the text than appears on the screen because the text can be rolled upward or downward. You perform scrolling on a standard typewriter whenever you roll the paper up or down.

Two or more can work on one document

Not all pieces of equipment that do heavy revisions have every one of these capabilities. Some have these and other features. For example, on the IBM 5520 Administrative System, and A. B. Dick S/L and Wang OIS models 115, 125, and 130, two or more people can be seated at separate machines and work on the same document.

Where reports are prepared for printing, some equipment has a **graphic spacing feature.** With this feature, blocks of white space can be inserted where the graphic art layout will be pasted down to complete a master that is being prepared for publication.

When an organization prepares a reference volume or maintenance manuals that have to be frequently updated, a feature is offered that will allow an operator to insert vertical bars called **change bars.** These bars appear next to the text to show where changes will occur (see Figure 3.12). Another feature puts **proofmarks** such as two vertical lines or two crossed lines over the old portion of text to show how the text read before it was changed (see Figure 3.13).

Form Documents For Repetitive Use

Some documents have large sections of information that does not change. This information is called the **constant.** Examples of such **form documents**

Before

After

Figure 3.8 Justification.

Ragged Right Margin

Justified Right Margin

```
adve    anag    arou    azzz    behe    bloo    brit    bzzz    casu    chew
aback abacus,es abandon,ed,ing,s,ment abase,d,ment,s abash,ed,ment,es abasing
abate,d,ment,s abbe,s abbess,es abbey,s abbot,s abbreviate,d,s abbreviating
abbreviation abdicate,d,s abdicating abdication abdomen,s abdominal
abduct,ed,ing,ion,or abed aberration,s abet,ment,s,ted,ting abeyance abeyant
abhor,red,rence,rent,rer,ring,s abide,d,s abiding abilities ability
abject,ion,ly,ness abjure,d,r,s abjuring ablaze able,r,st able-bodied abloom
ablution,ary,s ably abnormal,ity,ly abnormity aboard abode,s
abolish,ed,er,es,ing,ment abolition,ary,ism,ist abominable,ness abominably
abominate,d,s abominating abomination aboriginal,ly aborigine,s
abort,ed,ing,ion,ionist,ive,s abound,ed,ing,ingly,s about about-face above
aboveboard abrade,d,s abrading abrasion abrasive abreast abridge,able,d,r,s
```

Figure 3.9 Dictionary.

```
plaz    pree    pron    pzzz    qzzz    recy    rese    rzzz    segm    shie
perfect,ed,ible,ing,ly perfect,ion,ionist,ionists perforate,d,s perforating
perforation,s perform,ance,ances,ed,ing,s perfume,d,s perfunctorily perfunctory
periactin pericarditis pericolace peril,ed,ing,s perilous,ly,ness perimeter,s
perineal perineum period,s periodic,al,ally,als perioophoritis peripheral,ly
peripheries periphery perish,ed,es,ing perishable,ness,s peritoneal,ize
peritoneum peri-umbilical perjury perk,ed,ing,s permanence permanency
permanent,ly permeability permeate,d,s permeating permissible,ness permission,s
permissive,ly,ness permit,s,ted,ting pernicious,ly,ness perpendicular,ity,ly
perpetrate,d,s perpetrating perpetration,s perpetrator,s perpetual,ly
perpetuate,d,s perpetuating perpetuation,s perplex,ities,ity peritrate
peroxidase persantin persecute,d,s persecuting persecution,al,s persecutor,s
```

Figure 3.10
Medical dictionary.

Before

After

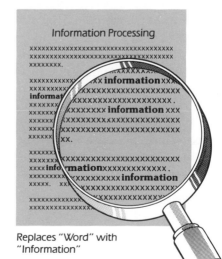

Figure 3.11
Global search and replace.

Global Searches "Word"

Replaces "Word" with
"Information"

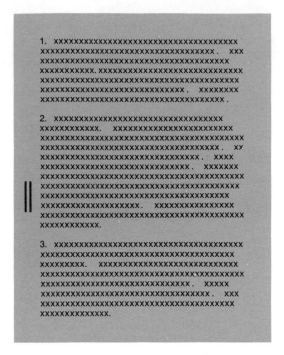

Figure 3.12 Change bars.

Catalogue No.   1241 Chair: Yellow and White. Price $42.50 ea.
                     1242 Table: White. Price $185.00.
                     ~~1243 Coffee Table: Oak. Price $95.00.~~
                     1243 Irish Linen Tablecloth: White only. Price $175.00
                     1244 Irish Linen Napkins: White only. Price $10.00 ea.

Figure 3.13 Proofmarks.

include form letters, contracts, leases, insurance policies, invoices, purchase requisitions, work orders, and job applications. In the traditional office, the constant portion of the document is often typed once and sent to a printer to have multiple copies made. The secretary's job is then easier; the secretary only inserts the information that changes (called **variables**). For example, in a form letter, the skeleton of the letter may exist as in Figure 3.3. The secretary types in only the name, address, and information where the blanks occur. The name and address is then retyped for the envelope.

Repetitive letters

Form letters are often referred to as repetitive letters because they are the same letters used over and over, sent to a number of different people. Forms are not very flexible. Every time a document is revised, the document has to be changed and sent to the printer.

Another method organizations use to add more flexibility is to create a number of standard paragraphs called **boilerplate.** To create a letter or other document using boilerplate, the boss simply tells the secretary the order in which the paragraphs are to appear. The secretary then assembles the paragraphs and types the new document.

If you work in an office that produces a great volume of repetitive letters or documents, word processing equipment aids in the production of these documents in several ways:

1. New form letters or documents can be made easily by typing one copy of the document. The document does not have to be sent out to be printed each time revisions are made.

2. The quality of the work is improved because each document looks like an original.

Figure 3.14 Document assembly.

3. After the names and addresses of customers are typed once, they can be combined with any form letter and used again for envelopes.

4. Entirely new documents can be created from standard paragraphs without having to retype the paragraphs.

The features found on equipment that make the production of these documents easier are:

Merging capabilities. Combines stored text, such as a list of names and addresses, with a stored letter.

Document assembly. Assembles paragraphs in any sequence to create a new document (Figure 3.14).

Equipment that performs volumes of repetitive work is sometimes exclusively used in offices for this particular application, although it may be capable of doing other kinds of work. Examples of such equipment include the IBM Displaywriter, the Dictaphone 2000, and the Syntrex.

Forms such as invoices and purchase/requisitions that contain horizontal and vertical printed lines pose another problem for the secretary. The secretary has to align the form carefully in the printer to make sure that the characters will print correctly on the line. When not lined up properly, the form is often hard to read.

Word Processing Handles Problems in Document Production

INFORMATION PROCESSING CENTER

ASSIGNMENT CHART

HOURS	MONDAY	TUESDAY	WEDNESDAY	THURSDAY	FRIDAY	SATURDAY
8:00						
9:00						
10:00						
11:00						
12:00						
1:00						
2:00						
3:00						
4:00						
5:00						
6:00						
7:00						
8:00						
9:00						

Figure 3.15 Form.

Forms packages enable you to prepare such items as invoices, purchase requisitions, and other types of forms. Using a forms package, you can create the standard part of the form and update it when necessary (see Figure 3.15). It also makes the placement of variables within the form easier. A feature of a good forms package is called an **edit check.** An edit check prevents you from making certain errors when filling in the form. For example, a zip code should consist of five numbers. A good edit check will allow the equipment to signal you if you try to insert six numbers where only five numbers will fit or if you try to insert a letter where a number belongs. An edit check can also be sure that a name that appears more than once in the form is spelled consistently.

Lists

In the traditional office, the secretary types many kinds of lists; for example, an employee list that contains the addresses, birth dates, salaries, number of children, and social security numbers of an organization's employees. Every time there is a change in an employee's status, however, the list has to be re-typed. If you work in any office, you will have occasion to prepare and use lists. The following features will help you produce them more easily:

Files capabilities. Creates and updates lists and prints them out according to any of the categories in the list. For example, if you have the names, addresses, age, sex, and social security numbers of your clients stored in

ID	LAST NAME	LAST NAME	STREET ADDRESS	CITY	STATE	ZIP	SEX	BIRTH	SOC.SEC.NO.
1	Clark	Nancy	13A New Avenue	Brea	CA	96812	F	02/06/51	556-73-5848
2	Evans	Clark	1942 20th Street	Napa	ID	91823	M	03/01/52	554-35-6848
3	Freeman	Marianne	2291 Oak Street	Santa Fe	NM	88622	F	07/03/51	556-47-3958
4	Gonzales	Marie	10781 Hamilton Rd.	Sterling	IL	66821	F	02/25/30	023-58-6749
5	Lyon	Larry	687 N. Elm St.	Rapid City	SD	67181	M	03/01/25	023-58-5832
6	Claffey	Patti	1506-D Canterbury Ct.	Placentia	CA	92670	F	07/03/51	557-53-6849
7	Rogers	Anita	8426 Walker	Cypress	CA	90630	F	12/09/51	552-45-3958
8	Hucker	Don	3424 Primrose	North Pole	ID	40503	M	12/11/40	453-59-1845
9	Appleby	Joan	108 Park Way	Phoenix	AZ	85038	F	11/05/48	442-53-6868
10	Zellers	John	4858 Spruce	Cypress	CA	90630	M	09/23/35	335-23-6948
11	Godwin	Lana	3456 Mural Drive	Santa Fe	NM	88385	F	02/23/47	495-35-2354
12	Huver	Betty	4701 Hillard	Cypress	CA	90630	F	07/04/40	458-63-5353
13	Aster	Dorothy	47 Cotuit Road	Phoenix	AZ	92994	F	03/03/30	558-64-6841
14	Carno	Mary Cay	701 Wagon Wheel Circle	Brea	CA	92621	F	06/08/63	445-23-6643
15	Brinski	Mary Ellen	4385 Birch	Brea	CA	92621	F	05/17/41	552-43-5823

Figure 3.16 Files capabilities: a list of client names and addresses can be created.

ID	LAST NAME	LAST NAME	STREET ADDRESS	CITY	STATE	ZIP	SEX	BIRTH	SOC.SEC.NO.
1	Clark	Nancy	13A New Avenue	Brea	CA	96812	F	02/06/51	556-73-5848
14	Carno	Mary Cay	701 Wagon Wheel Circle	Brea	CA	92621	F	06/08/63	445-23-6643
15	Brinski	Mary Ellen	4385 Birch	Brea	CA	92621	F	05/17/41	552-43-5823

Figure 3.17 Files capabilities: females that live in a certain city can be identified.

ID	LAST NAME	LAST NAME	STREET ADDRESS	CITY	STATE	ZIP	SEX	BIRTH	SOC.SEC.NO.
15	Brinski	Mary Ellen	4385 Birch	Brea	CA	92621	F	05/17/41	552-43-5823
14	Carno	Mary Cay	701 Wagon Wheel Circle	Brea	CA	92621	F	06/08/63	445-23-6643
1	Clark	Nancy	13A New Avenue	Brea	CA	96812	F	02/06/51	556-73-5848

Figure 3.18 Sort capabilities: rearranging lists in alphabetical order.

your equipment (Figure 3.16), you could have the equipment give you a list of the information that applies only to the females that live in a certain city (Figure 3.17).

Sort capabilities. Rearranges the information so that it appears in a different order. Using the previous example, you could not only list the females that live in a certain city, but could also rearrange that list in alphabetical order (Figures 3.18 and 3.19).

Word processing equipment not only makes updating lists easier to prepare because all of the information does not have to be retyped, but also makes the lists more valuable to the organization.

Once you have the lists, some equipment allows you to go a step further. For example, an insurance salesperson can arrange information pertaining to his or her clients, such as their birth dates, sex, car model, policy renewal date,

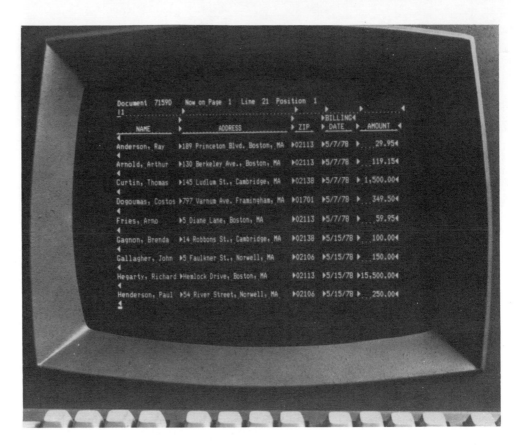

Figure 3.19 Sorting. Wang's new software for Word Processing Systems 20, 25, and 30 performs high-speed file sorting in the same sequences as a computer, but without complicated electronic data processing (EDP) procedures. *(Courtesy of Wang Laboratories, Incorporated.)*

and annual income according to birth dates and on the appropriate day merge that list with a standard letter wishing the clients a happy birthday. The list could also be arranged according to policy renewal dates, so that each client with an overdue payment would receive a late payment reminder. The list could also be used to solicit new business. For example, all the women 25 years or older with an annual income of $20,000 or more could be sent a letter telling them of new reduced rates for coverage on items of personal property.

Equipment with these capabilities include the Vydec 2000, Wang 20, Xerox 860, and IBM Office System 6.

Storage Media — Saving What You Have Typed

Processing a document would not be possible without the equipment's ability to store information. Information can be stored both internally and externally. Information storage occurs internally as it is being keyboarded; the information can then be transferred and stored externally on discrete storage media.

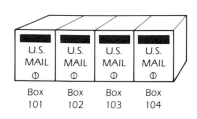

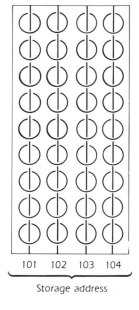

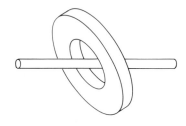

Figure 3.20 Internal storage.

Figure 3.21 Core memory.

Internal Storage

Storage of information (characters, numbers, symbols, spaces) electronically inside the automated equipment where it is not usually touched or handled is called internal storage or **memory.** It is also referred to as "main", "core", "primary", "buffer", or "working" storage. Internal storage resembles the arrangement of post office boxes shown in Figure 3.20. Imagine for a moment that each location within the memory has a permanent address like the number on a post office box. Information stored in these locations (addresses) inside the memory may be retained indefinitely, changed, or erased. When information is needed, it is copied from its address or location in the memory. The information at the location does not change. It can be used over and over again without having to be rekeyboarded. When you want to change information at a location, you can erase parts of it and make the appropriate changes or you can erase the entire memory. With the exception of core memory, the different types of internal storage described in the following paragraphs can be found on word and data processing equipment.

Core memory consists of large numbers of doughnut-like iron circles, each smaller than the head of a pin, that are strung together like beads on a wire (Figure 3.21). The iron circle (core) is magnetized and holds one **bit** of information. (A bit is the smallest unit of information that memory can store.) The magnetic core was once the most common type of internal storage used in computers. Now, technological advances are rapidly replacing core memory with other types. These newer types are cheaper to build, smaller, and less expensive than core memory.

A **computer-on-a-chip** is a chip of silicon containing a central processing unit and memory which stores one million bits or more of information. The chip is about one-fifth of an inch square and is also called a microcomputer

What is internal storage?

The impact of chip technology

Figure 3.22 Computer-on-a-chip. *(Courtesy of International Business Machines Corporation.)*

(Figure 3.22). One chip functions as a complete computer. Some computers formerly weighed 30 tons, took up about 1600 square feet of floor space, and cost $3,000,000. Today's microcomputer fits in the palm of your hand, may cost less than $300, has more power, speed, and memory capacity than most of our former computers, and consumes less energy than a light bulb. Some authorities believe the chip will have more impact on our society in the next 20 years than any other invention.

Another type of chip which functions as a central processing unit but has no memory is known as a microprocessor. Some chips store information but have no central processing unit. They are called Random Access Memory (RAM) chips.

Bubble memory is memory that has a greater potential storage capacity than any other form of magnetic memory. It also allows processing to take place at a greater speed than ever before possible. If you photographed a chip containing a bubble memory, you would see magnetic fields that move in loops and look like bubbles (Figure 3.23). To illustrate the capacity of bubble memory, an area one inch square can store about 100 pages of the Manhattan telephone directory. Bubble memory is solid-state—no moving parts to wear out. Also, bubble memory is nonvolatile—a sudden loss of electrical power will not wipe out the information it contains. Bubble memory is more reliable, more compact, and less expensive than most other types of internal memory, but is currently available from only a few vendors.

Holography is a lensless, photographic method for internal storage that uses laser light to produce three-dimensional images. The holographic method is important for manipulation and rearrangement of information which requires larger areas of storage than are available through traditional photographic stor-

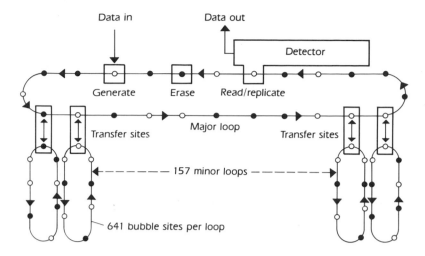

Figure 3.23 Bubble memory.

age processes such as microfilm. Equipment using holographic prototypes has shown the possibility of desk size libraries for storage having a capacity of one trillion bits of information (one terabit) or the equivalent of 10 million typewritten pages. Selection time for documents stored in a holographic memory would be only a few seconds. Holographic memories have high storage capacity, low storage cost, and fast transmission rates making them feasible for the design of information systems which do not require erasable memories.

External Storage

An important part of word processing equipment is the external medium on which information is electronically stored. It is also referred to as **auxiliary storage.** Some of the many forms of external storage media include paper tape, magnetic tape (in cartridge, reel, or cassette form), magnetic card, and magnetic diskettes or disks (floppy and hard disk). This medium is handled outside the word processor but may be inserted to allow the information stored on the medium to be transferred or manipulated by the equipment. All of the following external storage media can be found on word and data processing equipment.

Paper tape is a strip of paper on which characters are represented by combinations of holes punched across the strip (Figure 3.24).

Magnetic tape is plastic-like tape coated with a chemical compound (oxide-coated Mylar film) on which information may be stored. It is similar to the tape used with voice tape recorders. This medium may be purchased in cartridges, reels, cassettes, and magnetic tapes (Figures 3.25, 3.26, and 3.27). Users can store more text on cassettes and magnetic tapes than on a magnetic card (23,000 to 80,000 characters, or approximately 25 to 60 pages).[1]

A **magnetic card** is a plastic-like card coated with a chemical compound (oxide-coated Mylar film). It is useful for creating and producing short documents (5,000 to 10,000 characters). Approximately 50 lines of information may be

[1]Approximately 2,500 characters equals one page on magnetic media.

stored on one card (Figure 3.28). Some dual-sided magnetic cards also allow the user to record on both sides of the magnetic card, doubling the potential storage capacity.

A **magnetic disk or diskette** is sometimes called "**floppy**" to distinguish it from the rigid version often used in computer memories (disk pack). The circular diskette is always enclosed in a protective folder and resembles a 45 rpm record in size and shape. The floppy disk is rapidly replacing the magnetic card as a storage medium because of the ease of use and size of storage capability — approximately 250,000 to 325,000 characters, or 70 to 130 pages of text and codes, can be contained on one diskette. (See Figure 3.29.) A dual-floppy is a double-sided diskette that utilizes both of its sides for data storage. Mini-floppy disks have a smaller storage capacity of about 30 pages or 70,000 characters, and are smaller than a 45 rpm record.

Hard disks resemble a 33-1/3 rpm record in size, are rigid, and hold enormous quantities of data — frequently 2 million to 50 million characters or more on each disk. A disk pack contains one or more hard disks (see Figure 3.30). The disk contained in the disk pack may be nonremovable or removable to allow for replacement and adding more storage. Some disks are contained in cartridges, as shown in Figure 3.31. A **Winchester disk** is a hard disk which stores millions of characters per disk. The disks are usually contained in a box-like unit that rotates or drives the disks (Figure 3.32). The disks cannot be handled or removed from the box. Since they are sealed in this container, they are more reliable than floppies.

Many users need more performance and capacity than a floppy can provide. Rather than buy additional floppy disk units, a user may decide to purchase a Winchester. This magnetic medium stores more information than any other external medium in existence today. The 8-inch Winchester disk drives have storage capacities that run from slightly more than a floppy up to the capacity of a 14-inch hard disk drive. Compared to the floppy, the Winchester is five times more expensive but holds ten times as much information.

Several manufacturers predict that it will be possible to build a version of the Winchester that will have six platters that store up to 600 million characters in a space now occupied by two 8-inch floppy (600,000 characters) drives. This Winchester disk drive appears to be the beginning of a new era of storage media in the word/information processing industry.

There are specific phrases to indicate which type of storage medium is being used. For example, the term "key-to-cassette" means keyboarding onto a cassette storage medium. Other examples of similar phrases are key-to-tape, key-to-diskette, or key-to-disk. If keyboarded information is going directly into a computer for storage, this process is called on-line data/text entry.

Methods of Storing Information on External Media

Sequential storage and random storage are two basic methods of storing information on external storage media.

Tape and card media are **sequential access** recording media. They are sometimes considered difficult to use because information is stored in a sequential order (one item after another). When using magnetic tape, for example,

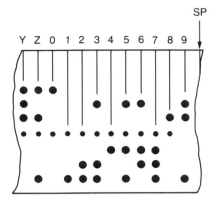

Figure 3.24 Paper tape.

Figure 3.25 Magnetic tape in a cartridge. *(Courtesy of Graham Magnetics Corporation.)*

Figure 3.26 Magnetic tape in a reel. *(Courtesy of Wabash Tape Corporation.)*

Figure 3.27 Magnetic tape in cassettes. *(Courtesy of Memorex Corporation.)*

Figure 3.28 Magnetic card. *(Courtesy of Graham Magnetics Corporation.)*

Figure 3.29 Floppy disk. *(Courtesy of Verbatim Corporation.)*

Figure 3.30 Disk pack. *(Courtesy of Athana.)*

Figure 3.31 Disk in a cartridge. *(Courtesy of Dysan Corporation.)*

Figure 3.32 Winchester disk.

the operator must wind or rewind the tape to find specific information. It is much the same as finding a particular song on a reel-to-reel tape player. If you want to play the fifth song on a tape, you must first pass through the first four songs. Also, if you want to insert more music between the second and third songs on the tape, you may have to delete or move the third song or put the new music at the end of the tape.

Diskettes, disks, and core memory are **random access** memories; information can be stored anywhere in the memory or on the media. Random access is like laying all the pages you are working with out on a flat surface to redistribute them. You can pick up individual pages or arrange them in any desired order without having to pass through all the pages on the table.

Knowing the difference between these two methods of storing and retrieving (accessing) information is helpful when selecting the appropriate media and equipment. With random access, the user can go directly from one record to another regardless of location and retrieve information in thousandths of a second rather than minutes. Random access is extremely important when records such as active criminal files and emergency medical files must be retrieved (accessed) constantly from large files.

Selection of the appropriate medium

Software Versus Firmware

The term **hardware** indicates the equipment (mechanical or electronic) that is combined with programs (software or firmware) to create a word processing system.

What is firmware?

Firmware relates to specific instructions that have been permanently placed or wired into the control memory of a piece of equipment. These instructions are usually located inside the equipment. The functions of equipment driven by firmware cannot usually be changed or upgraded without acquiring an entirely new or different piece of equipment. Therefore, it becomes extremely costly to upgrade equipment that is firmware-driven. Firmware is also referred to as **hardwired** because the program is wired into the equipment, usually on hard boards.

Why are software programs more flexible?

Software is a program that controls the operations of word and data processing equipment. Software is located externally, on magnetic media such as floppy diskettes. When you need to give your word processor instructions you may have to insert the diskette and press a button on the keyboard. The machine will then accept the instructions you need to perform your tasks. Then you may remove the software (diskette) and insert the diskette you are using for your project and continue with it. When you want functions not on one software program, you may upgrade your word processor simply by acquiring new software from the manufacturer, usually for a fee. Such new programs may have math capabilities, dictionaries, or a records processing program. The new instructions on diskettes are simply inserted into the equipment to provide new and greater capabilities.

Software provides greater flexibility than firmware because it is easy to switch from program to program by simply changing diskettes. For example, if you wish to add a software program that has a dictionary of your own terms to help you check the spelling of technical words in a document, all you do is to insert the diskette with the dictionary program. The ability to constantly update your system by adding the latest software enables you to keep your equipment from becoming technologically obsolete.

The cost for software-driven systems is generally less, for total program capabilities, than firmware systems. A firmware-driven system may be capable of global search and columnar interchange, but if you want to add a sort or math package, it may be necessary to purchase another piece of equipment which could cost as much as the first system. To add the software which performs a sort or math function to a software-driven system requires a new program on a diskette that usually costs far less than the price of an entirely new firmware-driven system.

Why is software-driven cheaper?

Many users of word processing systems are not aware of the difference between software and firmware driven systems and are very surprised when they realize the cost involved in upgrading to newer capabilities or options.

Software that allows a user to change functions to meet his or her needs is referred to as **interactive** software. With interactive software, the user can actually change a program or function of the software. Examples of this type of software include math pack and math edit, sort, forms packages, and dictionaries. Software containing a dictionary program may have 50,000 words in the dictionary and a capacity to add from 500 to 10,000 of the user's own technical words.

Some software features, however, cannot be changed. Some examples of software that enables equipment to perform certain functions that a user cannot change include automatic carriage return, centering, decimal tabulation, page numbering, headers and footers, global search and replace, and columnar interchange. If columnar interchange is a capacity of the software but you want the capability expanded so that the equipment will also verify or add columns, it may not be possible unless the manufacturer designs a new software program.

Summary

The equipment used in word processing consists of basic components used to perform inputting, processing and storage, outputting, and communicating.

Automated equipment has changed the way in which documents can be processed while they are internally stored and are in what is called the typewriter's memory. Different types of internal storage memory exists in different types of word and data processing equipment. Computer-on-a-chip and bubble memory are the most common types of internal memory found in word and data processing equipment.

Documents can now be stored externally on discrete, external storage media such as paper tape, magnetic cards, magnetic diskettes (disks), and Winchester disks.

Material can be stored sequentially or randomly in the memory or on the media. If information is stored on random access storage media, it can be retrieved (accessed) faster.

Firmware and software are programs or instructions which, when combined with hardware (mechanical or electronic equipment) enables the machine to perform certain functions such as centering or global search and replace.

Firmware instructions are wired into the equipment and cannot be removed or replaced by the user. Software instructions are located on magnetic media such as floppy diskettes and can be inserted by the user into the equipment to instruct the machine to do such things as check the spelling of technical terms in a document or perform basic equipment functions.

Software can easily be updated to perform new functions by adding a new software package. Equipment that uses firmware, however, cannot be updated as inexpensively. A new piece of equipment is usually needed if new capabilities are desired.

Some software features, such as a dictionary, may be changed or altered to meet the user's needs. This type of software is referred to as interactive software. Other software features, such as centering, cannot be altered by the user.

Key Terms

CPU
Short one-time documents
Form documents
Heavy-revision documents
Automatic carrier return
Automatic center
Automatic tab grid
Phrase storage
Pagination and repagination
Justified right margins
Columnar interchange
Decimal alignment
Table of contents update
Superscripts and subscripts
Headers and footers
Footnoting capabilities
Math packs and math edits
Dictionary
Global search and replace
Block
Scrolling
Graphic spacing feature
Change bars
Proofmarks
Constant

Bit
Boilerplate
Merging capabilities
Document assembly
Forms package
Edit check
Files capabilities
Sort capabilities
Storage
Memory
Core memory
Computer-on-a-chip
Bubble memory
Auxiliary storage
Paper tape
Magnetic tape
Magnetic card
Diskette/disk
Winchester disk
Random access
Sequential access
Hardware
Software
Firmware
Hardwired

Study Guide

This study guide provides you with feedback to find out how well you are doing. Use a separate sheet of paper to record your answers. When you have finished check your responses with the answers at the back of the book.

Matching: Choose the answer that best defines the word in the left column.

1. Memory

   a. Instructions for a word processor that are relatively easy to upgrade or change.

2. Winchester disk

   b. Where information is stored inside automated equipment.

3. Software

   c. A magnetic disk the size of a 45 rpm record that may contain approximately 70 to 130 pages of information.

4. Floppy diskette

   d. A hard disk that stores more characters of information than any other external storage device available today.

5. Change bars

   e. A strip of paper on which characters are represented by combinations of holes punched across the strip.

6. Boilerplate

   f. The ability to create and update lists and print them out according to any of the categories in the list.

7. Blocking

   g. Bars next to the text to show where changes will occur.

8. Files capabilities

   h. The ability to take information that has been keyboarded and save it for when it is needed.

9. Paper tape

   i. Paragraphs containing information that does not change.

Multiple choice: Select the letter or letters that best answer each question.

10. Bubble memory is:
    a. Memory made up of large numbers of doughnut-like iron circles that look like beads strung together on a wire.
    b. An external storage medium.
    c. Another name for a Winchester disk.
    d. A magnetic memory that has a greater potential storage capacity than any other form of memory.

11. Which of the following is considered internal storage?
    a. A random access memory chip
    b. Paper tape
    c. A magnetic card
    d. A diskette

12. Magnetic tape is considered to have:
    a. Random access storage capabilities.
    b. Sequential access storage capabilities.
    c. Less storage capacity than a magnetic card.
    d. Neither random nor sequential access storage capabilities.

13. Firmware is:
    a. Another name for hardware.
    b. Another name for software.
    c. A type of program permanently contained in certain word processing equipment.
    d. A type of external storage media.

14. Which of the following is **not** an editing feature found on equipment?
    a. Columnar interchange
    b. Table of contents update
    c. Global search and replace
    d. Boilerplate

Completion: Write the correct answer on a separate sheet of paper.

15. The feature found on automated typing equipment that sets up tabs at frequent intervals, such as every five spaces, is called _____ .

16. Equipment that can number or renumber all pages of text automatically has a _____ feature.

17. A math edit feature would allow you to _____ .

18. What would you be able to do if the equipment you were using had a dictionary feature? _____
_____ .

19. What capability allows equipment to combine a list of names and addresses with a stored letter?
_____ .

True/False: Write + for True, 0 for False for each question.

20. A forms package is a form of internal storage media.

21. A software function that can be changed is the automatic carrier return.

22. A random access medium is a disk.

23. Every piece of automated equipment has files capabilities.

24. A block feature would be helpful if you had a great deal of heavy revision to do.

Questions on Concepts

1. Describe four different categories of documents found in an office.
2. Discuss several equipment features that make the production of a heavy revision document easier.
3. Explain the difference between internal and external storage media.
4. Describe three types of external storage media.
5. Compare the storage capacities of magnetic cards and magnetic diskettes.
6. Compare the advantages and disadvantages of software-driven equipment and firmware-driven equipment.
7. Why is it important to know if the media you are using has random or sequential access?
8. Give two reasons why a company would choose to use magnetic card media rather than floppy disk media when selecting equipment.

Case and Activities

Meg Crutchfield, an attorney, purchased a piece of word processing equipment because she was told that it would help make the production of standard legal documents easier. After her secretary trained on the equipment, she told Ms. Crutchfield that the equipment could not do what she thought it could. Ms. Crutchfield called the equipment manufacturer and found out that the equipment she had purchased was designed for short one-time documents and not repetitive work.

1. What main feature or features did the equipment lack?
2. What features do you think the equipment probably had?
3. If Ms. Crutchfield also wanted the equipment to do heavy revision work, what other features might she want the equipment to have?
4. If Ms. Crutchfield wanted to make lists of her clients and store information about them, what features might she want the equipment to have?

Activities

1. Interview an equipment operator to find out the brand of equipment being used, the features the equipment has, and what kinds of documents the operator produces on the equipment.
2. Locate any business that uses either word or data processing and ask what type of storage media is used on its equipment.
3. Read any article concerning storage media and write a summary of it.

CHAPTER 4

Output

The objectives of this chapter are to:

1. Discuss the evolution of word processors.

2. Describe the advantages and disadvantages of display and nondisplay systems.

3. List the three main categories and functions of word/information processors.

4. Explain the reasons for the tremendous potential growth of the electronic typewriter.

5. Identify the basic components and categories of shared-system equipment.

6. Compare and contrast impact and nonimpact printing devices.

7. Describe the important factors to consider when selecting the appropriate printing device.

What appears to be a typewriter keyboard may be something quite different. It may be one of the many new word processors that has been developed over the past few decades. Operating this new equipment is like typing on a typewriter except that the newer machine has extra capabilities. Word processors are **natural language keyboards;** you do not have to learn any special computer language to make the machine work.

This chapter describes keyboards used for inputting, categories of word/information processors for processing and storage, and printing devices and printers for outputting to hard copy. As technology has developed, the capabilities of the equipment have expanded. With added capabilities, word processors can become word/information processors.

Evolution of Word Processors

Keyboarding on word processors today is similar to keyboarding done by typists on earlier equipment (shown in Figures 4.1, 4.2, and 4.3). The main difference today is that improved storage techniques permit the functions to be performed faster and more efficiently than ever before.

Figure 4.1 The Halda was an Early European typewriter manufactured in Sweden in 1890. *(Facit-Addo, Incorporated.)*

Figure 4.2 IBM's history of electric typewriters, 1933 to 1954. *(Courtesy of International Business Machines Corporation.)*

Figure 4.3 The first machine in history to make typing errors disappear from original copies with the use of a special "lift-off" tape. Also, it can switch from pica to elite pitch just by switching a "dual pitch" lever to change the pitch. *(Courtesy of International Business Machines Corporation.)*

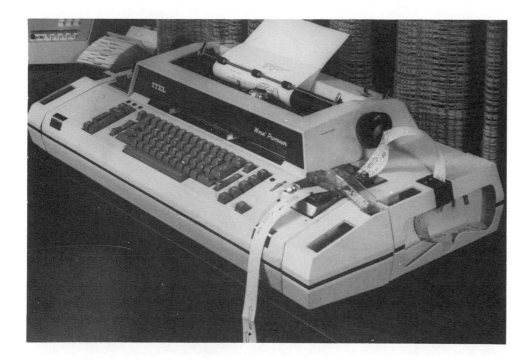

Figure 4.4 The ITEL 852 was first introduced in 1971. Still in use today, it uses an IBM Selectric as a keyboard/printer and a paper tape punch and reader to record the document on paper tape. Revisions can be made on a document by "playing out" a punched paper tape and punching a new one while making necessary changes. Although handling the media is cumbersome, paper tape is an inexpensive storage media. *(Courtesy of Automatic Word Processors. Photo courtesy of Michael G. Slack)*

One of the first steps in the evolution of the word processor came in the 1930s with the introduction of **automatic typewriters** like the Auto Typist. The automatic typewriter is one of the oldest, simplest, and least expensive of the word processing typewriters still on the market today. The automatic typewriter uses a paper roll similar to the old piano rolls for its medium. Punched holes in the roll represent the characters. During playback, air is forced through these holes in the medium, automatically driving the typewriter. The automatic typewriter was designed specifically for handling repetitive letters, form letters, and contracts. It was enhanced in the 1950s by the addition of punched paper tape as a storage medium and the addition of some machine logic which allowed switching between two tape punch/readers. Later, additional capabilities were added to paper tape word processors like the ITEL (see Figure 4.4). *Automatic typewriter*

During this period, another typewriter system, similar to a word processor, was introduced. It was called a **teletypewriter** and consists of a keyboard, a printer, and a paper tape punch/reader that records information onto storage media. The information can be sent over telephone lines to a teletype in another location. *Teletypewriter*

A **text editor** is a word processor developed in the 1960s that has the ability to store typewritten material and is capable of revision work (Figure 4.5). These first text editors were also called power typewriters or keyboards. The storage may be temporary (in an internal memory) or permanent (on such external media as cards, tapes, cassettes, or disks). The keystrokes are recorded electron- *Text editors*

Figure 4.5 The MT/ST (Magnetic Tape Selectric Typewriter) was one of the first text editors capable of automatically producing error-free copy. *(Courtesy of International Business Machines Corporation.)*

ically in the internal memory or on the external storage medium. Changes are made in the text by rerecording over the errors (this procedure also makes revisions on the media).

Since the mid-1960s, this category of word processing equipment has grown incredibly with respect to the number of manufacturers and the great variety of capabilities available on the equipment. Some of the characteristics of the newer word processors include microprocessors, screens, a storage capacity of millions of characters, and the ability to tie into computers and other equipment.

Nondisplay and Display Systems

The keyboard on a word processing system usually looks like an ordinary typewriter. The keyboard may be attached to a screen that is similar to a television screen, or it may be separate and hooked together by a hard wire. The keyboard and screen together is called a terminal or sometimes a work station. Word processing systems can have either display terminals or nondisplay terminals.

Nondisplay Terminals

Blind Terminals. Some terminals print output (hard copy) on the same piece of equipment as the keyboard, and are referred to as combination **input/output**

Input/output terminals

Output

Figure 4.6 A stand-alone nondisplay text-editing typewriter that prints at up to 350 words per minute in pica, elite, or proportional spacing. *(Courtesy of Xerox Corporation.)*

terminals. These input/output terminals do not provide the secretary with the opportunity to view the entire page of material as corrections or revisions are being made, and are therefore called **blind terminals** (Figure 4.6). Only the portion of the text that is changed appears on the printed page unless the entire text is played out on paper. These systems have edit capabilities, internal memory, and a magnetic media recorder. On these word processors, the printer is used to input text for editing functions as well as for the final document output.

Display Systems

Many word processing terminals now have a screen called a visual display terminal that shows the document being keyboarded (inputted) or what is being retrieved from storage. The screen makes it possible to produce a document in the document cycle without the use of paper and is referred to as a **CRT (cathode-ray tube).** Like the nondisplay systems, when an error is made, the operator backspaces and types over the error. The operator can then see corrections and changes as they are made. When the copy on the screen is error-free, it is placed on the storage media, from which it can be played back at a later time. This eliminates the need for a rough draft of all typed work. Figure 4.7 shows the advantages, disadvantages, and other features of display systems. Some display systems have a keyboard, CRT display, and printer. The printer located away from the terminal may do nothing but produce output and may or may not be attached to the terminal. The advantages of visual display screens will for the most part eliminate "blind" terminals in the 1980s.

VDTs or CRTs

The advantages and disadvantages of display stand—alone text editors are listed below:

Advantages

1. You see the document during its creation.
2. You can proofread, correct, and revise the document before it is printed out.
3. The process is done on a screen with no paper being used.
4. You can clearly see the correction when revising rather than striking over the change/error and waiting for a printout to see the revised copy.
5. You can keyboard the next page while the printer types the previous page.
6. Printout and keyboarding can occur simultaneously.
7. A proofreader can use a different CRT as a second monitor, revise if necessary, and begin the printout while the original text is still being keyboarded.

Disadvantages

1. Display systems are more expensive than nondisplay systems because initial "typing" shows up on a screen and not on paper, most CRT systems include a separate printer to create the final document.
2. Eyestrain is a factor. Considerable research has been done on these systems regarding the affect of working with CRT's.

Features of a display screen are:

1. Number of lines presented on the screen are from 1 to 50 at a time.
2. Wraparound capability (visual width expanse).
3. Scroll—up characteristics on the screen so that operator can bring lines into view from the top or bottom of screen.
4. Visual components: CRT or gas plasma.
5. Visual characteristics:
   a. Color (green on black; white on green; orange on black).
   b. Nonglare screens.

Figure 4.7 Advantages and disadvantages of display stand-alone text editors.

Figure 4.8 A stand-alone Dictaphone/Artec Display 2000. It features a thin-window display for prompting tasks, verifying commands, or highlighting a line you are working on; a 66-line CRT display for easy editing (including a zoom feature that allows you to focus on a magnified image of half the page); and a daisy wheel printer that produces bidirectional printing at speeds up to 480 words per minute. Optional features like communications, records processing, and math capabilities are available. *(Courtesy of Dictaphone Corporation.)*

One-line-at-a-time. An operator of a word processor can only correct or revise **one line at a time.** This situation has caused many manufacturers of word/ information processing equipment to develop stand-alone word processors with **"thin windows."** Thin-window systems are one-line, partial-line CRT or gas plasma displays, giving the operator a window into the memory (see Figure 4.8). Other manufacturers feel that an operator must "see" more than one line at a time while revising and that the larger the display the easier the learning and editing tasks.

Partial Displays. The visual display terminals today hold as few as one line, partial pages with 6 to 24 lines, and full displays with as many as 66 lines. The best argument used for promoting the full page display is that the operator is used to dealing with full pages and finds the editing process easier and adapts faster to the use of the equipment.

Full to partial displays

Dual Displays. One vendor developed a **dual display** that allows the operator to see two full pages, miniaturized, but next to each other on one screen. Another manufacturer has a system with a one-line display just above the keyboard and

Figure 4.9 The Micom 2000 partial page display terminal is shown with its Qume printer and two disk drives. In addition to the normal stand-alone word/information processor features, the Micom 2000 has the capability of designing and outputting limited graphics. It will draw vertical or horizontal lines around a text or may be used to build bar or flow charts or organizational diagrams. Other features of the Micom are automatic indexing, sort, file sort, selective search, library functions, and a math pack. *(Courtesy of MICOM Company.)*

also a full page display screen, and calls this combination a dual display.

Color and Graphics. Graphics will soon be a capability to choose from when selecting word processors (Figure 4.9). **Color display** stations are available and can present information in many **graphic forms** (charts, maps, and diagrams) in one to several colors with excellent clarity and brightness. Such color displays can emphasize and simplify information in many ways. Presenting sales or financial data or showing inventory shortages in graphic form would help clarify many business illustrations. A color printer using a multicolor ribbon must be used to provide color copies of the information available on the display screen.

Color helps emphasize information

Categories of Word/Information Processors

Word/ information processors

The term "**word processor**" is really too limited a description of the equipment which exists today. Word processors capture documents in memory or on storage media and manipulate the documents in many ways before they are turned into hard or readable copy. Many of the newer devices have been given "intelligence" that permits them to handle certain parts of document information in special ways in addition to the standard word processor editing chores of insertion, deletion, hyphenation, and pagination. So, word processors could more appropriately be called *text processors*, *records processors*, or even *information processors*. This discussion of equipment will not be limited to just word processors but will be expanded to include **word/information processors** to more accurately reflect the industry.

Many manufacturers

Since 1964 more than 100 manufacturers have flooded the market place with a huge array of word/information processors. Each word/information processor has special features and individual weaknesses. Many organizations selecting word/information processors do not take the time to conduct a thorough study of the organization to determine the document needs of the employees. As a result, users of word/information processors often purchase or lease equipment which does not meet their needs. The equipment that is selected can establish the direction the office will take in future automation plans. For example, an organization may purchase equipment that does not have the capabilities necessary to handle its document needs. Management may then have a negative attitude about word processing and may be reluctant to invest in additional word/information processing equipment. Perhaps the word/information processor has capabilities far greater than what the organization needs or uses and the equipment sits idle most of the time. Future automation plans are made easier if the selection of word/information processors is done in stages with a knowledge of the needs of the organization and the capabilities of the equipment.

This section describes the categories of word/information processors in order to provide a starting point for evaluating them. Word/information processors have evolved into a wide range of sophisticated and powerful equipment, but can be classified into three main categories: stand-alone systems, shared systems, and time-shared systems.

Three categories evolve

Stand-alone Systems

A **stand-alone system** consists of a single station (used by one person at a time). It is self-contained, meaning that it is not hooked up to or does not share the processing power of a central computer. A stand-alone nondisplay system may have a keyboard that acts as an input/output terminal or may be a display system with a separate printer (Figure 4.10). It may also, but not always, provide math or data processing capabilities and be software-driven.

Electronic Typewriters. A category of equipment entering the stand-alone market in the late 1970s was the **electronic typewriter.** Manufacturers leading this market segment are IBM with its Electronic 60 and 75; Exxon with its QYX

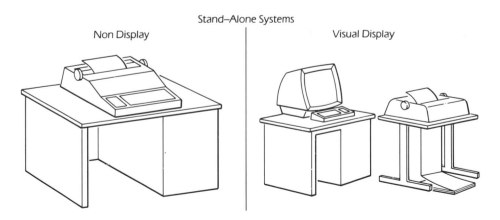

Figure 4.10 Stand-alone systems.

Nondisplay and Display Systems

Figure 4.11 Qyx, The Intelligent Typewriter, grows smarter without getting larger. Here Qyx is shown at its basic level. The electronic typewriter can be upgraded to a dual minidiskette text editor with communications and a 24-character minidisplay. The change is accomplished by adding electronic modules to the basic unit. *(Courtesy of Qyx, Division of Exxon Enterprises, Inc.)*

Figure 4.12 The Olivetti TES 401 is an electronic memory typewriter. It consists of an integral keyboard/printer with a 21-character gas plasma thin-window display and disk drive. *(Courtesy of Olivetti Corporation of America.)*

Levels 1, (Figure 4.11) 2, and 3; and the Contitronix and Olivetti TES 401 (Figure 4.12). This category is presently referred to as "electronic typewriters" but is no different than other stand-alone systems except that the capabilities of the electronics are now limited. The electronic typewriters cost between $1500 and $2500, have an internal storage of 7500 characters or less, and have very limited text entry and editing capabilities. One vendor has upgraded one version by adding 8000 characters of plug-in memory equalling a total of about 15,000 characters (6 typewritten pages). Other vendors have communication features that allow the typewriter to send information over the telephone to the same kind of machine, and some vendors have added single or dual mini-diskettes to bring the equipment capacity for memory and editing up to that of the regular "stand-alone system" market.

A replacement for electric typewriters

Even though the electronic typewriter has limited capabilities, its low cost and ease of operation will eventually find it replacing most electric typewriters in today's office as the electric typewriter replaced the manual typewriter. One model, IBM's Electronic 75 (Figure 4.13), designed for the average typing station, has many features made possible by chip technology. Included is a high-capacity memory that permits storage of documents in 26 locations and storage of frequently used phrases and repetitive sentences and paragraphs in up to 99 locations. Two tiny memory chips hold a total of 7,500 characters of working memory which may be doubled if the user wishes to pay a fee to add more storage capacity with additional chips.

Memory capacity increases

The stand-alone systems range from one of the first word processors (MT/ST) to today's highly sophisticated word/information processors. The newer equipment has the capability to utilize internal dictionaries, solve math problems, and assist in massive revision (see Figure 4.14).

Peripherals. Some stand-alone systems have optional peripherals available to them. **Peripherals** are additional pieces of equipment that can attach to a stand-alone or that the stand-alone can share. An example of a peripheral to a stand-alone is a faster printer or an OCR reader; or, the stand-alone system

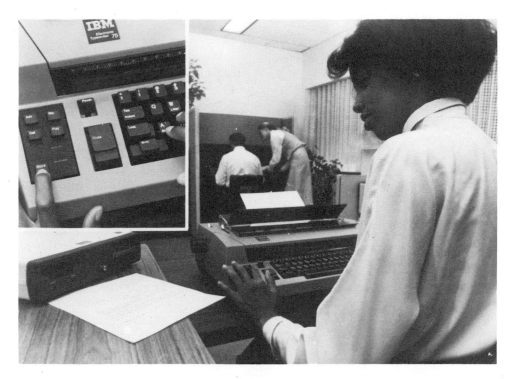

Figure 4.13 The IBM Electronic 75 has an upgradable memory capacity of 7,500 to 15,000 characters of working memory. *(Courtesy of International Business Machines Corporation.)*

Figure 4.14 The Displaywriter is a text processing office system with an electronic "dictionary" that checks the spelling of about 50,000 words, and that has the capability to transmit mail electronically. (Courtesy of International Business Machines Corporation).

Nondisplay and Display Systems

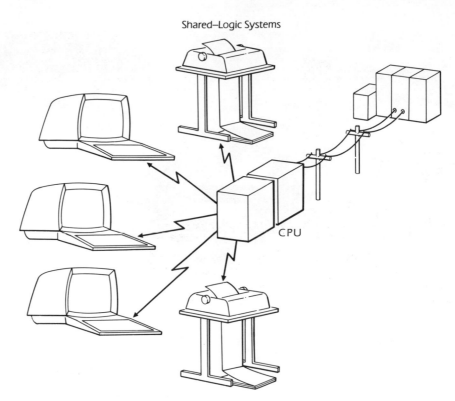

Figure 4.15 Shared-logic systems.

might have "**communications**" available on it. *Communications* in word/information processing is the process of moving or distributing the words or data from one location to another over telephone lines. It is often referred to as *distribution.*

Shared Systems

This category of word/information processing equipment includes CRTs, keyboards, printers, CPUs, and disk drives—basic components of word/information processing equipment that can be arranged in a variety of ways. Types of **shared systems** are shared-logic and distributed-logic.

Shared-logic. The "pure" **shared-logic** system combines pieces of equipment that use a common data base. There may be several terminals; each terminal has a keyboard and a visual display (CRT) that usually share the logic or intelligence of one computer, as well as storage and peripherals (Figure 4.15 and 4.16).

What is a "dumb" terminal? It is referred to as a shared-logic system when the terminals are "**dumb**" or are unable to work if the central computer ceases to work. Some shared-logic systems can handle from 2 to 35, or more, combined terminals and peripherals on one computer. What happens if the computer breaks down and there are 12 or more terminals dependent on it? None of the terminal operators can work on the equipment until the computer is operational again. This drawback forced vendors to come up with alternatives to shared-logic systems. But shared-logic systems do have some advantages, one of which is the ease of handling compli-

Figure 4.16 The A.B. Dick Magna SL offers full page display, a 550 word per minute printer, and a central processing unit with the flexibility of both magnetic cards and floppy disks. *ZCourtesy of A. B. Dick Company.)*

cated revisions. Several operators may be working on different parts of the revision at the same time (see Figure 4.17). In an office where the majority of the work is highly technical and constantly changing, material may be revised four or five times before a final document is prepared. Research development centers and legal offices are good examples of such a situation. A **clustered/shared-logic** system allows operators to share the same CPU, magnetic storage, and printers, but each operator has a separate disk drive. This allows for the integrity or security of central files. Each operator can function independently on "dumb" terminals using his or her own disk and disk drive, but, through the equipment, each is able to lock out other operators from visually or physically

Greater security of information

Figure 4.17 The Visual Type 3 shared-logic system from Xerox Corporation has a 66-line, full-page display screen and separate keyboard. A single system can serve up to ten work stations and ten printers. All system operations are independent and the system offers several hardware and software options. *(Courtesy of Xerox Corporation.)*

obtaining his or her own files (see Figure 4.18).

Distributed-logic. A **distributed-logic** system looks like a shared-logic system but is very different in that the logic or computer intelligence has been dispersed to the terminals, the printers, and the storage centers or other peripherals rather than concentrating all the intelligence in one computer. This creates what are called "**smart**" or "**intelligent**" terminals. Because intelligence or power is dispersed, a malfunction does not necessarily shut down the entire system. Each operator can access and control jobs freely because each terminal has its own computing power, but with central support when needed (such as for disk storage and printing). When a distributed-logic system is not tied into a central computer it is called a stand-alone system.

Shared resource. A shared resource is any independent workstation or "smart" terminal which can tie into another related piece of equipment to share resources such as volumes of hard disk storage, greater processor power, and peripherals.

The term "shared resource" may refer to connecting (through cables or tel-

What makes a terminal "smart"?

Terminal has its own CPU

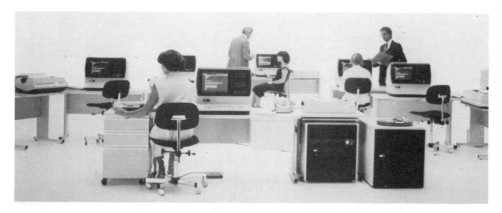

Figure 4.18 Lanier Business Products, Incorporated offers a family of nine shared and cluster typing systems with many system combinations ranging from a single unit to multistation typing systems sharing a central memory/processing unit (right bottom), magnetic storage, and printers. Shown is a shared system consisting of six typing stations, central processing units (right bottom) using floppy discs (capable of storing 200 pages) and magnetic disc cartridges (capable of storing 30,000 pages), and five printers. The No Problem LTE-3 electronic typewriter can be connected to the new units to form a cluster system. *(Courtesy of Lanier Business Products, Incorporated.)*

ephone lines) a stand-alone system to a shared-logic system. The stand-alone system then benefits from the increased power of the main logic (CPU), disk storage, and printers.

Manufacturers of word/information processing equipment have developed peripherals such as printers that can be shared by some of their systems. An example of a **shared printer** is where several word/information processing terminals can use one printer, as in a shared-logic system. Each of the terminals "asks" the CPU (central computer) to "tell" the printer to print. Media (magnetic diskettes and cards) may also be shared or used in more than one word/information processor if they are compatible. Another form of **shared media** is when the operator physically takes the magnetic media (like a mag card) recorded on one word/information processor and inserts it into a device called a mag card reader that works with another word/information processor. The reader uses the mag card as a **transfer media** to "dump" or read its previously recorded information onto the media of another word/information processor such as a diskette or into the memory of a printer or another computer. This is also referred to as **media conversion.**

Time-shared Systems

Since computers were first used, some organizations have sold a portion of their computer power to other organizations to use. These firms are often called time-sharing service bureaus. Organizations buying time on another organization's computer equipment are referred to as **subscribers.** There can be a few to several hundred subscribers using one **time-shared** system.

Subscribers to such systems call up the remote computer from their on-site

How does time-sharing work?

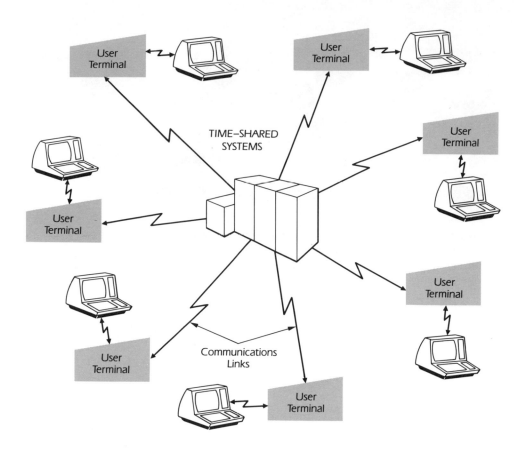

Figure 4.19 Time-shared systems.

terminals (keyboard and telephone connector) using ordinary phone lines (Figure 4.19). Charges for each subscriber are based on the time the user was on-line to the computer, the amount of computer power utilized, and the backup services provided by the vendor.

Many of the organizations who offer time-shared services for data processing now also offer similar services for word/information processing. Such organizations include Bowne Information Systems, PCS (Proprietary Computer Services), On-Line Systems, and GRW Time Sharing, Inc.

Why use time-shared systems?

Organizations who buy time from a vendor do so for several reasons. Maximum word/information processing power is available for a minimum financial commitment because of the organization subscribing to a time-shared system actually has the use of another organization's computer system. The subscriber is able to tie into levels of sophistication that an infrequent user could not justify on a purchase or rental basis. Also, additional capabilities are available, such as centralized text storage that allows an organization to send its text documents around the country to any branch time-sharing with the same organization. A backup system for organizations that experience user-owned computer equipment failure is also available through time-shared services.

How does a user tie into these services?

To tie in with time-shared systems, the user need only obtain a low-cost computer terminal (some of which are the size of a briefcase) or a communicating word/information processor. Usage of the service is billed on a monthly

The chart below outlines the hourly connect charges for 10 or 30 CPS dial–in usage to GRW Systems, Inc. timesharing services:

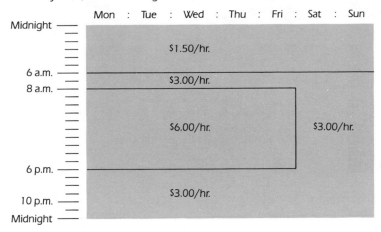

Figure 4.20 Hourly connect charges for a time-shared system.

basis, directly related to the time, degree, and type of service provided. The chart in Figure 4.20 is an example of hourly *connect charges* for 10 or 30 CPS (characters per second). If the equipment runs at 120 CPS, the rates are increased.

Another feature of time-shared systems is that through their use it is possible for different brands of equipment to send information to each other. For example, at the present time an IBM word/information processor cannot send information directly to a Vydec word/information processor and have its formats and keyboarded information accurately transmitted. But if Vydec and IBM can send information over phone lines to the same time-shared computer, they can, in effect, connect or send formats and all keyboarded information to each other. One organization that provides this connection is Bowne Information Systems.

Printing Devices: From Typebars to Lasers

The part of a word/information processor that transfers information to paper is called a **printing device.** Since some typewriters combine keyboarding and printer activities, they are known as input/output terminals. There are also separate pieces of equipment that can be used solely for printing and are physically separate from a keyboard. Each of these produce **hard copy** (paper) and are called **output equipment.**

A double-spaced keyboarded page contains about 200 words and is composed of about 1,000 individual symbols called **characters.** A typist who keyboards at 50 words per minute without any interruptions or errors produces one page every four minutes. Technological advances allow some pieces of equipment to print at speeds of 200 pages per minute or even faster.

The most important development contributing to advanced printing speeds is the printing device itself. Let's look at how technology has changed this device.

Figure 4.21 Typebar. The familiar curved well of typing keys that was the original printing device on the first typewriters and is still a popular device being manufactured today. *(Courtesy of Olivetti Corporation of America.)*

Figure 4.22 Element. The printing device that helped develop greater typewriting speeds than had been possible on typewriters using typebar devices. *(Courtesy of International Business Machines Corporation.)*

Impact Printing Devices

Device strikes the paper

The typebar, element, and print wheel are devices that transfer character images onto paper. The characters are transferred by the device striking a piece of paper through an inked or carbon ribbon against a platen.

These three devices are referred to as character **impact printers** and produce copies at 15 to 60 cps (characters per second) or 175 to 700 wpm (words per minute). If carbon copies of a document are needed, an impact printer is necessary to create these copies. Impact devices produce good quality printing but are relatively slow and noisy.

Typebar. Most of us who have a typewriter are familiar with the **typebar** mechanism (Figure 4.21), that originated with the invention of the first typewriter in 1868. Using this device, you strike a key on your typewriter and a metal bar emerges from a curved well of typebars. The metal bar has a letter on it corresponding to the letter on the key you struck. The typebar then hits the paper and produces a letter on the copy. Typebars are used on only a few word processing printers because they have difficulty moving fast enough to compete with newer printing devices.

Removable or interchangeable device

Element. A device commonly called a "ball", "golf ball", or "**Selectric element**" was developed by IBM in 1961 and is shown in Figure 4.22. Today the element is sold to other manufacturers to use in many of their products. Unlike the familiar typebar mechanism, the element contains all of the printing characters on one ball-shaped piece and is often called a single-element font. The selectric element strikes the paper through an inked or carbon ribbon. The element can be removed and **interchanged** with other elements to provide variation in type size and style. This is referred to as interchanging **fonts** or elements.

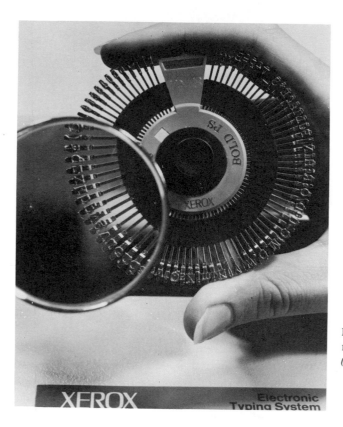

Figure 4.23 Print Wheel. A typing device that prints more rapidly than type typebar or Selectric element devices. *(Courtesy of Xerox Corporation.)*

Print Wheel. Diablo, a manufacturer, originally developed an inexpensive plastic printing device in 1974, called a **daisy print wheel,** that was purchased by Xerox Corporation. As shown in Figure 4.23, the shape looks like a flattened daisy with a different character at the end of each petal on a multispoked, rimless wheel. It is also referred to as a **single-element** typing device. The print wheel rotates in a vertical position until it arrives at the selected character, at which time a hammer hits the character against the paper to print through an inked or carbon ribbon. The originator of the print wheel started another company called Qume to make petal printers. The Qume print wheel and more recent brands like the IBM print wheel are refinements of the original daisy. They print rapidly, with good quality, and exceed the words-per-minute capabilities of the element device. Different typefaces can be obtained by removing one print wheel and interchanging it with another. Some equipment has print wheels that print **bidirectionally.** This means the printing device moves not only from left to right on the page, but continues printing from right to left for increased speed and productivity. These print wheel devices offer output speeds of 30, 40, 45, or 55 characters per second (350, 480, 500 or 650 words per minute) and a variety of typestyles. Some printers contain two print wheels for added speed.

A twin track printer contains two print wheels on the same printer that can simultaneously print two of the same or different type fonts, such as English and Greek/math.

NEC Information Systems, Inc. developed another single-element printing device called the NEC Spinwriter (Figure 4.24). Spinwriter printers are also known as **thimbles** because of their appearance. A thimble device allows you to

Another "single-element" device

Bidirectionality is faster

Twin track printer

Figure 4.24 The NEC Spinwriter is a fast, quiet, and durable printing device that resembles a thimble. *(Courtesy of NEC Spinwriter Systems, Inc.)*

print in from two to ten languages during the same print run at 55 cps. This device is quite durable and reliable.

High speed printers

Line Printers. **Line printers** are referred to as high speed printers and are most commonly used as a computer output device. They employ primarily chains, print wheels, or typebars as the printing device. They are driven by hammerlike objects that push the type against an inked ribbon to make a line of print against the paper. Speeds vary from 100 to about 3,800 lpm (lines per minute). In the past, print quality was sacrificed for speed and the output was used primarily for internal communications in an organization. The continued development of line printers is providing high speed and good quality so that higher quality documents can be produced for the external communications of an organization. Line printers are usually separate pieces of equipment and are often called peripherals.

Some line printers use a print wheel similar to the daisy print wheel device described above, but when used on line printers the print wheel achieves speeds of 150 lines per minute or greater (Figure 4.25).

Loop of metal

Chain Printers. A **chain device** on a line printer looks like letters embedded on a continuous loop of metal as in Figure 4.26. The chain moves through the printer horizontally and usually has four complete sections of characters (numbers and letters) following each other. As a desired character passes the position where it is to be printed, a hammerlike device presses the paper against the type. Speeds of up to 1,200 lines per minute can be attained using a chain printing device.

Matrix Printer. Another type of impact printer occasionally used is a matrix or **dot matrix printer,** consisting of a grouping of tiny rods mounted like hairbrush bristles in a rectangular base called a matrix. Characters are printed by selected rods being pushed against the paper. This results in a group of closely spaced dots with a printed pattern that looks like the shape of the desired character. The speed of a dot matrix printer varies from 150 to 600 cps or 230 lpm and can also produce multicolor printing on paper.

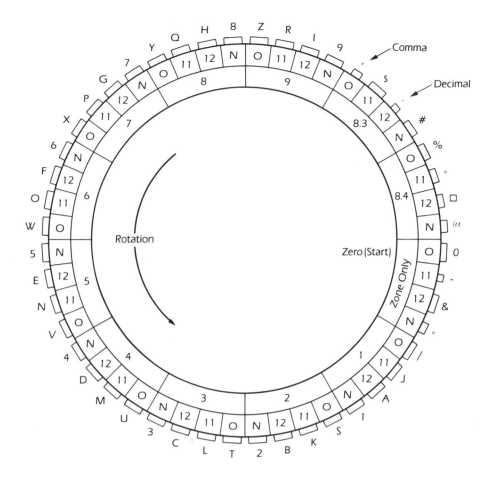

Figure 4.25 The print wheel printer has 120 of these rotary wheels, each of which has 48 characters. All 120 wheels are positioned to represent the characters to be printed, and the complete line of 120 characters impacts the paper at a speed of 150 lines per minute.

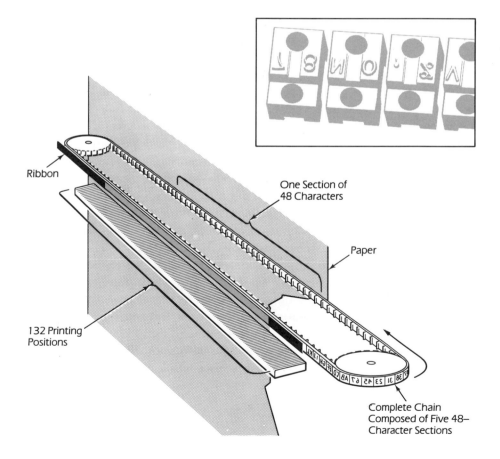

Figure 4.26 The train printer uses a type chain that travels horizontally. As a desired character passes the position where it is to be printed, an electromagnetic hammer presses the paper against the type. Speeds up to 2000 lines per minute are attained, with 132 characters per line.

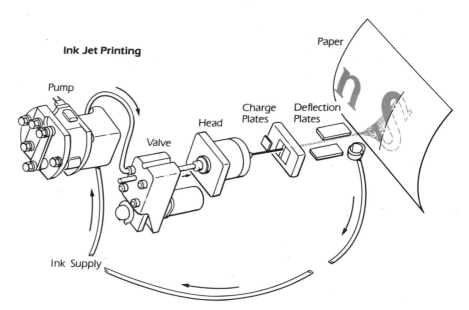

Ink Jet Printing

Figure 4.27 Ink jet printing. Ink jet technology uses a process that combines a special fast-drying ink and a nozzle to spray ink on a sheet of paper in patterns which are formed by electrically charging certain droplets.

Nonimpact Printers

The **nonimpact printer** has no printing device hitting a platen and is therefore almost noiseless. It can be located anywhere in an office and is generally faster than the impact printer.

Ink Jet Printers. An **ink jet printing** mechanism was developed before 1976 by A. B. Dick and was used in the computer industry. Figure 4.27 shows the process of ink jet printing. The characters are shaped by electrostatically spraying a very fine hairlike stream of ink onto paper. The quality of type is similar to that of a typewriter. The ink must dry by being absorbed into the paper. The IBM ink jet printer uses two different pitches and proportional spacing in nine type styles and one symbol font. Features that make the ink jet printer in great demand are high-volume form letters with automatic paper and envelope handling, very high playout speed, and excellent original print quality. The limitations of the ink jet printer are that it does not create carbon copies or masters for reprographics equipment and the quality range of paper that can be used is limited. The latest refinements of the ink jet printing device have opened new technology possibilities for equipment such as composers and electronic copiers. In 1976, IBM refined this unique mechanism for playback printout. It has speeds of 92 to 184 characters per second (approximately 1100 to 2200 words per minute). Other types of printers can print faster when driven by a computer.

Intelligent Printers. Printers combining laser, computer, and some photocopying technology are often called intelligent printers. Some of these page printers are also called copier/printers because they combine both photocopying and printing features. One example of an **intelligent printer/copier** is the IBM 6670 Information Distributor. It can link word processing and data processing by ac-

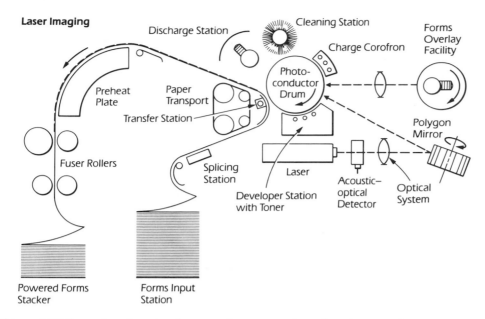

Figure 4.28 Laser imaging. An electrostatic process, laser imaging uses low-powered laser beams as the light source which exposes the photoconductor.

cepting input or information from IBM magnetic cards or through communication lines (telephone) from a computer or another word processor.

The IBM 6670 Information Distributor is also known as a **laser printer.** Laser printing is accomplished by an intense, narrow beam of pure red light capable of carrying millions of messages simultaneously (see Figure 4.28). A laser beam is merged with a process that uses light to shape a character on a photosensitive surface (high speed electrophotography). A toner is then used to transfer the image to paper. Speeds of laser printers vary from 8,000 to 18,000 lpm (90 to 600 pages per minute), and are often referred to as page printers. The Xerox 9700, a type of laser photocopier, can print on both sides of the paper, provide output on film, and print information being sent to it from a film or from compatible pieces of word processing equipment. This equipment offers such options as a mixture of type styles and can print type sizes from 4 point to 24 point. It is possible for the user to design and store in the printer custom-made company logos, type styles, letterheads, business forms, and even signatures.

Laser printer

An intelligent printer developed by Wang is called the Intelligent Image Printer. A copier is combined with electronics and fiber optics and joined to a Wang word/information processor as a high-speed, quality printer. **Fiber optics** consist of glass-like tubes as thin as strands of human hair that send a light source from one location to another (Figure 4.29). The light source changes machine signals into light pulses that are transmitted along the tubes. At the end of the tube, a device changes the varying intensities of light into signals that the receiving machine can recognize. The light being transmitted could be a laser beam.

Fiber optic printer

Lasers and fiber optics are creating higher quality documents at greater speeds and reducing the cost of word/information processing.

Printing Devices: From Typebars to Lasers

Fiber Optic CRT Imaging

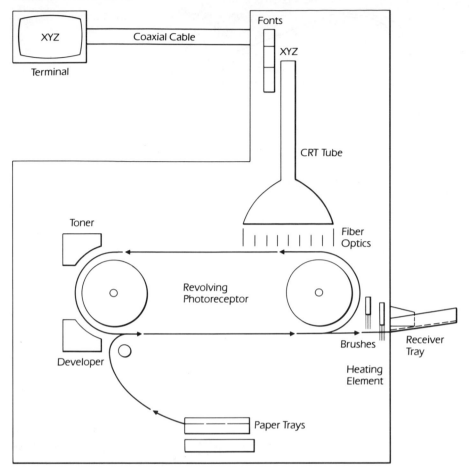

Figure 4.29 Fiber optic CRT imaging. Fiber optics is an electrostatic process that exposes the photoconductor by sending a CRT image through fine glass or plastic rods.

The electrostatic process has been used in the copier industry for years. Here's a simplified explanation of how it works:

1. A photoconducting surface (drum or belt) is electrically charged and made light-sensitive.
2. An image is reflected onto the surface.
3. Ink (toner) particles adhere to the charged areas of the photoconducting surface forming a latent image.
4. A piece of paper is charged, comes in contact with the photoconducting surface, and attracts the toner.
5. The photoconductor is desensitized and cleaned.

Typeface Sizes and Style

Pitch

There are three basic typeface sizes (referred to as **pitch**) that are used on the element, print wheel, and ink jet devices. Pitch is the number of characters per horizontal inch (cpi). Figure 4.30 shows samples of typeface sizes and styles. Pica type has a pitch of 10 cpi, and Elite has a pitch of 12 cpi. Proportional spacing is a typewriter feature that gives the alpha-numerical characters horizontal spacing related to their natural size. For example, an *i* is narrower than

```
|m|a|r|g|i|n|


|m|a|r|g|i|n|
```

Sample of proportional spacing.

Figure 4.30 Sample of typeface sizes and styles.

```
10   Pitch
     Artisan
     Courier
     Prestige pica

12   Pitch
     Courier
     Letter gothic
     Prestige elite

Proportional Spacing
     A r c a d i a
     B o l d f a c e
     E s s a y
```

an *m*; therefore, the *i* takes up less space in proportional spacing.

Some manufacturers of word/information processing equipment offer a special feature called dual or triple pitch, which allows switching from one type size and style to another on the same piece of equipment.

As word/information processing equipment becomes integrated with aspects of the printing industry, the terminology for type size takes on a new look. For instance, type size is referred to as point size and the word "font" relates to type styles. Operators of word/information processors who input material will want to become familiar with this terminology to develop flexibility for operating other types of equipment.

Point size

Production Speed, Print Quality, and Cost

When selecting the appropriate printing device it is important to consider production speed, print quality, and cost. If printing speed is the most important factor, then a larger computer-type printer can be considered. If print quality is the main consideration, then slower equipment with high quality, such as automatic composing equipment, must be considered. Finally, if cost is the most important factor, printers such as the nonimpact ink jet, laser, and fiber optic printers (Figures 4.31, 4.32, and 4.33) may be ruled out because they are more expensive than some of the other devices, although, if the volume of output is extremely high, the cost of these per unit of output could actually be cheaper. The most important consideration is to select the speed or quality that is most appropriate for your application or your dollars.

Selecting a printing device

Summary

This chapter covered the output aspect of information processing. The evolution of the original word processor into today's word/information processor

Figure 4.31 Office System 6 using the IBM 6/450 model features high-speed ink jet printing and automatic paper and envelope handling with electronic communication capabilities. In the background are an IBM 6640 Document Printer (left) and an IBM Mag Card/A Typewriter. *(Courtesy of International Business Machines Corporation.)*

Figure 4.32 The IBM 6670 Information Distributor prints with a laser and receives and transmits documents electronically over ordinary telephone lines. It also links word processing and data processing, printing computer-based information in typewriter-like quality letter-size originals using customized formats. The new intelligent printer also prints on both sides of a page, electronically changes typefaces, and can print multiple sets of documents at speeds of up to 1,800 characters per second in original print quality. *(Courtesy of International Business Machines Corporation.)*

Figure 4.33 Wang's intelligent Image Printer, prints 1,600 quality characters per minute without operator intervention. A selection of type fonts, specified during document input, offers unprecedented printing flexibility. Clean, quiet, and extremely easy to use, the Image Printer provides typewriter-like results at high speed in virtually all applications. *(Courtesy of Wang Laboratories, Incorporated.)*

(Figure 4.34) was described. All word/information processing equipment processes information, uses printing devices, and utilizes a form of storage media. Some have display terminals and others use nondisplay terminals. There are three main categories of word/information processors: stand-alone systems, shared systems, and time-shared systems. The shared systems are of two types: shared-logic and distributed logic. Media and printers are components that may also be shared.

The only constant in the word/information processing industry is change. Change in printing devices, storage media, printers, peripheral devices, and computer technology continues to transform and broaden the definition of word processing to word/information processing. This newer term is being used while the industry is in the transition from word processing to information processing.

Figure 4.34 The Wang OIS/130 is a hard disk system with storage of up to 4,000 full pages on the master disk to automate practically any office task. Totally compatible with other Wang word processing and OIS systems, OIS/130 operates with up to 14 diverse peripherals for complete versatility in any office environment. *(Courtesy of Wang Laboratories, Incorporated.)*

Summary

Key Terms

Automatic typewriter
Teletypewriter
Natural language keyboard
Word processor
Text editor
Power typing
Nondisplay system
Visual display
Input/output terminal
CRT
Blind terminal
Dual display terminals
Thin windows
Word/information processor
Stand-alone system
Electronic typewriter
Shared systems
Shared-logic system
Clustered/shared-logic
   system

Distributed logic
"Smart" terminal
"Dumb" terminal
Time-shared systems
Output equipment
Printing device
Impact printer
Font
Line printer
Print wheel
Thimble
Bidirectionality
Chain printer
Nonimpact printer
Dot matrix printer
Ink jet printer
Intelligent printers
Laser printing
Fiber optics
Pitch

Study Guide

This study guide provides you with feedback to find out how well you are doing. Use a separate sheet of paper to record your answers. When you have finished check your responses with the answers at the back of the book.

Matching: Choose the answer that best defines the term in the left column.

1. Word processor   a. A terminal that can no longer function if the computer it is tied to ceases to operate.

2. "Dumb" terminal   b. An impact printing device that looks like a flattened daisy with a different character at the end of each petal.

3. Text editor   c. A single station word/ information processor (used by one person at a time) that is not hooked up to or does not share the processing power of a central computer.

4. Ink jet printing   d. Any grouping of the basic components (CRTs, keyboards, printers, CPUs, disk drives) where one or more of the components is shared or hooked to another component.

5. Shared system   e. A cathode ray tube used to display information.

6. CRT   f. A nonimpact printer that prints characters by spraying a stream of ink onto the paper.

7. Time-shared system   g. A machine that captures a document and, through its use, manipulates the information in many ways before it is turned into hard or readable copy.

8. Stand-alone system   h. One of the names given to an early word processor that was designed primarily for revision of text.

9. Daisy print wheel   i. A service bureau whose subscribers share the cost and time usage on computers and peripheral devices that are in a location remote from the subscribers.

Multiple choice: Select the letter or letters that best answer each question.

10. The most important initial advantage of the word processor was:
    a. Its ability to automatically play back materials while unattended.
    b. Its ability to revise and/or edit information.
    c. Its ability to make decisions about revisions.
    d. How much information it could store in its memory.

11. One of the categories of shared systems is called a:
    a. Dictation system.
    b. Shared-logic system.
    c. Output system.
    d. Text editor.

12. The development of the laser printing device is very important in the information processing industry because it:
    a. Allows for more typing on a line.
    b. Creates a light image that shows you where to print the characters as it moves across the paper.
    c. Increases production speed considerably over the other printing devices.
    d. Increases the line count per page.

13. A major advantage in using visual display equipment over nondisplay equipment is:
    a. More lines can be proofread on a screen at one time than on a nondisplay text editor.
    b. If paper is needed at all, it is only when it is necessary to produce a final document in hard copy.
    c. The visual screens can be converted to televisions.
    d. There is no eyestrain using the visual screen.

True/False: Write + for True, 0 for False for each question.

14. The print wheel devices on word/information processors can produce copy at speeds comparable to the laser printer.

15. Computer technology is the basic technology of the word/information processing industry.

16. The angle you hold a print wheel when installing it on a printer is called pitch.

17. The automatic typewriter developed in the 1930s was designed primarily to handle repetitive documents.

18. Hard copy is copy that is stored inside a computer.

19. The ink jet printer is a device that has printing speeds greater than any of the other printing devices that are revolutionizing the word/information processing industry.

20. Word/information processing terminals with visual screens show whatever is typed on the keyboard or is retrieved from storage.

21. An operator of a word/information processor can only correct or revise one line at a time.

22. Because electronic typewriters have such limited capabilities, they will not easily find a place in today's office.

23. Color display stations for word/information processing terminals have not yet been developed.

Questions on Concepts

1. Describe the advantages of using a visual or display screen word/information processor as compared to a nondisplay word/information processor.
2. Name the three main categories of word/information processing equipment.
3. For what reasons would a manufacturer design a word/information processor with only a one-line or partial display screen?
4. Define the term "shared systems" and list the categories within this equipment group.
5. What were the main functions of the first text editor?
6. Explain the term "intelligent printer".
7. Compare a shared-logic system to a distributed-logic system.
8. Discuss the advantages of subscribing to a time-shared service bureau.
9. Explain the importance of production speed, print quality, and cost when selecting a printing device.
10. Compare the advantages and disadvantages of nonimpact printing devices to those of impact printing devices.

Case and Activities

W. E. Balsukot Associates, Inc. is a Seattle-based investment counseling and research firm that has been managing other people's money since 1937. Assets total approximately $7 billion. Currently, the management of these assets requires an enormous research effort and numerous statistical support services. A variety of data is processed and used throughout the firm in order to best serve each client. Word processing is invaluable to W. E. Balsukot because it provides an effective means of arranging and recording volumes of up-to-date information in a clear, easily readable form. The word processing center allows one of the firm's overall objectives to be met: that of providing accurate and concise information and documents to each client.

The work load directed to the word processing center consists of a number of statistical projects, daily dictation and one-time correspondence, heavy revision of large investment proposals, forms requiring five carbon copies, and mass mailings. The center has three word processing operators and one supervisor.

At the present time the word processing center has one electric typewriter and three IBM text editors called MT/STs.

1. What type of word/information processors would you select to replace the existing keyboards in this center? Why?
2. Indicate the type of printer and printing device you would select for outputting based on the processing needs of this organization. Why?

Activities

1. Attend a local office products show. Visit the booths of vendors displaying word/information processing systems. Collect brochures on the available products and write a report comparing the features and prices of the various categories of equipment as described in this chapter.
2. Visit the word processing center of a local organization in your community. Find out what categories of word/information processors they use and why.
3. Read two articles in recent word/information processing literature on topics that relate to output and prepare abstracts of them.

CHAPTER 5

Alternative Methods of Input and Output

The objectives of this chapter are to:

1. Explain the purpose of a multifunction workstation.

2. Describe three types of voice processing systems and their uses.

3. Compare the basic document cycle with and without the use of OCR.

4. Discuss the primary advantage of using OCR.

5. Explain what is meant by media incompatibility.

6. Define reprographics.

7. List the six major reprographics alternatives.

8. List two advantages and two disadvantages of the copying process.

9. Give three reasons why copiers are misused and list three possibilities for copy control procedures.

10. Describe the basic principle of the offset printing process.

11. Describe the phototypesetting process.

12. Identify five factors to consider when choosing a reprographics method.

13. Compare the offset process with the stencil and fluid processes.

Most inputting to word/information processing equipment systems is done by keyboarding onto storage media using a keyboard similar to a typewriter. The keyboard is generally designed for one function: editing text to produce a final document. Inputting, however, can be done on keyboards designed for this and other functions. These keyboards are referred to as **multifunction workstations**. Inputting to word/information processing can also be done using the voice instead of a keyboard. This method is referred to as voice processing. A hard (paper) copy document, one that has been typed on a regular typewriter keyboard, can be used for input to a word/information processor because equipment has been developed that can scan (read) the typed copy and transfer the contents to storage media.

Machines once used primarily by court reporters are now also becoming a means of inputting to word/information processing systems. These machines input whole words into the system at one time, using letters of the alphabet as shorthand symbols. This chapter discusses alternative methods of inputting and shows how they differ from the traditional way of producing a document.

Reprographics is another method of achieving a form of hard copy output in the word processing system. This chapter describes the various reprographics methods and discusses some factors to consider when choosing a reprographics process.

Additional Methods of Inputting

Multifunction workstations, voice processing equipment, optical character recognition equipment (OCR), and machine shorthand equipment are all being used for inputting information into word/information processing equipment systems.

Multifunction Workstations

Equipment that can be placed on a desk, looks like a small television set, and has a keyboard may be called a **multifunction workstation**. A multifunction workstation allows many tasks to be completed at one workstation in addition to the "normal" editing chores of processing information. Tasks may appear on the screen or in several sections called "**windows**." A screen divided into four windows or sections may be used by a word/information processing operator at one time to create a new document, refer to stored paragraphs, see a document related to the one being answered, and see messages or news of incoming mail.

Screen is sectioned into windows

The primary applications of current and future multifunction workstations are entering words and data, processing, communicating, retrieving, and storing and exchanging files without going to **hard copy**.

Document production

If the multifunction workstation is placed on a manager's desk, it may be called a **managerial workstation**. This system allows managers to communicate electronically inside and outside their organizations. No hard copy or paper is created except when necessary. Mail is delivered immediately from the sender to the receiver and can be read at any time from any location. An administrative support person or a manager might use a multiwindow screen, as shown in Figure 5.1, with as many as eight sections to read incoming mail, file and retrieve stored documents electronically, list appointments and review the calendar, set up a reminder file (tickler file) of important deadlines and review it, update lists, create new documents from one standard text, and send outgoing messages.

Some manufacturers call multifunction workstations interactive workstations and see them developing into personal-use tools, much like calculators. Some equipment has a conventional keyboard similar to a word/information processor, while other types have only a 12-key pad similar to a calculator. The equipment also may be designed to recognize a limited spoken (voice) vocabulary. This equipment would allow the manager to speak directly into the workstation. Other multifunction workstations have pressure-sensitive areas on the

Personal-use tools

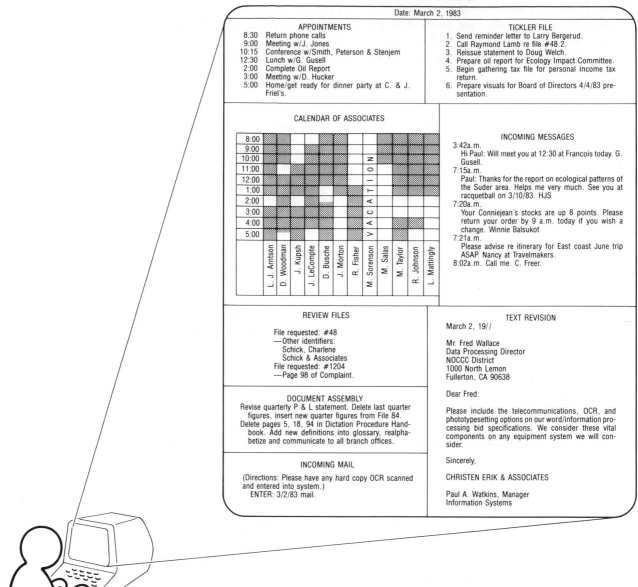

MULTIFUNCTION WORKSTATION

Date: March 2, 1983

APPOINTMENTS

8:30 Return phone calls
9:00 Meeting w/J. Jones
10:15 Conference w/Smith, Peterson & Stenjem
12:30 Lunch w/G. Gusell
2:00 Complete Oil Report
3:00 Meeting w/D. Hucker
5:00 Home/get ready for dinner party at C. & J. Friel's.

TICKLER FILE

1. Send reminder letter to Larry Bergerud.
2. Call Raymond Lamb re file #48.2.
3. Reissue statement to Doug Welch.
4. Prepare oil report for Ecology Impact Committee.
5. Begin gathering tax file for personal income tax return.
6. Prepare visuals for Board of Directors 4/4/83 presentation.

CALENDAR OF ASSOCIATES

	L. J. Arntson	D. Woodman	J. Kupsh	J. LeCompte	D. Busche	J. Morton	R. Fisher	M. Sorenson	M. Salas	M. Taylor	R. Johnson	L. Mattingly
8:00												
9:00												
10:00							N					
11:00							O					
12:00							I					
1:00							T					
2:00							A					
3:00							C					
4:00							A					
5:00							V					

INCOMING MESSAGES

3:42a.m.
  Hi Paul: Will meet you at 12:30 at Francois today. G. Gusell.
7:15a.m.
  Paul: Thanks for the report on ecological patterns of the Suder area. Helps me very much. See you at racquetball on 3/10/83. HJS
7:20a.m.
  Your Conniejean's stocks are up 8 points. Please return your order by 9 a.m. today if you wish a change. Winnie Balsukot
7:21a.m.
  Please advise re itinerary for East coast June trip ASAP. Nancy at Travelmakers.
8:02a.m. Call me. C. Freer.

REVIEW FILES

File requested: #48
—Other identifiers:
   Schick, Charlene
   Schick & Associates
File requested: #1204
—Page 98 of Complaint.

DOCUMENT ASSEMBLY

Revise quarterly P & L statement. Delete last quarter figures, insert new quarter figures from File 84. Delete pages 5, 18, 94 in Dictation Procedure Handbook. Add new definitions into glossary, realphabetize and communicate to all branch offices.

INCOMING MAIL

(Directions: Please have any hard copy OCR scanned and entered into system.)
   ENTER: 3/2/83 mail.

TEXT REVISION

March 2, 19//

Mr. Fred Wallace
Data Processing Director
NOCCC District
1000 North Lemon
Fullerton, CA 90638

Dear Fred:

Please include the telecommunications, OCR, and phototypesetting options on our word/information processing bid specifications. We consider these vital components on any equipment system we will consider.

Sincerely,

CHRISTEN ERIK & ASSOCIATES

Paul A. Watkins, Manager
Information Systems

Figure 5.1 Managerial workstation.

visual screen that may be labeled "search" or "get file". When the manager touches the spot, the designated function takes place.

An advanced level of sophistication in multifunction workstations will allow them to be connected to peripherals such as printers, phototypesetters, and **scanners** (a device that reads typed characters from hard copy). This connection will give these workstations the capability of performing many kinds of work that will result in a complete information processing system.

One of the most important tools human beings use to communicate with one another is speech. We have been able to extend our powers by inventing mechanical and electronic equipment such as the typewriter, calculator, and computer to help make work easier. However, until recently, we have not been able to speak to the equipment and have it respond to our spoken word. Therefore, manufacturers developed cards with punched holes, magnetic media, and machines that could "read" the printed word. All of these devices have served in place of speech between people and machines. Recently, however, developments in voice processing technology have changed this situation. Machines can now recognize and respond to words spoken by a person (they are *voice actuated*).

Talking to machines

In some instances, voice processing refers to using the voice rather than keyboarding as a method of inputting information into the word/information processing system. Such devices today have limitations: the vocabularies they recognize are not extensive, the person speaking must be trained in how to speak the words, the machine usually only recognizes words but not continuous speech, and the accuracy is not always perfect. However, since speech is the fastest means of originating a message, these limitations will eventually be overcome. We will use our voice more and more to communicate with machines and the machines in turn will respond.

A common form of voice processing is machine dictation. Speaking over the telephone is another method of voice processing. In addition to dictation systems and telephone systems, many voice processing systems have been developed recently.

New developments

Voice Message Systems. These systems provide callers with an alternative to speaking directly with the person they call. A form of a voice message system already in use is the telephone answering machine. With a telephone answering machine, the person receiving the call regulates the incoming call and the person calling has no choice but to leave a message or hang up. If you are using a **voice message system**, when you call another person you will make the choice of whether to talk to the person or leave a message.

Voice Reminder Systems. These systems allow an executive to program reminder messages into a machine. **Voice reminder messages** allow someone to make a recorded message that will serve as a reminder of appointments, meetings, and other scheduled activities. Voice reminder systems handle a part of the job that traditional secretaries did, or can be used to lighten the administrative secretary's responsibilities.

Voice Recognition Systems. These systems recognize human speech and are referred to as **voice data entry** or **automatic speech recognition** (ASR) systems. Two classes of ASR systems are speaker-dependent and speaker-independent. If the ASR requires a sample of how each person says each vocabulary item before it can recognize that person speaking the item, it is called a **speaker-dependent system**. The process of providing an ASR with the necessary samples of words for the system to recognize is called "training" the system. A **speaker-independent system** recognizes what is being said without ever hav-

Figure 5.2 This voice data entry system allows an operator using natural language to send data from oil well logs directly to the computer. Using this type of system eliminates errors that are often made when transferring data because all data can be verified. *(Courtesy of Interstate Electronics, Inc. a subsidiary of A-T-O.)*

ing been previously supplied a sample of how that specific speaker says each vocabulary item. Examples of speaker-dependent systems (Figures 5.2 and 5.3) in the developmental stages include the operators of a word/information processor using the system to repetitively perform function commands such as paragraph indent, line delete, center, search, replace, and justify by speaking into the equipment. This development may have a significant impact on the ease of entering function commands into word/information processing systems and on operator training. Speaker-independent systems are required when the operator is a casual user and there is no requirement to validate that the operator is authorized to perform the task, such as determining the flight weather between two locations.

In voice recognition systems there are two ways in which the speaker-dependent and speaker-independent systems will recognize words. They are known as **discrete word recognition** and connected or **continuous word recognition**. In discrete word recognition, the operator must pause between speaking each vocabulary item. In some forms of automatic speech recognition systems, the system responds to the caller's voice.

Connected or continuous word recognition does not require the operator to pause between vocabulary items and can recognize a sequence of spoken commands in a natural speech pattern. This is also known as continuous

Types of word recognition

Figure 5.3 The intelligent Voice Data Entry System with a Voice Recognition Module enables an operator to speak into the system using a limited number of words. The machine reacts with a prompt or question on the screen. The operator then provides a natural language verbal response. *(Courtesy of Interstate Electronics, Inc. a subsidiary of A-T-O.)*

speech recognition. These systems are able to recognize continuous human speech sound patterns and, in the future, will not be limited to a restricted vocabulary. Such systems have not been perfected yet, but the ultimate goal is a system that will keyboard a person's words as they are being continuously spoken, eliminating the need for a typist.

Continuous speech recognition is the most difficult of the voice processing systems to develop because there are many variables to deal with, such as voice speed, high and low voices, and different ways of pronouncing words.

Speech recognition in voice processing systems is useful because it is not always practical for workers to use their hands to control equipment or to enter data. For example, workers may be away from the equipment, using their hands for other tasks like holding a measuring device, unable to use their hands because they are soiled, or forbidden to use their hands for health reasons such as when packaging foods. Also, speech recognition systems are particularly good tools for business executives like doctors and lawyers who may refuse to use keyboards.

Optical Character Recognition (OCR)

The process of reading a typewritten page using an optical character reader is called **optical character recognition (OCR)**. An OCR reader is an optical character recognition machine that scans (reads) pages of documents. The reader can actually copy an originally typed document onto magnetic media. Just as a photocopier copies an originally typed document onto another piece of

What is OCR?

Additional Methods of Inputting

Figure 5.4 *(left)* The Typereader 2 Optical Character Recognition Scanner allows scanning of 14″ legal size pages as well as smaller size paper. It reads OCR-B and Hendrix Gothic typefaces, pages with any line spacing, and either 10 or 12 pitch. *(Courtesy of Hendrix Corporation.)* **Figure 5.5** *(right)* An Alphaword Optical Character Recognition Scanner with a keyboard. *(Courtesy of CompuScan.)*

paper, OCR readers read many types of documents. This section covers only the kind of OCR reader that reads typewritten pages (Figures 5.4 and 5.5). OCR page readers are very accurate and make fewer than 1 error in 10,000 characters. They electronically send information to a computer or word/information processor at 25 times the speed of manual rekeyboarding. Several types of OCR readers with varied applications are manufactured by companies such as Hendrix, Context, DEST, Kurzweil, and Compuscan.

Past uses of OCR

OCR is technology that has been used in the data processing industry for years. You see evidence of its use every day on your credit card statements, electric bills, blank checks, at the checkout stand in the supermarket, and on magazine labels. Firms such as IBM, NCR (National Cash Register), and Honeywell have refined OCR techniques for data processing over the past 20 years and reduced the cost of the machine from $100,000 to about $15,000 or less. The cost reduction has resulted in greater use of OCR by organizations with word/information processing systems who can now afford to take advantage of the unique benefits of optical scanning.

Why use OCR?

Workflow of a Document Using OCR. OCR can reduce keyboarding and turnaround time, lower equipments costs, increase equipment productivity, reduce organizational problems and training costs, and ease conversion of magnetic media. Figure 5.6 shows how this is accomplished.

STEP 1 The word originator generates the document (by dictating to a secretary, writing in longhand, or using machine dictation).

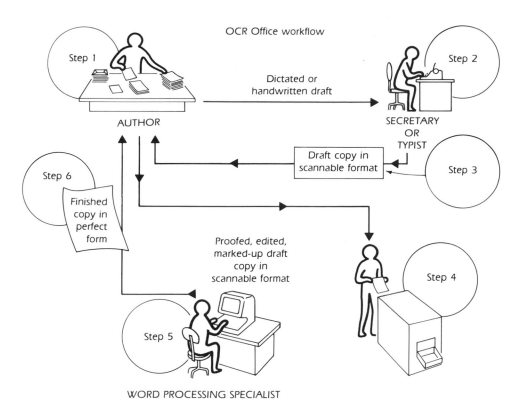

Figure 5.6 Workflow of a document using OCR.

STEP 2 Any office worker using an electric typewriter with an OCR element (font) or print wheel prepares a draft at rough-draft speed. For maximum accuracy, most OCR page readers require typewriters that are 10 pitch and use film ribbon. The method of correcting typographical errors varies with the kinds of OCR page readers used. Many newer OCR readers are now able to read several type styles and sizes, and some are reading handwriting as well as hand-printed material.

STEP 3 The typed draft is then returned to the word originator for review. The originator can edit and correct the typewritten draft, using handwritten notations as needed. While editing the draft, the word originator may use a blue or red pencil.

STEP 4 The marked-up typewritten draft is scanned by the OCR reader. The OCR reader only copies the originally-typed draft. It does not pick up any of the handwritten changes the originator makes on the draft. At the same time, the typewritten text is being scanned, it is automatically being duplicated onto a magnetic storage medium.

STEP 5 The draft is instantly ready to be corrected on a word/information processor. A trained operator revises the document that appears on the screen by looking at the marked-up rough draft. The operator has to keyboard only the revisions and manipulate the recorded information to match the revised draft. The operator does not have to spend any time doing original keyboarding of the document.

STEP 6   The corrected document may then be returned to the originator. It may be obtained by using a line printer located next to the OCR reader or one found in another location. It can also be printed out on a stand-alone word/information processor or a shared printer. If a printed copy is needed, the information can be transferred (converted) to typesetter tape and printed out on a phototypesetter.

Benefits of OCR. Using an OCR reader in a word/information processing system reduces the time it takes to return the document to the word originator. A secretary can keyboard on an electric typewriter at top rough-draft speed and immediately return the draft to the originators. Had this draft gone to a word processing center and through the basic document cycle without the use of OCR, the word originator may have had to wait twice as long for any of these reasons: The originator might be on a priority work list and have to wait for another originator's work to be finished; the transcriptionist might be unfamiliar with the dictation habits of the originator; the transcriptionist might have to spend a good deal of time playing out a corrected copy of the draft after making corrections for typographical errors, and so on. Therefore, OCR eliminates time-consuming retyping and allows the corrected copy to be handled more efficiently.

Reduces turnaround time

When OCR is used, the traditional boss/secretary relationship does not have to be disrupted. Therefore, both people accept the change to word/information processing. Since the secretaries doing the keyboarding are familiar with the originator's dictation style, handwriting, and spelling, they are able to produce rough drafts faster. These secretaries are able to take advantage of the benefits of word/information processing without having to be trained on new equipment.

Make the change to word processing easier

Using OCR equipment makes better use of expensive word/information processing equipment. With OCR added, this equipment is used mainly to revise text and do other work that cannot be done with a regular electric typewriter. The most time-consuming part of producing the document, the original keyboarding, is still done on the less expensive electric typewriters. Every office typewriter thus becomes an input device for the word/information processing equipment, and fewer word/information processors are required.

Typewriters become input devices

Problems to Consider When Implementing OCR. There are many benefits of using OCR but there are also some disadvantages. Sometimes it takes many days to get the OCR equipment installed and serviced to run properly. Secretaries inputting on their regular electric typewriters need to be trained to input correctly for OCR. One problem to be aware of for some OCR equipment is inserting paper into the typewriter correctly so that the characters print in a straight line across the paper. If this is not done properly, an OCR reader may not pick up any of the typed information. The error rate in reading pages may be very high if the paper does not feed properly through the machine and valuable time would be lost in rekeyboarding the information. Also, the method of correcting errors

Handwritten additions or insertions can be made with a red Pentel fine line ballpoint pen. Scanner will ignore red ink insertions, but they will be a flag to scanner operator who will make the insertion at our editing terminal.

Correction & addition instructions

Deletions (cross outs) can be made with a black Pentel medium ballpoint pen. If copy has been triple spaced, you can reinsert the page in the typewriter and type the correction in the space below the line with the error.

Errors detected during initial typing can be corrected by using "delta" symbol which looks like this Δ.

Use of delta symbol

A single "delta" cancels the character immediately preceding "delta".

Two consecutive "deltas" cancel the word immediately preceding the two "deltas", including the word space. Insert one space before typing the corrected word.

Three or more consecutive "deltas" cancel all characters and spaces preceding the three "deltas" to the beginning of the line.

Erasures, opaque liquids or correction tapes **cannot** be used.

```
//02There is nothing quite like the tatΔste of ripe, red tomatoes
straight fΔout of the garden. They are rich, almost trΔart, and
thiΔeir pulp glows with a deep orangeΔy red lusciousness. And not-
hing is as sweet tastyΔing on a summersΔ evening as the just-picked
salad of letuceΔΔ lettuce, onions and cucumbers from your onwΔΔ own
```

Text with corrections inserted

There is nothing quite like the taste of ripe, red tomatoes straight out of the garden. They are rich, almost tart, and their pulp glows with a deep orangy red lusciousness. And nothing is as sweet tasting on a summer evening as the just-picked salad of lettuce, onions and cucumbers from your own

Phototypeset output

Figure 5.7 Preparing copy for some OCR scanners.

while doing the original keyboarding is time-consuming for some types of OCR readers. Secretaries may have to learn special methods for correcting and coding documents that must be inserted while doing the original keyboarding. These codes are read by the OCR reader and become format instructions such as paragraph, indent, or underline (Figure 5.7).

Media conversion

When an OCR reader is scanning text, it usually does not allow other machine operations to occur simultaneously on a word/information processor. This ties up the use of one terminal for the period of time necessary to complete the scanning. Figure 5.8 shows a connecting device (interface) developed by one manufacturer that allows the scanning to operate at the same time as all other word/information processing functions.

Media Incompatibility. One of the problems in the word/information processing industry has been that of **media incompatibility** — one type of magnetic media may not work on another word/information processor. Therefore, if you were to have all of your documents stored on one type of media and decided to trade in your present equipment for machines that use a different type, you would not be able to do anything with the information stored on your original media. You would not be able to revise it or even to see what was stored on it. Manufacturers have had to develop some way to transfer information stored on one type of media to another type. This method of moving the information is called **media conversion.** Using a card converter, it is now possible to move the in-

Magnetic card converter

Figure 5.8 An on-line OCR interface lets users optically scan information at local or remote terminals via telecommunications. It operates simultaneously with all other word processing functions such as text entry, revision, and print-out. *(Courtesy of Wang Laboratories.)*

Can OCR assist in media conversion?

formation stored on magnetic cards to magnetic disks. The cards are inserted into the word/information processor and are read onto the magnetic disk. Another device used for media conversion is called an on-line interface (see Figure 7.26). It connects most word/information processors, computers, OCR readers, and phototypesetters. Organizations that have a great deal of information stored on media often have to send it to a place that specializes in media conversion.

Another method for handling media conversion is with the use of an OCR reader. For example, you may wish to use your existing type A diskettes on a different word/information processor. That word/information processor will use diskettes, but the diskettes may be type B. Both diskettes A and B are available from the same magnetic media supplier but cannot be used interchangeably. Neither word/information processor manufacturer has a diskette media converter. How do you convert all of your information from one diskette to another diskette if they are not compatible? You use an OCR reader to convert the information. You place your existing type A diskette into a word/information processor to print out the pages of information you wish transferred. The only new item added to this old procedure is that you change your printer element or print wheel to an OCR typeface. Then you take all pages printed with an OCR typeface and have them read by an OCR reader which automatically copies the pages onto the new media (type B diskette).

Some OCR readers will now read pages printed with typefaces other than

Figure 5.9 Keystrokes are captured by the shorthand machine and transmitted to the automated transcription system. *(Courtesy of Stenograph Corporation.)*

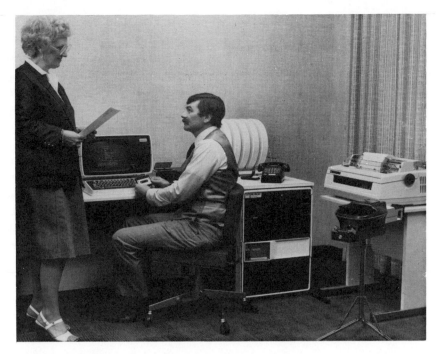

Figure 5.10 The automated transcription unit instantly transcribes the machine shorthand notes into English. The transcript can be displayed on a screen, printed, or recorded electronically for later recall. *(Courtesy of Stenograph Corporation.)*

OCR, such as Courier or Letter Gothic typefaces. Media conversion using an OCR reader will cut costs greatly because information will not have to be sent out for media conversion.

Media conversion can also be done between two word/information processors which have compatible media by using a central computer. The information stored on media is placed in one word/information processor and sent over telephone lines to a computer. The computer makes the necessary conversion and sends the information over telephone lines to another word/information processor.

Media conversion through a computer

Machine Shorthand

Machines such as the one in Figure 5.9 are becoming an alternative to the typewriter keyboard as a means of inputting information into word/information processing systems. The standard shorthand machine once used primarily by court reporters to take notes in court is now used in word/information processing because the keystrokes made on the equipment can be captured on magnetic tape and transcribed using **computer aided transcription (CAT)** as shown in Figure 5.10. If you were to use this method for inputting, you would need a shorthand machine that would allow you to insert magnetic tape cassettes before you take notes. You would also have to learn a shorthand system composed of letters that allow you to write whole words by depressing one or more keys at a time. For example, you could write the word "sat" in one stroke, because the letters on the keyboard are arranged in such a way that this is possible. The word "ready" (RED/EU) would have to be written in two strokes.

The advantage of using this method is that the traditional boss/secretary relationship does not have to be disrupted. The boss can dictate to a secretary who takes machine shorthand at speeds of anywhere from 200 to 230 words per minute and have the document transcribed by the computer. This method eliminates the need for the secretary to type the document. Once the magnetic tape is read into the computer, needed revisions can be made using a word/information processor with a screen just as if the document had been keyboarded directly. The words appear as words, not as shorthand symbols on the screen. The advantage over a keyboard is that whole words can be inputted to the system rather than individual characters. This method doesn't do away with machine dictation, but instead enhances its use. Secretaries or specialists in a word processing center can listen to machine dictation, take notes, and have the computer transcribe their notes immediately. This method reduces the time needed to transcribe notes taken at long business meetings, seminars, and conventions. The machine is portable, unlike most typewriter keyboards. The secretary can take notes at a convention, return to the office, use the computer, and produce pages of text that might have taken days to transcribe.

Additional Methods of Outputting

Reprographics is another method of achieving a form of hard copy output in the word processing system. Available methods of reprographics range from the familiar carbon process to very sophisticated phototypesetting equipment connected to computers.

The terms "duplication" and "reproduction" are commonly used for this area of output; however, the names "reprography" and "reprographics" are acceptable. We will use the term reprographics.

An organization depends upon paperwork to carry on its work. Just as the original copy is necessary, many organizations must provide one or more copies of the same document. Therefore, offices use various types of equipment to meet the demands of reprographics.

The cost savings that word/information processing provides is eliminated if the cost reduction does not continue from origination through distribution—the final stage of the document cycle. The office worker must know how to make decisions about the most economical method of reproduction to save time and money and to produce the quantity and quality of copy needed in each situation. Word/information processing equipment is able to produce copies that look like individually-typed correspondence. Other methods discussed in this chapter produce copies that vary in quality.

Reprographics is an area in which decision-making ability is required. An important decision is choosing the correct process; not all office correspondence demands high-quality copies.

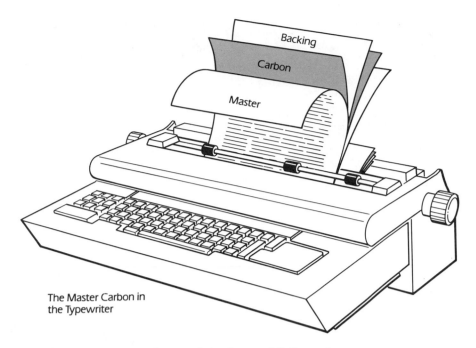

The Master Carbon in the Typewriter

Figure 5.11 The master carbon pack in the word/information processor.

Carbon Process

Carbon copying is a traditional method of producing a limited number of copies. The carbon can be a tissuelike paper treated with ink, wax, oil, and lampblack; or a film called Mylar. The top sheet (the original) is usually a high-quality bond paper. The copies are made on thin tissuelike paper called onionskin. The carbon is placed with the treated side facing the copy, creating a carbon copy of the original as the typist types (Figure 5.11).

Approximately eight legible copies can be made by using additional carbon paper and copy sheets to create a *carbon pack.* The impression and carbon copy controls on the typewriter should be adjusted to produce the desired number of readable copies.

Commercially prepared carbon packs or *copy sets* are also available that contain the original, carbons, and copy sheets.

New ways to produce carbon copies

Figures 5.12 and 5.13 show two word/information processors that make producing carbon copies easier. For example, the documents can be keyboarded on the word/information processor and revised before the carbon pack is inserted into the impact printer. This method produces error-free copies and eliminates correcting messy carbon copies. Many organizations still require the use of multicolored copies for various departments. Some insurance companies, for example, may require a claim form that is yellow for accounting, pink for the claims adjuster, and green for the customer's copy. It is important for the user to keep this in mind when considering which type of printer or word/information processor is best because a nonimpact printer only produces original copies, and it is necessary to have an impact printer to make carbon copies.

Figure 5.12 The Royal 7000 partial page display word/information processor with detached printer. *(Courtesy of Royal Corporation.)*

Figure 5.13 A word processing specialist uses a Xerox 850 full-page display word/information processor to revise a page on the screen. After the material is proofread on the screen, a carbon pack or original copies may be printed out on the separate printer. *(Courtesy of Xerox Corporation.)*

Fluid and Stencil Processes

The **fluid process** is also known as the spirit, liquid, direct, or Ditto process. The fluid duplicator is used with a three-sheet pack of paper called a *master set* (shown in Figure 5.14). The top sheet of the master set is glossy white paper connected to a bottom sheet of carbon coated with a purple dye. Red, green, blue, and black carbons may be used to produce different colored copies.

Fluid process

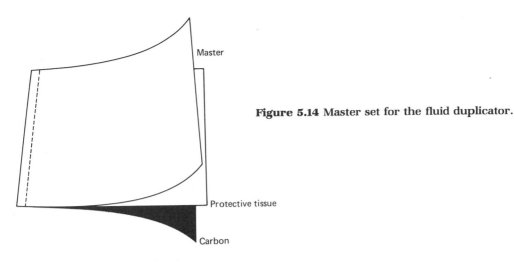

Figure 5.14 Master set for the fluid duplicator.

Figure 5.15 An electric fluid duplicator. *(Courtesy of Standard Duplicating Machines.)*

The typist removes a protective tissue separating the two connected sheets before typing or drawing on the top sheet of paper. After the master is prepared, the two sheets are separated and the top white sheet is clamped to the drum of the fluid duplicator (Figure 5.15), where the dye contacts the fluid to produce the desired number of copies.

For longer runs, fluid duplicating becomes even more economical when coupled with a word/information processor. The documents can be keyboarded and revised before the master set is inserted and played out. Also, masters can be reproduced from stored magnetic media. New masters thus do not have to be retyped when they wear out.

Stencil process

Stencil duplicating is often referred to as *ink process* or *mimeographing*. The stencil pack consists of a transparent film (optional), a stencil sheet (a porous sheet of tissue coated with a waxlike substance), a wax-coated cushion

Additional Methods of Outputting

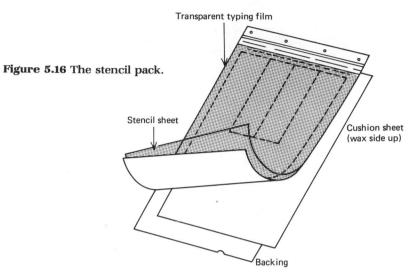

Figure 5.16 The stencil pack.

Figure 5.17 A table-top model 466 stencil duplicator. *(Courtesy of Gestetner Corporation.)*

sheet, and a backing sheet (Figure 5.16). The process involves disengaging the ribbon on a typewriter and allowing the keys to hit directly on the stencil. This typing action removes the wax coating and leaves an impression on the stencil. Drawing with a hard pen or stylus will produce the same results. When the stencil is clamped to the rotary drum of the duplicator, as shown in Figure 5.17, ink passes through the impression and prints onto the paper.

Electronic stencil makers or scanners have helped the stencil duplicating process greatly. Electronic scanning (Figure 5.18) reproduces an original document on a special stencil. As the special stencil rotates on a cylinder, images are scanned at up to three inches per minute and are electronically burned into the stencil.

The fluid and stencil processes no longer are important methods of dup-

Figure 5.18 An Electronic Scanner Model 7500 for reproducing stencils. *(Courtesy of Heyer.)*

licating. They are used primarily in government and education as an inexpensive method of duplicating where the quality of the copy is not the most important factor.

Offset and Phototypesetting Printing Processes

As far back as the eighth century, single letters appeared on clay tablets and were arranged or rearranged into different phrases. Thus, **movable type** (typesetting) and printing began. There are four ways of setting type for printing that are done manually, mechanically, or electronically (Figure 5.19).

Setting type

One method of printing called **offset** uses a raised or depressed surface on the master in which the printing surface is level with the nonprinting surface.

The principle used in the offset process is that oil and water do not mix. Inks used in offset duplicators are oil- or grease-based and made to adhere to master (plate) images. The master has a nonimage area on its flat surface on which printing cannot be reproduced, and an image area on which printing can be reproduced. As ink is applied to the master, it is attracted by the image. When water is applied to the master, it is repelled by the image area and attracted by the nonimage area. The proper mixture of ink and water determines the quality of print on the finished areas of the master.

Operators of word/information processors may prepare the master for the offset but probably will not be involved in running the equipment (Figure 5.20). It is important to select the offset master suited to meet specific job needs. Three basic types of masters to choose from in the offset (**lithography**) process are metal, electrostatic, and paper, as shown in Figure 5.21.

Phototypesetting is a printing process that uses film rather than the lead or brass plates used in hot lead printing. Some mechanical typesetters are driven by punched paper tape on computer communications terminals. The methods described are slow and the equipment is noisy, hot, heavy, and bulky.

Figure 5.20 A table-top model 310 offset duplicator. *(Courtesy of A. B. Dick Corporation.)*

FOUR METHODS OF SETTING TYPE

Movable type. The traditional method of setting individual pieces of molded type by hand (1440 A.D.).

Hot metal or linecasting. The familiar linotype machine which sets lines of type with hot molten lead being poured over type (1885).

Cold type/strike-on. Using a direct impression typewriter device (monotype system 1887).

Phototypesetting. The fastest, lowest-cost method of setting type through the use of a photographic master image which produces high-quality type for printing.

Figure 5.19 Four methods of setting type.

OFFSET PRINTING MASTERS

Metal plates. The aluminum plate method uses a camera to produce the master. This master is the most expensive of the three kinds of offset masters and produces the longest run (approximately 50,000 copies).

Electrostatic master. A coated paper master made on high-quality electrostatic photocopiers (also called xerographic master). These masters are used for medium length runs (approximately 25 to 5000 copies per master).

Direct-impression master. A smooth paperlike material which is handled like a regular sheet of paper. You may use a typewriter, pen, or pencil to produce impressions on this master. This master will produce the shortest run of copies from one master — 25 to 2500).

Figure 5.21 Offset printing masters.

These factors influenced the development of a photographic technique to "set" type that is used in phototypesetters. This process is called phototypesetting. The machines are often referred to as photocomposers and the process can be called photocomposition.

Some phototypesetters operate in this way: The font is rotated into position at high speed. A light is projected through the negative character images on the font, enlarged, and passed through a prism, or reflected by mirrors onto the photosensitive paper (Figure 5.22). This process is done repeatedly to create a column of text on the paper. There are a variety of type font masters, including rotating discs, film strips attached to a revolving drum, revolving multidisc turrets, or matrix grids (Figure 5.23). Figure 5.24 is a picture of a disc that fits into the disc turret inside a phototypesetter shown in Figure 5.25.

A phototypesetter is nothing more than a printer. Instead of striking the paper with a typewriter key, characters are printed optically one at a time at very high speeds onto photosensitive paper. It is like taking pictures of individual characters to form words. Phototypesetters are not difficult to operate and have less than a dozen moving parts.

A phototypesetter produces high-quality type with a wide variety of type sizes, but the major advantage is speed. The machine also can get at least two pages of typing onto a single phototypeset page. Therefore, paper, handling time, printing time, filing time, weight, and mailing costs can be cut in half.

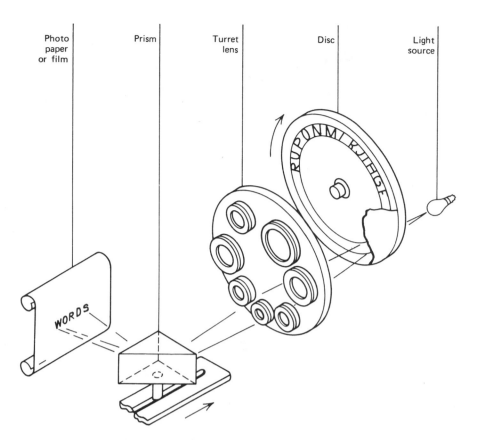

Figure 5.22 The phototypesetting process.

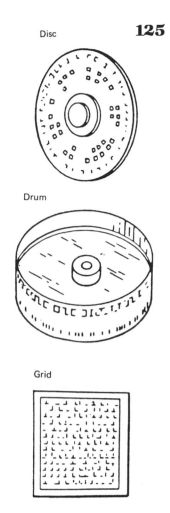

Disc

Drum

Grid

Film strip

Figure 5.23 Master fonts for phototypesetting.

A way that many organizations are reducing their reprographics costs when they have material that must be phototypeset is by using word/information processors tied into phototypesetting equipment. Figure 5.26 shows a portion of the visual display on a word/information processing terminal. This example shows what the display screen might look like when being given word/information processing keyboard commands. The commands in this example tell the machine to print what has been keyboarded on 66-line paper in the phototypesetting device with 12 pitch and an unjustified format. With phototypesetting machines (Figures 5.27 and 5.28), printing can be done in-house rather than sent out to be printed.

Generally, when an organization has to prepare material for printing either outside the organization or in an in-house print shop, the following steps are taken:

1. The document is sent to the print shop from an engineering department.

2. The secretary must keyboard the document, which usually involves considerable time depending upon the size of the document.

3. Someone must proofread the document and revisions must be made.

4. The document is sent back to the department for any changes.

5. The changes are made, final proofreading is done, and final approval of the document takes place.

Preparing material for printing

Figure 5.24, Figure 5.25 A disc that fits on the Comp/Edit disc turret in the photo-typesetter shown in Figure 5.25. *(Courtesy of AM Corporation.)*

Figure 5.26 A portion of a display screen showing formatting instructions for outputting to photocomposition. *(Courtesy of Wang Laboratories, Inc.)*

Figure 5.27 The Omnitech/2000 typesetting machine combines digitized type faces, laser beam scanning technology, and a dry output system with paper platemaking capabilities. *(Courtesy of Mergenthaler Linotype Company.)*

6. The document is sent out to a printer. A considerable amount of time is wasted because the document must be rekeyboarded with the typesetting codes inserted, reproofread, and returned to the originator.

7. In case of changes or errors, the document has to be returned to the printer, then the printer has to make corrections and return the document upon completion.

Figure 5.28 The EditWriter 7700 is a photocomposition system containing an editing screen, magnetic disk storage, keyboard, and simultaneous input and output capability. *(Courtesy of Compugraphics.)*

∠ID3   <UF2 I, <, a resident of the county of <, State of California, being of sound and disposing mind and memory, and not acting under menace, duress, fraud, or undue influence of any person do make and declare this to be my LAST WILL AND TESTAMENT, and revoke all other Wills and Codicils previously made by me. <FL

<UF2 I declare that at the time of making this my LAST WILL AND TESTAMENT, I am married and my <wife's/husband's name is <. I have < now living as a result of my marriage whose name is < and whose date of birth is <. The terms "my child" and "my issue" as used in this WILL shall include any other children hereinafter born to or adopted by me. I have < deceased children. I have taken into consideration all of my relatives including < _____. <FL

<UF = Use format "X" (for each style, size, font, or leading change a format number is assigned.)
<FL = Flush left or end of paragraph
<ID = Indent "X" picas
<XI = Cancel Indent
<ET = End of take (Chapter, page, or galley batch)
≤ = stop code for insert

Figure 5.29 Codes that need to be inserted on a word/information processor in order to be read by a phototypesetter.

Word/information processors allow the organization to draft the document and store it on media. When the final copy is ready for printing, a special device called an interface (that may or may not be connected to the word/information processor) allows the organization to take the edited text and send it directly to the phototypesetter. Then, special typesetting codes are added to the document from a marked draft as in Figure 5.29 and the phototypesetter produces

Additional Methods of Outputting

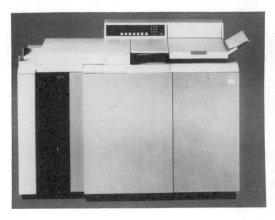

Figure 5.30 The IBM Series III Copier/ Duplicator, Model 20 shown with collator. *(Courtesy of International Business Machines Corporation.)*

Figure 5.31 The Xerox 9400 has a 200-capacity automatic document handler. *(Courtesy of Xerox Corporation.)*

camera-ready copy. The camera-ready copy can then be photographed onto a master and printed.

Combining technologies

The process of producing in-house printing combining the technology of word/informaton processors with phototypesetters has several advantages that affect costs. In-house printing can reduce the time involved in preparing final copy because the material is only keyboarded once; reduce the effort involved in keyboarding a second time and reproofing material; and store material electronically in a computer memory or on magnetic media for future revisions.

The Copying Process

Copying technology is rapidly taking the place of offset and other traditional methods of duplicating. Copiers can increase employee productivity and reduce costs. Copies of an existing document are made on equipment shown in Figures 5.30 and 5.31 without preparing a master. In many organizations, however, increased costs and lower productivity through equipment misuse have occurred.

The copier, when improperly used, can inflate budget costs overnight. Misuse of copiers ranges between 30% and 60% of the copies made on a single machine in an average company. Some of the reasons for copier misuse are:

Personal use

Copying material for personal use or nonbusiness applications.

Using less economical method

Copying materials (in large quantities) that could have been copied more economically by other reprographic methods.

Duplication

Duplicating files because of an unwillingness to release the office copy to a centralized filing system.

Many copies

Making more copies than needed.

Poor techniques

Wasting copies because of careless operating techniques.

In order to reduce copying costs, procedures for copy control must be used. A few ways organizations are controlling the use of the copier include:

Placing the copying machine in a central location.

Providing a notation book where those who use the copier must identify themselves and indicate how many copies they make.

Hiring an operator for a busy machine.

Limiting the use of the copier to certain types of work and certain people.

Copying technology has been combined with other technologies such as microcomputers, lasers, and fiber optics. The intelligent printer/copiers mentioned in Chapter 4 are examples of this new copying technology. These copiers are a new type of peripheral device that can be used as an output printer for word and data processing systems in place of or in addition to daisy wheel printers, matrix printers, or even phototypesetters.

Once the document has been keyboarded, whole pages can be printed out at one time. The speed is expressed in terms of pages per minute, compared to the traditional characters per minute. Another characteristic is the system's ability to use many fonts or typefaces. The intelligent printer/copier can print many sets of multiple page documents with little operator assistance, greatly increasing efficiency and productivity.

Factors to Consider When Selecting a Reprographics Process

Those whose responsibility it is to decide which reprographics process to use (Figure 5.32) must take into account the following factors.

Copy Appearance. One of the first considerations in selecting a process is to determine what the quality of the final copy should be. Some methods produce higher quality reproduction than do other methods. Some methods are limited to reproducing one color only. Others permit you to use several colors economically and/or enable you to reproduce pictures and illustrations.

Economic Length of Run. The most economical copy range for each method varies from 1 to 50,000 or more. There is usually a point where an economical length of run dictates the method used unless overruled by other considerations.

Paper Size Range. The size of the original to be copied or the size of the paper to be duplicated or printed will help determine the methods you should use.

Speed. Various reprographic methods differ in the amount of time involved in producing a copy. When choosing a method, an important consideration should be how much of the office worker's time will be required to use various processes. The worker's time could add considerably to the cost of the method. Since some information is needed more urgently than other information, the urgency of the need is another factor to consider when choosing an appropriate process. Speed is referred to in different ways: copies per minute, impressions per hour (iph), and pica newspaper lines per minute.

Copy Cost Range. The cost per copy varies with the method of master prepara-

Frequently people in offices must decide which reprographics process to use. That person must know something about the following factors:

Appearance
Copy Appearance. One of the first considerations in selecting a process is to determine what the quality of the final copy should be. Some methods produce higher quality reproduction than do other methods. Some methods are limited to reproducing one color only. Others permit you to use multicolors economically and/or enable you to reproduce pictures and illustrations.

Length of run
Economical Length of Run. The most economical copy range for each method varies from 1 to 50,000 or more. There is usually a point where an economical length of run dictates the method used unless overruled by other considerations.

Paper Size
Paper Size Range. The size of the original to be copied or the size of the paper to be duplicated or printed will help determine the methods which you should use.

Speed
Speed. The various reprographic methods differ in the amount of time involved in producing a copy. When choosing a method, an important consideration should be how much of the office worker's time will be spent when the various processes are used. The worker's time could add considerably to the cost of the method. Some information is needed more urgently than other information. The urgency of the need is another factor when choosing an appropriate process. Speed is referred to in different ways: copies per minute, impressions per hour (iph), and pica newspaper lines per minute.

Cost
Copy Cost Range. Cost per copy varies with the method of master preparation, types of supplies, paper used, and length of run. Quantity purchasing can affect costs.

Masters
All of the above factors will directly influence the type of master you choose. Each reprographics method varies according to the manner in which the master is produced.

Figure 5.32 Factors to consider when selecting a reprographics process.

tion, types of supplies, paper used, and length of run. Quantity purchasing can affect costs.

Masters

All of these factors will directly influence the type of master you choose. Each reprographics method varies according to the manner in which the master is produced.

Summary

Inputting to word/information processing can be done on a keyboard designed specifically for that purpose, or it can be done with other types of equipment. Some of these types of equipment are multifunction workstations, voice processing equipment, machine shorthand equipment, and optical character recognition (OCR) equipment.

Multifunctional workstations change the traditional office functions because they provide the manager with a keyboard. Voice processing affects the traditional functions because the voice, rather than keyboarding on a typewriter, becomes the method of inputting.

Optical character recognition (OCR) and machine shorthand provide little disruption to the traditional boss/secretary relationship. OCR allows every secretarial workstation to become an input workstation because an electric typewriter with an OCR font can produce copy that can be electronically scanned (read) by an OCR reader and stored on magnetic media. Machine shorthand used with computer aided transcription (CAT) eliminates keyboarding on a typewriter and provides a faster method of transcription.

Reprographics is another method of outputting a hard (paper) copy in the word/information processing system. The methods of reprographics used in word/information processing still include some very traditional ways of copying. However, newer methods can eliminate many of the problems associated with these traditional methods.

Material prepared for printing used to be keyboarded once in the office for the manager's approval and then rekeyboarded at the printer. Rekeyboarding can now be eliminated when word/information processors are used with new reprographics equipment. One way is by using the storage media from the word/information processor and adding special codes to it which allow the media to be read by a phototypesetter.

Key Terms

Multifunction workstation	Scanner
Windows	Media incompatibility
Voice message system	Media conversion
Voice reminder system	Computer Aided
Voice recognition system	Transcription (CAT)
Voice data entry	Reprographics
Automatic speech recognition	Carbon copying
Speaker-dependent system	Fluid process
Speaker-independent system	Stencil duplicating
Discrete word recognition	Offset process
Continuous word recognition	Lithography
OCR (optical character	Phototypesetting
recognition)	Copying

Study Guide

This study guide provides you with feedback to find out how well you are doing. Use a separate sheet of paper to record your answers. When you have finished check your responses with the answers at the back of the book.

Matching: Choose the answer that best defines the word in the left column.

1. Optical character reader
   a. One type of media may not work on another word/information processor.

2. Windows
   b. A printing process that uses film rather than lead or brass plates.

3. Multifunction workstation
   c. A piece of equipment that can transfer typewritten copy onto magnetic storage media.

4. Phototypesetting
   d. A station that can provide the manager with a keyboard.

5. Media incompatibility
   e. Sections on a screen used on a multifunction workstation.

6. Magnetic card converter
   f. Moving information from one type of media to another.

7. Metal, electrostatic and paper
   g. Methods of voice processing.

8. Speech recognition, dictation, voice message systems
   h. Types of offset masters.

9. Fluid master set
   i. A piece of equipment that takes information stored on cards and places it on disks.

10. Media conversion
    j. A carbon sheet coated with a dye attached to a glossy sheet.

Multiple choice: Select the letter or letters that best answer each question.

11. Which of the following is a method of outputting used in word/information processing?
    a. Phototypesetting
    b. Optical character recognition
    c. Machine shorthand
    d. Keyboarding

12. Which reprographics method guarantees the highest quality output?
    a. Carbon copying process
    b. Fluid process
    c. Phototypesetting process
    d. Optical character recognition

13. Which is **not** one of the functions of a multifunction workstation?
    a. Scanning (reading) documents and transferring the information to storage media.
    b. Filing and retrieving documents electronically.
    c. Updating lists.
    d. Sending outgoing messages.

14. Which of the following terms are associated with voice processing?
    a. Voice message systems
    b. Machine dictation
    c. Machine shorthand
    d. Speech recognition

15. Which of the following is **not** an advantage of optical character recognition (OCR)?
    a. The organization has to buy fewer typewriters.
    b. OCR does not disrupt the traditional boss/secretary relationship.
    c. OCR provides an efficient method of inputting information.
    d. The secretary does not have to learn how to operate new equipment.

Completion: Write the correct answer on a separate sheet of paper.

16. Four types of voice processing systems are _____ , _____ , _____ , _____ .

17. Five reprographics processes are _____ , _____ , _____ , _____ .

18. What does "CAT" stand for in the information processing industry? _____ .

19. Name four methods of setting type:
    _____ , _____ , _____ , _____ .

20. List five factors to consider when choosing a reprographics method: _____ , _____ , _____ , _____ .

True/False: Write + for True, 0 for False for each question.

21. An example of a voice message system is an optical character reader.

22. The difference between discrete word recognition and continuous word recognition systems is that continuous word recognition systems can only recognize a limited vocabulary.

23. Using optical character recognition as a method of inputting information to word/information processors disrupts the traditional boss/secretary relationship because the secretaries must be located in a center near the OCR equipment.

24. Machine shorthand with computer aided transcription (CAT) is a slower method of inputting information than a typewriter keyboard, but it is more convenient because the notes can be transcribed by a computer.

25. Reprographics is an alternate method of inputting information into a word/information processing system.

26. Machine shorthand with computer aided transcription (CAT) is being used as a new reprographics method.

27. The various reprographics methods generally produce the same quality reproductions.

28. Optical character recognition can assist in media conversion.

29. An important piece of equipment used for optical character recognition is a magnetic card converter.

30. Punched paper tape media is sometimes used on phototypesetting equipment.

Questions on Concepts

1. Identify some of the tasks a manager or secretary can perform on a multifunction workstation.
2. Explain what is meant by voice processing.
3. Explain how a voice message system operates.
4. Compare speaker-dependent to speaker-independent voice recognition systems.
5. Discuss the difference between discrete word recognition systems and continuous speech recognition systems.

6. Describe optical character recognition and explain some of its uses.
7. Discuss the advantage of using optical character recognition in an office.
8. Discuss how OCR can assist in media conversion.
9. Discuss what is meant by media incompatibility.
10. Compare and contrast the five reprographics processes.
11. Describe the phototypesetting process.
12. Identify the major reasons for copier misuse.

Case and Activities

Madison, Pfiffner, Flinn and Kassi is a law firm of 80 attorneys based in Washington, D.C., with another office in Los Angeles, California. The practice, mostly litigation and corporate law, is suitable for word processing because of continual ongoing editing and the importance of high-quality final drafts. The word processing center in this law firm consists of three operators using three word/information processors. In addition to the word processing center, there are 60 secretaries working directly with the lawyers.

A backlog of work began to develop because the operators were unable to keep up with entry and editing work created by the lawyers. There was little time for text editing as word/ information processors were continually tied up with original keyboarding or text entry work. Turnaround time on projects was very high and each operator averaged 100 hours of overtime each month.

1. What recommendations would you make to this law firm to assist with the backlog of paperwork? Explain.
2. How would your recommendations, if implemented, affect the traditional boss/secretary relationship? Explain.

Activities

1. Investigate the reprographics processes used in an office located nearby. Determine whether the most cost-effective method for producing copies is being used for such documents as letters, reports, interoffice memoranda, and form letters.
2. Read three articles in recent word/information processing literature on the subjects of voice processing, optical character recognition, and word/information processors tied into phototypesetter. Prepare an abstract on each of the articles.
3. Create an example of a company that needs to use the carbon process as a reprographics method. Explain why.

CHAPTER 6

Distribution

The objectives of this chapter are to:

1. Identify the reasons why distribution is the most costly link in the workflow of a document.

2. Describe the technology that will gradually cure the problems of speed and cost in distribution.

3. List the two methods of distributing information.

4. Identify the four most common microforms.

5. List several advantages and disadvantages of using microfilm for storing information.

6. Explain why electronic methods of distributing information are growing in importance.

7. Define the four ways information is communicated electronically.

8. Explain why today's information carriers have caused distribution costs to increase.

9. Describe the kinds of technology that will help speed up distribution and reduce distribution costs.

Managers need information to assist them in making decisions. Several difficulties arise in the process of providing them with information:

1. The amount of information is so massive it is difficult to sort out needed information.

2. Managers must receive information when they need it. If the information cannot be found quickly, it is of no use to them.

3. People must share information. Consequently, it must be sent (distributed) from one place to another.

This chapter discusses why the cost of distribution of information is so high, what is being done to reduce distribution problems, and what methods of distribution are used.

Automation has been added to the origination, production, and reproduction of documents to speed up productivity and decrease costs. The efficiency ends there unless the document can be distributed quickly, and many times it is not. The following example illustrates the problem of obtaining efficient **distribution**.

A costly link

A document is delivered to a manager's in-basket. It stays there until the manager reviews it and decides what action to take. The manager may decide to have a secretary type a response to the document. If so, the document goes to the manager's out-basket and stays there until the secretary picks it up. After the secretary types the document, it goes back to the manager for review. The manager eventually signs it and places it again in the out-basket, where the secretary picks it up and prepares it for mailing. It then goes into the secretary's out-basket until it is delivered to the mailroom where it goes into the in-basket to be sorted. Finally, it goes into the out-basket and leaves the organization. The document then goes to the post office, is put in a basket to be sorted, and finally is delivered (or lost).

After a document reaches its destination, it goes through another mail room. Again it is placed in another secretary's in-basket to be sorted and then placed in another manager's in-basket. The process continues to repeat itself.

This example shows the amount of time wasted by the physical handling of paper. A study conducted by Exxon in the mid-1970s showed that 74% of the time spent on a document was taken up by distribution. Nevertheless, word processing equipment manufacturers in the 1970s spent their greatest effort developing input and output equipment. The equipment they developed increases productivity for only 26% of the time spent on the document—the time between its origination and its distribution. The reason manufacturers concentrated on developing equipment for these two areas was that they wanted to produce equipment that would show visible increases in *productivity*: larger volumes of finished paperwork. However, as organizations began to use the equipment, it became clear that a faster way was needed to handle a document after it was produced. Making secretaries more productive can reduce costs, but organizations began to realize that they could derive greater savings by making their managers more productive. The problem, however, is that it is easier to measure how productive a secretary is by counting the number of lines or pages of type that person produces than it is to measure a manager's productivity (Figure 6.1).

Documents spend 74% of time in distribution

Productivity was visible

Management's productivity not as easily measured

With the world's information doubling nearly every six years, the traditional methods used to communicate are inadequate. In the United States alone, 70 billion pages of information are distributed each year between business and government locations. Nearly the entire amount is transported from point to point by physical means (post office, courier, hand delivery). Only one out of every hundred pages is distributed electronically (over telephone wires). This creates a **paper overload**.

The distribution function of an office remains one of the most important aspects of processing information. Unless the information compiled or accumulated by the office is immediately available and delivered rapidly to the people who need the information, costs will continue to increase and efficiency will continue to decline.

Impacting Principal Time:
Examples from a current study
at a large oil company
(66 principals, 35 support staff)

Source	Hours/ Week	Yearly Cost
Principals spent at copier	79	$113,760
Principals try to reach someone on phone	104	149,760
Principals could save by delegating to secretary	200	288,000
Principals spend doing longhand:		
at office	499	718,560
at home	165	237,600
Principals say work is not getting done due to lack of secretarial support	Yes: 25%	
	No: 75%	

Figure 6.1 The chart shows specific tasks affecting a manager's productivity and costs. *(Courtesy of Office Systems Research Group.)*

Physical Methods of Distributing Information

In the traditional office, the telephone is used to distribute the spoken word; paper is used to distribute the written word. Using paper creates at least two problems: Our ability to use the information contained in paper is limited by how fast the paper can be physically handled by everyone who has contact with it, and paper continues to affect an organization's costs long after the document is created and distributed. It costs the organization money because as long as paperwork remains in existence, it must be physically stored somewhere. Therefore, filing equipment, space, and records managers are needed to maintain the files.

Filing

Transaction documents

The paperwork generated by a correspondence center is but a portion of an organization's total paperwork. In this section, we reclassify documents to include all the paperwork that exists in an organization's filing and retrieval system, also known as a records management system.

Traditional Methods. The paperwork that gets filed in an organization falls into two categories: **transaction documents** and reference documents. Active correspondence with customers and suppliers is an example of transaction docu-

Figure 6.2 Easy access to numerically arranged files. *(Courtesy of Acme Visible Records, Incorporated.)*

ments produced by a correspondence center. Other examples of an organization's transaction files are checks, invoices, and order forms. Transaction documents generally comprise from 75% to 90% of an organization's paperwork. Filing and retrieving these documents is comparatively simple because they can be arranged numerically or alphabetically to be accessed easily (Figure 6.2). The main filing consideration is providing a rapid means of access, an easy way of expanding the files, and adequate protection for the records.

The longer documents produced by the correspondence center or reprographics departments comprise the category called **reference documents**. Reference documents include research data, reports, brochures, legal documents, and catalogues. Managers make more use of these documents than of transaction documents. Therefore, they must be easier for management to locate. The manager must be able to select information from some source or from a well-designed records management system.

Organizations are approaching records management problems in several ways:

1. Designing records management systems whereby people exercise control over the creation, distribution, retention, use, storage, retrieval, protection, preservation, and final disposition of all types of records in an organization.

2. Using motorized or automated filing equipment and modern supplies which improve the records management methods used in the traditional office.

3. Experimenting with alternative methods of filing made possible by advanced technology. Electronic methods are replacing traditional records management systems in some organizations.

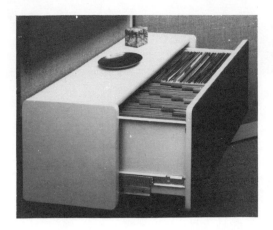

Figure 6.3 A lateral file. *(Courtesy of G. F. Business Equipment.)*

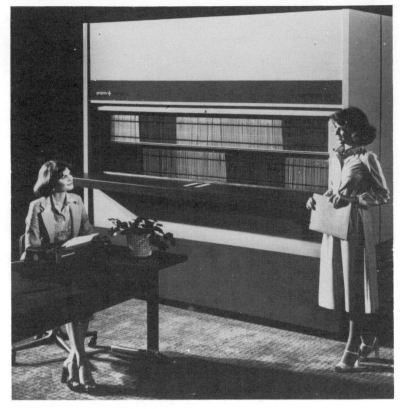

Figure 6.4 Automated shelf files. *(Courtesy of Kardex Systems.)*

Many organizations still rely to a large extent on traditional records management systems for physical distribution. These systems keep records in a variety of storage equipment such as cabinets, suspension folder equipment, rotary files, open shelves, and lateral files (Figures 6.3 and 6.4).

The traditional method of physically filing hard copy (paper) documents has made finding adequate storage space for the millions of pieces of recorded information in organizations an overwhelming task. One solution to the problem is to miniaturize records, so organizations have begun to consider a new technology called **micrographics**.

New technology

Microfilm

Legality

Film. Micrographics is the method of filing information on film (microfilm) using miniaturized images. It eliminates the need to store bulky paperwork because the paper records are photographed on microfilm and reduced to microfilm images. **Microfilm** is used for keeping old records that are referred to infrequently (Figure 6.5). These records can then be kept in less space than hard copy. Many organizations considered microfilm an unnecessary, expensive step for filing and storing old records, but now organizations are converting to micrographics to store their documents because governmental agencies will accept microfilm in place of hard copy.

Micrographics can save approximately 95% to 98% of the space needed for storing records in office areas. It can reduce letter-size documents at a ratio of 10 to 1. One shoebox-size microfilm file cabinet can hold the equivalent of the contents of about 160 four-drawer, letter-size files. For example, a 100-foot roll of

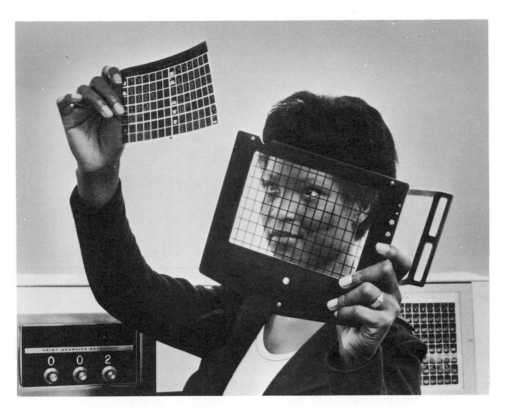

Figure 6.5 A micrographics technician examines film to be converted from microfilm to hard copy at nearly a page per second. *(Courtesy of Xerox Corporation.)*

16mm film will store 3,000 photographed letters, 5,800 6″ by 4″ cards, or 13,000 bank checks.

The use of microfilm copy rather than hard copy for information storage and retrieval of records was designed to solve some of the following filing and storage problems by:

Reducing the number of misfiled records and lost documents. The original copy never has to leave the area. Documents once filed in the correct sequential order remain that way permanently. — *File integrity*

Reducing the space necessary to file documents. Because of miniaturization on microfilm, it is possible to file more documents in an area than was possible with a paper-based system. — *Storage*

Aiding in the preparation of reports using a process called **computer output microfilm (COM)**. Computer output can be microfilmed directly by COM for immediate distribution without first producing a hard copy (Figure 6.6). It provides the latest, up-to-date information to individual terminals that may be at a distance from the central processing unit (CPU). **Computer assisted retrieval (CAR)** enables the reports reproduced on COM to be retrieved from the computer files at rapid speeds (Figure 6.7). A process of updating information once it has been filmed is known as **computer input microfilm (CIM)**. It is a method of producing new microimages through the use of a computer using existing microimages on film as the source document. — *COM, CAR and CIM*

Figure 6.6 This picture shows part of the equipment that comprises a Computer Output Microfilm (COM) unit. The Memorex 1644 Auto Viewer allows rapid scanning of microfilm reports through an 11″ x 14″ screen. It contains a manual scanning wheel for fine screening, a hood to prevent overhead light glare, and a movable line finder. *(Courtesy of Memorex Corporation.)*

Filing and retrieval

Reducing filing time. Most modern microfilm readers have ways of scanning the microfilm that make it possible to locate a document in a few seconds.

Distribution

Decreasing the cost of mailing. With microfilm, a book-length report or catalogue can be mailed for less money. Microfilming is faster than imprint paper publishing; therefore, the information gets distributed faster. Organizations can improve cash flow by distributing daily reports rather than weekly reports. Customers are better serviced if information can be processed faster.

Security

Duplicating sets of records that can be stored on microfilm and kept in a safe in another location for maximum security (Figure 6.8).

Problems still exist in the use of microfilm. These include the following:

No margin notations

Making notations in the margins or correcting mistakes when reading reports is difficult.

Difficult to compare pages

Comparing two microfilm pages or sections simultaneously is difficult. Unless the user works with multiple readers placed side by side or a reader and an information processing retrieval terminal, the reports will have to be reconverted into hard copy (Figure 6.9).

Difficult to reproduce colors

Reproducing colors cannot be done on regular microfilm. If records are color-coded, either more expensive microfilm must be used or alternative coding methods must be developed.

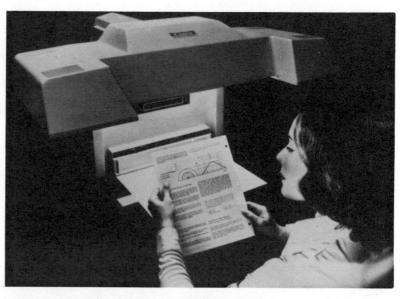

Figure 6.7 The Ragen 95 is a system that will internally store millions of pages of source document images and COM, while providing a ten-second retrieval or access. *(Courtesy of Ragen Precision Industries.)*

Figure 6.8 A records technician decides how to film a document on the 161G Processor Camera. *(Courtesy of Canon Incorporated.)*

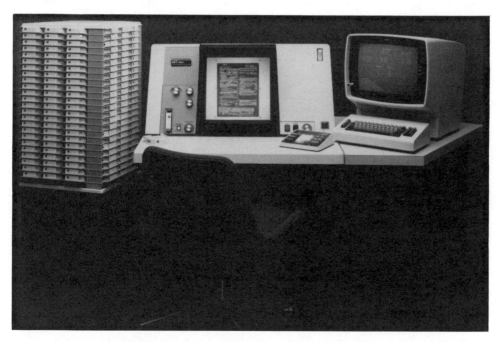

Figure 6.9 The microimage terminal allows an operator to view one image, store it in a memory, and recall it by simply pushing a button. *(Courtesy of Eastman Kodak Company.)*

Figure 6.11 A microfiche printer which handles filming up to 10″ x 10″. *(Courtesy of The Micobra Corporation.)*

Figure 6.10 Thorough indexing on microfilm assists administrative support secretary in finding information. *(Courtesy of Microform Data Systems, Incorporated.)*

Indexing must be thorough

Indexing must be done more thoroughly than for paper records. The ability to browse through the records is limited because of the thousands of images contained in the microfilm formats. Microfilm needs in-depth indexing and thus has higher preparation costs than a paper-based system (Figure 6.10).

Updating microfilm

Updating microfilm files because of the addition of a new record or a revision of an existing one may require remicrofilming the entire file. Updating might also be slowed by the filming process (Figures 6.11 and 6.12).

Film expense and time

Filming is expensive and requires time. If the filming is not done in-house, the problem of having the files unavailable during filming is an important consideration.

Viewing equipment needed

Microfilm requires viewer or reader equipment that is expensive (Figure 6.13). If the reports are to be outside the office, portable equipment will have to be used and transporting the equipment becomes another consideration.

The miniaturized images (**microimages**) are stored in four categories called **microforms**. These categories should be considered when converting from hard copy to microfilm. The microforms are as follows.

Roll film is a roll of microfilm that may or may not be housed in a cartridge or cassette. It is suitable for large volumes of paperwork that can be numbered in sequence. Roll film is often used for work that is not referred to often. It is the oldest and most economical method of microfilming (Figures 6.14 and 6.15).

An **aperture card** is a card that has an opening in which a strip or frame of microfilm is mounted. A single frame of film can be handled

Figure 6.12 The SRC 1050 Camera is a step-and-repeat microfiche camera capable of generating microfiche as rapidly as an operator can place documents on its copy board. *(Courtesy of 3M Company.)*

Figure 6.14
A roll of film.
(Courtesy of Bell and Howell.)

Figure 6.15 A cartridge of microfilm. *(Courtesy of Bell and Howell.)*

Figure 6.13 A dry-silver process reader/printer, used only for microfiche, that cuts the paper using a switch selection to either 8 1/2″ x 11″ or 11″ lengths. *(Courtesy of 3M Company.)*

Figure 6.16 Aperture cards leave room for indexing on the paper portion of the card. *(Courtesy of 3M Company.)*

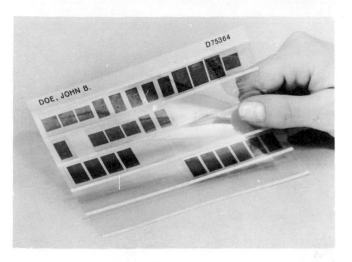

Figure 6.17 A microfilm jacket. *(Courtesy of Bell and Howell.)*

individually much like a paper document. Cumbersome engineering documents can be easily mounted on the cards, as can letters or other documents (Figure 6.16). The card also provides a writing area for indexing.

A **microfilm jacket** is a folder consisting of clear material sealed together on two sides. Within the folder are channels into which microfilm can be slipped from one open end. One sheet of a microfilm jacket can store approximately 60 to 70 documents. Individual frames are easily inserted at any time, making the updating of files a simple task (Figure 6.17).

Microfiche is a sheet of film that may contain several hundred exposures. Microfiche is frequently used for publications or reports that must be referenced frequently and distributed widely (Figure 6.18). Additions and deletions to the information on microfiche can easily be done. A fast way of updating is to discard old microfiche and replace it with corrected fiche. Another type of microfiche (PCMI Microfilm System) developed by the National Cash Register Company is called **ultrafiche** or ultramicrofiche. The fiche produced by this method permits tremendous reduction rates to be used in filming material. For example, over 1,200 printed pages of the Bible can be reproduced on approximately two square inches of film. **Ultrastrip** is another filmstrip of micro-images. It is 8″ long and contains five segments. Each segment is partitioned into 2,000 images and the entire strip contains 10,000 images of 8½″ × 11″ typewritten pages (Figure 6.19).

A new storage medium

Video Disc. Another innovation in technology that is being considered as a records storage medium is the **video disc**. Video disc technology makes possible the high-density storage of visual images and sound on a durable plastic disc about the size of a longplaying record. A video disc player can locate any one of up to 54,000 frames on a disc within five seconds. The player optically

Figure 6.18 A microfiche. *(Courtesy of Image Systems.)*

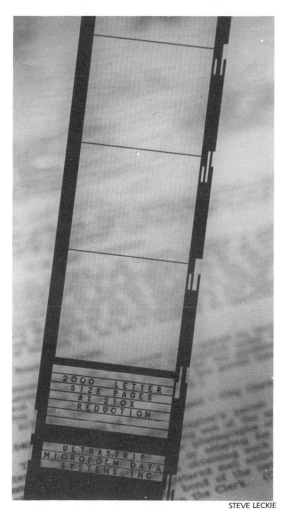

STEVE LECKIE

Figure 6.19 An ultrastrip holds 10,000 8 1/2″ x 11″ documents. *(Courtesy of Microform Data Systems, Incorporated.)*

Physical Methods of Distributing Information

scans the recorded information to play out the picture and the sound on a television receiver. Disco Vision is a company manufacturing video discs.

Holography. The area of technology with the potential for storing the greatest amount of information in the future is the nonerasable storage method called **holography**. Millions of characters of information can be stored internally without ever being output on paper, film, or magnetic media. One of the major drawbacks of holography is that the government does not presently accept it as a legal form of storage.

Post Office and Private Carriers

Mail carriers

The U.S. Postal Service uses mail carriers for physical distribution, and the Yankee Group, a consulting firm, predicts that the cost of an ordinary first-class letter will be 50¢ in 1985.

Private carriers

The increasing cost of distributing information through the U.S. Postal Service and the time involved have caused organizations to seek other ways of moving information from one point to another. One of these is by courier. Two examples of courier service companies are Federal Express and Emery Air Freight Corp. These organizations offer guaranteed delivery of mail to a destination by a certain time. The use of Federal Express or Emery Air Freight Corp. does shorten delivery time, but the cost is high.

Electronic Methods of Distributing Information

Electronic distribution of information

Since paper causes many of the problems associated with the speed and cost of distributing information, electronic methods of sending information are becoming more popular. Information can be sent electronically through space, such as with radio frequencies, or over a hard wire like a telephone wire. The distribution of information, physical and electronic, has been redefined to mean *communications*. The idea behind sending information electronically is to keep the information in the form of electronic signals until it is necessary to convert it into hard copy. Information can flow faster when it is distributed electronically because it does not have to be physically handled as much. Moreover, offices throughout the world can be linked together by phone. Any information distributed electronically over telephone lines is called **telecommunications**.

Information can be sent electronically in the form of voice, data, graphic or image, and video communications. You send **voice communications** electronically every time you use the telephone to call someone (Figure 6.20). If you dictate over phone lines to a central recording system, you are also transmitting your voice electronically. Data (words, symbols, numbers) as well as voice can be sent electronically. Sending data electronically is referred to as data or digital communications. It is possible to have a secretary type a document at one location and have it electronically play back at another location (Figure 6.21). This method of sending data is a form of **data communications**.

Managers often need graphics or images in addition to text and tables. It is possible to take a picture at one location and electronically send that image to a

Figure 6.20 Voice communications.

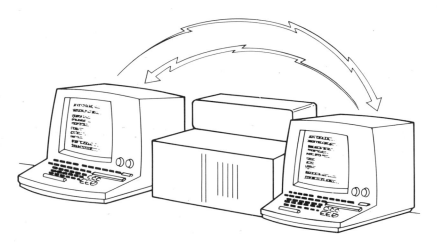

Figure 6.21 Data communications.

screen or a printer at another location. The image can appear on the screen in up to eight different colors. To achieve colored printouts, some manufacturers have developed printers that contain four or more colored ribbons. Sending graphics electronically is referred to as **graphic communications**. Graphic communications is used to send such items as sales territory layouts, maps, line or bar graphs, and log or pie charts. Another term for sending some types of graphics electronically is **facsimile (FAX)** — a device that reads (scans) hard copy in one location, sends it through space or over telephone wires, and produces a hard copy of the document in another location (Figure 6.22).

Pictures of people involved in a phone conversation can be sent electronically and appear on a screen in another location. This method of communications is referred to as **video communications** or teleconferencing (Figure 6.23). With teleconferencing, people in several locations can exchange ideas. Teleconferencing is not as personal as face-to-face communications, but it is a better method of communicating than a telephone because it allows the participants in a conversation to see each other's facial expressions. Teleconferencing is used instead of face-to-face meetings to solve such problems as the breakdown of equipment, settlement of legal questions, and handling labor/management difficulties.

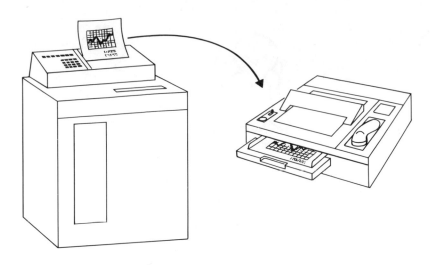

Figure 6.22 Graphic communications.

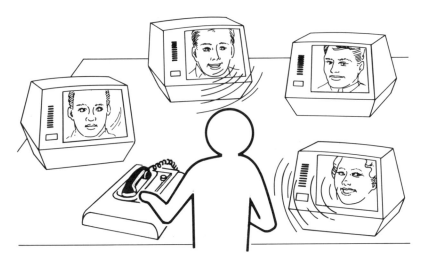

Figure 6.23 Video communications.

Information Carriers for Electronic Distribution

Most information is transmitted (sent) electronically through thousands of twisted-pair telephone lines passing through a facility supported by junction boxes, switching panels, and massive wiring. Organizations spend thousands of dollars on miles and miles of wire and cable to create these communication links. Not only is the capacity of the wire and cable method inadequate, but not enough of it exists to handle present needs. This method is a major factor in the increase of distribution costs.

Types of carriers

Part of the reason for the problem is the way in which information is sent. Information is sent electronically from one location to another location through **information carriers**. Information carriers are referred to as narrowband, voiceband, and wideband. Narrowband, voiceband, and wideband describe how information is carried as it travels through space or over telephone wires. Think of narrowband as a narrow diameter garden hose and wideband as a wider diameter hose. The speed and quantity of water as it flows through the narrow pipe is limited no matter how much the water pressure is increased. More water can flow through a wider garden hose at a higher speed. The speed information moves is measured in bits per second (bps) and is referred to as a Baud rate. Today's word/information processing equipment has the capacity to transmit information at speeds much greater than can be handled by the narrowband and voiceband carriers.

Narrowband carriers are cables or telephone lines (private or leased) that have slow transmission rates up to only 300 bits per second. They are used primarily for telephone companies' teletypewriter exchange services (TWX), which cannot operate at faster speeds.

Voiceband carriers are upgraded telephone lines which cannot send information faster than 10,000 bits per second. These lines are referred to as **voice lines** because they are used primarily for sending voice communications.

Wideband or **broadband carriers** are designed to handle data communications and are called **data lines**. Data, therefore, can travel faster over data lines than over voice lines, but voice lines are still sometimes used to send data because telephone lines are more available. Voices can also travel over data lines, but the primary purpose of the data line is to send data, not voice communications. Wideband carriers provide for data transmission at rates from several thousand to several million bits per second. Data communications generally use cables, microwave frequencies, or satellites for transmitting information (Figure 6.24).

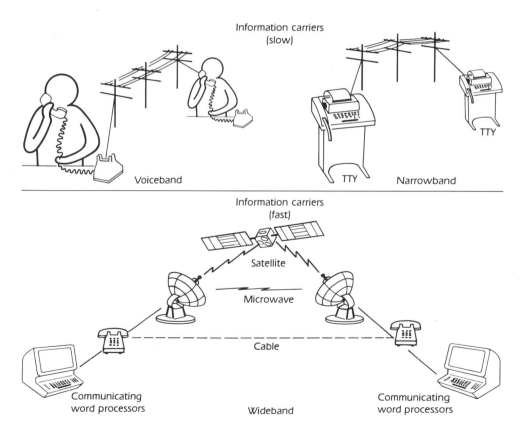

Figure 6.24 Information carriers (voiceband, narrowband, and wideband).

More information can flow through a wideband carrier than through a narrowband or voiceband carrier at a higher speed with fewer transmission errors. A transmission error is something received differently from the way in which it was sent; for example, a transmission error occurs if you send the message, "The cow jumped over the moon," and it is received, "The cow jumped over the spoon."

A consideration in deciding whether to choose a voice or data line is how the choice will affect distribution costs. For example, when using voice or data lines, you are charged for the actual time you use the line (**connect time**). Since data can travel faster over data lines than voice lines, when you use data lines your actual charges are less.

Technology to Cure the Distribution Problem

The problems of speed and the high cost of distribution will be reduced by the continued development of microprocessor, laser, fiber optic, and satellite technologies.

Microprocessors

Microelectronics have been largely responsible for the advances in information processing technology. Today, a tiny chip smaller than the tip of your finger contains the equivalent of 15,000 transistors. It is predicted that in the 1980s, the number of transistors will increase to 400,000 per chip. The chip takes up less space than a computer and costs less to house (Figure 6.25).[1]

Since the one-chip CPU (Central Processing Unit) containing 2,250 transistors was introduced in 1971, the capacity of the single memory chip (RAM) has doubled every 18 months. Also, the cost of these chips has been going down at a rate of approximately 20% per year.[2]

Today's **microprocessor** selling for $100 has about the same computing power as the $1 million computer of the 1950s. The speed of the computer has increased ten times every eight years in that same period of time. As processing speeds increase, distribution costs decrease.[3]

Lasers

Laser technology is offering new ways to move information rapidly. The laser, a beam of pure red light, is capable of carrying millions of messages simultaneously. A laser beam is merged with a process that uses light to shape characters on a photosensitive surface, then a toner is used to transfer the image to paper. Some of the intelligent copier/printers in word/information processing are able to achieve their high printing speeds because of laser

[1] "The Computer Society: Thinking Small," *Time*, February 20, 1978, p. 50.
[2] "The Computer Society: The Numbers Game," *Time*, February 20, 1978, p. 59.
[3] "Toward An Intelligence Beyond Man's." *Time*, February 20, 1978, p. 59.

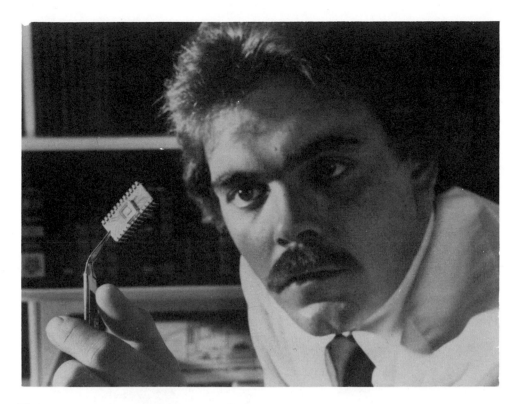

Figure 6.25 A tiny microcomputer checks memory location in seconds and tells an operator the cause of equipment problems. (*Courtesy of Xerox Corporation.*)

technology. The laser is used to increase printing speeds, with speeds ranging from 8,000 to 18,000 lines per minute.

Fiber Optics

Fiber Optics, smooth glass-like thin tubes as fine as human hair, send a light source generated from electric power. The tubes are about 10 to 80 times smaller in size than copper or other cables carrying the same information. Fiber optics are used in several areas of the document cycle in word/information processing. The light source may expose a document to be copied (see inset in Figure 6.26) or to provide a path for communications.

Glass-like thin tubes

In the word/information processing industry there are several categories of fiber optics or fiber cables being used. Fiber optics are used in word/information processing to provide a new method for sending and receiving video, audio, and data. The wide acceptance of this new technology is due to its reliability, energy savings, low cost, less maintenance (usually has fewer moving parts), and less required space.

When properly connected to a word/information processor, fiber optics can also read directly from a video screen to create images on paper. Fiber optics technology holds the greatest promise for solving the problems of high cost and inadequate communicating links in the local distribution of information. It per-

Solving the cost problem

Figure 6.26 A revolutionary fiber optic wafer replaces traditional lens and mirror systems of conventional office copiers, as in this Electrographictm 301 office copier. (*Courtesy of Minolta Corporation.*)

mits 1,000 times more communication traffic than an ordinary twisted pair of wires the same size. Also, fiber optics and laser technology can be combined, with fiber optics acting as the tube or channel for the laser light source.

Satellites

Who owns satellite systems?

During the 1960s the United States developed space programs that sent men to walk on the moon and satellites into space. Soon afterward, many large organizations talked of future plans to use satellites to act as a nationwide computer and enable mail services to be channeled through the sky. Most of these satellites provide services for their customers that simply substitute for traditional land lines. In the late 1970s, only a few organizations owned complete satellite systems: RCA-Americom, Western Union, and American Satellite Corporation. Other communication carriers such as American Telephone & Telegraph and General Telephone & Electronics employ satellites, but the Federal Communication Commission (FCC) did not allow them to use satellite channels for private-line service to users until after 1979. Xerox is proposing an electronic message service called Xten (Figure 6.27) and Advanced Communications Service (ACS) is a data communications service proposed by the Bell System (Figure

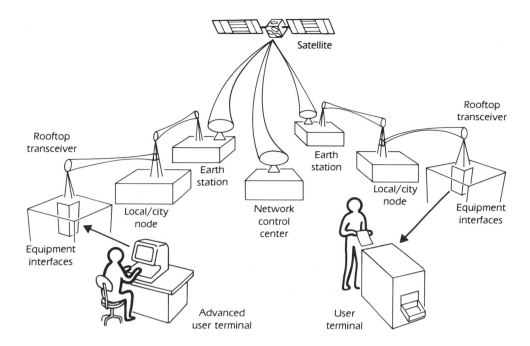

Figure 6.27 The three main applications of the XTEN satellite are rapid distribution of documents, data transmission, and teleconferencing.

6.28). International Business Machines Corporation (IBM), Comsat General, and Aetna Life and Casualty are a group of companies that have cooperated to form another organization called Satellite Business Systems (SBS). SBS (Figure 6.29) will be a total communications network that will allow users to send voice, data, graphic, or video transmissions.

An SBS satellite will bypass land lines and broadcast directly to antennas small enough to fit into a two-car garage. These antennas can be located anywhere a customer wants. The satellite's capacity is so large that customers will be able to send 6.3 million bits of data per second between points, compared with only 2,000 bits per second over conventional telephone lines.[4] This satellite will allow an organization to tighten its control over remote operations by increasing the amount and timeliness of inventory, sales, and production data it can gather. This system could change the way America does business.

Tremendous speed of transmission

The basic principles of the SBS system are simple. Earth stations, generally on top of office buildings, beam radio waves through space at a satellite that amplifies the signal, and, from about 22,300 miles in space, broadcasts those radio waves to all stations in the continental United States. The satellite is like a microwave tower with wings to capture solar energy and a small rocket motor for repositioning it into orbit. The data can flow fast enough to send the book *War and Peace* —every second. Conceptually, satellites may be thought of as reflectors for bouncing radio signals back to earth. One of the reasons for excitement about communications satellites is their ability to broadcast from one point to many points, facilitating the electronic movement of mail and providing opportunities for other business applications such as teleconferencing and facsimile transmission.

Earth stations beam radio waves

[4]"Information Processing: SBS Casts A Wider Customer Net," *Business Week*, July 21, 1980, p. 156.

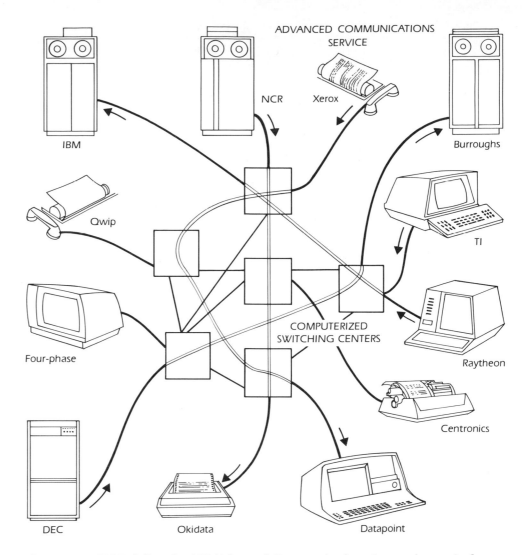

Figure 6.28 AT&T defines its ACS (Advanced Communications Systems) as a single service that allows its users to "talk" to incompatible terminals.

Satellite communication systems will enable users to have cheap wideband services to connect their offices and plants to satellites in space. This hookup will make more extensive and efficient use of computers and other office equipment.

Summary

After a document moves through the steps of origination, production, and reproduction, the workflow of the document slows down at the distribution step. Distribution is the movement of information from one location to another. Since distribution is a critical point in the workflow of a document, slower movement of the document and larger hard-copy storage needs can be a problem.

In the traditional office, the telephone is used to electronically distribute the spoken word but is quite slow. Paper is used to physically distribute the

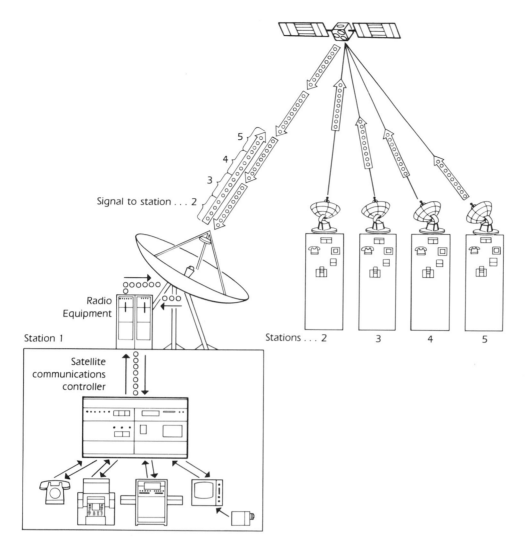

Figure 6.29 SBS will be a fully switchable network with full communications service (voice, narrowband, and wideband).

written word but requires costly storage space.

Information flows faster when it is distributed electronically because it is not physically handled as often, or perhaps not at all. Moreover, newer technology allows information to be miniaturized and stored on film rather than on hard copy.

The most common methods for transmitting information are voice, graphic, data, and video. These are made possible through advances in microprocessor, laser, fiber optics, and satellite technology.

Three types of information carriers for moving information are narrowband, voiceband, and wideband. The type of information carrier chosen will determine how fast information can move.

Today's word/information processing equipment has the capacity of moving information at speeds much greater than the telephone.

Summary

Key Terms

Distribution
Paper overload
Information carriers
Facsimile (FAX)
Reference documents
Transaction documents
Micrographics
Computer output microfilm
   (COM)
Microforms
Telecommunications
Voice communications
Data communications
Computer assisted retrieval
   (CAR)
Computer input microfilm
   (CIM)
Aperture card
Roll film

Microfilm jacket
Microfiche
Ultrafiche
Ultrastrip
Video disc
Holography
Graphic communications
Video communications
Fiber optics
Satellites
Microprocessor
Laser
Data line
Narrowband carriers
Connect time
Voiceband carriers
Microelectronics
Wideband carriers

Study Guide

This study guide provides you with feedback to find out how well you are doing. Use a separate sheet of paper to record your answers. When you have finished check your responses with the answers at the back of the book.

Matching: Choose the answer that best defines the word in the left column.

1. Distribution

   a. documents such as research data, reports, brochures, and catalogues.

2. Data communications

   b. a method of filing information on microfilm using miniaturized images.

3. Voice lines

   c. any form, either film or paper, that contains microimages.

4. Fiber optics

   d. an information carrier designed to handle data communications.

5. Reference documents

   e. movement of information from one location to another.

6. Microfiche

   f. a sheet of film containing possibly several hundred exposures.

7. Wideband

   g. words, symbols, and numbers being sent electronically.

8. Microform

   h. satellites proposed to act as a nationwide computer and provide total communications networks channeled through the sky.

9. ACS, Xten, and SBS

   i. voiceband carriers that use telephone lines for sending voice or data.

10. Micrographics

   j. glass-like thin tubes as fine as human hair that send light from one location to another.

Multiple choice: Select the letter or letters that best answer each question.

11. Which of the following microform holds the greatest numbers of microimages?
   a. Aperture card
   b. Microfilm jacket
   c. Ultrafiche
   d. Microfiche

12. The following is considered a problem when using microfilm:
   a. Storage space
   b. Mailing costs
   c. Computer output microfilm
   d. Margin notations

13. What do the letters FAX stand for?
   a. Foreign auxiliary exchange
   b. Facsimile
   c. Facts (a teletypewriter abbreviation)
   d. None of the above.

14. The two methods of distributing information are physical and:
   a. Electric
   b. Electronic
   c. Mechanical
   d. None of the above

15. Which of the following information carriers is the fastest means of moving information?
   a. Voiceband
   b. Wideband
   c. Narrowband
   d. None of the above

Completion: Write the correct answer(s) on a separate sheet of paper.

16. Information can be sent electronically in the form of
_____ , _____ ,
_____ , and _____

17. Another word for voice communication carriers is
_____ .

18. Three types of information carriers for electronic distribution are _____ , _____ , and
_____ .

19. Four kinds of technology that are helping to speed up distribution of documents are _____ , _____ , _____ , and _____ .

20. Another term for facsimile is _____ .

graphic communication

True/False: Write + for True, 0 for False for each question.

21. Distribution is the most costly step in the workflow of the document cycle.

22. The best solution to the problem of finding adequate storage space for filing hard copy is to store files in boxes in a rented building.

23. A transmission error refers to something received differently from the way in which it was sent.

24. Data communications can be transmitted over voiceband or wideband carriers.

25. Any information distributed electronically over telephones is called telecommunications.

Questions on Concepts

1. Compare the four most common microforms.
2. Describe what is meant by voice, data, graphics, and video communications.
3. Compare the three information carriers with respect to speed of transmission.
4. Explain the four kinds of technology that will help speed up distribution and reduce distribution costs.
5. Why is the cost of computer technology going down? Explain.

6. Who owns the major satellite systems in the United States?
7. Narrowband and voiceband carriers of information are inadequate for high-speed data communications. Explain.

Case and Activities

Louisville's Harris Bank has 40 locations and maintains savings information on nearly 500,000 cards in several files containing names, addresses, telephone numbers, and other important information. The bank also produces about 50 daily, weekly, and monthly reports on paper ranging from a total of 200 to 30,000 pages per month. Checking account names, addresses, and special instructions are filed on nearly 250,000 cards. Printed information of the data in the files is available at only four bank locations due to cost and limitations in producing copies.

1. What recommendations would you make to this bank to create a more efficient and cost-effective way of handling its paperwork problem? Explain.
2. Discuss the advantages of your method of handling the bank's paperwork problems.
3. What backup system for the security of files would you suggest implementing?

Activities

1. Visit a library or office that uses microfilm readers. Use the reader to find some item of interest related to word/information processing.
2. Write to either IBM, Comsat General, Aetna Life and Casualty, American Telephone & Telegraph, Western Union, or Xerox to acquire any consumer information they have available related to their satellites.
3. Visit the U.S. Postal Service to see how mail is physically handled.

CHAPTER 7

Telecommunications Systems

The objectives of this chapter are to:

1. Define telecommunication.

2. Compare the patterns of office communications in the first, second, and third stages of office automation.

3. List the most important piece of automated equipment in the third stage of office automation.

4. Identify the five major categories of electronic mail systems.

5. Describe the equipment specifications that determine whether communications can occur.

6. Explain how unlike systems can communicate.

7. Contrast word processing with data processing as they were originally defined.

8. Describe the integration of word and data processing.

9. Describe the integration of word processing and photocomposition.

10. Discuss the main reasons for integrating word processing and micrographics.

11. Explain the purpose of a management information system.

The telephone is one of the most important tools in information processing technology. It electronically moves information from one location to another. Most electronic distribution of information is called telecommunications and involves the use of telephone lines. Every telecommunication method has the purpose of exchanging information between two or more points accurately and quickly. To accomplish this task, equipment must have compatible modems, protocols, and languages.

Telecommunication methods, referred to as electronic mail systems discussed later in this chapter, include carrier based systems, public and private teletype, facsimile, communicating word/information processors, and computer-based message systems.

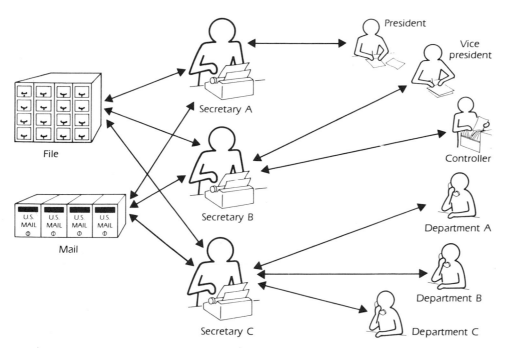

Figure 7.1 Patterns of office communications are not affected by the use of the typewriter in the first stage of office automation.

Evolution of Office Communications

The purpose of office automation technology is to communicate more accurately and quickly. The typewriter was one of the first pieces of office equipment in the initial stage of office automation. It increased the productivity of the secretary, but had no effect upon the pattern of communication in the office. The pattern of communication for the **first stage** shows information moving back and forth between the manager and the secretary throughout the steps in the document cycle (Figure 7.1). The manager originates, the secretary keyboards, the manager proofreads and revises, the secretary rekeyboards, the manager signs the document, the secretary prepares it for mailing. Within the distribution step alone, this exchange of information occurs several times. The secretary physically handles the mail and filing; when the manager needs a file, the secretary gets it from the area where records are kept. The file has to be physically delivered to the manager. When the manager is finished using the file, a secretary or a messenger has to physically return it to the file room. The same procedure occurs when mail comes or is ready to be distributed.

The **second stage** of office automation came about when the typewriter was given some logic, memory, CRTs, and floppy disks. This stage of automation created documents more rapidly, causing a considerable increase in the productivity level of the secretary, but the pattern of communication between the manager and secretary during the origination, production, and distribution of the information still did not change (Figure 7.2).

The **third stage** of office automation added a central processing unit (CPU). People were then able to store information in a central location and access it

Stages of communication

160

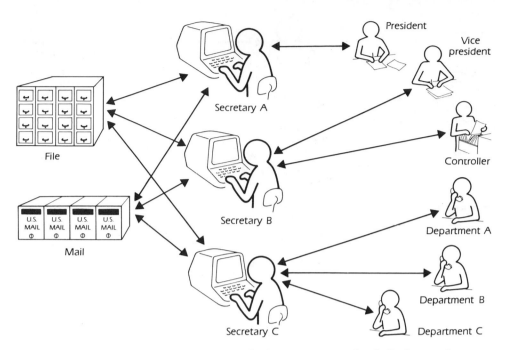

Figure 7.2 The typewriter is given some logic, memory, a visual display, and storage media in the second stage of office automation, but the patterns of office communications remain unchanged.

easily. Several common components in each of the word/information processing systems in the third stage of office automation are:

Central processor is key component

    A central processing unit (CPU)
    Some form of storage media
    A CRT display
    A printer for hardcopy output
    A keyboard for information input (some form of direct access)
    Capability to add one or more of the following options:
- Telecommunications
- OCR
- Photocomposition
- Special function keyboards

Replaces less capable devices

The third stage of office automation starts with the same common types of components in each system. These components are computer parts from the data processing industry. They allow for massive replacement of the existing less-capable devices of earlier office automation like typewriters, paper-based word processors, telecopiers, and calculators.

Easy to learn

    One of the major advantages that equipment in the third stage of office automation has over similar data processing systems is that the equipment is relatively simple to operate. There is no complex data processing terminology such as system utilities, report generators, or I/O processors commonly found in computer technology. Instead, the third stage of office automation systems simplifies the operation of the equipment by using simple, easy-to-learn two-key commands. The equipment has computer functions, and, with minimal training, its power is now available to the office staff.

In office automation, the equipment can be instructed to search and re- *Easy to use*
place words or insert and delete characters, words, or lines using a few keystrokes. Functions such as "search/replace" and "insert/delete" are easy to
understand and use, yet they are often executed with very sophisticated
software and instructions.

Unlike equipment in the data processing industry, the third stage of *Easy to install*
equipment in word/information processing is packaged into small, sometimes
desktop-size units that are connected with small cables. The equipment uses
standard electrical outlets, but it may function better when an electrical line is
dedicated solely for its use. Installation generally is not difficult and neither
special air conditioning nor site preparation are usually necessary.

Moreover, the third stage of office automation changes the traditional pat- *Patterns of communication*
tern of office communications drastically (Figure 7.3). The *central location for* *change*
storage and distribution of information causes a tremendous increase in productivity. People in the office can communicate with each other through a computer. Using the computer, they can rapidly exchange information and can easily find the information they need when it is located in the computer files. The
flow of information is no longer between the secretary and manager, but between a person and a computer. For example, a manager wishing to examine a

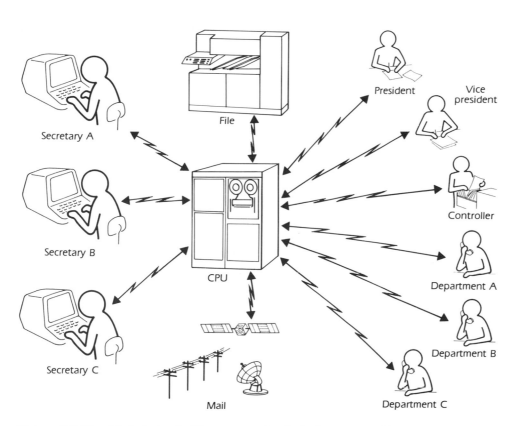

Figure 7.3 The third stage of office automation includes a central location for storage
and distribution in information. It can increase productivity significantly and drastically
change the patterns of office communication.

Evolution of Office Communications

file need only give a two-key command such as "search/files" to a desktop terminal and an index of the organization's files appears on a screen. The manager rapidly scans the index to locate the needed file and presses another key on the terminal which brings to the screen the actual file needed. Then, the manager can review the file page by page on the screen without ever leaving the office. The manager does not use the secretary's time to retrieve the files. No hard copy is moved around the office. The third stage of office automation has affected patterns of communication by moving information electronically.

Electronic Mail Systems

Word processing and office automation are two terms often used interchangeably. Moreover, the term "word processing" is often used to mean automated typewriting equipment. Many managers, therefore, think of word processing or office automation as primarily secretarial tools because the process is associated with typewriters. Acceptance of automation depends on managers. Therefore, for office automation to be successfully implemented, attitudes toward it must change. For example, electronic mail is a form of office automation, but many managers and executives who could benefit directly from faster communications available through electronic mail have little knowledge of it.

Electronic mail is a way in which information moves between two locations over hard wires or telephone lines. When this movement or transfer of information occurs it is often called "**telecommunications**." A small core group of experts know and understand the concepts, products, and uses of this new technology, but electronic mail or office automation for the masses still is the wave of the future. Today it is still misused, misunderstood, and many times unprofitable.

Types of systems

The five major categories of electronic mail systems are carrier-based systems and public postal services, public and private teletype, facsimile, communicating word/information processors, and computer-based message systems.

Carrier-based Systems and Public Postal Services

In 1979 President Carter gave the Administration's go-ahead to the U.S. Postal Service to become active in electronic mail beginning in 1985. Under the electronic mail concept, letters are not physically carried from the senders to the receivers. Instead, modern electronic technology is used to bounce computerized messages off satellites or send them over wires. Then, a facsimile or copy of the original message is printed at a receiving post office and delivered with the regular mail. Using electronic mail technology, organizations can use private companies that provide electronic technology to send messages to specially equipped post offices.

One form of the U.S. Postal Service electronic mail is called **ECOM** (Electronic Computer Originated Messages). To use ECOM, magnetic media (magnetic disk, card, tape) must be keyboarded into one of the 25 post offices in the

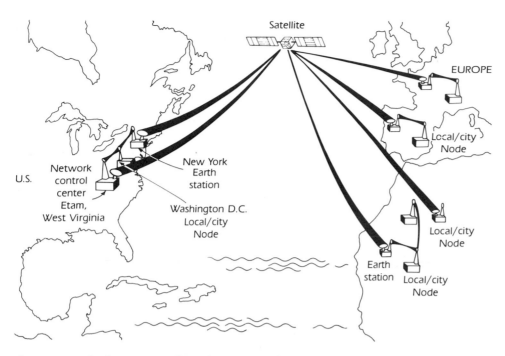

Figure 7.4 United States Postal Service project of international electronic messages.

ECOM System. The message will then be delivered by postal employees. ECOM is one of the five forms of electronic mail available during the 1980s.

For international electronic messages, the Postal Service signed an agreement with Communications Satellite Corporation (COMSAT) to develop both high- and low-speed facsimile and OCR overseas transmissions. This plan operates as follows: The U.S. earth station will be transmitting from Etam, West Virginia to a selected group of 101 countries involved in the project, named **INTELSAT**. The message path will use land communication links between New York and Washington post office "nodes" (computers) and the Etam facility (Figure 7.4). Physical delivery of messages (by users to the post offices and by couriers from the post offices) will speed mail circulation through the nodes. This system could be tied into our internal U.S. mail services in the future. A rough cost for international electronic message service today ranges from $1 to $4 per page. The goal is to offer next-day delivery at a reasonable cost. INTELSAT should become a means for expanding distribution capabilities in word/information processing. Information stored on media in organizations may be moved electronically across the United States and even internationally with the assistance of the U.S. Postal Services.

The U.S. Postal Service will expand its minicomputer mail forwarding systems, designed to reduce the cost and delivery time associated with mail that is addressed to locations from which people have moved. Each system is comprised of a minicomputer, a keyboard with a video display, a label printer, and a storage area for disks on which address changes are recorded.

A service offered by Western Union for distribution of information combines telephone service and the U.S. Postal Service in a **Mailgram**. Mailgrams can be used in sending messages to customers, suppliers, and distributors who are not

Nodes

Figure 7.5 A terminal for sending Mailgrams. *(Courtesy of Western Union.)*

on a teletypewriter network. The message is sent over a screen and keyboard (terminal) as shown in Figure 7.5 from the post office sending the Mailgram to the post office closest to the intended destination. Western Union takes care of the transmission over satellites by using its own land, microwave, and cable links. The post office physically delivers the final message. Mailgrams provide *Guaranteed one-day delivery* guaranteed one-day transmission of a document in an envelope resembling a telegram. Mailgrams save internal writing, typing, sorting, and posting time and thus speed the communication of the message. Also, the service is available after the secretaries have left the office.

Another service of Mailgram is called a **Stored Mailgram**, which allows the user to store material for repeated use in units called a Telepost. Letters, paragraphs, address lists, and other stored information are available 7 days a week, 24 hours a day. A telephone or Mailgram terminal can make it possible to use this information.

If applications do not require original copy letters on company stationery with high-quality printing, organizations that use mailgrams can have next-day delivery of repetitive letters. Organizations with limited word/information processing applications may use the Mailgram and Stored Mailgram service rather than invest in their own word/information processing equipment.

Public and Private Teletype

Telex and **TWX** were sending information electronically long before the term "electronic mail" was ever used. TWX and Telex are two teletypewriters provided by Western Union since 1958. The main difference between them is that Telex has three rows of keys and TWX has four. TWX transmits slightly

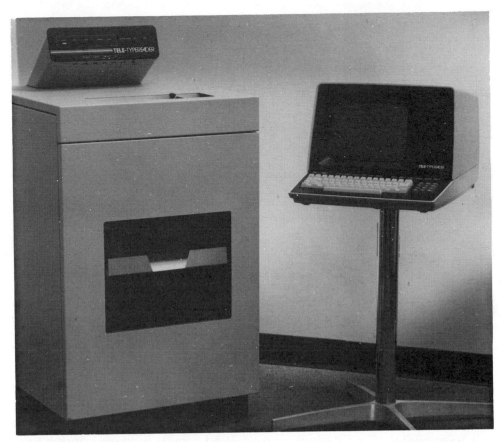

Figure 7.6 A tele-typereader consists of an OCR reader, an intelligent user-programmable editing terminal, and an optional paper tape punch. *(Courtesy of Hendrix.)*

faster than Telex, but both are able to communicate with their own terminals or with each other. Both are generally used to transmit brief messages that move slowly (300 bits per second or slower) on narrowband information carriers.

Telex/TWX can be used as an alternative to many routine telephone calls. A Telex/TWX call costs about one-half that of a regular telephone call, provides the receiver with a permanent record (hard copy), and the person receiving the message does not have to be near the phone.

Telex/TWX is also an economical way of sending international messages to teletypewriter subscribers overseas. If the intended receiver is not a subscriber, then an International Telegram (Cablegram) can be sent, eliminating the time involved in getting an overseas phone connection.

Some word/information processors have an optional device which allows them to communicate with a Telex machine. This device gives word/information processing users access to approximately 720,000 Telex/TWX terminals all over the world that can be reached through their word/information processors. Also, some OCR readers now use a programmable editing terminal or a paper tape punch that can be used to generate a Telex message (Figure 7.6). The text message is prepared by an author and keyboarded with an OCR element on an ordinary office typewriter. The text is then read by the OCR reader and displayed on the visual screen. The Telex/TWX address of the receiver is

Word/information processors can communicate with Telex machines

Figure 7.7 *(left)* The dex^R 5100 high speed digital facsimile transceiver communicates full pages of text or graphics in as little as 20 seconds. *(Courtesy of Graphic Sciences, Inc., a Burroughs Corporation Subsidiary.)* **Figure 7.8** *(above)* The dex 1100 facsimile communicator is receiving a page of information. *(Courtesy of Graphic Sciences, Inc., a Burroughs Corporation Subsidiary.)*

added and the text is changed (formatted) to fit requirements for Telex or TWX transmission. The text is then sent to a paper tape punch. After the tape is punched, it is removed from the punch unit and read into the Telex machine for transmission to the desired location. Hard copy is produced during transmission.

Facsimile

FAX

Copies an original

Since the late 1970s, **facsimile** or **FAX** has become one of the major elements of "electronic mail." It is essentially a type of copier that electronically sends an original document from one location to a remote location where it is reproduced as a copy or "facsimile" of the original document (Figure 7.7). The transmitting copy is scanned by a light source (lens, laser, or fiber optics) that converts original material into electronic signals. The signals are sent to a receiving unit where they are converted to sound signals by placing a telephone receiver into a nonvisual unit, which then reverses the process and produces a hard copy (Figure 7.8). These documents are sent over public or private telephone lines. Text and numbers have been sent over telephone lines since the 1940s in the form of wirephotos for newspapers or law enforcement agencies.

Facsimile units are also referred to as *telecopiers*. Facsimile may be used in place of teletype message transmission or as a higher speed alternative to the mails.

Facsimile has speed advantages

Recently, the concept of "electronic mail" for business applications caused managers to look carefully at the relative slowness of the U.S. Postal Service and the speed advantages of facsimile. Now, not only are text and numbers sent over facsimile but so are handwritten text, photographs, signatures, drawings or charts, and graphs.

The sending facsimile unit accepts documents in their original form without any rekeying of information. Graphic material as well as printed material can be transmitted with ease and documents can be signed or verified. Users are accepting facsimile as an important means of moving information. The cost of the units is decreasing, quality is increasing, and there is a trend among vendors for increased compatibility between equipment. Compatible facsimile units between different vendors allow the units to send and receive to each other.

No rekeying of documents

Portable facsimile equipment is available and can be carried to a work site or used on business trips.

Portable

Facsimile does have a few limitations that should be considered. Regardless of how much of the page is typed, the facsimile process sends the entire page, white space included. Therefore, no matter how much typed material is on the page, it still takes the same amount of time to transmit it. Manufacturers are developing new devices for facsimile to compress the information in order to speed up the transmission. The compression operation is called **white-space skipping** and is particularly useful when the volume of documents transmitted is high enough for communication costs to be a major issue.

Transmission needs to be faster

Another limitation is that once you have received a facsimile document, all you have is a hard copy. Unlike word/information processors, you have no magnetic recording of the information and any revisions (editing) in the document would require it to be rekeyboarded and then revised.

No magnetic recording is made

A third limitation of facsimile is the quality of print. It is usually readable, but not always of high quality. Although facsimile units may send and receive documents unattended (without a worker present), a great deal of effort is still required to accomplish this task.

Quality of print is not high

A further limitation is that many of the devices still cannot communicate with each other, although there is a growing trend toward increased compatibility.

Facsimile is used in many departments in businesses to send documents or photos from one office to another in a different location. For example, in accounting, facsimile is used to send customer credit information, process invoices, and forward statistical data without data errors resulting from rekeyboarding the numbers (Figure 7.9). In sales, it is used to send delivery schedules, specification sheet drawings, proposals, and price quotes. In purchasing, it is used to speed bids, quotes, specifications, and orders. Some facsimile units like the one shown in Figure 7.10 can automatically receive or send documents by telephone overnight without an attendant.

Transmission speeds on facsimile units vary from less than one minute to six minutes or more. The reason for slow transmission speeds is because telephone lines are used. Because of slow transmission time, charges for use of transmission lines are high and the operation of equipment is inefficient. With some satellite transmission of facsimile, even the slowest machine could send copies over a satellite system for 15¢ per page, including the rental of the machine. Newer and faster machines of tomorrow and higher volumes of information to be transmitted could drop the cost to 1.5¢ per page for facsimile transmission.

Satellite transmission of facsimile

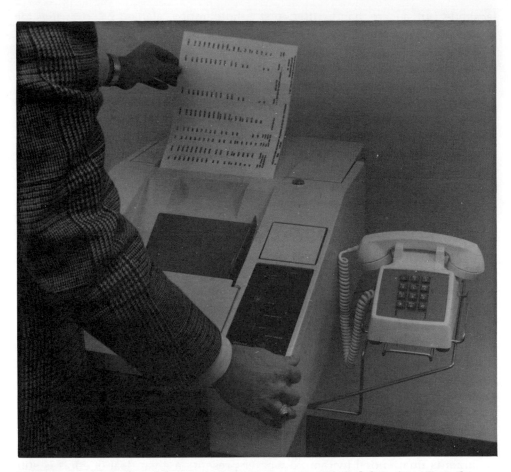

Figure 7.9 A facsimile unit assures receiving accurate statistical data. *(Courtesy of Xerox Corporation.)*

One-third of intracompany postal expense goes for movement of information that satellites could handle using FAX and communicating word/information processors. Communicating word/information processors are pieces of equipment that can send information to one another. An example of an organization that needs to transmit information at very high speeds would be a user of a computer system who has an overloaded computer in Los Angeles. They could use a high-speed satellite channel to transfer elaborate jobs to an underused computer in New York. Using this method would eliminate bottlenecks and increase the workload capacity without requiring heavy expenditures for new equipment.

Can poll satellites

Some newer facsimile units can **poll satellites.** With this capability, unattended facsimile units are ready to send documents automatically via satellite when called upon by another remote facsimile machine.

Communicating Word/Information Processors

Electronic mail

To many users of automated equipment, the words "**communicating word/information processor**" and electronic mail have the same meaning. Communicating word/information processors allow equipment to "talk"—that

Figure 7.10 Xerox Night Caller. Before leaving the office or home at night, documents can be stacked in the feeder trays of the self-dialing facsimile system or the Xerox Telecopier 410 in the upper left hand corner. After 11 p.m., when interstate telephone rates are 60% lower, these facsimile units will call other telecopier units and send trayloads of documents, in sequence, to designated locations around the world. *(Courtesy of Xerox Corporation.)*

is, to transfer documents electronically between two points (terminals). The communicating word/information processor shown in Figure 7.11 can exchange information with another communicating word/information processor (Figure 7.12), or a computer, over telephone lines or via other telecommunication hookups. When a communicating word/information processor is connected to another piece of equipment that also communicates, it is **on-line.**

When on line, text can be exchanged much faster than by keyboarding manually. The exchange of documents from one communicating word/information processor to another at great speeds makes it possible to send and receive written communications faster than by mailing these documents. Documents that have been exchanged by communicating word/information processors are received in the form of a printout or may be received on magnetic media without ever being printed. To be considered equipment that is part of electronic mail, the machine has to have the capability of entering, editing (revis-

What must electronic mail be able to do?

Figure 7.11 A communicating word/information processor preparing to communicate to another system. *(Courtesy of International Business Machines Corporation.)*

Figure 7.12 A person working with a display terminal on a shared-logic system, revising information after it has been received through communications. *(Courtesy of Basic Four Corporation, an MAI Company.)*

ing), sending, and receiving text. Most of the job of setting up documents for sending and receiving systems must be performed manually and with operator control at some point in the operation. Some sophisticated word/information processors can be receiving a message while other word/information processing functions occur.

Tasks Performed by Communicating Word/Information Processors. In the future, the need will increase to connect word/information processors to provide the communications function of electronic mail and to permit word/information processors to be part of an overall information processing system. It is predicted that the number of communicating word/information processors will increase by 1900% between 1979 and 1984. By 1984, 500,000 pieces of this equipment will be in use representing the most growth of any electronic mail system.[1]

Eliminates need for some U.S. mail

Using communicating word/information processors has several advantages: delivering a document electronically from one word/information processor to another over telephone lines or satellites eliminates the delivery time required by the U.S. mails. Electronic delivery avoids the need for a hard copy of the document, although the document might be printed on paper at the receiving end. The communicating word/information processor such as those shown in Figures 7.13 and 7.14 can operate at night and take advantage of low-cost evening or night telephone rates. The receiving units can operate completely unattended and can receive more than 20 pages of text. The information received

[1]"Business Communication: Alternatives for the Eighties," *Fortune*, January 13, 1980, p. 24–25.

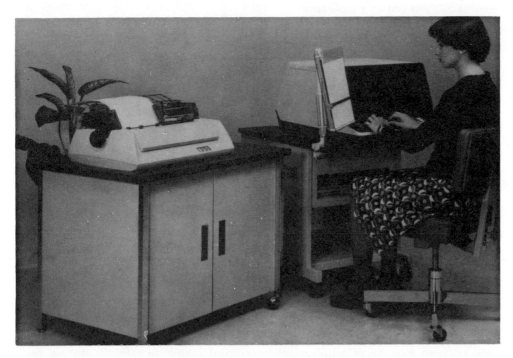

Figure 7.13 The Word Station 78 (WS78) can act as a stand-alone word/information processor or communicate with other WS78 terminals or certain computers as part of a distributed processing network. *(Courtesy of Digital Equipment Corporation.)*

Figure 7.14 Telecommunications provides a fast and accurate network between compatible word/information processors and computers regardless of their locations. *(Courtesy of Wang Laboratories, Inc.)*

Eliminates need to maintain and update files

can be played out at a later time.

Communicating word/information processors provide a central point (CPU) which can be used by different departments in an organization as a common storage area to receive updated information and eliminate duplication of work. Material already typed on magnetic media in one department can be transmitted electronically to and from departments from the common storage area without additional keyboarding.

Eliminates rekeyboarding

A communicating word/information processor may be able to connect (interface) to peripheral equipment such as OCR scanners or phototypesetters for increased capabilities. This connection will eliminate the rekeyboarding of information used in more than one department of an organization.

Eliminates revision on-line

Before a document is communicated, changes can be made on a magnetic medium while it is inside the communicating word/information processor. If changes are made while the equipment is not connected to the equipment that communicates, the changes are made **off-line.** Revising documents using this procedure does not tie up telephone lines; consequently, costs are reduced.

Eliminates physically transferring work

A communicating word/information processor permits text or data keyboarded in one location to be edited and printed in another location. This method is not only useful to move information from the equipment in an organization to equipment in several locations, but also to transfer work from one correspondence or administrative support center to another during peak periods.

Communicating word/information processors helped Litton, Dunaway, and Schick Research Laboratories in Tahway, Connecticut when they first realized they had an information handling problem. The problem started when the computer printouts of statistical information from data processing were being rekeyed in the company's word processing center. When the computer printouts were rekeyed, errors were made, and, for the quality control of research information, errors were unacceptable. Quality control of information is carried out through checking procedures to assure that data is correct. Therefore, it was decided to upgrade the word processing equipment, if possible, and acquire equipment with communications capabilities such as those shown in Figure 7.15. Then, instead of the word processing center rekeying computer printouts, the information would be called up from the computer into the word/information processor and the needed information would be displayed on a CRT. Any necessary reformatting of the text could take place and the chance of introducing errors through rekeying would be eliminated.

Computer-based Message Systems

Networks

A **computer-based message system** allows messages to be sent over a telephone wire or cable to a computer and saved until the person to whom the message is sent wants to receive it. Pathways over which message traffic is sent are referred to as networks. Switching equipment enables a pathway to be used for voice, data, graphic, and video traffic. Some computer-based message systems use remote computers and time-sharing firms with the aid of switching networks that handle data communications covering the entire United States. The networks are usually quite expensive, but are one of the few costs that

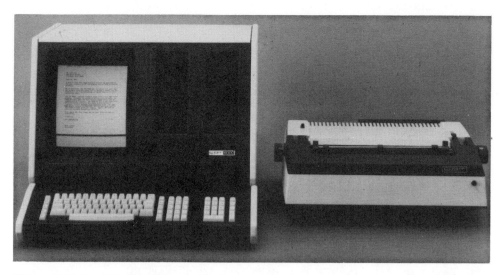

Figure 7.15 The CPT 8000 is a stand-alone word/information processor with communications capabilities. It can also share hard disk storage and some of the peripherals of a shared resource system. *(Courtesy of CPT Corporation.)*

directly increase office efficiency. For example, neither secretary nor manager handles paper containing the incoming messages. Messages do not take up any physical space, do not need to be repeated, rewritten, or attended in order to be received.

No hard copy messages

One type of internal message system operates from a central location that has a computer-based system with an operator who handles incoming and outgoing calls. The message center operator keys into the system the telephone number of the called party. A CRT display shows the name of the party, his or her calendar, who the party works for, who works for him or her, and other important information. With this information, the message center operator can more efficiently handle the call. The system reduces the number of return calls managers have to make and saves secretarial time. Once information is placed into the system, other scheduling and coordinating tasks can be done as needed.

An explanation of a computer-based message system (CBMS) is provided in Figure 7.16. Imagine a computerized telephone device as the center of all voice and electronic message traffic. The CBMS has computer capabilities and stores, processes, and delivers office communications. The message processor can be connected to video display or printer terminals using the standard office telephone wiring. Users can send or receive messages by plugging compatible terminals into the telephone. Users gain access to the CBMS by a special password code assigned to each person using the system. Floppy diskettes are one kind of media used for message storage. Rolm is one company producing this type of system; their unit is called the Rolm CBX Electronic Message System.

Telephone center of traffic

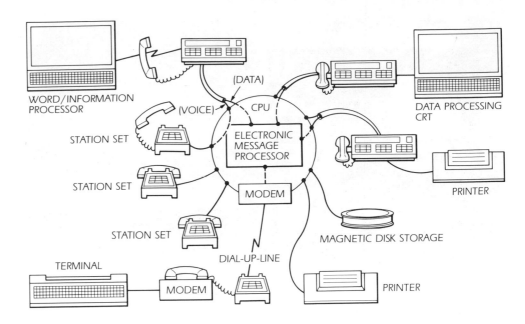

Figure 7.16 A computer-based message system.

Communication System Requirements

To acquire word/information processing equipment with just the internal capability to communicate is not enough. Each communicating device in the electronic mail systems must meet certain requirements before it can communicate to another device. Usually devices must have matching electronic signals as well as other equipment specifications.

Communicating with Modems

Creating usable signals

In order for the output of electronic mail systems to be communicated over information carriers, the output must first be changed. The language of the machine must change to signals that can be sent over a telephone line by using a device called a modem. A **modem** is a device for changing signals between an office machine and a communications line. The information to be communicated from the office machine is not suitable for sending directly over telephone lines to a computer. The modem changes the information to signals that can be transmitted easily over a distance and supplies power to get the information to the receiving end. At the receiving end, the modem changes the information back to a signal that the office machine will recognize (Figure 7.17).

You use a modem in your telephone receiver daily. It sends your voice over telephone lines but it changes your voice sounds first so that the communications line can recognize the voice, transmit it, and receive it on the other end of the line.

A modem is sometimes called an **interface**, which may be defined as the point at which two different pieces of equipment connect.

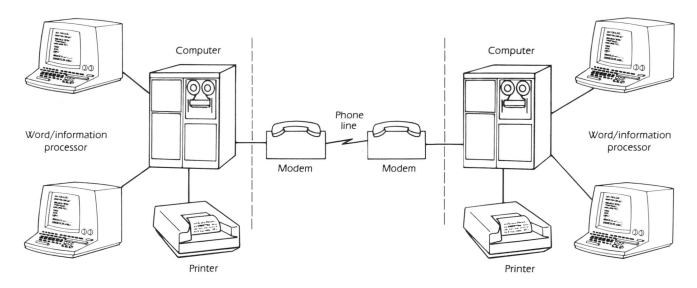

Figure 7.17 Communicating with modems.

Equipment Specifications

When information is transmitted, it has to be changed from a visually readable form to a **machine-readable form.** To accomplish this, four factors on the equipment must be compatible. They are defined below to assist you in understanding the problem of information transfer between devices with unlike specifications. If each of the factors mentioned is not the same (**compatible**) on both pieces of equipment trying to talk to each other, then no communication can take place. The single biggest inhibitor to equipment compatibility and the transfer of information between unlike units is the code assigned by each of the manufacturers to be used on their equipment. When considering the use of different manufacturers' units in an existing word/information processing network or when considering capabilities of new equipment, the user must be aware of the problem of incompatible codes.

The method by which pulses or **signals** are moved along the telephone line *Mode of transmission* is called the **mode of transmission.** It influences the speed the information moves and the amount of information that can be moved along the line. The two major modes of transmission are *asynchronous* and *synchronous*. Imagine both modes to be methods of moving characters of information along a telephone line. Asynchronous communications (Figure 7.18) can be compared to moving a string of individual characters with a "stop" and "start" signal on either side of each character one at a time along the line.

Synchronous communications, as shown in Figure 7.19, move faster than asynchronous communications. In this mode, a group or block of many characters move together or are sent along the line with a single "stop" and "start" signal bracketing the entire block of characters. Synchronous communications are sometimes referred to as "bisynch," or binary synchronous.

Signals that control the procedures of sending and receiving of information (transmission) between different devices are referred to as **protocol.**

The speed information moves is measured in bits per second (bps) and is

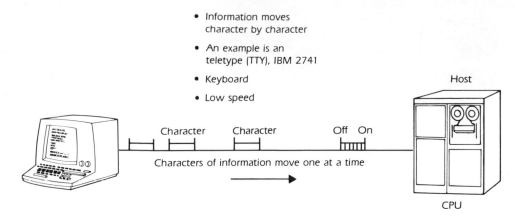

- Information moves character by character
- An example is an teletype (TTY), IBM 2741
- Keyboard
- Low speed

Character   Character   Off On

Characters of information move one at a time

Figure 7.18 Asynchronous communications.

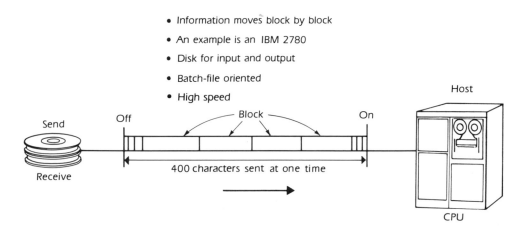

- Information moves block by block
- An example is an IBM 2780
- Disk for input and output
- Batch-file oriented
- High speed

Send   Off   Block   On

400 characters sent at one time

Receive

Figure 7.19 Synchronous communications.

Speed/Baud rate

Coding

often referred to as a **Baud rate**. Common telephone lines can handle a Baud rate of up to 4800 bps.

The bits travel along the telephone line in a **specific order** or **code.** When the information is received, the bits are decoded or changed back into characters. The most common code used is called ASCII (American Standard Code of Information Interchange). This code requires seven bits to make up a character. Two other common codes are EBCD (Extended Binary Coded Decimal), a six bit code; and EBCDIC (Extended Binary Coded Decimal Internal Code), an eight bit code. These codes control information content and signals for controlling the printer, formatting, and text editing functions.

Must insert format instructions

Unlike Systems Can Communicate. It is possible for word/information processors with **incompatible codes** to communicate. For example, through a modem, one system receives only previously keyboarded numbers, symbols, and letters from another system. Margin settings, paragraph indentations, and other format instructions are not communicated to the receiving system. These format instructions must be inserted by the person receiving the information.

Another way for unlike systems to communicate using any kind of communicating device is to pay a fee to a satellite communication network. The network will distribute information wherever the user chooses. The interface provided by the network works with any device chosen to receive the user's message. It may be important for an organization to have two unlike systems within the organization communicate to each other. Communication between these two unlike systems allows information that is stored on each system's magnetic media to be shared immediately. The transfer of information between the two systems is accomplished through a computer in a time-shared service bureau. One unlike system communicates with the computer and the computer then communicates back to the other unlike system.

Satellite communication networks for distribution

IBM developed a communications method to eliminate the need for machines to be identical to communicate accurately. The method is called SNA, which stands for Systems Network Architecture.

SNA

Common Methods of Communicating with Word/Information Processors

The most common method of communications that users of word/information processors are exposed to is called **point-to-point** communications. It means information moves from one terminal (point) to another terminal (point). For documents to be transmitted, two pieces of equipment with modems are required, with a communications controller/processor connecting them over a telephone line or a hardwire. Some word/information processing managers hold meetings of operators who use communicating equipment in different offices located across the country. These meetings bring together the point-to-point operators who communicate daily with one another, but have never met face to face. One necessity in utilizing communicating word/information processors is standard operating procedures among all operators. Uniformity in the manipulation of documents is a must. These meetings give operators the opportunity to meet one another, exchange ideas, knowledge, and experiences, and gain an understanding of the overall plan of communications in their organizations and how they fit within its framework.

Use of modems

Operator meetings

Point-to-computer is a communications method between word/information processors and computers. Point-to-computer communications began in the mid 1960s. Limitations in the early systems were that the magnetic media was recorded sequentially and the word/information processors had limited storage capacity. Today each communicating word/information processor has up to 64,000 characters of random access memory (RAM). As long as word/information processors are provided with compatible modems, protocols, code sets, and Baud rates, point-to-computer communications will assist management with increased productivity.

Increased productivity

Another method of communicating between word/information processors is an intraoffice communication network developed by Xerox Corporation called **Ethernet.** It is designed to transmit information between connected workstations and support devices at high speed. Using Ethernet, a document can be created at one word/information processor, sent to another for review and approval, and then sent to an electronic printer for hard-copy generation or to an on-line library for retention and subsequent retrieval. Ethernet is a coaxial cable strung down office corridors or in hallway ceilings between pieces of word/

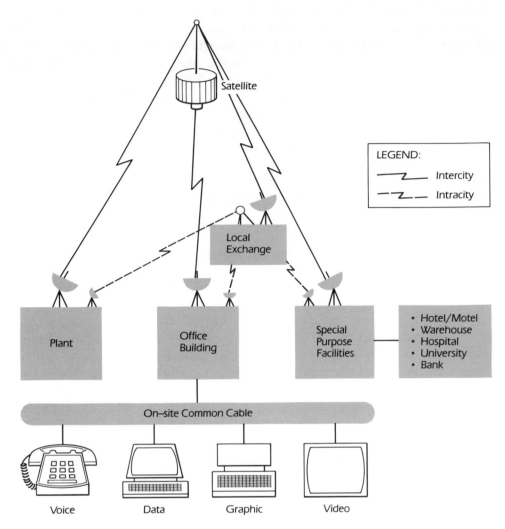

Figure 7.20 Multipoint communications using satellite systems to send and receive voice, data, graphics, and video.

Intraoffice network

information processing equipment. It can connect up to 128 workstations. Other devices called "gateways" will allow Ethernet to connect to computers and other communications networks.

In the telecommunications industry the shortest distance between two points is not always the fastest. This is true in many instances in satellite communication systems. For example, a satellite user sending data 1,800 miles from Chicago to San Francisco first sends many communications signals 23,000 miles into space. These are beamed back to earth in San Francisco, as a complete signal, in less time than it would take to transmit the same data over continuous land communications paths.

Speed is only one of the advantages of satellite communication systems. Satellite vendors claim that users will find fewer errors in the information transmitted. Also, users will find that communication costs are less using satellites to transmit information rather than telephone lines. One of the many options available to users of satellite communications is that they can send a signal from point to point, or to an unlimited number of (**multipoint**) receiving stations across the country as shown in Figure 7.20.

Integration of technologies using telecommunications is the trend for offices of the future. Voice processing, word processing, data processing, records processing, and reprographics are technologies that will continue to be the focus of integration.

Most computers use some form of telecommunications. Word/information processors communicate with other word/information processors and with computers, copiers, and phototypesetters. Microforms and paper are transmitted over telecommunication networks. Teleconferencing makes possible face-to-face communications through telecommunications. By integrating these technologies, information entering a telecommunications network through any one machine can be moved and made available to any other machine without rekeyboarding.

Word Processing and Data Processing Integration

It is not appropriate to call today's office equipment "word processing" equipment when it has computer components and possibly the same capabilities as a computer. This equipment is not just for data processing, either, because the new capabilities are better adapted to handling text than was data processing equipment. Because newer word processing equipment has so many features that extend its uses, the term "word/information processing" better describes today's automated office equipment.

Producing documents such as letters, memos, and reports for correspondence support is considered a word processing function. Payroll, general ledger, and inventory control for administrative support are considered data processing functions. When equipment has both word and data processing capabilities, it is considered integrated word and data processing.

Handles both word and data processing

If your document requirements call for some word processing and some data processing, then you should investigate the new integrated technology. Manufacturers of word processing and data processing have now developed new systems that are a combination of the two technologies without compromising either of them.

One of the most exciting and important concepts that makes communicating word/information processors the link to information processing is the natural language English keyboard. At no time in the past has society had such easy access to the wealth of information stored in computers. People only need to use one of these keyboards and they can reach and manipulate information never before available except to a small group of people specially trained in data processing. Now people in word processing departments can communicate with computers and other people in data processing departments (see Figure 7.21). Their ability to use the information in the computer (data bases) is the reason for the development of word/information processing as the total or complete picture with voice processing, data processing, word processing, and records processing as parts of the whole.

Link to information processing

An example of the integration of word and data processing is the introduction of the intelligent printer to the automated office. Figure 7.22 shows the

Figure 7.21 A word processing manager loading a hard disc into a word/information processing system for additional storage or retrieval of information. *(Courtesy of Digital Equipment.)*

movement of information between word and data processing through the link of the IBM 6670 Information Distributor (printer/copier). The printer accepts input in the following forms:

—Magnetic cards that have been keyboarded on a compatible word/information processor plus a control card that tells the printer how the job is to be set up (spacing, indents, type style, etc.).

—Communications that are accepted over communication lines from computers or communicating word/information processors.

—As a copier that accepts originals through a paper feeder and produces copies at the rate of 36 copies per minute.

Merging variable and constant data

The printer can merge variable data (names, addresses) with constant data (the body of the letter). This may be done through either of the first two methods mentioned above or it may be accomplished through a combination of input types. The constant may be fed to a printer from a magnetic card while the variable data can be fed over a communications line directly from a computer. This system is one type of integration of word and data processing technology.

Integrating word and data processing

Another method of integrating word and data processing technology is through the use of Ethernet. Figure 7.23 shows the Ethernet cable connecting many combinations of input/output devices as well as a host CPU into an elec-

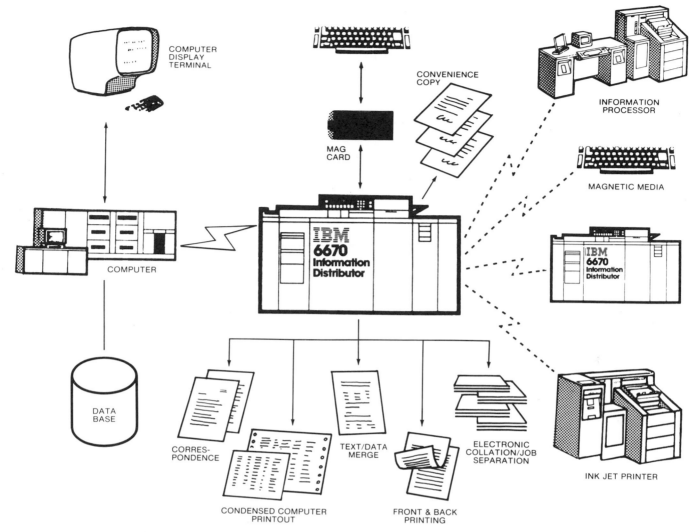

Figure 7.22 The IBM 6670 Information Distributor can become a link between word and data processing systems. *(Courtesy of International Business Machines Corporation.)*

tronically integrated office system.

The following are examples of how organizations can use integrated word and data processing effectively:

—An organization that has time-sharing terminals that are used for data processing can replace those terminals with WP/DP terminals. These terminals are used for both word and data processing.

Replace time-sharing terminals

—An organization may have a high volume of work that requires data processing and may need a mainframe computer (host computer or CPU) to handle it. With the addition of integrated word and data processing equipment (word processors), some of the data processing work that is inefficient to process on a mainframe computer can be processed on a word processor. This type of work can include adding numbers and creating mailing lists.

Handles former DP work

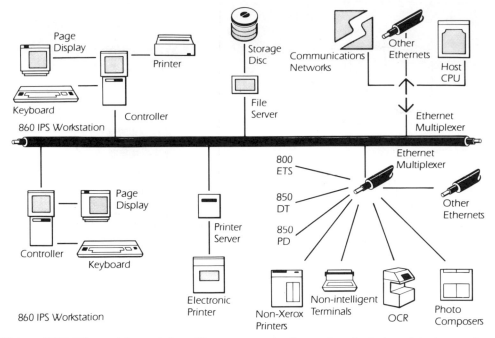

Figure 7.23 Ethernet is an intra-office communication network designed to transmit between connected workstations and support devices at high speed. Using Ethernet, a document can be created at one workstation, sent to another for review and approval, and then sent to an electronic printer for hard-copy generation or to an on-line library for retention and subsequent recall.

Combines WP/DP

—A small organization that does not have a high enough volume or work to require data processing equipment can still have data processing capabilities for its payroll, general ledger, and inventory control. Using a word/information processor, the organization can do this work and satisfy both its word processing and data processing needs.

With the introduction of integrated word and data processing systems, managers and word processing specialists will need to understand the principles of both technologies. Organizations need to combine key people from each of the disciplines—word processing, data processing, records processing, and voice processing—into task forces to solve the problems of the organization. A person who can assume the role of generalist is required to guide the information processing group effectively.

Word Processing and Phototypesetting Integration

Organizations that print a large volume of their documents in-house are integrating their word processing equipment with their phototypesetting equipment. Some organizations have not integrated word processing and phototypesetting because they are still uncertain about what procedures to use to integrate the two. Although manufacturers have equipment available for the integration, organizations still must conduct a feasibility study and combine existing terminals, printers, typesetters, and peripheral equipment from several vendors into a unified system.

The purpose of integrating word processing and phototypesetting is to ob-

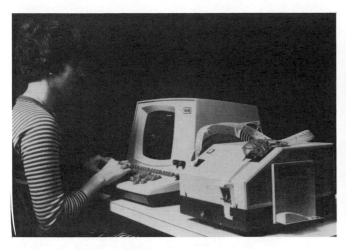

Figure 7.24 An operator keyboards into a word/information processing terminal that outputs onto punched paper tape. *(Courtesy of Wang Laboratories, Inc.)*

Figure 7.25 Some word/information processors function as keyboard entry and editing devices and are connected to a photocomposition system through an on-line interface. *(Courtesy of Wang Laboratories, Inc.)*

tain higher quality documents, to use less paper, and to eliminate the need to rekeyboard information for the phototypesetting system.

The typesetting function is very similar to the inputting and editing function in word processing. Material is rekeyboarded into a terminal with a screen and transferred to a magnetic medium such as tape or diskette (Figure 7.24). Changes can be made on the material in the same way they are made in the editing portion of the document cycle in word processing. A variety of methods are used for inputting to phototypesetting equipment. These methods include communicating from a word processing machine to a typesetter (Figure 7.25), keyboarding on any typewriting device and using an OCR reader to scan the copy, and using diskettes prepared on a word processing system with an interface as shown in Figure 7.26.

The primary difference between preparing information for word processing and preparing information for phototypesetting is that the material to be typeset has to contain instructions (codes) that inform the typesetter of such things as the size of characters (type size) and the amount of space between the lines (leading). If you keyboard information to be processed and printed out on word processors, you do not have to insert these instructions. If you keyboard material onto word processing equipment to be printed out on phototypesetting equipment, you can insert the typesetting codes where they are needed if you know them (Figure 7.27). If you do not know the exact typesetting codes, you can insert a symbol on the copy as you keyboard it every place a typesetting code is required. The typesetter then has to go back and replace the symbols with the proper codes. This method frees the person who operates the word processing equipment from having to learn typesetting codes.

Some manufacturers who have focused on word processing/phototypesetting integration and have made their equipment usable in this area are AM International, Bobst Varisystems, Compugraphic, CompuScan, Digital

Figure 7.26 An interface device or "black box" that acts as the link to integrating word processing and other technologies such as data processing and phototypesetting. *(Courtesy of Shaffstall Corporation.)*

Equipment, Itek, and Wang.

Involving the word processing operation in typesetting material saves time, reduces costs, and increases productivity. Figures 7.28 and 7.29 show the time saved by the elimination of production steps with the word processing photo-typesetting connection. The integration of word processing and phototypesetting is another step in integrating technologies.

Word Processing and Micrographics Integration

Manuals, legal documents, and medical records are examples of work keyboarded on word processing equipment. Work is keyboarded on word processing equipment because the keystrokes can be saved for future use and because the magnetic medium on which the keystrokes are captured can store more information than hard copy. However, magnetic media (floppy disks) are an expensive way to store large volumes of information for long periods of time. Therefore, a major concern in word/information processing is more efficient storage methods.

Video disc

One answer to this concern is video discs as discussed in Chapter 6. A video disc is a hard disc on which tiny codes are burned by a writing laser device. Visual access to information on video discs is over a CRT. The drawbacks of this medium are its high cost and the fact that the discs cannot be erased. Therefore, the primary use of the video disc is for archival storage or records that do not require revising. A single file drawer full of disc recordings could replace a building full of files.

Michrofiche costs less

Micrographics is an immediate answer for the storage problem. Storing information on magnetic media such as a floppy disk can cost around $10, and storing the same information on a fiche can cost about 10¢. In this case, the cost of the storage media is 100 times less expensive with fiche.

COM (computer output microfilm) allows film to become the medium for

```
                    ‹UF1FACTS


‹ID2    ‹UF2( 1 )XUF3 The Partnership will be formed under the
        California Uniform Limited Partnership Act, and a Certi-
        ficate of Limited Partnership will be filed with the Los
        Angeles County recorders office.‹FL

          ‹UF2( 2 )XUF3 W.D. Amber-Cal Corporation, a New York corpo-
        ration; Detre Natural Resources, Inc., a New York corpo-
        ration; and Jonathan B. Gardner will serve as General
        Partners to the Partnership.‹FL

          ‹UF2( 3 )XUF3 The Limited Partners as a group will share 80%
        in all income gain, loss, deductions and credits of the
        Partnership; and the General Partners as a group will
        share the rest (i.e. 25%).‹FL

          ‹UF2( 4 )XUF3 In 1976, the General Partners as a group will
        contribute cash of $10,000 and an interest in an oil well
        property with a cost basis of $10,000 and the Limited
        Partners as a group will contribute cash of $100,000 to
        the capital of the Partnership.  The General Partners have
        substantial net worth (excluding their interest as General
        Partners in the Partnership) which could be reached by
        creditors of the Partnership.‹FL

          ‹UF2( 5 )XUF3 In 1977, the General Partners as a group will
        contribute cash of $12,900 and an interest in an oil well
        property with a cost basis of $10,000 and the Limited
        Partners will contribute cash of $43,000 to the capital of
        the Partnership.‹FL

          ‹UF2( 6 )XUF3 In 1976, the Partnership will acquire a certain
        coal mining lease which the Partnership will pay substan-
        tial advance mineral royalties. These advance mineral
        royalties will consist of cash payments and the issuance
        of a non-recourse promissory note from the Partnership to
        International Coal.‹FL

   ‹ET
```

KEY:
   UF = Use format "X" (for each style, size, font, or leading change a format number is assigned.)
   FL = Flush left or end of paragraph.
   ID = Indent "X" picas
   ET = End of take (Chapter, page, or galley batch).

Figure 7.27 A page keyboarded on a word/information processor with inserted codes for typesetting.

recording information. COM is the ability to record computer output directly onto microforms, rather than print it out onto paper (see Figure 7.30). COM equipment operates faster than computer printers and produces output that can be reproduced, moved, and stored much more economically. Studies show savings to be in excess of 90% when COM is substituted for regular computer printouts.

Computer output microfilm

A major consideration in an information storage medium is the ease with which specific information can be found. Many approaches have been used to make the location of specific records stored on microforms easier. The most recent of these is called a CAR (computer assisted retrieval) system. A CAR system is used in the following way: An index to information retained in microforms is stored in a computer. When this information is needed, the index is

Computer assisted retrieval

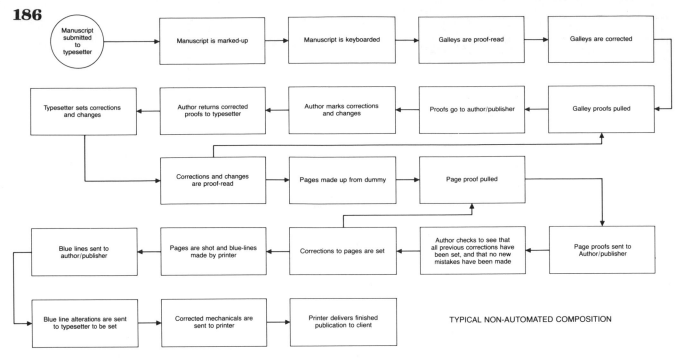

Figure 7.28 The necessary steps in producing a phototypeset document without composition being automated. *(Courtesy of The Rand Corporation.)*

reviewed on the screen of a microimage terminal (Figure 7.31) or on the screen of a word/information processing or data processing terminal. The computer address of the microform is then determined. After determining the address, the record can be called up to be reviewed on a screen. CAR is one of the most important developments in office automation technology.

Micronet, Inc. in Washington, D.C. is an example of an office attempting to demonstrate the feasibility of "the paperless office." The goal of the company is to design an office environment in which paper is replaced by the use of electronic data terminals and other automated means of accessing and using stored information. Micronet claims an average office can save 1 million dollars in filing costs alone over a ten-year period.

The typical work station for an employee at Micronet's paperless office includes a terminal to access a computer, a desktop dictation system wired into a centralized endless-loop recorder, a telephone, and a microfiche, reader/terminal. The dictation system is used to generate letters, memos, and internal reports. The transcriptionist keyboards the dictated material using a word/information processor. If a copy must leave the facility (such as an outgoing letter), an impact printer is used to create hard copy. Otherwise, the material is stored on floppy disk and transferred, if desired, to the main storage area of the computer. An active file of stored data in the computer is maintained for up to 90 days, after which a decision must be made as to what to do with the information. If it is no longer needed, the material can be erased. If the stored material should be kept in a permanent file, it is converted to microfiche via computer output microfilm equipment. Microfiche is important in the scheme of the paperless office. In Micronet's application, all incoming correspondence is im-

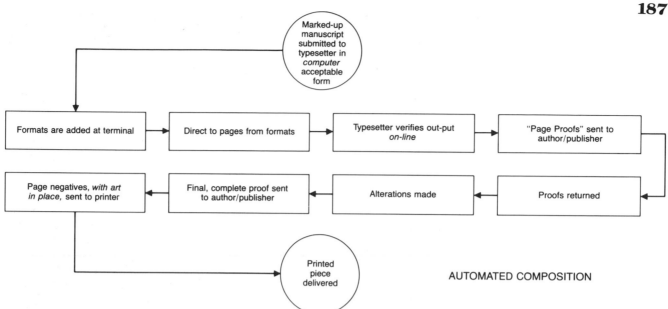

Figure 7.29 The reduced number of steps in the automated composition point out the advantages of the word processing/phototypesetting connection: the elimination of re-keyboarding, proofing time, and correcting time. *(Courtesy of The Rand Corporation.)*

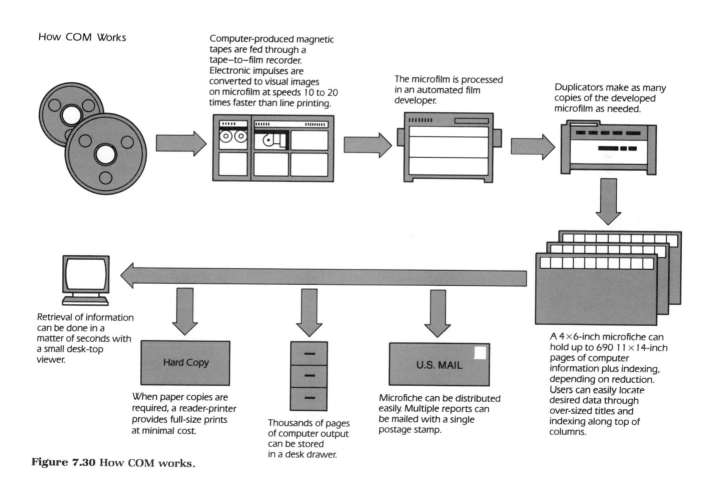

Figure 7.30 How COM works.

The Integration of Technologies

Figure 7.31 The Kodak IMT-150 microimage terminal can function as an on-line peripheral to most computers and provides immediate retrieval and hard-copy output. *(Courtesy of Eastman Kodak Company.)*

mediately transferred to microfiche; the receiver never sees the original hard copy of the material. Why did Micronet choose to depend on microfiche so heavily? The answer is simple: micrographics is a fairly mature technology and the equipment is readily available to perform automatic storage and retrieval functions at a reasonable cost.

Management Information Systems (MIS)

An **MIS** is similar to a multifunction or managerial workstation. It has a CRT, some type of keyboard to access information, it is connected to a computer, and there may be a printer nearby. The MIS may have the managerial functions described earlier, such as a calendar, a tickler file, a schedule of other managers, etc. But the primary function of a true MIS is to provide information to executives in an accurate, rapid, and readable form at any management level through a central computer system. Some of the usable information needs of management are shown in Figure 7.32.

An MIS has a display terminal that is tied into a computer to give management immediate information upon request. Managers can get up-to-the-minute answers concerning the status of a broad range of activities such as sales inventories and costs of a product or service at many locations. Managers can be informed of plans, schedules, comparisons, and operational trends. MIS can

The purpose of MIS

Immediate information

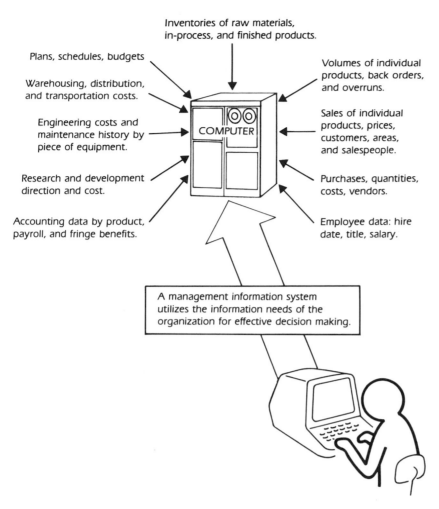

Inventories of raw materials, in-process, and finished products.

Plans, schedules, budgets

Warehousing, distribution, and transportation costs.

Engineering costs and maintenance history by piece of equipment.

COMPUTER

Research and development direction and cost.

Accounting data by product, payroll, and fringe benefits.

Volumes of individual products, back orders, and overruns.

Sales of individual products, prices, customers, areas, and salespeople.

Purchases, quantities, costs, vendors.

Employee data: hire date, title, salary.

A management information system utilizes the information needs of the organization for effective decision making.

Figure 7.32 Information needs of any company can be accessed through a management information system.

help point out where management's attention is most needed if a product line is to continue. The MIS is a comprehensive file of information that gives a very fast response to managers for assistance in decision making.

Aid in decision making

Some managers have MIS equipment that they personally operate. Others have a secretary who operates the equipment, which may diminish its effectiveness since the manager will tend to ask less of the system and therefore not be as informed. Unfortunately, the operation of terminals by persons in the upper levels of management is generally not accepted. But the development of natural language keyboards, as available in word/information processors, makes inquiries more meaningful to the manager and the technology is becoming more popular.

Managers use terminals

An MIS must be designed to fit the management style of its users. Perhaps the greatest cause of failure of an MIS is the lack of management's understanding of the capabilities and potential of the system. Managers may be unsure of what the system can do, fail to ask for what they really need from it, and do not get deeply involved in using it properly.

Managers understand capabilities

Whether small or large, businesses cannot survive without information. A

The Integration of Technologies

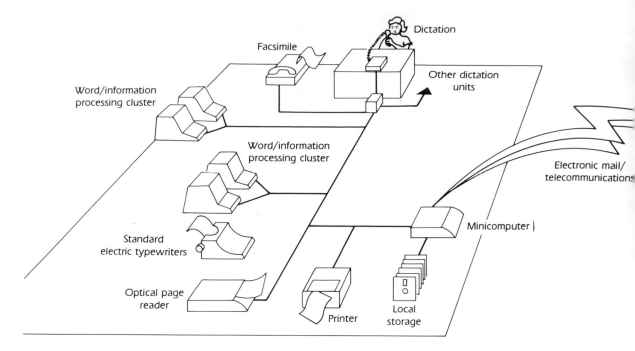

Figure 7.33 Integrating technologies for the office of the future.

MIS needed to compete

good MIS will enable small organizations to compete with large volume competitors. Decision making and problem solving requires that managers have access to information that is broad in scope, voluminous but concise, and, most important, up to date. MIS is a means of satisfying these needs.

MIS will increase opportunities for improving an organization's performance and will soon be used by all areas of business and government. It is possible that an organization's competitive and economic position in the 1990s will be directly related to the manner in which it handled the challenges of office automation in the 1980s.

Summary

Electronic mail is a form of office automation technology in which information is distributed over telephone lines, cables, or by satellite. There are five major categories of electronic mail: carrier-based systems and public postal services, public and private teletype, facsimile, communicating word/information processors, and computer-based message systems. Each of these categories is an important aspect of electronic mail.

One of the problems in directly communicating from one piece of equipment to another piece is that the equipment must have four specifically compatible features. These features for compatibility include the mode of transmission, protocol, speed or Baud rate, and coding.

The most important link in information processing is the communicating word/information processor. By 1984, installed communicating word/information processors will have experienced the greatest growth of all electronic mail systems. Therefore, any person able to use a natural language

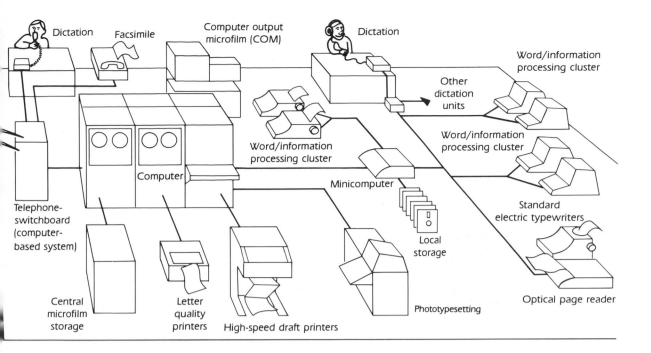

Dictation • Facsimile • Computer output microfilm (COM) • Dictation • Word/information processing cluster • Other dictation units • Word/information processing cluster • Word/information processing cluster • Computer • Minicomputer • Telephone-switchboard (computer-based system) • Standard electric typewriters • Local storage • Central microfilm storage • Letter quality printers • High-speed draft printers • Phototypesetting • Optical page reader

keyboard on the communicating word/information processors will be able to access the wealth of information stored in computers in other locations without having to learn programming or computer languages.

Patterns of communication between a manager and a secretary in the automated office have changed from the implementation of yesterday's typewriter to today's word/information processing systems. Now, information can move electronically from origination through the distribution of a document.

Word processing is no longer just a clerical tool for increasing productivity, evening workloads, and decreasing costs. It has evolved into a machine that can handle both word and data processing functions. This integrated equipment is now more appropriately called a word/information processor. It has capabilities which not only handle clerical functions but act as a tool for managers for the dissemination or distribution of ideas.

Integrating the technologies using telecommunications is the trend for offices of the future (Figures 7.33 and 7.34). The focus of combining the technologies is to integrate word processing with data processing, phototypesetting, or micrographics. The purpose in any integration is to allow information entering the telecommunications system through any one machine to be moved and made available to any other machine without rekeyboarding.

Summary

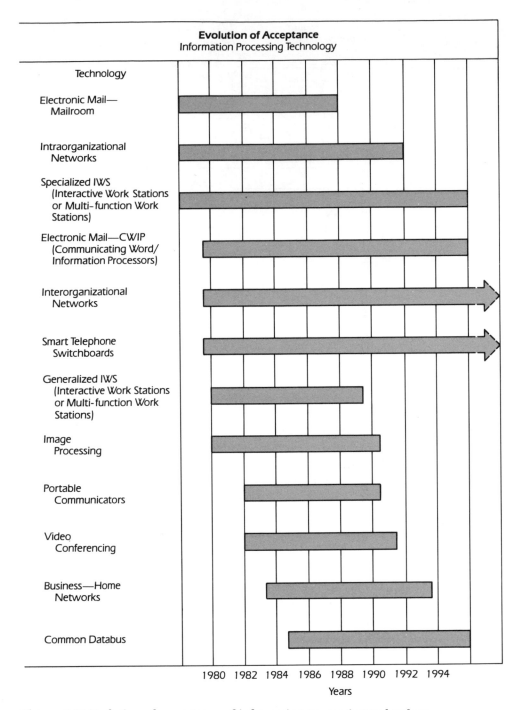

Figure 7.34 Evolution of acceptance of information processing technology.

Telecommunications
Electronic mail
Carrier-based systems
Mailgram
Stored Mailgrams
ECOM
TWX
Telex
White-space skipping
Polling of satellites
Communicating word/
   information processors
On-line
Off-line

Interface
Computer-based message
   systems
Modem
Mode of transmission
Protocol
Baud rate
Codes
Point-to-point
   communications
Point-to-computer
   communications
MIS
Ethernet

Study Guide

This study guide provides you with feedback to find out how well you are doing. Use a separate sheet of paper to record your answers. When you have finished check your responses with the answers at the back of the book.

Matching: Choose the answer that best defines the word in the left column.

1. Electronic mail

   a. an electronic mail system provided by Western Union.

2. Communicating word/information processors

   b. a way in which information is sent over a telephone wire or cable to a computer and saved until the person to whom it is sent wants to receive it.

3. Modem

   c. the method by which pulses or signals are moved along the telephone line.

4. Telecommunications

   d. a way in which information moves between two locations over hard wires or telephone lines.

5. Computer-based message system

   e. the system predicted to experience the greatest growth of any electronic mail system.

6. TWX and Telex

   f. electronic distribution of information using telephone lines.

7. Mode of transmission

   g. a device for changing signals between an office machine and a communications line.

8. Point-to-point communications

   h. the speed information moves, measured in bits per second.

9. Coding

   i. one terminal communicating to another terminal.

10. Baud rate

   j. the specific order information moves along a telephone line.

Multiple choice: Select the letter or letters that best answer each question.

11. The pattern of communications in the office between the manager and the secretary changed most drastically in the:
   a. First stage of office automation.
   b. Second stage of office automation.
   c. Third stage of office automation.
   d. None of the above.

12. One major difference between FAX communications and communicating word/information processors (CW/IP) is that:
   a. FAX output is hard copy.
   b. CW/IP output is hard copy.
   c. CW/IP output may be revised at the receiving end as it is stored onto magnetic media when it is communicated.
   d. CW/IP may have visual or nonvisual display terminals.

13. MIS stands for:
   a. Management Insurance Systems
   b. Mailing Information Systems
   c. Merging Interest Systems
   d. Management Information Systems

14. Information entering a telecommunications network through any one machine can be moved and made available to any other machine without:
   a. Record keeping
   b. Rekeyboarding
   c. Recording
   d. Revising

15. The following is the most important reason organizations are now beginning to convert to COM:
   a. The ability to record information directly onto microforms and bypass hard copy entirely.
   b. The ability to output faster through COM than through a computer.
   c. The ability to keyboard faster as a result of using COM.
   d. None of the above.

Completion: Write the correct answer(s) on a separate sheet of paper.

16. The four equipment specifications that must be compatible in order to communicate are: _____ , _____ , _____ , and _____ .

17. In order to be considered part of an electronic mail system, equipment has to be able to _____ , _____ , and _____ test.

18. Five electronic mail systems are: _____ , _____ , _____ , _____ , and _____ .

19. Telecommunications is _____ .

20. Two services provided for by the U. S. Postal Service combined with the telephone service are: _____ and _____ .

True/False: Write + for True, 0 for False for each question.

21. A modem is a device that changes the keystrokes on media to punched holes so a machine can communicate.

22. Mailgrams are sent electronically from their origination to their final distribution.

23. A node is another name for a computer in satellite communications.

24. The CPU caused the most significant change in the pattern of communication between the manager and the secretary.

25. The U.S. Postal Service has been active in electronic mail since the early 1970s.

Questions on Concepts

1. Define telecommunications and electronic mail.
2. Describe the main cause of the change in patterns of communication between the manager and the secretary in the third stage of office automation.
3. Describe the five major categories of electronic mail systems.
4. Explain how INTELSAT will work.
5. Discuss the difference between facsimile units and communicating word/information processors.
6. Discuss the four equipment specifications that must be compatible for equipment to communicate.
7. Explain ways in which unlike systems can communicate.
8. What does SNA mean and who developed it?
9. How are point-to-computer communications different from point-to-point communications?
10. Summarize the reasons you would integrate word and data processing technologies.
11. List some advantages for integrating word processing with phototypesetting.
12. Discuss some advantages of integrating word processing and micrographics.
13. Compare microfilm and magnetic media as storage media.
14. Describe the uses of an MIS.

Case and Activities

Perkins-Smith corporate headquarters, located at Erikson's Ranch near Las Vegas, Nevada, is a worldwide mining and manufacturing operation in the building, wood, and paper industries. These industries incorporate seven major businesses: fiberglass products, nonfiberglass insulation, pipe products and systems, roofing products, asbestos fiber, industrial products and services, and paper and wood products. The 18 offices of Perkins-Smith are located in the United States, Canada, Paris, and Beirut.

The word processing department at Perkins-Smith began in the early 1970s, with no central planning or control. It contained magnetic card, nonvisual stand-alone word processors, and a phone dictation system with centralized transcription. The department did a great deal of overload typing for other secretaries in the company. In 1975, memory typewriters were installed, and later that year four additional stand-alone word/information processors were acquired. The latest additions were visual display, floppy disk terminals with some logic. Perkins-Smith also has teletypewriters in most of its branches and is time-sharing with Data General Nova Computers.

Perkins-Smith's objectives for its word processing department include linking the administrative, correspondence, and operating portions of the business into some type of electronic network; using its computers to solve problems; reducing costs for communications; and providing for growth in applications and the number of users.

If you were the manager of communications planning and felt it was necessary to develop a plan to expand the word/information processing capabilities in order to meet company objectives, how would you design a basic telecommunications network between two locations? Use the following parts to make up the network.

1. Terminals (CRT, floppy disk) at two locations.
2. Printers at two locations.
3. One central processing unit (CPU).
4. Modems wherever necessary.
5. Facsimile units at two locations.

Activities

1. Read an article in recent word/information processing literature on each of the electronic mail systems described in this chapter. Prepare abstracts on each of the articles.
2. Visit a local office that uses communicating word/information processors and facsimile. Write a report on your findings regarding the type of equipment, number of operators, the size of the office, and the type of integration of office systems.
3. Visit a local office that uses a computer-based message system. Write a report on how it is used.

PART III

MANAGING THE CHANGE TO INFORMATION PROCESSING

Organizations that are beginning to integrate some of the new technologies are calling their systems "information processing systems" and refer to the centers where information processing occurs as "information processing centers." In some organizations, complete information systems may be introduced. Other organizations may have only word processing systems (the term "word processing system" generally refers to the keyboarding, editing, and printing of documents).

The new technologies will create a number of changes in the traditional office. When any of the new technologies are considered, steps are taken to prepare for these changes. People are alerted to the possible changes and a study is conducted of the present organization. If the study shows that any information processing system would benefit the organization, the results of the study are used to design a proper physical environment and select appropriate equipment. The study can also help place existing personnel in newly created employment positions. Selecting, training, and directing employees and creating procedures and controls for the new system are also factors that have to be considered when a new system is adopted.

The choice of personnel to staff the system will affect the success of the new system. The people who work with the new technologies need new skills and different attitudes toward their work. The manager's role is important because the manager has to motivate people, help employees develop the necessary skills and atttitudes, and provide leadership. Often, the manager is newly promoted from within the organization and may not possess management skills. He or she must be given an opportunity to develop these skills.

CHAPTER 8

Planning the Change

The objectives of this chapter are to:

1. Describe what a feasibility study is and how it provides a framework for implementing word processing.

2. Discuss why someone within an organization might be chosen to do the feasibility study.

3. List several reasons why top management's support is needed for word processing.

4. List several things a task force leader would want to know about an organization before beginning a feasibility study.

5. List two methods of getting information for document analyses.

6. List three methods of surveying administrative tasks in an organization.

7. List two methods of conducting opinion surveys.

8. Describe three examples of different ways of organizing data in pie charts.

9. List some considerations that should be included in making a presentation and report to employees and management on the results of the feasibility study.

10. Describe several factors to consider when selecting equipment.

11. Discuss the furnishings and office layout, lighting, color, air conditioning, and acoustics used in environments where information is processed.

12. Describe how office automation may be implemented in a large and a small organization.

Information processing is a new way of doing things. Equipment used in the new technologies—voice processing, word and data processing, reprographics, micrographics and records processing, and telecommunications—is costly and has a great effect upon the organization. A careful study of the organization's present system is needed before bringing in these new systems. An important part of this study focuses on the organization's paperwork. The types of documents an organization produces affect the type of equipment selected. The study, however, is not limited to finding out what kinds of documents exist. It also determines how the documents can be handled more effectively and how managers and secretaries can use their time more efficiently. The study, therefore, plays an important part in helping to introduce any new information processing system.

What Is a Feasibility Study?

An important part of planning is conducting a **feasibility study.** A feasibility study is used to determine if any of the new technologies are needed. Once the study is performed, the results provide data useful in selecting equipment, designing an environment, creating procedures, and placing people in newly created employment positions.

Who Conducts the Study?

A feasibility study may be done by an equipment manufacturer (**vendor**), a consulting firm, or someone within the organization itself. An equipment manufacturer generally conducts a feasibility study, but probably will recommend the equipment it sells. A vendor most likely will not reveal the inadequacies of its equipment, nor will it compare the cost of its products with those of other vendors.

A consulting firm may also conduct the study for the organization. The experience and objectivity a consultant brings often gives the organization a good insight into its problems. A consultant will probably be more unbiased than an equipment manufacturer but is often very expensive.

Someone from the organization is often chosen to do the study. Many times several persons, often from different parts of the organization, are chosen to act as a **task force.** One person is usually appointed as the task force leader. The task force leader sometimes is a person who works as a systems analyst for the organization.

Someone within the organization itself

In most organizations, information processing systems are **implemented** (installed) in stages. When people from within the organization perform the study, the experience they gain helps in planning future installations. Moreover, people from within the organization also have the advantage of knowing how the organization operates, the type of work it does, and the people who work there.

The disadvantage is that the people involved have to be trained to conduct the study. Their training and participation will take them away from their work.

Frequently a consultant is hired to work with and guide the task force leader. Such an approach combines the advantages of using people from within with an experienced consultant from outside the organization.

Combined responsibility

Setting the Stage for the Feasibility Study

For the feasibility study to be successful, a number of preliminary steps are taken. The persons performing the study should be endorsed by top management. Top management has to feel that the information processing system is an acceptable alternative to the current method of handling communications, and must recognize that the organization will have to undergo major changes if an information processing system is adopted and used to its fullest potential. It must also realize that costs are involved in adopting the new system. The lead person conducting the study must be given adequate authority to do the job. That person should not have to report to others within the organization nor have to be bothered with secondary responsibilities. The lead person conducting the study must also be given the full cooperation of middle management and operating personnel. Employees must understand what they are being asked to do and why. They must provide an accurate picture of how they spend their time and the type of work they perform. Since the employees are asked to reveal information they may feel is confidential, such as their attitudes toward their superiors, coworkers, or their jobs, they need total confidence in the person performing the study. Employees, moreover, are more likely to cooperate if they see the change as beneficial to them. Chapter 11 describes a number of methods used to prepare employees for change when the actual decision is made to implement any information processing system.

Before beginning the study, the head person conducting the study often uses a questionnaire such as shown in Figure 8.1 to find out more about the organization.

How Feasibility Studies are Performed

Before a feasibility study can be performed, the departments in the organization have to be studied and a **time line** established. A time line is a schedule of data collection activities that are to take place. The person who conducts the survey is selected and assigned the responsibility for assuring prompt collection of data and checking the accuracy of the results.

The feasibility study is primarily concerned with the types and volume of documents a firm produces. Data collection methods vary according to the type of information that is hoped will be gained from them. Some data collection methods are document analyses, activity surveys, and opinion surveys.

Document Analyses. Two types of document analyses are paper surveys and secretarial logs.

Paper survey. To evaluate typewritten documents, samples of documents are collected from each secretary. Samples can be obtained by having the secretary place a carbonless tissue or carbon set called an **action paper** behind each page to be typed. All sheets are numbered to provide an accurate account of all typing activity. The secretary also fills out the top of each sheet with the following information (see Figure 8.2).

1. The number of lines typed per document.

2. The kind of document.

3. The number of times the document was retyped.

4. The author of the document.

Figure 8.1 Questions about the organization.

Questionnaire Used To Obtain Information About The Organization

1. Where can organizational charts be found that show all departments and personnel?

2. Does the organization have any remote departments or locations, and if so are they going to be considered in the word processing plans?

3. What is the organization's growth potential? What are its future staff needs? How much money can the organization afford to invest? How much of the ideal system can the organization afford? How much can be implemented immediately?

4. Who has the authority for ordering equipment? Is this person or persons on the corporate level or the departmental level?

5. Does a list of all present office equipment exist? Does it include copiers, facsimile, time-shared terminals, dictation, and computing equipment? Where is the equipment located?

6. Is the study to include the executive level? How much reorganization of staff and procedures will be accepted? (Some organizations find the total concept of separating secretarial work into the two areas of word processing and administrative support entirely satisfactory and economically feasible. In other organizations, this division might be totally unacceptable even though the total word processing concept might be the best way to utilize equipment.)

7. How many private secretaries does the organization have? How many secretaries are assigned to work groups? How many are assigned to a centralized typing department? What are the secretarial reporting relationships? Do secretaries report directly to an individual or to an office manager or supervisor?

8. Who hires the secretaries? What are their job descriptions? What criteria are used in hiring? What criteria are used to determine if new staffing is necessary?

9. How is typing now being processed?

10. What is unsatisfactory about the present system? What should the new system accomplish?

11. How much money is spent on overtime and temporary help?

12. What are the present salary costs and floor space costs?

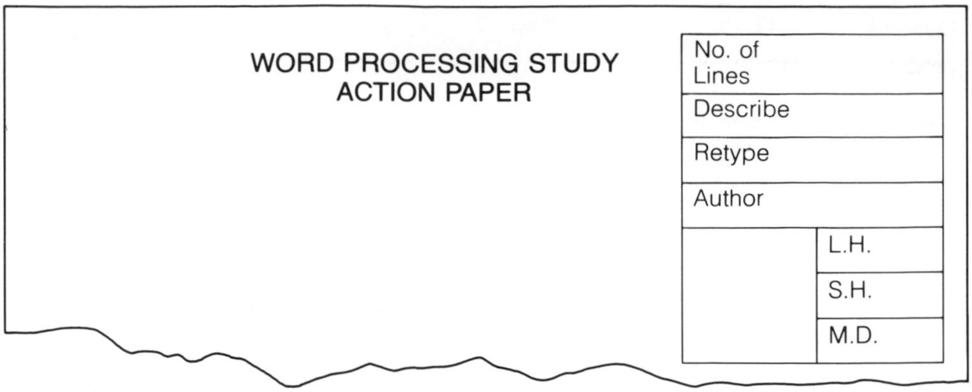
WORD PROCESSING STUDY
ACTION PAPER

No. of Lines	
Describe	
Retype	
Author	
	L.H.
	S.H.
	M.D.

Figure 8.2 Action paper. Provides a record of actual keystrokes, false starts, discarded typing, and a sample of the document the secretary produces.

5. The form in which the document was received: longhand, shorthand, machine dictation.
6. The time taken to type the document.
7. The secretary's initials.

What do paper surveys do?

Copies of all work are collected daily for some specific time period, usually two weeks. Such surveys provide an accurate account of the number of accurate keystrokes a secretary keyboards in a day, the number of false starts and discarded typing, and a sample of the document the secretary produces.

Once the surveys are collected, the task force leader or task force counts the work by volumes either by quarter-pages, half-pages, or full pages, or by lines using a line ruler. Some even assign different values according to the difficulty of the document.

Secretarial log. Another means of analyzing documents is by having secretaries keep a log or record of their daily typing activities such as the one in Figure 8.3. The secretarial log can be designed to reflect any information that is desired concerning each document. For example, the secretary can be asked to list the number of times a document had to be retyped before a final copy is produced or request the reason for retypes. The log may also include information as to whether the document was created on a rush or normal workload basis. A properly designed log can provide a good indication of how much revision is taking place as well as a summary of all daily typing activities.

Why use a log?

Although the log may be more efficient than the paper survey, it may not provide as accurate results as the paper survey, depending upon how reliable the employees are in logging activities. Sometimes both the log and survey are used together. The log can be designed to provide information not readily accessible in the paper survey, and the two act as a check upon each other. Later, the organization will use the information from both the log and paper survey to determine the amount and type of equipment that is needed and where it should be placed to be most beneficial. The information will also be important in determining how many secretaries are needed for typing activities. The secretaries who engage in these typing activities provide what is referred to as **correspondence support**. Paper surveys and secretarial logs, therefore, pro-

Activity	Who is Activity done for?
How many revisions are made?	Reason for retypes
Briefly describe Activity	
Activity	Who is Activity done for?
How many revisions are made?	Reason for retypes
Briefly describe Activity	
Activity	Who is Activity done for?
How many revisions are made?	Reason for retypes
Briefly describe Activity	

Figure 8.3 Secretarial log. Records the name of the originator, the number of times the document is typed before a final copy is produced, and reasons for retypes.

vide information on how much correspondence support is needed.

Activity Surveys. Another type of information that is needed is the time spent on administrative tasks (nontyping) and nonproductive tasks such as waiting for work. A variety of different forms can be used to determine activities other than typing.

Job analysis or task list. Using this form, secretaries indicate the kinds of work they do and estimate the amount of time spent on each task (see Figures 8.4 and 8.5).

Time ladder. Secretaries fill in a chart recording the exact time it takes to perform each activity. The ladder can be gridded in minutes, 5-, 10-, or 15-minute block segments (Figure 8.6, p. 204). A time ladder gives a more accurate approximation than a task list of the amount of time a secretary engages in various work activities.

Random or *work sampling.* Observing employee work habits can give such information as how much time employees spend in slack periods waiting for work or in activities away from their desks. In **work sampling,** someone enters the office unannounced at various times of the day over a given period of time and notes the activities that are taking place (Figure 8.7, p. 205). These observations may be accurate as to time but less specific in determining what is being done. For example, the survey may reveal that the secretary was away from his or her desk, but would not reveal whether the period away from the desk was being spent in work activities. The secretary might be away delivering a message or talking with someone about something unrelated to work. Random sampling surveys are often used together with time inventories to get a complete picture of how each secretary spends the day.

Activity surveys provide information concerning the amount of time that is

Keeping track of nontyping tasks

What do activity surveys do?

Job Analysis Form

Name: Job title:

Dept.:   Typewriter make:

Location: Pica   Elite   Executive

A. Principals You Support

Name of Principal	Title	Typing Hrs. per Day	Admin. Hrs. per Day

B. Your Activities

Examine the time you spend doing each of the following activities during an "average" day. Include personal time and the time you spend waiting for work to account for the total hours you are at work each day.

Hours per Day

Administrative duties
- Sorting-handling the mail
- Telephone calls
- Taking shorthand dictation
- Filing
- Reproduction work
- Business errands and message delivery
- Clerical posting, record keeping, calculations
- Personal service (coffee, watering plants, etc.)
- Other (include special projects; describe)
- Total hours for administrative duties

Typing hours total
Waiting-for-work time
Personal time
- Total hours per day

C. Nonroutine and Work Assignments

List the work of nonroutine nature, such as special reports or projects, that you perform occasionally or once a week, month, or year. List the principals for whom this work is performed and the frequency (weekly, etc.), and estimate the hours per project.

Principal	Type of Project	Frequency	Hrs. per Project

D. Narrative

Describe briefly the nature of your job and how your principals work. If there are special work situations (much travel, peak-and-valley situations, etc.), describe them here. Include any recommendations you now have.

Figure 8.4
Job analysis form.

TASK LIST
WORD PROCESSING SURVEY

Name	Operator Number	Position
Department	Department Number	Section
Supervisor		Date

TASKS	DESCRIPTION	Quantity	Hours per week
Shorthand			
Filing			
Mail			
Telephone			
Copy Machine			
Posting			
Special			
Miscellaneous			
TYPING			
A - Memo			
B - Letter			
C - Report			
D - Outline			
E - Statistical			
F - Forms			
G - Guide Letters			
Miscellaneous			

COMMENTS:

Figure 8.5
Task list form.

spent on duties other than typing and are important in making decisions about how many secretaries are needed for nontyping activities. The secretaries who engage in nontyping activities provide what is referred to as **administrative support.** Some managers within an organization may have their secretaries do little other than typing tasks. If an activity study revealed that this is the case, there would be no reason to plan for both correspondence and administrative support.

What is a Feasability Study?

Name: _____

Date:

8:00
15
30
45
9:00
15
30
45
10:00
15
30
45
11:00
15
30
45
12:00
15
30
45
1:00
15
30
45
2:00
15
30
45
3:00
15
30
45
4:00
15
30
45
5:00
15
30
45
6:00

Comments: _____

Figure 8.6 Time ladder.

Opinion surveys. Two types of opinion surveys are questionnaires and interviews.

Secretaries and managers are asked questions to find out potential typing and nontyping needs of originators as well as the degree of satisfaction with present work methods. In an **originator's questionnaire,** the originators are asked questions that reveal their work habits and how they feel about the type of secretarial or administrative support they receive (Figure 8.8). They are also often asked to make recommendations. A similar survey for secretaries is called a **typist's questionnaire.** It relates to the actual typing done. Such a survey asks for details such as the number of carbon copies requested, the correction tech-

Questionnaires for originators and typists

Name	Start							
	Finish							
	Typing	Filing	Mail	Telephone	Planning/ Working Alone	Away from Desk	Waiting for Work
Total							

Figure 8.7 Random or work sampling sheet.

niques used, and the use of copiers in the process (Figure 8.9).

Interviews

One way opinion surveys are conducted is by oral interviews. Interviews are an excellent way of determining the attitudes of employees toward word processing, work, coworkers, management, and secretarial support. Interviews help in determining how employees perceive their roles and the roles of others. Often what management thinks secretaries do is no more accurate than what secretaries think management does.

Interviews with various employees often clarify, verify, or help bring together information gained through other methods. Interviews with department heads help establish administrative priorities and identify potential problems as well as clarify the relationship between departments. Interviews with supervisors reveal information about the workflow, quality standards, backlogs, peaks and valleys, deadlines, dependability of employees, and help identify potential workers for word/information processing. Interviews with originators and secretaries describe the workflow and clarify relationships between originators and secretaries.

What information do interviews provide?

How Data is Organized, Analyzed, and Sorted

The data from the feasibility study answers questions such as those found in the checklist in Figure 8.10, p. 208.

The data from the preceding surveys can be organized, analyzed, and sorted in different ways. Often the information is organized in pie charts such as the ones in Figures 8.11, 8.12, and 8.13, p. 209, and is used in presentations made about the results of the study.

Different ways of organizing data in pie charts include the way the secre-

Name: Dept:

Title: Secretary:

Is your current secretarial support sufficient? _____ Yes _____ No

If no, explain:

1. How do you create work that is typed?
   Longhand _____ % Shorthand _____ % Machine dictation _____ %
2. How long do you create correspondence each day?
   Less than 1 hour/day _____ 1 to 3 hours/day _____ 3 to 5 hours/day _____
3. Do you originate work away from the office? _____ Yes _____ No
   If yes, how often? _____
   How do you generate this work?
   Longhand _____ % Shorthand _____ % Machine dictation _____ %
4. Do you ever request that any of your material be typed in rough-draft form?
   _____ Yes _____ No If yes, how often? _____ % Total material
   Why?
5. Do you occasionally revise letters that are sent to you in "finished" form?
   _____ Yes _____ No If yes, how often? _____
   Why?
6. How long does it take to get your letters typed?
   Less than 1 day _____ About 2 days _____ More than 2 days _____
7. Do you ever wish you could revise finished material but do not because of a deadline?
   _____ Yes _____ No
8. Do you have peak periods? _____ Yes _____ No
   When do they occur?
9. Are there backlogs in typing?
   Frequently _____ Occasionally _____ None _____
   If so, how long? _____ 1 day _____ 2 days _____ 3+ days
10. Are you satisfied with the appearance of the documents leaving your office?
    _____ Yes _____ No
11. Do you send out original repetitive letters? _____ Yes _____ No
    Do you send out any form letters with fill-ins? _____ Yes _____ No
12. Do you compose letters that might include "standard or stock" paragraphs?
    _____ Yes _____ No
13. Are you now performing any administrative tasks that could be delegated to a secretary if the time were available? _____ Yes _____ No
    Copying _____ Composing _____
    Filing _____ Sorting _____
    Research _____ Posting and bookkeeping _____
    Other _____
14. Is there necessary work not currently being done which you could perform?
    _____ Yes _____ No
    If yes, would this work generate additional typing? _____ Yes _____ No
15. Are you anticipating any personnel changes in the next 6 to 12 months?
    _____ Yes _____ No
    If yes, what type of changes? _____

Comments:

Figure 8.8 Questionnaire for originators.

Name: _____ Dept: _____

1. Is typing your primary job function? _____ Yes _____ No

2. What kind of typewriter do you use?
   _____ Electric _____ Manual _____ Brand name

3. Is it located at your desk? _____ Yes _____ No

4. How much of your typing is rough draft?
   _____ 10% _____ 25% _____ 50% _____ 75%

5. Is there retyping due to author change? _____ Yes _____ No

6. Is typing ever revised more than one time? _____ Yes _____ No

7. How does work to be typed arrive at your desk?
   Machine dictation _____ %   Longhand _____ %
   Shorthand _____ %   Copytyping _____ %
   Self-composition _____ %

8. Does work come in peak periods at certain times of the year?
   _____ Yes _____ No
   If yes, when? _____

9. Normal deadline requirements: _____ Same day _____ One day
   _____ Two days

10. Are erasures prohibited in any of the typing you do? _____ Yes _____ No
    If yes, in what work? _____

11. Number of carbon copies normally required: _____

12. Do any of the people you work for travel? _____ Yes _____ No

13. Do you work overtime? _____ Yes _____ No
    If yes, how many hours per week? _____

14. Do you use transcription equipment? _____ Yes _____ No
    If yes, brand name: _____

15. If you use the copy machine, how far is it from your desk?
    _____ Same floor _____ Different floor
    If a different floor, please give floor number _____

16. Do you often have to wait in line? _____ Yes _____ No
    If so, how long? _____ 1-2 min. _____ 3-5 min. _____ Longer

Figure 8.9 Questionnaire for typists.

tary spends the day, the types of documents that are produced, or the way work is originated.

The information from such surveys as task lists, time ladders, and random sampling can be used to construct a pie chart that reveals how a secretary spends the day (Figure 8.11). The chart can show the percentage of a secretary's time that is spent on a certain activity and how many hours a week a certain activity consumes. A chart can also reveal both productive and nonproductive time. **Productive time** is time that the secretary spends doing actual work such as typing, filing, and answering phones. Nonproductive time is the time the secretary spends doing such things as walking to the copying machine or waiting for work. From this chart, the organization can get an idea of the actual costs involved in secretarial (administrative and correspondence) support.

The information from the document analysis can be used to construct pie

How secretaries spend their day

Figure 8.10 Checklist of questions a feasibility study should answer.

CHECKLIST OF QUESTIONS A FEASIBILITY STUDY SHOULD ANSWER

1. What types of documents are being produced, where are they being produced, and how frequently are they being produced?
2. Are some periods busier than others?
3. What are the costs of producing the current paperwork?
4. Is there duplication of work?
5. Should similar work be consolidated in a similar area?
6. What procedures should be revised?
7. What standards and features are necessary on new equipment?
8. Where is administrative support needed? Where is typing support needed?
9. Is the majority of the secretary's typing one-time, revision, or repetitive?
10. How much time is spent on typing activities?
11. How much time is spent on revision typing? What amount of revision typing is caused by errors or interruptions? What is responsible for revisions — is it secretarial error or managerial revision?
12. Which managers generate the most typing?
13. How long are documents? Could some of these documents be more efficiently processed by people who specialize in typing these documents?
14. Could some of the manager's duties be delegated to a secretary?
15. What kinds of nontyping tasks occupy the secretary's day?
16. Could a group of secretaries more efficiently perform some of the activities that constantly disrupt the secretary's typing tasks?
17. How much time does a secretary spend away from the office?
18. Should word processing equipment be tied into other systems? For example, is there a need to print manuals or reports that will be keyboarded on information processing equipment? If so, perhaps the organization should consider word processing equipment that will tie into phototypesetting equipment to eliminate rekeyboarding of material.
19. What is the turnaround time for documents or the time it takes for a document to be created by an originator, keyboarded, and returned to the originator? Is a faster turnaround time necessary?
20. What are some types of work originators cannot presently do but would like to do if they had the proper equipment and secretarial support?
21. Does the organization do work that requires equipment with special features? For example, if an organization does a volume of statistical work, it might want equipment that could do such things as move columns of figures, check accuracy of a column of numbers, and automatically align decimal points.

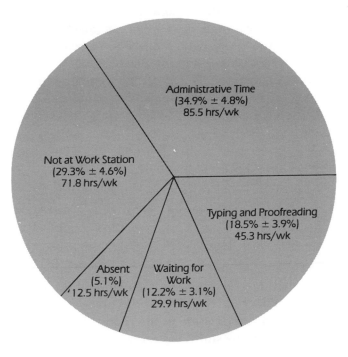

Figure 8.11 How the secretary spends the day.

Figure 8.12 Type of documents.

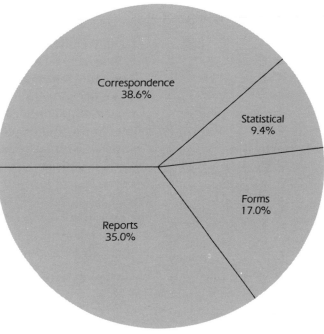

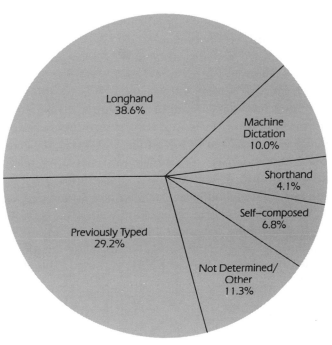

Figure 8.13 How work is originated.

What is a Feasability Study?

charts that reflect the types of documents the organization most frequently produces (Figure 8.12). This chart can determine the type of automated equipment that is needed. For example, if the chart shows that the organization produces a volume of repetitive correspondence, the organization will want to choose a type of automated typing equipment that can handle repetitive documents.

Other data that is gathered from opinion surveys and secretarial logs can be used to construct a pie chart showing how managers originate their work. A pie chart containing this information reveals whether or not dictation equipment should be considered. For example, the pie chart in Figure 8.13 shows that the majority of documents submitted have been previously typed and require heavy revision. They are not original documents. This information suggests that the organization probably does not need dictation equipment.

Reporting the Results. Everyone should be informed about the results of the feasibility study. To inform top management, the person who conducts the feasibility study should prepare a written report. In addition, an oral presentation is usually made for the benefit of all employees. This presentation will help successfully implement the recommendations made in the report. The presentation often contains a discussion of why the study was undertaken, how it was carried out, how the data was analyzed, and what the data revealed. It also points out to the employees how work is being done and what problems are associated with the present way of doing things.

The study may or may not reveal that any of the new technologies are needed. It may just indicate that new procedures should be used to improve work flow. If the study does show that any of the new technologies are needed, the presentation should indicate where they can be implemented.

The following example shows how the information obtained from the feasibility study is used in deciding what recommendations to make.

> Marge Fleming, a regional office manager of Moped Unlimited in Cheyenne, Wyoming, was appointed to conduct a feasibility study for her small sales organization. The opinion survey revealed that several managers who worked in the corporate headquarters felt that they spent too much of their time doing detail work. The task list showed that one secretary within the organization often duplicated the work of another secretary. A document analysis determined that a significant portion of the correspondence consisted of one-time documents that had to be error-free. The secretaries who keyboarded these documents frequently restarted them when they made keyboarding errors at the beginning of the document. Secretaries spent an average of a half hour on each document because each one had to be typed perfectly. The survey also revealed that the documents were often submitted to the secretaries in handwritten form. Many of the secretaries' errors resulted from their inability to read an originator's writing. The document analysis also showed that the organization had a high volume of repetitive correspondence.
>
> As a result of these surveys, Marge made the following suggestions. Based on the opinion survey, she recommended that the organization provide

administrative as well as correspondence support for the managers. Based on the information the task list revealed about the duplicated activities, she recommended that the organization change its procedures. Based on the document analysis, she suggested that a less expensive type of automated typing equipment be used for the one-time documents. The equipment would improve the quality and cut down on restarts. She also recommended that another type of more expensive automated equipment be used for repetitive correspondence. For the managers who dictated one-time correspondence, Marge recommended dictation equipment.

Selecting Equipment

Feasibility studies aid in determining the types of documents produced in an organization. This information helps in the selection of equipment. Other factors that are also considered important are: people, equipment location, vendor support, future needs, and equipment costs.

People

Employee skills and employee turnover rates are important considerations that may determine the kinds of equipment an organization chooses. Several different levels of equipment are available. Some equipment is easy to operate; some is not. Both difficult and easy-to-operate equipment are used in some organizations. Highly skilled workers operate the more complex equipment, and those who are less highly trained handle the easier tasks. The less highly skilled workers handle the repetitive typing tasks or initial keyboarding on less sophisticated and less expensive equipment; the more highly skilled do the complex, heavy revisions on more expensive equipment. Moreover, if an organization's employee turnover is high, equipment that is simple to operate may be chosen because of the cost of training new employees on complex equipment.

Why consider the skills of employees?

Equipment Location

A decision has to be made about where to place the equipment. A special environment can be designed where several pieces of equipment can be located, or the equipment can be located in the present environment. This decision is important because one type of equipment is inexpensive enough to be used in a traditional office environment. Another type of equipment may be quite expensive. Such equipment requires an area designed especially for its use.

Another factor affecting the placement of equipment is the equipment itself. For example, a shared-logic system presents the choice of whether to:

How does equipment location affect choice of equipment?

1. Select complete systems with a smaller capacity that have their own input terminals, central processors, storage units, and printers, and locate them near the appropriate departments or geographic areas they will service.

2. Locate only the terminals that input to a large central system in the areas they will service. The terminals may have their own printers operating in the departments in which they are located or their printers may be in a central area.

3. Use a shared-logic system for the centrally located information processing system with compatible stand-alone equipment assigned to departments.

Vendor Support

Why is vendor support important?

An important consideration is how much vendor support will be provided before and after equipment selection. Some vendors have very good equipment but do not have an adequate staff to provide organizations with the kinds of support they need to make sure that the implementation of the new technology is successful. Some considerations when choosing equipment from a particular vendor are:

1. Will the vendor conduct a study to determine the appropriate equipment and best system design for the organization?

2. Does the vendor have enough service people, and how responsive will its service people be when equipment needs repair?

3. Will the vendor help implement the new system by helping to create procedures and controls necessary for the organization to get the best use of the equipment?

4. Will the vendor provide training for managers and secretaries?

5. Will the vendor provide training for new employees as long as the organization uses its equipment?

Future Needs

What future needs should be considered?

The future needs of the organization have to be considered. Therefore, the equipment selected must be upgradeable. The advantage of using equipment that is upgradeable is that as the needs of the organization grow, new features can be added. Old equipment does not have to be traded in for newer models.

The media the equipment uses must be compatible with the media that future equipment will use. It is also important to consider what present features are necessary, what would be nice to have, and what features will be needed in the future. If no immediate plans to integrate technologies exist, future plans for integrating such technologies as word processing and data processing, word processing and phototypesetting, or word processing and micrographics have to be considered. Future plans for telecommunications and electronic mail systems should also be taken into account.

Decisions have to be made concerning the most economical way to meet the needs of an organization. For example, the initial cost of installing equipment can be lowered by using text editing units that share a printer. Selecting less expensive nondisplay stand-alone equipment for the initial keyboarding of documents and more expensive equipment with display screen and editing capabilities for reports requiring extensive revision can also reduce equipment costs.

Cost is a factor

Environmental Considerations

The technologies of voice processing, word and data processing, records processing, micrographics, and reprographics affect the traditional office environment. Planning an environment for the new technologies is important. Moreover, if employees are to be productive using the new technologies, they need to work in an environment planned for their physical and psychological well-being. Proper furnishings, office layout, lighting, color, air conditioning, and acoustics are environmental factors that should be considered. The term **ergonomics** is used to describe the planning of the workspace and the environmental design that covers these factors.

A productive environment

Furnishings and Office Layout

The environment for processing information using the new technologies has furnishings that create a feeling of open space. Designing an open atmosphere for offices is called **office landscaping.** Landscaped offices aid the workflow and promote productivity.

The furnishings for the landscaped office are designed to provide people with comfort, privacy, and convenience. In landscaped offices, modular, easy-to-move office furnishings are used. The furnishings consist of decorative partitions (Figure 8.14), acoustical panels, credenzas, tables, over-desk filing cabinets, and work stations with add-on drawers (Figure 8.15). The acoustical panels serve to decrease noise. Both acoustical panels and storage units serve as partitions to cut one area off from another and provide privacy.

Lighting

Lighting is an important consideration in planning an environment for the processing of information because of the nature of the work performed. Poor lighting is often responsible for decreased productivity, poor quality work, eyestrain, and mental fatigue. These factors ultimately affect employee morale and the image of the center.

Lighting can affect productivity

Light has to be properly directed to the work area to prevent glare. Glare is created several ways. It can be produced by sunlight, artificial light sources that are too bright, too numerous, or too low, or reflections from light striking a

Glare is easily created

Figure 8.14 A manager's landscaped office with decorative partitions. *(Courtesy of Vogel Peterson.)*

surface. In an environment where information is processed, care is taken to reduce glare, especially any that might be created on CRT screens.

Often, glare is produced when visual screens are introduced into an existing office without altering the environment. A study was done at the Loughborough University of Technology (London) because there is a question about whether screens actually are detrimental to eyesight. The group's findings show that the real problem is not the screen, but visual defects that have not been corrected.

The researchers pointed out that between 20% and 30% of the population have uncorrected or inadequately corrected visual defects. When these people use a CRT screen, the screen causes discomfort. Using a CRT simply brings existing visual defects to light. Proper lighting, moreover, removes much of the discomfort caused by glare on a CRT.

Two types of lighting sources are incandescent or fluorescent lighting. Fluorescent lighting is used more often than incandescent lighting in these environments because it uses less electricity, produces less glare, and generates less heat.

In areas that process information, **task** and **ambient lighting** are used to provide a more comfortable and pleasant environment for employees. Task lighting is lighting that is required for an employee to perform a specific task. Task lighting is usually provided by light fixtures built into the furniture (Figure 8.16).

Ambient lighting is the lighting used in the background. Task lighting does not provide sufficient light for the entire area, so ambient lighting is used in the background to complement task lighting (Figure 8.17).

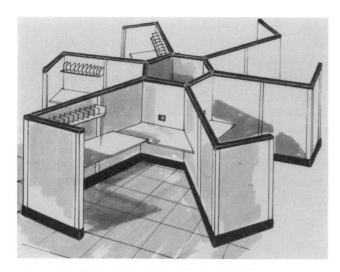

Figure 8.15 Freestanding hexagonal cluster provides six work stations. Work tops may be installed at any height. Work stations may be fitted for administrative or correspondence activities. *(Courtesy of Rockway Metal Products Corporation.)*

Figure 8.16 Task lighting is built into the work station furniture. *(Courtesy of Hauserman, Incorporated.)*

Figure 8.17 Ambient lighting is set in a vaulted ceiling that has an acoustical surface to soak up sound. Lighting, air distribution, sound masking system, and fire control are all contained in the ceiling. *(Courtesy of Armstrong Cork Company.)*

Color

Color has a significant effect upon people by influencing our moods. Color can be used to create an atmosphere that stimulates employees to be more productive, creates enthusiasm, and reduces fatigue. The ultimate result is less absenteeism and less employee turnover.

Color can also be used to achieve special effects such as making small work areas appear larger by adding lighter colors or making large open areas appear cozier by adding darker colors (Figure 8.18).

An expert should be consulted for both lighting and color considerations when planning the environment for processing information because the two directly affect each other. For example, the color of carpeting in one light may appear completely different in another light.

Air Conditioning

Air conditioning encompasses humidity, temperature, purity, and circulation. In addition to the way that temperature affects people's health, comfort, and morale, proper temperature is also important to the proper functioning of equipment. Much of the equipment emits a considerable amount of heat. Some of the equipment can operate at a high temperature, but the environment may become too uncomfortable for the workers. In this case, it will be necessary to install auxiliary air conditioning in this area. Special humidifying equipment may also be necessary, especially in the northern parts of the country where winter humidity levels drop.

Acoustics

Noise control is important to keep the environment comfortable for employees. Employees must be able to hear well and conduct private conversations. The aim of noise control, however, is not to eliminate all noise. Some noise is important to maintain a proper work environment. Excessive noise, however, is distracting. The following design criteria should be implemented for proper acoustics.

1. A good level of background noise should be provided to mask out minor noises. Air conditioning units are often used to provide a fairly continuous sound. Some organizations use music for this purpose or simulate the sound of nature such as wind whistling through the trees. These noises are known as **white sound.**

2. Sound-absorbing materials such as acoustic ceilings and panels, carpeting, draperies, and upholstery should be used to soften unpleasant noise (Figures 8.19 and 8.20). For example, carpeting is used to decrease typing clatter but not eliminate it.

3. Special acoustical shields can be used that are designed to control noise on equipment.

Figure 8.18 Work station is designed in shades of blue with contrasting yellow and orange chairs. *(Courtesy of Hauserman, Incorporated.)*

Figure 8.19 Carpeting and paneling absorb sound. *(Courtesy of Armstrong Cork Company.)*

Figure 8.20 A combination of acoustical paneling and carpeting absorbs sound. *(Courtesy of Armstrong Cork Company.)*

Environmental Considerations

4. Reverberation can be controlled through the use of wall fabric, tile, carpeting, and draperies. Reverberation is the ability of sound to bounce off the walls (Figure 8.21).

Implementing Office Automation

To some organizations, office automation may mean implementing only a word processing system. To other organizations, it may mean implementing a total information processing system consisting of integrating voice processing, word and data processing, records processing, reprographics, and telecommunications. Not all organizations choose to implement office automation to the same extent. The size of the organization is an important consideration, for it will determine how much the environment might change.

Implementing Office Automation In A Small Organization

Provides more originators with support

If the organization is very small with perhaps one secretary, the addition of some office automation equipment may not alter the environment very much. The secretary will still probably do both the administrative and correspondence work. The addition of dictation equipment, automated typing equipment, and new procedures, however, will make the secretary more productive and capable of assuming more responsibilities.

In a small organization, the addition of some office automation equipment might also allow the secretary to do work for a greater number of originators (Figure 8.22). For example, in a small sales organization that consists of a regional sales manager and five salespeople, only the manager might have a private secretary. Before the addition of office automation equipment such as a stand-alone word processor, the salespeople might have to spend their time in unproductive ways such as typing their own letters and preparing their sales reports. After the addition of automated equipment, the secretary might be able to provide the salespeople with the secretarial support they need.

Secretaries specialize

If this organization is large enough to have at least two secretaries (one who is a private secretary to a sales manager and one who does work for the five salespeople) and adds word/information processors, each secretary might specialize. One secretary might handle administrative work such as preparing the sales reports, dictating original responses to customers, and tabulating weekly and monthly sales. The other secretary could specialize in correspondence work so the equipment can be kept in constant use (Figure 8.23). The secretary who specializes in correspondence work might use the equipment for one application such as repetitive form letters to customers who request sales information, or for several different applications such as repetitive letters, original correspondence, sales reports, and proposals. For this specialization to occur, the sales manager must be willing to give up his or her private secretary.

Figure 8.21 Acoustical ceilings, carpeting, draperies, and paneling absorb sound and control reverberation. *(Courtesy of Armstrong Cork Company.)*

Figure 8.22 The secretary can become more productive. *(Courtesy of Comptek Research, Incorporated.)*

If an organization is large, office automation may be implemented in one department, in several departments, or in the total organization. Moreover, the size of the word processing department varies from organization to organization (Figure 8.24). Sometimes word processing is introduced on a small scale, department by department. Gradually, as more technologies are added, the organization might progress from word processing toward total information processing. Whether personal secretaries are eliminated will depend upon the organization. In some organizations, personal secretaries will be removed from the entire management staff and divided into two groups (secretaries who perform correspondence tasks and secretaries who perform administrative tasks) and each group will be assigned a supervisor. In such cases, the secretary will no longer report to a manager, but will report to the supervisor. Other top executives may keep their personal secretaries but personal secretaries may be removed from middle and lower management.

Still other executives may retain personal secretaries and use the correspondence centers only for overflow work from all departments or to provide secretarial support for people who normally would not be assigned a personal secretary. For example, in a large law firm only the partners may have personal secretaries; junior partners will not. Correspondence centers can provide these people with a degree of secretarial support.

Summary

The best way to lay the foundation for successfully introducing any information processing system is to conduct a feasibility study. The feasibility study can be conducted by either an equipment manufacturer (vendor) or an organization itself. For the new technologies to be successful, top management must support the concept, the person conducting the survey must have the proper authority necessary to conduct the survey, and employees must give the person who conducts the survey their full cooperation.

First, the feasibility study is scheduled and undertaken. Interviews, activity surveys, and document analysis are performed and data are collected. Data are then analyzed. The activities of the organization are determined and the amount of time spent doing them is calculated. Estimates are made of what typing is to be done in the information processing area and what will continue to be handled by individual secretaries. A final presentation, including a written report, is prepared. Recommendations are given, costs are estimated, and proposed benefits are explained.

Several factors are considered before equipment is selected. These factors include types of documents created, the people involved, equipment location, vendor support, future needs, and equipment costs. The feasibility study is important to provide information for equipment selection.

The new technologies require a different physical environment from the traditional office. The furnishings and layout consist of modular easy-to-move furniture in open areas rather than heavy furniture behind fixed walls. Furnish-

Figure 8.23 An administrative secretary is working in the background; a correspondence secretary is transcribing in the foreground. *(Courtesy of Dictaphone Corporation.)*

Summary

Figure 8.24 A word processing center. *(Courtesy of Wang Laboratories, Incorporated.)*

ings and office layout, lighting, color, air conditioning, and acoustics are factors to consider because new technologies require a new environment and because the employees' physical and psychological well-being are affected by their work environment. Taking into consideration physical and psychological well-being in the planning of work is called ergonomics.

Key Terms

Feasibility study	Random/work sampling
Vendor	Administrative support
Implementation	Opinion surveys
Task force	Originator's questionnaire
Time line	Typist's questionnaire
Document analysis	Interviews
Paper survey	Vendor support
Action paper	Ergonomics
Secretarial log	Office landscaping
Correspondence support	Task lighting
Activity surveys	Ambient lighting
Job analysis/task list	White sound
Time ladder	

Study Guide

This study guide provides you with feedback to find out how well you are doing. Use a separate sheet of paper to record your answers. When you have finished check your responses with the answers at the back of the book.

Matching: Choose the answer that best define the words in the left column.

1. Job analysis   a. A survey taken by someone who walks through an office and notes the activities taking place.

2. Time ladder

   b. Samples of correspondence obtained by placing carbonless sheets behind each page to be typed.

3. Random or work sampling

   c. An activity survey that is used to estimate the time secretaries spend on each task for the purpose of determining administrative support requirements.

4. Interview

   d. A chart that secretaries use to indicate the exact time it takes to perform each activity.

5. Implementation

   e. One method used to determine employee's opinions and their attitudes toward such things as word processing work, coworkers, management, and secretarial support.

6. Paper survey

   f. Introducing word processing to an organization.

Multiple choice: Select the letter or letters that best answer each question.

7. Which statement is **not** true about feasibility studies?
   a. Feasibility studies can be conducted by someone in the organization itself.
   b. Feasibility studies can help to ensure that word processing is implemented properly.
   c. Feasibility studies are only conducted once.
   d. None of the above.

8. The best reason for having a consultant conduct a study is:
   a. When you hire an expensive consultant, you are sure of getting good results.
   b. No one in the organization is capable of conducting the study.
   c. Consultants work better with secretarial staff.
   d. None of the above.

9. Which of the following statements is **not** true about planning for word processing?
   a. Provisions should be made to handle management's nontyping needs if word processing is to be successful.
   b. Feasibility studies will help the organization make decisions about the types of equipment that will be best for its particular applications.
   c. Task force leaders should not know anything about the organization and the work applications so they can be totally objective.
   d. None of the above.

10. Which is a factor an organization should be concerned with when selecting equipment?
    a. The skills of its employees.
    b. The support it will receive from a vendor.
    c. Where the equipment will be located.
    d. All of the above.

11. What is true about a time ladder survey?
    a. It tells only the amount of time a secretary spends on typing tasks.
    b. It tells only the amount of time a secretary spends on activities other than typing.
    c. It shows the amount of time a secretary spends doing all activities during a day.
    d. It provides a way to observe the work habits of a secretary without the secretary being aware that his or her activities are being charted.

12. A random or work sampling survey:
    a. Can reveal employee slack periods.
    b. Can reveal the types of work a manager would like the secretary to handle.
    c. Is conducted at 5-, 10-, or 15-minute intervals throughout the entire day.
    d. None of the above.

13. Task lighting:
    a. Is often built into office furniture.
    b. Is background lighting used in centers.
    c. Eliminates ambient lighting.
    d. None of the above.

True/False: Write + for True, 0 for False for each question.

14. An office considering word processing should first examine its present system of handling paperwork.

15. Surveys provide useful information and statistics about the office and the habits of its employees.

16. Every organization needs word processing.

17. The only workload covered in a feasibility study is that of the secretary.

18. An organization should keep the results of the feasibility study from the employees until it has selected equipment.

19. A feasibility study can be conducted to find out if an organization should use micrographics equipment.

20. An important decision an organization should make before selecting equipment is where it will be located.

21. Vendors are the people who may conduct feasibility studies for organizations that are thinking about implementing word/information processing.

22. An important part of the feasibility study is analyzing the data that is gathered.

23. When vendors conduct feasibility studies, they are usually objective and will recommend another vendor's equipment if they think it will be best for an organization's needs.

24. The best furnishings for an environment where information is processed consist of fixed walls and heavy furniture.

25. Controlling noise is an important consideration in environments where information is processed.

26. Studies have proven that CRT screens cause eyestrain.

27. Word processing is implemented in all organizations in the same way.

Questions on Concepts

1. Explain what a feasibility study is.
2. Discuss why an organization might do its own feasibility study.
3. List some questions a feasibility study should answer.
4. Describe how a random sampling survey is conducted.
5. List several things a task force leader would want to know about the organization before beginning a feasibility study.
6. Describe three examples of organizing data into pie charts.
7. Describe several factors to consider when selecting equipment.
8. Discuss the furnishings and office layout, lighting, color, air conditioning, and acoustics used in environments where information is processed.
9. Describe how office automation may be implemented in a large and a small organization.

Case and Activities

In a large insurance organization, the potential benefit of using word processing in the underwriting and claims de-partments was investigated. The study was conducted using interviewing as the method of gathering data. A secretary who worked for the organization was given release time for two hours a day to do the study in her particular department and report the findings. Her findings were compiled and a decision was made about what equipment to choose for several departments.

The secretary did not tell the people she interviewed why she was conducting the study. She met immediate complications. Some people refused to give her information.

When she finished the study, she was unable to make a decision about what type of equipment to choose, so she let a vendor recommend appropriate equipment.

1. Did the secretary make a good task force leader? Discuss why or why not.
2. Discuss the approach to conducting a feasibility study.
3. How might resistance to the survey have been eliminated?
4. Why was the secretary unable to make appropriate recommendations?
5. Explain your reaction to allowing vendors to select the equipment.
6. Why were people unwilling to give the secretary information?

Activities

1. Conduct a random sampling survey of any office worker using a form similar to one in Figure 8.7.
2. Prepare a time ladder survey of your activities for one day in 15-minute segments. How much time do you waste in one day?
3. Suppose you had to choose a piece of equipment for a small office. List several types of equipment that would fit on a desk top.

CHAPTER 9

Organizing the Change

The objectives of this chapter are to:

1. Describe a custom and a production environment and the category of work done in each.

2. Discuss three system designs.

3. Trace the movement from centralization toward decentralization in word processing.

4. Describe several models of administrative support systems.

5. Discuss why an area that processes information needs procedures.

6. List four methods of filing and indexing in centers.

7. List several benefits of a procedures manual.

The kind of atmosphere in which the processing of information occurs is referred to as the **work environment.** To have the environment function efficiently, the equipment, staff, and office furnishings must be arranged in a certain design within the organization. The people are given procedures to follow and work is measured (work measurement). From the results of work measurement, information (feedback) is received to determine how efficient the environment is.

Selecting the Proper Environment

The type of work environment that needs to be created for processing information is determined after examining the results of a feasibility study and finding out what type of work exists. A relationship exists between the type of work that an organization has and the type of environment that provides the best way to handle that work. The two major categories of work are routine and nonroutine. **Routine work** is work that recurs frequently. It usually does not vary much. **Nonroutine work** is work that recurs infrequently. It usually varies from time to time. Often an organization has both categories of work. If this is the case, an environment is designed that handles both routine and nonroutine work.

Routine work requires little skill. An example of a routine task is washing dishes. If you wash dishes at home, you know that certain characteristics apply to the description of the job. Once the job is initially learned, you really do not have to concentrate on doing it. If you were a dishwasher for a restaurant, you would have to wash a certain volume of dishes to keep your job. In all probability, you would be highly supervised and you would have little contact with the customers who used the clean dishes.

The work environment that describes the environment in which routine tasks are performed is aptly referred to as a **production environment.** In this environment, a person is often expected to conform to certain procedures to make sure that everyone is doing the job the same way and that the job is being done as efficiently as possible. Work is often measured in these circumstances to see that sufficient work is being produced. The work being done must also be worth more than the cost of doing it. In such an environment, the cost attributed to error is not very high. For instance, if you happen to break a dish or two, the cost of replacing it would not be very much.

Production Environment. In an organization, a production environment is used if a great deal of highly repetitive work such as a number of form letters exists. Such work is easy to do, has few revisions, and requires little skill on the part of the secretary. The directions the originators give are clear. In such an environment, the secretaries follow routine standard procedures with very few exceptions. Work is handled on a first-in, first-out basis. The emphasis is on quantity, more than on quality. The work is always predictable, and the employees are not expected to rush to meet deadlines. All originators can expect to receive the work they submit in a standard number of hours or days. Most of the work is not confidential.

Type of Work

A collection department produces the type of work that could best be handled in a total production environment. In a collection department, many routine letters are sent each month to remind customers that their bills are due. Collection letters are usually sent out in a number of stages. First customers are gently reminded that their accounts are overdue. Then they are sent letters of inquiry to find out if they have some problem that is preventing them from paying. Next, they are sent anywhere from one to a number of letters appealing to them to pay and finally they are issued an ultimatum, "pay up or else" (Figure 9.1).

In a production environment, a schedule could be set up to review delinquent accounts and automatically forward to the customer the appropriate letter. This type of work fits all the criteria for work done in a production environment.

Criteria

1. The letters have very few variables—perhaps only names, addresses, and amounts due.

2. Since the letters are standard, they are easy to process.

3. The quantity of work is important. All customers who need to receive notices are notified.

4. The work is predictable and as long as a schedule is kept, there is no reason for originators to make last-minute changes.

5. Since the letters are all similar, they can be expected to take about the same amount of time to prepare.

Patti-Ruth Originals
378 CAROLET LANE, ORANGE, CA. 92669
TELEPHONE: (714) 639-7991

Amount Due _____
Date Due _____

Dear Friend:

We are writing because our good customers like you generally like to be reminded if they have overlooked a payment.

Your account is overdue, but you can easily take care of this matter by sending your check in the envelope we have enclosed.

Sincerely yours,

Collection Department

Patti-Ruth Originals
378 CAROLET LANE, ORANGE, CA. 92669
TELEPHONE: (714) 639-7991

Amount Due _____
Date Due _____

Dear Friend:

Since you did not respond to our last notice, we hope there is no reason why you are unable to make the payment on your account. The payment is twenty days overdue and another will soon be due.

If for some reason, you are unable to make this payment, will you let me know by telephone or by writing an explanation and returning it in the enclosed return envelope.

Otherwise, please let us have your check right away.

Cordially,

Patti Claffey
Collection Manager

Patti-Ruth Originals
378 CAROLET LANE, ORANGE, CA. 92669
TELEPHONE: (714) 639-7991

Amount Due _____
Late Charge _____
Total Due _____

Dear Friend:

Your account is now seriously delinquent. The above amounts represent your last two monthly payments and a late charge.

We must hear from you immediately. Please call us at (714) 826-7027.

Cordially,

Carolee Freer
Division Manager

Patti-Ruth Originals
378 CAROLET LANE, ORANGE, CA. 92669
TELEPHONE: (714) 639-7991

Amount Due _____
Late Charge _____
Total Due _____

Dear Customer:

Your payment is now three months overdue.

Unless we hear from you within 24 hours, a penalty will be added and your account will be turned over to a collection agency.

Call us at (714) 826-7027.

Cordially,

Vicki Cunningham
District Manager

Figure 9.1 An example of a series of form collection letters; routine production work.

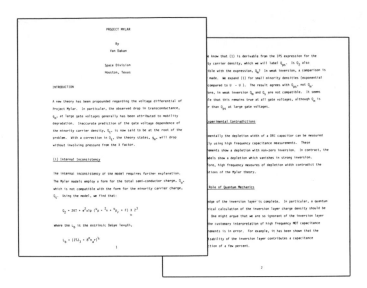

Figure 9.2 An engineering document is an example of non-routine custom work.

Nonroutine Work

What is nonroutine work?

Nonroutine work requires a great deal of skill. An example of a nonroutine task is performing a surgical operation. If you were a surgeon, your range of duties would be varied. Even though certain parts of your task are repetitive, a great part of your job may involve new complications. The term **custom environment** describes the environment in which nonroutine tasks are best performed. In this environment, you may have a set of guidelines, but you are on your own with little supervision. Your job demands high quality and your work is measured according to how well you perform the given operation rather than how many operations you are able to perform. Your work is very unpredictable and errors involve a high cost. For example, if you make an error in judgment, your patient's life is at stake.

Custom environment

Custom Environment. A custom environment is often used if an organization has a great deal of highly complex, widely varied work with little or no repetition. In a custom environment, the work can be expected to have a high value per item. The work is generally difficult and unpredictable. Secretaries follow procedures, but have to cope with originators' wishes. Originators generally need the work to meet deadlines so employees can expect a great deal of rush work. Since the work is usually vital to some project, the work must be done accurately and the result of missed deadlines, sloppy work, or errors is costly. The secretaries generally are expected to use their own judgment at times and often are given few or no directions.

An example of where a custom environment is desirable is in an engineering department. In an engineering department, engineers write and submit proposals and other documents that require a great deal of skill to produce. Usually, the documents are very technical and often contain many numbers, formulas, and statistics (Figure 9.2). Often the documents have to be revised as

Production Environment

Procedures	Secretaries use standard procedures set up to ensure that work is produced uniformly. The supervisor has to make sure that the originator and the secretary conform to procedures.
Supervision	The secretaries are closely supervised.
Secretarial skills	Secretaries with entry-level skills are acceptable.
Working relationships	Secretaries do work for many originators.
Communication	Secretaries and managers have very little reason to talk to one another.
Work measurement	Secretaries' work is measured to see how productive the environment is.
Turnaround Time	Originators expect their work in a standard amount of time.
Configuration	Work such as this is best done in a centralized area. In this way, all expensive equipment can be kept in one area and used to the fullest capacity. It is unnecessary to have the same equipment in several areas.
Emphasis	The emphasis is on reducing secretarial costs.

Custom Environment

Procedures	The secretaries respond to originators' requirements and do not always follow standard procedures.
Supervision	The individual manager usually supervises, not the supervisor. Secretaries usually have a minimum of supervision.
Secretarial skills	The secretaries need high level skills.
Working relationships	The secretaries do specialized work for a limited (or dedicated) number of originators.
Communication	Secretaries and managers must work together, since secretaries often have to ask managers questions and managers often must explain how they want the work done.
Work Measurement	Work is measured by quality and timeliness, not by volume.
Emphasis	The emphasis is on reducing managerial costs by making managers more productive.
Turnaround Time	Deadlines must be met so turnaround time is a high priority.
Configuration	Work such as this is best done in decentralized or small work groups, with few controls and a high level of skilled workers.

Figure 9.3 Summary of production and custom environment.

engineers add new ideas, think of better ways of presenting their ideas, or as new developments occur. Engineering work fits all the criteria for work done in a custom environment. The work is never the same. The quality of each document is important. The documents are difficult to produce, and the employees must work under constant deadlines and often with incomplete instructions. The items are very valauble, and missing a deadline can be critical.

A custom environment, therefore, is chosen if the primary goal of an organization in processing information is to make the highly paid manager more effective. The chart in Figure 9.3 summarizes the characteristics of both a custom and a production environment.

Designing The System

Equipment is arranged in different patterns (configurations) within the organization after the type of work environment needed has been determined.

The process of arranging the equipment to handle various work environments is called designing the system. Three types of system designs commonly

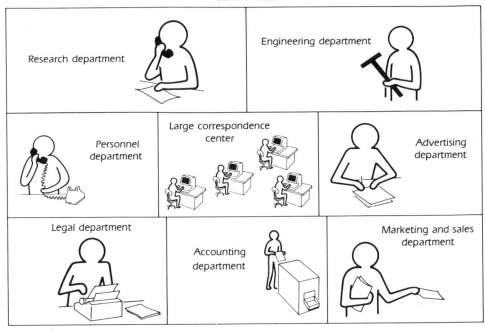

CENTRALIZED

Figure 9.4 Centralized system design.

used in areas where information is processed are centralized, decentralized, and hybrid. (Figures 9.4, 9.5, and 9.6).

In **centralized systems,** all the word/information processing equipment is located in one area. The area may not be close to where the work is originated. In **decentralized systems,** however, the equipment is usually located close to where the work is originated. In decentrelized systems, the equipment may be located in **mini-centers,** centers that have only a few pieces of equipment. An organization may have several mini-centers. The mini-centers may be located on several different floors throughout the organization.

Hybrid systems are a combination of centralized and decentralized systems. In a hybrid system, the organization may have one large center and several mini-centers. Sometimes the mini-centers consist of only one person on one piece of equipment. These mini-centers are referred to as **satellites** of the large center.

Equipment in large centers (centralized) or mini-centers (decentralized) is arranged to provide a particular type of work environment. Large centers are often total production environments. Mini-centers located near the departments they service are often custom environments.

Centralized Systems. A centralized system is an effective design for a high volume production work environment (Figure 9.7). Centralized systems provide several advantages for this type of work. For heavy volumes of repetitive work, secretaries frequently store, update, and retrieve media. They must, therefore, have speedy access to filed material. For example, the Great Mutual Insurance Company in Tucson, Arizona has a large center for 250 originators. It has some 5,000 paragraphs stored on magnetic disks from which the originators can choose when creating a document. If the same type work were done in mini-

Advantages

Speedy access to filed material

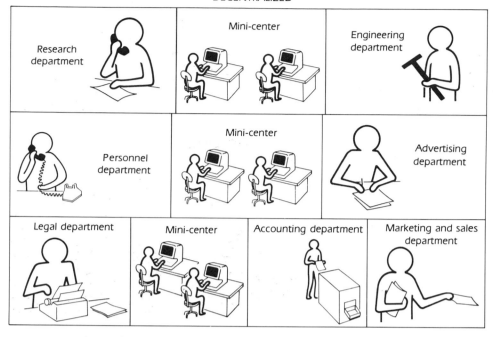

Figure 9.5 Decentralized system design.

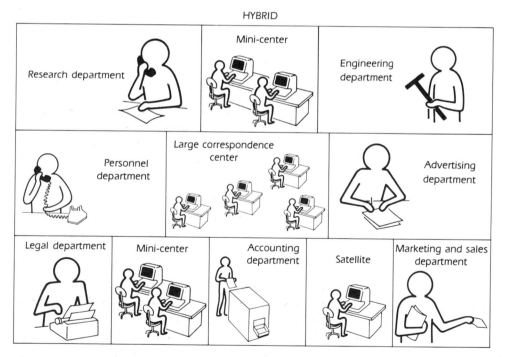

Figure 9.6 Hybrid system design.

Figure 9.7 A centralized system. *(Courtesy of Wang Laboratories, Incorporated.)*

centers, each mini-center would need copies of the stored media.

Effective use of equipment

Another advantage is that in this environment, equipment can often be more effectively used. For example, a high speed printer may be too expensive an item to have unless it is located in a centralized area where it can get the most use.

Advantage for secretaries

Centralized systems also provide an advantage over the traditional office for secretaries and originators. Secretaries can become specialists on equipment. They do not have to be distracted by having to do such things as answer phones or deal with other office interruptions. They have more even workloads because they are generally supervised by one person. In a central system, secretaries who are ambitious and desire to move up in an organization are less likely to become locked into one position. Career paths are generally available. The secretaries' work is usually more fairly evaluated and their promotions are based on merit.

Advantages for originators

Originators, on the other hand, receive the correspondence support they need. The amount of correspondence support has nothing to do with the position they hold in the organization. They are able to have uninterrupted support. Their work will not pile up when a secretary is absent or on vacation.

Specialize in work

Decentralized systems. Decentralized systems, however, are located near the departments they service; therefore, secretaries can become more specialized in the terminology used in a particular department (Figures 9.8, 9.9, and 9.10). When secretaries are specialized in a particular type of work such as legal or financial, they can become more efficient. Secretaries often become so skilled that they may move into higher level positions in these areas.

Since decentralized systems are located near originators, the turnaround time is improved. (The **turnaround time** is the amount of time it takes for a document to be returned to the originator after it is submitted for keyboarding.)

Figure 9.8 A decentralized system. *(Courtesy of Wang Laboratories, Incorporated.)*

Figure 9.9 A decentralized system. *(Courtesy of International Business Machines Corporation.)*

Figure 9.10 A decentralized system. *(Courtesy of Oxford Pendaflex Corporation.)*

In large centralized systems, the turnaround time may be much longer because the work might have to be delivered and returned from a center that could be located in a separate building.

Near originator

Decentralized mini-centers are located near the originators and originators often feel more comfortable working with smaller groups. In a decentralized system, originators are encouraged to deal with the people who prepare their documents. Consequently, originators develop more confidence in the services provided and secretaries get personal recognition for the work they do. Since originators are closer to secretaries, secretaries often receive better instructions and can get answers to their questions.

Decentralized systems may fit the needs of some organizations better than centralized systems. For example, the Sun Engineering Firm in Louisville, Kentucky has four mini-centers located on four separate floors. Two of the four centers specialize in engineering, one in financial matters, and one in legal documents. For this organization, decentralization is effective. The secretaries in each of the centers can specialize in the terminology used in the departments they service.

Production and custom work

Hybrid Systems. Hybrid systems are often used when an organization has available both a production and a custom environment to fit the work that is done in different departments. For example, the Stewart Engineering Corporation has a great diversity of highly specialized work such as financial, legal, scientific, and engineering documents. It also has high volumes of original dictation and long repetitive documents. Therefore, four mini-centers containing three secretaries in each were created. In the mini-centers, secretaries work on documents up to ten pages in length and transcribe minicassettes prepared on portable dictation equipment. Stewart Engineering Corporation also created a main center with 20 secretaries on the day shift and 17 on nights. This center handles all long repetitive documents and most nontechnical dictation.

The Movement From Centralization Toward Decentralization

Reduces costs

When any of the information processing technologies are implemented, the question of whether to centralize or decentralize equipment arises. Word processing was centralized in the early installations for several reasons. The early emphasis was on reducing secretarial costs, and word processing was initially implemented for this reason. Word processing equipment, however, was expensive, so it was centralized so the equipment could be placed in one location to service many departments. If it were centralized, the equipment could get the

Increased efficiency

best use, secretaries could be trained to operate it and use it more efficiently, and every department would not have to have its own equipment. Moreover, the early applications of word processing were the kinds of applications that best fit into a production environment—work of a repetitive nature. Centralization of word processing meant that all equipment was placed in e central location and secretaries, with the possible exception of those who worked for top management, no longer worked for individual managers. They were placed in a correspondence center called a word processing center. Eventually, technology developed to the point that the center could handle work other than production work, such as long, complex reports with large amounts of revision typing.

Another consideration in the early installations was that managers were getting their routine correspondence processed, but many of them were without any administrative support. Later, specialists who were trained specifically in administrative support were added to centralized word processing. The word processing center then became the center for both the correspondence and administrative support secretaries. Where this plan was not feasible, the word processing center became just a correspondence center. The administrative secretaries were grouped in other locations, either in an area where they would function as receptionists or close to the managers for whom they worked. Many organizations still refer to the correspondence center as the word processing center.

No administrative support

Word processing centers were not always readily accepted. Originators often resented giving up their personal secretaries, losing control of their work, and having their work go out of the area, especially if the material was confidential. The work the originator submitted was often work that was not suitable for a production environment. Although the equipment could handle revisions and lengthy reports better than standard typewriters, the production environment was not always best for the given application. For example, a long complex engineering document might require that the secretary be near enough to the engineer to ask questions. Yet, with centralization, the engineer might be located floors away from the word processing center or perhaps even in another building. Since the centers were often too far away, efficiency was lost because material had to be picked up and delivered. Moreover, secretaries often did not like being isolated in centers.

Centers not always accepted

In many organizations, equipment was decentralized to help word processing gain more acceptance. Decentralized word processing became more popular as the price of equipment dropped, as the emphasis in word processing began to be placed on making the highly paid manager more efficient, and as machine capabilities increased.

Decentralization becomes popular

Along with the change from centralization to decentralization, word processing has also undergone other changes. For example, as equipment becomes more sophisticated and can do more than the production work of the document cycle done by stand-alone word processors, the term "word processing" is less likely to remain an accurate term for what is happening in the center. Word processing centers that have equipment with greater capabilities are being called "information system centers" or "information processing centers." In some organizations, the centers remain word processing centers because they are not designed to handle such things as electronic document distribution, telecommunications, and records processing that would make them information processors.

The development of technology has also caused a greater use of hybrid systems, a combination of both a large center (centralized) and a mini-center or satellite (decentralized). In information processing, the equipment in a hybrid system is often tied into high powered computers located in large centers. The mini-centers or satellites do not have to be connected by hard wire or telephone to equipment in the large center. They may consist of stand-alone equipment or shared-logic equipment tied into the equipment in the main center. When the word or data processing equipment is tied into a central computer, the systems are often referred to as **distributed systems.**

Hybrid system

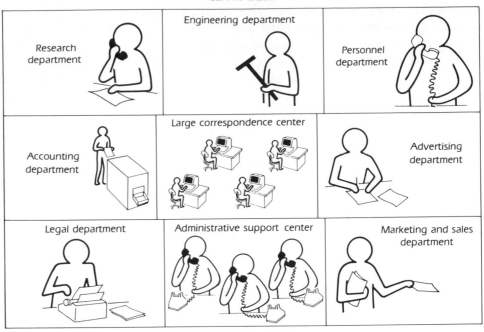

Figure 9.11 Centralized administrative support systems.

Models of Administrative Support Systems

Administrative support is provided for managers in many organizations. An example of administrative support activities for a manager might range from simple responsibilities such as photocopying and collating documents, answering phones, taking and delivering messages, to more complex responsibilities such as composing original correspondence and compiling reports.

Managers delegate time-consuming activities

Managers are able to delegate many of the routine time-consuming activities that keep them from doing the work they are highly paid to do when provided with administrative support.

Secretaries who work in an administrative support position are also able to become more knowledgeable of the organization and capable of moving into positions of more responsibility. Secretaries who provide administrative support are arranged in many different patterns (configurations), as shown in Figures 9.11, 9.12, and 9.13.

Support is in different patterns

Centralized. Administrative support may be located with the correspondence support in a large center (Figure 9.11). The administrative support can also be located in a separate large administrative support center (Figure 9.11). When administrative support is located in one area, it is called a centralized administrative support system. The advantages of centralized administrative support centers are similar to the advantages of centralized correspondence centers. Since all nontyping clerical work is done in one area, administrative secretaries have more even workloads and someone is always available to handle an originator's work.

Work varies in complexity

Since administrative support centers usually have work that varies in levels of complexity from simple to difficult, a number of different job levels are pro-

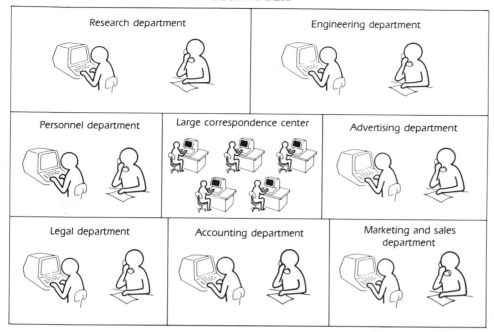

Figure 9.12 Decentralized administrative support systems.

Figure 9.13 Work group support systems.

Figure 9.14 Work group. *(Courtesy of Hauserman, Incorporated.)*

vided within the center. Secretaries in lower job levels can, therefore, develop their skills and move into higher paid, more challenging positions.

The same disadvantages also exist in centralized administrative support centers that apply to centralized correspondence support centers. Managers might feel that they lose control when their work leaves the area. Secretaries might feel isolated. They might not feel that they receive enough recognition from individual managers for the work they do.

Decentralized. In some organizations, the traditional boss/secretary relationship is not disrupted at all (Figure 9.12). Managers retain secretaries near their offices. This model of administrative support is called decentralized administrative support. In the decentralized model, the secretary often sends overload correspondence work to a centralized correspondence support center.

Work Group. A **work group** is an alternative to centralized administrative support (Figure 9.13). It is a unit that provides both decentralized administrative and correspondence support (Figure 9.14). In a work group, a few administrative secretaries and one or two correspondence secretaries supporting the group may be near the people for whom they work. Work groups require the least amount of change in the way managers operate, yet they bring managers additional efficiency. In work group designs, the secretarial support is increased but the secretaries remain outside the manager's door. The manager is still able to submit work and request help on a face-to-face basis. It is not necessary for managers to learn new procedures; they can operate much as before. Work groups are people doing like tasks and are generally identified with a department. Several groups may share one word/information processing team or have

Alternative to centralization

its own team as an integral part of the group. The important consideration is that the manager/secretary relationship need not be drastically altered.

Work groups are increasing in popularity as more and more equipment is used for data and word processing that makes it possible to tie together work groups throughout the organization. For example, a central computer might be the link between several work groups. The tie-in to the central computer might make it possible for secretaries to be involved in both data and word processing applications. The chart in Figure 9.15 provides examples of several different administrative support systems.

Setting Up Procedures

A goal in processing information is increasing efficiency and decreasing costs. Setting up procedures plays an important part in achieving this goal. In the following example, you can see how a lack of procedures can add to the cost of producing the document and affect the morale of the people involved.

Why are procedures necessary?

Figure 9.15 Administrative support systems in industry.

Examples of Administrative Support Systems

One center

A *mortgage/banking company in Minneapolis, Minnesota.* In this average-sized organization, only one center handles all administrative and correspondence services. Correspondence secretaries store and update all accounts on card and tape media, using automated equipment.

Administrative secretaries have no typewriters. Their desks are equipped with phones and calculators. They handle all customer calls, filing, readjusting accounts, and problem solving. They dictate replies to customers' requests into an endless loop dictation tank.

Correspondence support center

A *dental school in Los Angeles, California.* Correspondence secretaries in the center handle all educational papers, lecture notes, publication materials, school grants, and personal correspondence for professors. They do mostly large jobs, utilizing automated typewriters. They have recently added an ink jet printer to free the automated typewriter for more keyboarding.

Administrative support center

Administrative secretaries are in open reception areas, handling school budgets, personnel payroll budgets, and office management, and acting as assistants to department heads. Professors and doctors are in classrooms, labs, and offices, and drop off their work as they pass the center.

Work groups

A *government agency.* Administrative and correspondence secretaries all are in the same area, in work groups near management. The work is highly technical. Management's needs are constantly changing. Each correspondence secretary specializes in one type of work. They do legal documents, brochures, special confidential correspondence, graphs, and tables. The administrative secretaries have to prepare audiovisual material for presentation.

All secretaries are cross-trained, using different types of automated equipment such as standalone word processors and shared-logic systems.

They must all know how to copy documents using several different reprographics methods.

Correspondence support center and decentralized satellites

A *large law firm in New York City.* Some correspondence secretaries work in a central correspondence center on one floor, but others work in satellite centers on three other floors. All correspondence secretaries use the same type of automated equipment. Their function is to play out legal documents that are permanently stored on magnetic media, merging it with the information that is necessary to create a new client's file.

Decentralized administrative support

Individual administrative legal secretaries are outside attorneys' doors. Some are training to become paralegal assistants; others have their own automated typewriters and do special applications and high priority work. Word/information processing serves over 150 attorneys in this organization.

The North and Young Company recently opened its correspondence center. Since employees were told that they could begin submitting work, by 11 o'clock each day the center is inundated with work marked "rush" from 210 originators. The work comes to the center in many ways: dictated, handwritten, and typewritten in rough-draft form. The center cannot be reached by phone because the lines are tied up by originators calling in with things they forgot to mention. For example, one originator called in to say he needed to have his work produced on blue paper; another to specify that she needed 300 copies.

The center itself is in chaos. The correspondence secretaries argue over who does what work. None want to do the long revision documents. Originators are often being sent the wrong work. Work is sent back to originators before it is proofread. Originators call to ask if their work has been done, and the center is unable to give them an answer. Dictation recorders in the center often are unable to receive dictation because the cassette media gets filled up and no one changes them.

The secretaries have difficulty using the media that the other secretaries record because nobody keyboards and records media in the same way. Therefore, the secretaries have to guess how the document stored in the media will look when it is played out. All those requesting copies get photocopies, totally disregarding the costs involved in reproducing work.

The center also needs to purchase additional storage media because the secretaries record all documents on media and the work from the 210 originators used up all the storage media that had been purchased. Work that has been previously recorded cannot be located when the originator requests that the work be revised, and the correspondence secretaries have to re-keyboard many documents that have previously been recorded.

Urgent messages that should be sent immediately finally emerge from the stack of work days later.

Turnaround time

The correspondence secretaries complain that they cannot understand the originator's dictation. The originators complain about the quality of the work being done, turnaround time of the documents, and the length of time it takes to get their work done after they have requested it.

You can see from this example that the center has several problems because it has no rules and people have no procedures to follow. Consequently, documents do not move smoothly through the stages of workflow (origination, production, reproduction, filing, storage and retrieval, and distribution), and the people are unhappy about processing information.

To remedy the situation, procedures need to be set up and communicated to people within the organization.

Types Of Procedures

Workflow

Procedures are necessary to make sure that work flows smoothly through the stages of origination, production, reproduction, filing, storage, retrieval, and distribution.

Origination Procedures. In considering procedures for origination, decisions must be made whether handwritten, rough draft typewritten documents, or dic-

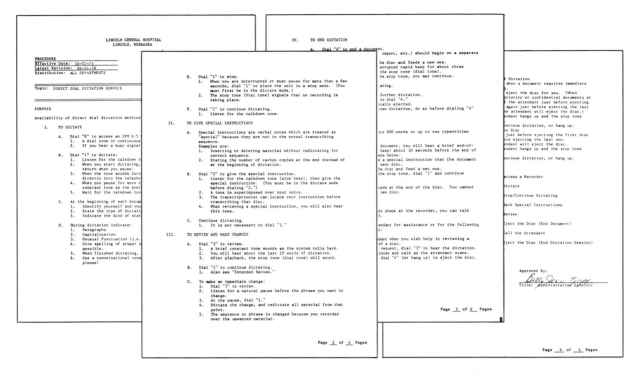

Figure 9.16 Origination procedures: guidelines for operating dictation equipment.

tated documents are acceptable as a means of origination. Some centers might limit origination to dictation; others might accept several methods. The deciding factor may be the type of equipment available. For example, one law firm in Los Angeles uses only rough-draft typewritten copy as input because it has an OCR scanner that reads the copy in typewritten form. After the copy is scanned and read, the originators can just insert any changes they want and make as many revisions as needed.

Some other center considerations when planning procedures include the following.

1. What hours will the center be available? If it will be open 24 hours a day, what are the procedures for using the center after regular working hours?

2. How will the center inform people about the best time to submit work? One center puts a green flag up when the center is not busy and a red flag when it has a backlog of work.

3. What procedures will be set up for the attendant who monitors recording procedures within the center?

Within a center, procedures are also necessary for handling rush or confidential work, and originators need to know what procedures to use to have their documents processed accordingly. In addition to general dictation procedures, originators also need to have a set of procedures for dictating the types of documents that the center processes. Finally, originators should have a set of guidelines or procedures for operating dictation equipment (Figure 9.16).

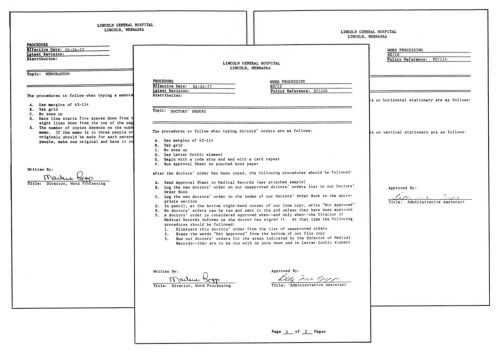

Figure 9.17 Procedures for setting up documents.

Production Procedures. In considering procedures for production, decisions must be made as to what type of work the center will produce and what standard formats will be set up to provide uniformity in the center's work (Figure 9.17). Procedures must be provided for the originator to request formats other than standard formats if deviations are accepted in the center.

The workflow within the center must also be considered. For example, the steps after work is logged into the center might be as follows.

1. Work is sent to a correspondence secretary to be keyboarded.

2. The correspondence secretary sends it to the proofreader.

3. The proofreader sends it to a supervisor for logging out.

4. The supervisor returns it to the originator.

Revision procedures should not waste time

If any revisions occur, the originator must also have a set of revision procedures. If the originator does not use proper procedures when submitting revisions, the result will be much wasted time, confusion, and added costs. The three time wasters in revision are retyping parts that have already been typed, reproofreading parts that have already been proofread, and playing out documents after the new corrections are made. The originator should provide as little repetition of these time wasters as possible. For example, when submitting the document, the originator should not cut and paste because the document is recorded on magnetic media and the paragraphs are in a certain order. If the document comes back to the correspondence secretary revised by the cut-and-paste method, the entire document will have to be rekeyboarded. In some centers, the originator returns original documents to the center because often the entire document does not have to be revised, and the revised pages may just be reinserted in the original.

Centers need to have procedures for proofreading. Some centers will make their operators responsible; others will have people designated as proofreaders. Procedures concerning how copy is to be proofread is important to maintain the quality of documents within a center.

Secretaries within the center need to have procedures for keyboarding, recording, and playing back documents. Any secretary in the center should be able to work on any media recorded by someone else in the center.

Reproduction Procedures. Having procedures for copying documents helps keep the high cost of reproduction down. Both correspondence and administrative secretaries may be involved in reproducing documents, and center procedures might outline and describe how the document leaves the correspondence secretary and is sent to the administrative secretary for reproduction.

The center needs procedures that describe how work is to be reproduced. For example, the procedures may state that all work will have one carbon copy, unless otherwise requested. Procedures for operating the various types of reprographics equipment and procedures for deciding which reprographics method is to be used are important considerations.

Filing, Storage, and Retrieval Procedures. Sometimes certain documents are to be reproduced in the center and others are to be reproduced in other parts of the organization or sent to an outside printing firm. Procedures are necessary to outline how these documents are to be handled.

Filing and indexing media such as magnetic cards and diskettes is important to the efficient operation of any center. Media that have been filed properly can be easily located and reused. When media have not been filed properly, documents have to be rekeyboarded and time and money is wasted. Procedures also help to eliminate the unnecessary storage of documents. Unnecessary storage is very costly to an organization.

Procedures are often provided that outline what should be permanently stored and what should be temporarily stored. In many centers, work such as letters, memos, and documents that may be used one time are temporarily stored on media. Temporarily stored media may be retained anywhere from two days to a week to allow originators to make revisions. In certain centers, schedules are set up to reuse media (depending upon the type of documents stored on them) at various intervals—daily, weekly, monthly, semiannually, and annually. In some centers, a document is stored until the originator says it is no longer necessary. Periodically a form such as the one in Figure 9.18 will go out to originators asking them if a document that is stored temporarily should be kept any longer. If the originator requests it, the document is placed in **archive** or permanent storage. In some organizations, originators are assigned their own archive storage diskettes.

When media is temporarily stored, some system of identification is used for logging in the media and filing it. In some centers, the originator's name and code number are recorded on a log sheet. The media is filed according to the code number (Figure 9.19). When a revision is requested, the secretary refers to the log sheet to determine the code. The media is then located and the docu-

Proofreading is an important part of production

Permanent and temporary storage

Media is filed in various ways

Setting Up Procedures

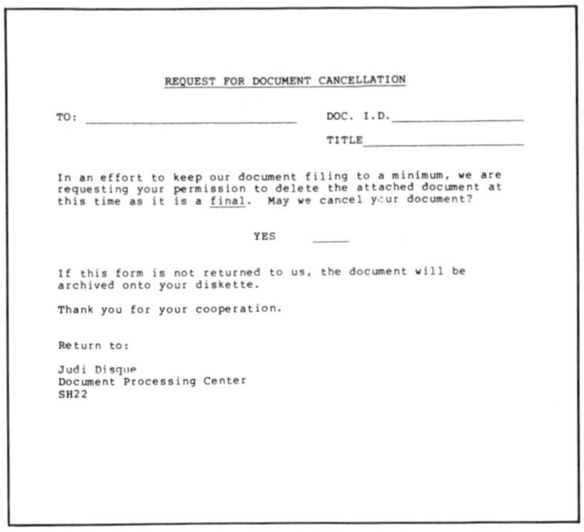

Figure 9.18 Request for document cancellation.

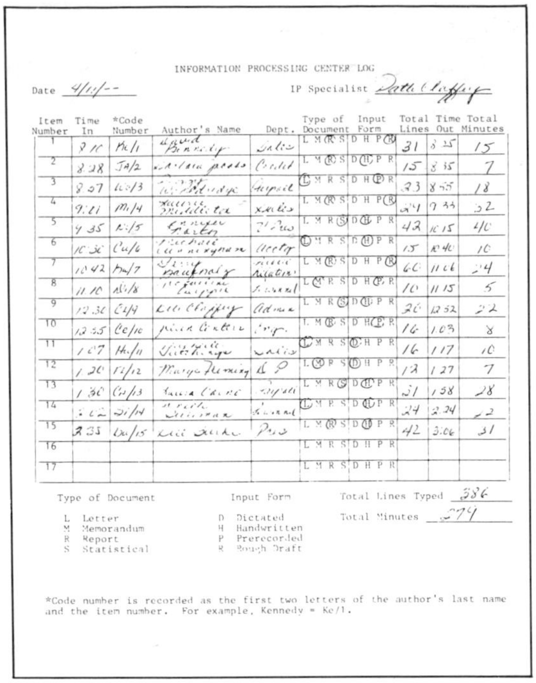

Figure 9.19 Information processing center log.

ment is played out and revised. One method used in some organizations to determine when temporary media should be reused involves the secretaries' storing certain information as part of the text that is keyboarded. For example, at the end of a document, secretaries indicate their initials, day of the week (Monday = 1) and the date and time the document was prepared. For example, if Jan Jones recorded a document on Thursday at 2:00 p.m., the media would contain the code JJ/4/2 (Figure 9.20). Media is held a week and then reused. In other organizations, the code number of a standard document becomes part of the secretary's reference initials at the bottom of the letter. For example, if Jan Jones produced a new letter from a recorded form letter number 126, the reference initials at the end of the document would read: JJ/126.

Permanently stored media is often kept in a central location so every secretary will have access to the files. Permanent files are made up of such items as standard forms that are constantly reused. Law firms, for example, usually have many such documents on permanent file.

The system of filing and indexing for temporary and permanent stored media varies. Media is generally filed and indexed in four basic ways.

1. The media and typewritten text are filed together in a central file in a convenient area. The advantage of filing documents in this way is that the documents can become part of the organization's entire records processing system. The documents can be used for reference by both administrative and correspondence secretaries who need to use them. Traditional filing cabinets are often used for this purpose. Filing media and typewritten text together in file folders, however, is often bulky and cumbersome.

2. The media and the documents they represent are filed in separate or

Figure 9.20 Document with codes recorded to indicate when media should be reused.

decentralized filing units. Media filed in this manner are often located more conveniently for individual operators. Traditional filing cabinets may also be used when the media and documents are filed together in a decentralized area. However, many new storage devices are being developed that allow hard copy and media to be stored together (see Figures 9.21 and 9.22). In some organizations, hard copy is still filed because hard copy can be marked where the person who recorded the document inserted special machine codes. An example of a special machine code is a stop code placed where the operator is to insert a variable in a repetitive letter. Revising or playing out is easier for the next person who works on the document if the person can see a hard copy version of the text.

3. The media is filed in one place (either centrally or decentrally located) and the hard copy may be filed separately in a loose-leaf binder. New storage devices such as the ones in Figures 9.23 through 9.26 are used for storing just the media. Loose-leaf binders or file cabinets store the file copy.

4. The media is stored either in a centralized or decentralized location, using such storage devices as the ones in Figures 9.23 through 9.26, but the hard copy is not retained. In a center, a combination of these methods may be used when filing storage media.

Administrative secretaries are often involved in converting documents to microfilm for permanent storage. In those centers where microfilming is done, procedures describe which documents are to be microfilmed and which ones are to be stored by other means.

Distribution Procedures. Work that leaves the center must be handled by certain procedures. For example, in some organizations, work is sent back to the originator for a signature and then sent to the administrative secretaries for mailing. Procedures must also be developed that outline what work is to be sent physically through the mails and what work is to be distributed electronically

Handling the mail

by other means such as facsimile machines, communicating word/information processors, and Telex/TWX machines.

When documents are distributed through an electronic mail system, the person who is responsible for distributing the work must have operating procedures for the equipment. For example, administrative secretaries might operate facsimile equipment and correspondence secretaries might operate communicating word/information processors.

Control with forms

Workflow Control Procedures. Forms are used to control the workflow and provide managers with immediate information about the progress of any document through the stages of workflow. The information derived from the forms filed after the job is complete becomes a source of feedback to aid in reports that are sent to management. The way that one organization uses a system of forms control starts when work comes into the center, in either dictated or hard copy form. If the work is dictated, the supervisor must manually log in the dictation. If the work arrives in longhand or hard copy, it is accompanied by what is referred to as a work requisition slip, job ticket, or job request form. These forms vary from organization to organization.

The job request form one organization uses contains two sections and consists of an original and two copies (Figure 9.27). Section I of the form provides a space for basic information about how to do the job. For example, the originator is asked what line spacing should be used. Section II contains such information as who will do the work, whether the work is an original or a revision, the name of the originating department, the kind of input, the date and time the job arrived, and what equipment is to be used.

The following steps take place after the document arrives in the center (see Figure 9.28).

1. If the work requisition form is not filled out, the supervisor fills it out. If it is already filled out, the supervisor checks the completeness of the form.

2. The supervisor gives all three copies and the dictation or hard copy to the correspondence secretary.

3. The secretary keyboards the work.

4. The secretary fills in the production date and files the production copy of the work requisition form.

5. The secretary sends the remaining two copies, along with dictation media or hard copy, to the proofreader, who makes corrections on the work and records the number of errors on the work requisition form.

6. The proofreader sends copy that needs changes back to the correspondence secretary.

7. The correspondence secretary makes the changes and returns the material to the proofreader.

8. The proofreader who accepts the material sends it to the supervisor.

9. The supervisor sends the top copy of the work requisition form to the originator, along with the typewritten work and the original or hard copy documents.

Figure 9.21 *(left)* Track-back cassette ring binder. *(Courtesy of Wilson Jones Company.)* **Figure 9.22** *(middle)* Mag card jackets and packets. *(Courtesy of Wilson Jones Company.)* **Figure 9.23** *(right)* Rotary diskette storage stands. *(Courtesy of Eichner Systems.)*

Figure 9.24 *(left above)* Mag card storage module. *(Courtesy of The Morley Company.)*

Figure 9.25 *(middle)* Mag card storage module. *(Courtesy of Wilson Jones Company.)*

Figure 9.26 *(right)* Cassette media storage module. *(Courtesy of Wilson Jones Company.)*

```
WORD PROCESSING JOB REQUEST

                                                              DATE _____
SECTION 1                                                     JOB NO. _____

ORIGINATOR:                              | ROOM    | BLDG.    | EXT.
-----------------------------------------------------------------------------------
DEPARTMENT/UNIT                          | SUBJECT OR REPORT TITLE
-----------------------------------------------------------------------------------
PAPER: [] INTEROFFICE [] CO. LETTERHEAD _____ [] BOND, [] OTHER:
                                          NAME
[] RETURN IN SEALED ENVELOPE  SPACING: [] SINGLE, [] DOUBLE, [] ONE AND ONE-HALF
-----------------------------------------------------------------------------------
ORIGINAL AND _____ COPIES | [] WILL BE REPRODUCED | WHEN NEEDED:
-----------------------------------------------------------------------------------
        NOTE: TEXT WILL BE RETAINED ON TAPE FOR THREE WORKDAYS UNLESS REQUESTED OTHERWISE.
SPECIAL INSTRUCTIONS:

                                    [] SPECIAL RETENTION ____/____/____
                                                                DATE

   ATTACHED IS YOUR JOB TYPED IN ACCORDANCE WITH THE ABOVE INSTRUCTIONS. PLEASE RETAIN THIS
   PART OF THE JOB REQUEST AND ATTACH IT TO THE WORK IF REVISION OR CORRECTION IS NECESSARY


SECTION II
ASSIGNED TO:     | INPUT: DEPT. _____   | CATEGORY:
                 | [] MACHINE DICTATION     | [] CORRESPONDENCE   [] PRE-RECORDED
                 |    TAPE NO. _____       |
GENERATION:      | [] LONGHAND              | [] TEXT             [] OTHER:
[] ORIGINAL      | [] HARD COPY             | [] FORMS            _____
[] REVISION      | [] EDITED COPY           | [] STATISTICAL      _____
-----------------------------------------------------------------------------------
        PRODUCTION DATA    LINE COUNT _____    PAGE COUNT _____
          TYPING                          ERRORS
MEDIA NO. | MACHINE NO. | FIRST PROOF | SECOND PROOF | THIRD PROOF

QUALITY CONTROL  _____|_____   _____|_____   _____|_____
-----------------------------------------------------------------------------------
REMARKS:


PRODUCTION TIME
   HARD COPY          DATE/TIME       MACHINE DICTATION       DATE/TIME
JOB ARRIVED         _____|_____      JOB ARRIVED           _____|_____
PROOFING COMPLETED  _____|_____      PROOFING COMPLETED    _____|_____
JOB DELIVERED       _____|_____      JOB DELIVERED         _____|_____
TURN-AROUND TIME    _____|_____      TURN-AROUND TIME      _____|_____


COPY 1 ORIGINATOR'S COPY    COPY 2 SUPERVISOR'S COPY    COPY 3 PRODUCTION COPY
```

Figure 9.27 Job request form.

10.   The supervisor files the remaining copy of the form and logs the job out of the control log.

Work Measurement Procedures. The work that employees do is measured to determine how well people's needs for processed information are being met. The process of measuring work is nalled **work measurement.** Work measurement is an important aid in providing management with information for making

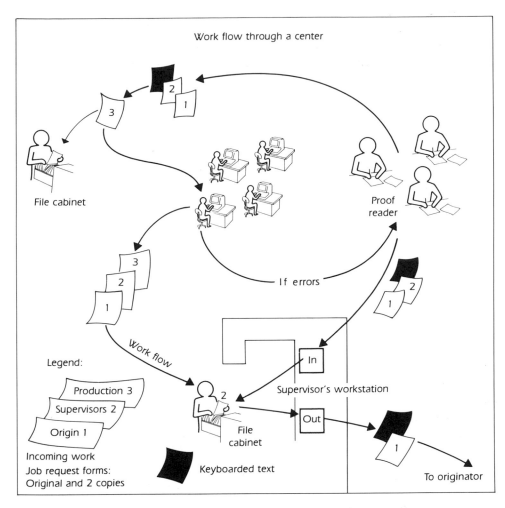

Figure 9.28 Control procedures: workflow of document through a center.

future decisions regarding equipment and staff increases and for planning budgets. It can also justify the addition of staff and equipment. For example, the information from work measurement could show that the organization was saving a certain dollar amount by using word processing. Managers could then argue that the addition of three or four more pieces of equipment could increase cost savings.

The information derived from work measurement helps managers make decisions about their present operations. For example, it can tell them if their operation is running efficiently. If the information from work measurement shows a lack of efficiency, managers can decide how to remedy the situation. Low production, for example, might indicate that originators are unhappy with the quality of the work produced in a center. Steps such as providing training seminars or adding proofreaders might then be taken to improve the quality of work. The information can also be used to bill individual departments for the use of the center services. Charging departments for work done by service departments such as word, data, or information processing is called **chargeback.**

Before establishing work measurement procedures, standards have to be set up. A standard is something against which work can be measured. For

Helps managers make decisions

Standards must be established

example, a center might establish a standard of 400 lines a day per operator. Secretaries are then encouraged to meet that standard daily. Right now, there are no universally accepted work measurement standards in word processing or some of the other information processing technologies.

To establish standards, the following factors are considered:

1. How much volume is required? What unit of measurement will be used when determining the volume? Will volume be determined by characters, lines, pages, or documents produced?

2. In what amount of time can originators expect to receive their finished work after they submit it (turnaround time)?

3. What are the projected costs of producing a unit of work such as a page or a document?

Once these goals are established, they are reviewed periodically to see that they are realistic. For example, if it is decided that a secretary should produce 2,000 lines of copy a day, but after a year the average secretary was only able to produce 400 lines a day, the standard should be revised.

Some procedures are informal

Procedures for work measurement differ from organization to organization. In some organizations, work measurement is done very informally; the secretaries may just jot down the number of pages they type in a day. In other organizations, a word processing supervisor might count the number of lines produced. From this data, production can be figured using a chart such as the one in Figure 9.29. Some organizations have the secretary keep a daily log in which the originator's name, a description of the overall work, and a breakdown of the pages according to the nature of the work are recorded (Figure 9.30). For example, the log might say "John Jones, Statistical Report, keyboarded 23 pages, revised 6 pages." The secretary would then get a certain amount of credit for keyboarding the 23 pages and another amount for revising the 6 pages. When credit is based on different amounts for different types of work, the work is said to be weighted. One organization gives a secretary 15% credit for playing out a prerecorded letter because the job requires little skill. However, it gives the secretary 50% credit for doing revisions and 75% credit for keyboarding material that is handwritten. A daily log showing the amount of weighted material that is done can help in producing a report that tells the total amount of work produced, the weighted amount of work produced, and the percentage of material that is revision, hard copy, and hardwritten from each department.

Contents of a Procedures Manual

User's manual

The procedures for workflow are usually outlined in what is known as a user's manual or a **procedures manual.** The term "procedures manual" is usually used when all the procedures for the users and the administrative and correspondence secretaries are contained in the same manual. The term "user's manual" applies only when the procedures that apply to the originator are included in the manual and the administrative and correspondence secretaries have their own.

A procedures manual has many benefits, including the following.

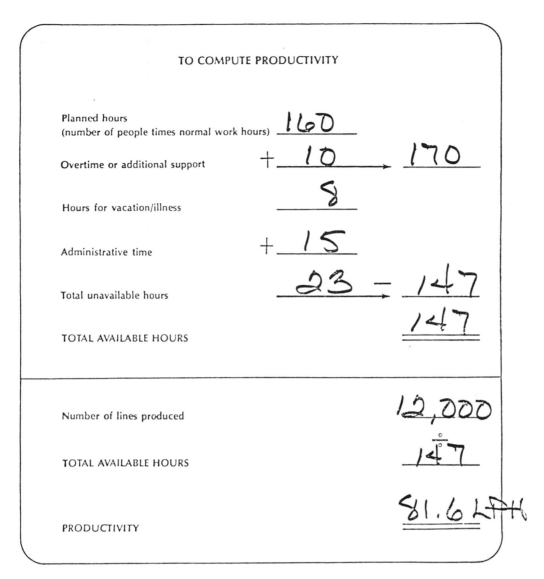

Figure 9.29 Production chart.

1. It is a reference tool for originators, administrative secretaries, and correspondence secretaries.

    Benefits

2. It is an available training tool to hand to new employees or employees who are introduced to word processing for the first time.

3. It establishes uniform procedures.

4. It contains suggestions for upgrading dictation skills.

5. It provides labor-saving and time-saving forms.

The manual consists of three parts: general information about the center, information for the originator, and information for the administrative and correspondence secretaries.

```
                          WPC LOG SHEET

                                        LINE COUNT

         AUTHOR: _____    Handwritten_____

         DATE IN: _____TIME_____   Copy Type_____

         DATE OUT: _____TIME_____   Machine
                                        Dictation_____
         DATE
         REQUESTED:_____TIME_____   Prerecorded_____

                                        Revisions_____


         START        STOP         START        STOP
         TIME         TIME         TIME         TIME

         _____    _____    _____    _____

         _____    _____    _____    _____

         _____    _____    _____    _____

         _____    _____    _____    _____


         (PLEASE PUT CHARGEABLE TIME & INITIALS FOR ITEMS LISTED BELOW)


         Selectric    _____  _____    Text Printer    _____  _____
         Proofread    _____  _____    Communication   _____  _____
         Scanned      _____  _____


         _____ FOR COMPUTER INPUT _____

         APPLICATION                    TOTAL LINES: _____

         Correspondence_____            TOTAL OPERATING TIME: _____

         Form Letters  _____            TURNAROUND TIME: _____

         Tech. Report                   REQ. VS. OUT: _____
         (paper, etc.) _____
                                        PRIORITY: _____
         Statistical   _____
                                        CHARGEABLE TIME: _____
         Legal         _____
                                        PROJECT NUMBER: _____


         _____

                              OPERATOR: _____
```

Figure 9.30 Secretarial daily log sheet.

The manual usually sets forth the goals of the system. It tells what work the center will accept and how the work is to be submitted. The responsibilities are outlined for all employees involved. The manual also presents organizational charts and shows the person to whom the people in a particular job category report.

The manual tells about the operation of the system by listing the hours of operation, showing a workflow diagram, and describing how rush, confidential, and routine work will be treated. It also describes how proofreading will be handled and how work will be picked up and delivered.

The manual also provides information specifically for the originator. The originator is given instructions for filling out forms. If dictation equipment is used, the originator is given instructions for using the dictation equipment and hints to improve dictation skills and business communication skills. For example, the manual might give a checklist of what to include and what to avoid in letters or reports. The originator is also given instructions for dictating special documents such as an original letter for several people, a tabular format, and variables for prerecorded material. The manual also contains samples of stored paragraphs, stored documents and variable sheets, lists of proofreader's marks, a standard phonetic alphabet, frequently misspelled words, frequently confused words, and samples of special forms the center uses such as routing revision cards and special request cards.

Information for originator

Preparing a Procedures Manual. Employees can participate in preparing the procedures manual. Some employees may help design the manual; others type, edit, proofread, and review it. The pride that people take in their system is often reflected in the quality of their procedures manual. An effective procedures manual is easy to read, uses simple vocabulary in a simple format, and has wide margins with lots of open space. Employees have to be able to find material in the manual easily. Therefore, a simple indexing system and index tables should be used. The material is spread out and broken into logical topics and subtopics. Good quality paper, a good binder, and quality illustrations are used to make the manual attractive.

Employees can participate

The following are three formats that are frequently used in preparing a procedures manual: **item, role,** or **action.** In an *item* format, the items are set off to the left and a few brief sentences or words explain the item. A *role* format sets off people to the left, with a few brief sentences telling what they do. The *action* format sets off the action, with a few brief sentences to explain it. (See Figures 9.31, 9.32, and 9.33.)

Formats

Figure 9.31 Item format. The items are listed on the left; an explanation is on the right.

```
            ROUTINE TREATMENT OF DOCUMENTS

Unless you specify otherwise, your letters will be typed as
follows:

     Paper:              Letterhead

     Format:             2-inch top margins;
                         1-inch bottom margins;
                         6½-inch typing line;
                         block format, single
                         spacing

     Envelopes:          white, #10

     Typing:             all final copy

     Original:           Returned as final copy

     Retention of        Documents held for ____
     Media:              days in case revisions are
                         necessary.  After ____
                         days, media will be reused
```

```
              WORKFLOW OF DOCUMENTS

Originator:           Dictates from remote
                      locations to endless
                      loop recording dictation
                      tanks

Transcriptionist:     Transcribes documents
                      on a "first-in," "first-
                      out" basis

Proofreader:          Checks for typographical
                      spelling, grammar, and
                      punctuation errors

Center                Prepares material for
Supervisor:           delivery clerk

Delivery Clerk:       Returns dictation to
                      orignators at scheduled
                      intervals from 9 a.m. to
                      4 p.m.

Originator:           Reviews, signs, gives to
                      administrative secretary for
                      enclosures and mailing
                      or
                      Marks changes and returns
                      copy to center
```

Figure 9.32 Role format. The people are listed on the left; an explanation of what they do is on the right.

```
              COPIES TO BE COLLATED

The steps to take to have your copies collated are:

Send:               All copies to the
                    administrative
                    support center

Attach:             Form No.  2176

Check off:          When you want copies
                    Color of paper?
                    Three-hole punched?
                    Three-ring binder?

File:               Carbon copy of form

Return:             Service evaluation
                    form to the center when
                    you receive your copies
```

Figure 9.33 Action format. Action words are listed on the left; an explanation is on the right.

Summary

In organizations, office automation is often implemented in varying degrees. In some organizations, word processing is introduced, while in others, information processing is implemented. The size of the organization is often a factor in determining to what extent office automation will be used.

The type of work that an organization does often affects the type of work environment that is created for information processing systems. Two categories of work are routine and nonroutine work. Routine work is best handled in a production environment. Nonroutine work is best handled in a custom environment.

Equipment is arranged in different patterns (configurations) within an organization. The process of arranging the equipment is called designing the system. Three types of common system designs are centralized, decentralized, and hybrid. The early word processing systems were centralized; however, like other of the information processing technologies, word processing is now often decentralized.

Standard procedures are necessary for the efficient operation of the new system. Procedures are made available to employees in procedures manuals.

Key Terms

Routine work	Standards
Nonroutine work	User's manual
Production environment	Procedures manual
Custom environment	Turnaround time
Centralized system	Distributed system
Decentralized system	Archive storage
Hybrid system	Chargeback
Mini-center	Satellites
Work group	Administrative support
Work measurement	

Study Guide

This study guide provides you with feedback to find out how well you are doing. Use a separate sheet of paper to record your answers. When you have finished check your responses with the answers at the back of the book.

Matching: Choose the answer that best defines the word in the left column.

1. Production environment
   a. Environment that best handles nonroutine work.

2. Custom environment
   b. Environment that best handles routine work.

3. Chargeback
   c. The process of determining the amount of work employees do.

4. Turnaround time
   d. Charging departments for work done by service departments.

5. Work measurement
   e. The amount of time it takes for a document to be returned to the originator after it is submitted for keyboarding.

6. Archival storage
   f. Keeping information stored in permanent files.

Multiple choice: Select the letter or letters that best answer each question.

7. Which of the answers is **not** true of early word processing installations?
   a. Early installations emphasized the centralized approach to word processing.
   b. Early installations emphasized reducing clerical costs.
   c. Early installations emphasized the need to make managers more efficient.
   d. None of the above.

8. Which of the following is **not** true of decentralized systems?
   a. They often fit the needs of some organizations better than centralized systems.
   b. They are usually located near the secretaries they service.
   c. They allow originators and secretaries to interact.
   d. None of the above.

9. Which is a good reason for decentralizing equipment?
   a. Equipment costs will be lower.
   b. Originators like to have control over their work.
   c. Routine work can be handled better.
   d. None of the above.

10. A hybrid system
    a. Is a type of administrative support system.
    b. Is a combination centralized and decentralized system.
    c. Was the first type of system design used for word processing.
    d. None of the above.

11. A work group
    a. Provides both centralized administrative and correspondence support.
    b. Provides decentralized administrative and correspondence support.
    c. Consists only of administrative secretaries.
    d. Consists only of correspondence secretaries.

12. Work measurement
    a. Determines how well people's needs for processed information are being met.
    b. Is an aid in providing management with information for making future decisions regarding equipment and staff increases.
    c. Can justify the addition of staff and equipment.
    d. All of the above.

Completion: Write the correct answer(s) on a separate sheet of paper.

13. Two categories of work within an organization are _____ and _____ .

14. Three types of system designs commonly used in word/information processing are _____ , _____ , and _____ .

15. When word or data processing equipment is tied into a central computer, the systems are often referred to as _____ .

16. Three formats used in preparing a procedures manual are _____ , _____ , and _____ .

True/False: Write + for True, 0 for False for each question.

17. Before establishing work measurement, standards need to be set up.

18. Work measurement standards need to be realistic.

19. A custom environment is the best environment for handling highly technical work.

20. A system that has a large center and several mini-centers is called a hybrid system.

21. Decentralized systems are often criticized because the turnaround time of documents is usually greater than for centralized systems.

22. Centralized word processing became possible when equipment costs decreased.

23. Work groups are composed of just administrative secretaries.

24. Standard filing procedures are used in all word processing centers.

25. A job request form is a request secretaries fill out when they request a particular type of work.

26. Most organizations have both routine and nonroutine work.

Questions on Concepts

1. Describe a custom and a production environment and the category of work done in each.
2. Describe three system designs.
3. Trace the movement from centralization toward decentralization in word processing.
4. Describe several models of administrative support systems.
5. Discuss why an area that processes information needs standard procedures.
6. List four methods of filing and indexing in centers.
7. List several benefits of a procedures manual.

Case and Activities

John Stewart is a candidate for City Council in the June election. In January, he decided to send a personalized campaign letter to each of the 40,000 voters in his district. To do this, he obtained a list of the names and addresses of the voters in his district through the County Registrar of Voters and rented two word processing typewriters on a rental/purchase contract for a period of six months.

He assigned Sarah, who answered the telephones in his office, to operate the typewriters to produce the letters. As far as he knew, her only duty was answering the telephone, so he assumed she would be able to insert the addresses, play out the letter, type the addresses on the envelopes, and stuff them. The salesperson told him that if his secretary worked eight hours a day, using both machines she would be able to produce approximately 400 letters per day and would, therefore, be able to easily send out all of his letters prior to election day. In actuality, she produced approximately 100 letters a day because she did other chores for people in the office and took numerous coffee breaks.

In May, one of the machines broke. Sarah called the repair person, who took the machine into the shop to be fixed. She did not inform Mr. Stewart that the machine was out for service. During this time, her output decreased to about 50 letters a day.

The day before the election, Sarah informed Mr. Stewart that she had sent only 9,000 letters since January. When he asked her why she was 31,000 letters short of the goal he had set, she said it was because one of the machines was broken.

1. How could Mr. Stewart have implemented word processing more successfully?

2. Mr. Stewart needed 40,000 letters. Did he have a realistic goal?
3. How could work measurement procedures have benefited Mr. Stewart?
4. Discuss the kind of work Sarah did for Mr. Stewart and the kind of work environment that is best for producing this type of work. Did Mr. Stewart provide the proper kind of work environment?

Activities

1. Visit a word or information processing center and inquire about what method of work measurement they use.
2. Read an article and write a two-page report on procedures used in word or information processing centers.
3. Write the following procedure using a format that will make it easier to read. Use one of the three formats discussed in this chapter.

An information processing center accepts a number of different types of work. Revision work that the center accepts are documents of five or more pages of material that requires revision. Multiple letters are identical letters with or without variable information sent to different addresses. All dictation work is work that will be dictated into the central recording system or dictated on portable equipment provided by the center. Prerecorded material includes standard letters, memoranda, paragraphs, or sections, with or without variable information.

CHAPTER 10

Staffing the Area

The objectives of this chapter are to:

1. Describe three job positions in word processing.

2. Describe the criteria used for determining job titles and descriptions.

3. Contrast the traditional office role of the generalist with that of the specialist in a word processing center.

4. Compare the responsibilities or tasks of a correspondence position with the tasks of an administrative position.

5. Compare the special qualities required for a correspondence position with those needed for an administrative position.

6. Describe the duties of a manager.

7. Describe the special qualities needed for the job of manager in a word or information processing center.

8. Explain why some people question the ability of secretaries to move from secretarial to managerial positions.

9. Explain what a lateral career path is and give an example.

10. Explain what is meant by vertical career paths.

11. Describe the kinds of equipment that help special employment groups such as people with visual or auditory impairments.

12. Describe several types of training used to prepare people for jobs in information processing.

13. Describe several sources of employment information.

The new technologies have created a variety of new career opportunities for the office worker and for special employment groups such as paraplegics, quadriplegics, and people with auditory or visual impairments. Moreover, the role of the traditional office worker has also changed. Prospective employees need to know the new job titles and understand new job descriptions. Employers need to know where to go to find employees with the skills the new jobs require.

An important consideration when staffing information processing technologies is matching the right employee to the right job. Often employees do not have the skills for the new environment and have to be trained. An ongoing training program, moreover, is essential to the success of information processing.

The role of the office worker has changed because of the new technologies and the new work environments in offices; employees must have different skills and attitudes from those possessed by employees in the traditional office. Therefore, job titles and descriptions have also changed. For example, the term "secretary" once meant someone who was a generalist. A **generalist** is a person whose job description contains several different types of duties. A job description for secretary's duties in a traditional office might include the following: taking dictation, running errands, typing, proofreading, filing, greeting clients, scheduling appointments, preparing itineraries, and reproducing materials.

Generalist to specialist

In some work environments today, secretaries often are specialists, not generalists. A **specialist** is a person whose job description contains one type of duty. For example, employees perform either administrative (nontyping) or correspondence (typing) activities. In these environments, the secretaries are often supervised by someone in a management role.

The transition of the secretarial role from generalist to specialist is a drastic change that poses many questions for the secretaries involved in the transition. Some of their typical concerns are:

Does specialization mean that secretaries sit at a typewriter and type?

No. Specialization means that employees work in one of the following categories: administrative (nontyping), correspondence (typing), or management (directing people).

Does specialization cause boredom for secretaries?

No. On the contrary, secretaries are usually stimulated by specializing because the job now may bring them into contact with several originators instead of just one exclusively. Secretaries may have similar work tasks; they may have a variety of work that comes from many different departments.

Why would secretaries choose to specialize and move away from the comfortable, traditional one-to-one working relationship?

They can select the career path that best suits their personality and preferences. For example, some people enjoy typing; others do not.

Secretaries can move upward based on merit (competence and achievement), rather than being brought along with a boss who was just promoted. Previously the secretary's career path was tied to the career path of the boss.

People have discovered that specialization is the basis for achievement of individual productivity and personal job satisfaction.

Why do some traditional secretaries resist the change from generalist to specialist?

They fear working on automated equipment; they don't like to type and are afraid of being "found out" (they don't realize that there are typing as well as nontyping roles in a word processing center); or they may be afraid of losing the personal communication between boss and secretary.

What are the greatest benefits to the organization derived from specialization in a word processing center?

Specialization provides efficiency, productivity, cost reduction, and better utilization of human resources.

Are jobs in centers always specialized?

*Yes. Jobs in most centers are specialized. Each center must organize its staff to best fit the needs of the organization. Some centers adhere closely to nontyping versus typing-related tasks. Others have a versatile approach where all secretaries in the center learn all the jobs and periodically rotate to different positions. This is referred to as "***cross-training***" —the secretarial jobs are specialized, but the secretaries are not.*

Does the separation of administrative and correspondence functions in an organization better utilize human talent?

Yes. Traditionally, many secretaries did not stay in secretarial positions because they had low status, low pay, and dead-end jobs that were often associated with positions that required typing skills. The secretary would move into a nontyping job for more salary and status and the organization would thus lose this person's good typing skill. Now there is a potential new area for secretarial advancement. The administrative function needs secretaries with language skills and general secretarial abilities, and the correspondence function needs secretaries with keyboarding, formatting, and language skills.

Are the traditional skills of filing, shorthand, and use of office machines required for employment in word processing?

To a certain extent. In the correspondence function, the traditional secretarial skills such as filing, computation, and shorthand are usually considered important but are not required. An administrative secretary, however, may take dictation and type one-time correspondence so the traditional secretarial skill of shorthand is usually considered important and may be required as a job prerequisite.

Numerous job titles and descriptions

Several job titles can arise from an attempt at labeling the administrative, correspondence, and management functions (Figure 10.1). As yet, however, no standard job titles exist. For example, a survey was done by Deutsch, Shea and Evans, Inc., a New York human resources consulting firm, with the cooperation of the IWPA (International Word Processing Association). The consulting firm asked, "What job title is used for people who operate word processing equipment?" A few titles such as "word processing operator" and "word processing secretary" were presented for checkoff and space was left to indicate other titles. A total of 91 different titles appeared in answer to this question. Consequently, job applicants who desire to apply for positions in word processing and other information processing areas are often confused. Job applicants should understand that the positions fall into three categories: administrative, correspondence, and management. To function in these positions, job applicants must possess certain skills and qualities. Matching the right person to the right job is critical because the person must be suited to the job function. The following paragraphs describe administrative, correspondence, and management positions and the skills and qualities needed for them.

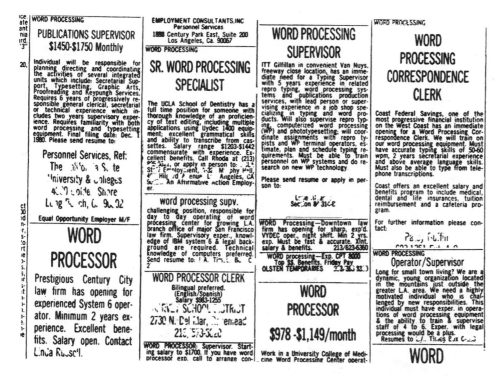

Figure 10.1 Job titles used in advertising for word/information processing positions.

Administrative Positions

Employees in administrative positions generally act as assistants to executives and handle nontyping activities such as research, compiling and writing reports and speeches, attending meetings in place of the executive, handling and originating dictation and correspondence. These people are often referred to as administrative secretaries. However, their job titles and descriptions may be more specific as they get involved in areas such as records processing or micrographics.

Employees in administrative positions (Figures 10.2 through 10.5) need skills in oral and written communications, human relations, supervision, organization, and equipment operation.

Oral and written communication skills. In an administrative position, employees must be able to proofread, spell, compose original correspondence, answer phones, and meet and talk with people. Sometimes administrative employees must edit and revise rough draft copy prepared by originators. Therefore, administrative employees need oral and written communication skills.

Human relation skills. Employees in administrative positions need to interact with a number of different people in various job levels and positions. For example, administrative secretaries might have to work closely with managers from several departments, staff from the correspondence center, and supervisors from both administrative and correspondence centers.

Figure 10.2 An administrative assistant filing and retrieving information on the Micrapoint System from 3M Company's Micrographic Products Division. *(Courtesy of 3M Company.)*

Equipment operation skills. Employees in administrative positions may do some light typing. Some positions, therefore, may require some typing ability. Shorthand may also be a requirement in some organizations. Employees in these positions often are required to compose original correspondence using dictation equipment. Therefore, dictation skills are necessary. In some organizations, administrative employees are also required to know how to use a variety of equipment to perform calculations. In organizations where the technologies of word and data processing are merging, administrative employees must know how to operate some data processing equipment. In organizations where micrographics and records processing are becoming computerized, the administrative employees may have to become familiar with equipment designed for that purpose (Figure 10.2). Administrative employees may also be responsible for handling such things as sending documents by facsimile or other communications equipment (Figure 10.3).

Special qualities. Employers look for people to fill administrative positions who are self-motivated, like working with people, and enjoy detail work. Administra-

Figure 10.3 An administrative secretary sending information using the QWIP Two facsimile equipment. *(Courtesy of QWIP Systems, a Division of Exxon Enterprises Incorporated.)*

Figure 10.4 An administrative secretary performing calculations. *(Courtesy of Graphic Sciences, Incorporated.)*

Changing Roles of Office Workers

Figure 10.5 An administrative secretary photocopying. *(Courtesy of Eastman Kodak Company.)*

tive employees must be able to establish self-imposed deadlines and adhere to them with little supervision, and perform a variety of tasks. Employers often desire people in these positions to have college degrees or to be willing to obtain more formal education since these employees often move into management positions.

Supervisory skills. An administrative employee often might have to supervise administrative or correspondence staff members. For example, several levels of administrative positions might exist in a center. The person in the top-level administrative position might be called the lead administrative assistant and might be responsible for supervising administrative secretaries in the entry level positions. In some organizations, the lead administrative assistants are responsible for supervising temporary or part-time administrative or correspondence employees brought in to help finish special projects.

Organizational skills. In administrative positions, employees need organizational

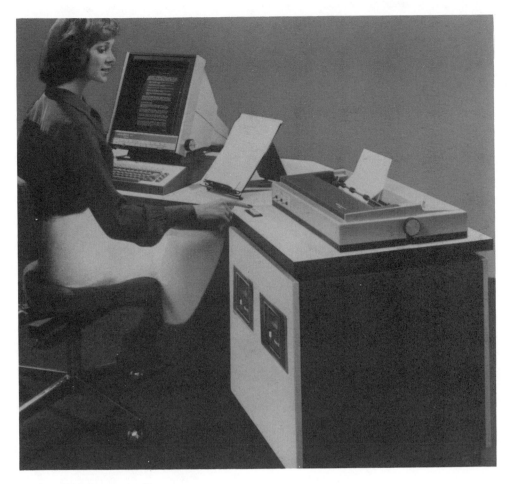

Figure 10.6 A correspondence secretary needs to index material properly on disks. *(Courtesy of Lexitron Corporation.)*

skills because they often have to arrange meetings, set up calendars, sort the mail, determine what mail can be answered without the manager's assistance, and determine work load priorities. They often have to do extensive research and, after gathering the material, organize it in a logical manner.

Correspondence Positions

Employees in correspondence positions (Figures 10.6 through 10.9) need skills in oral and written communications, human relations, organization, and equipment operation.

Oral and written communication skills. Employees in correspondence positions need oral and written communication skills because they have to communicate with people on several different job levels. For example, employees in correspondence positions often have to discuss work with originators and center supervisors. They may have ideas for doing work more efficiently and must be able to express these ideas to their supervisor. Often correspondence employees, because they know the equipment, are asked to accompany managers

Figure 10.7 A correspondence secretary often needs a knowledge of data processing as well as word processing. *(Courtesy of National Cash Register Corporation.)*

to trade shows, conventions, and equipment demonstrations, and to participate in equipment selection. Consequently, they have to be able to express their ideas well.

Human relation skills. Employees in correspondence positions need to work well with people because the work they do often requires a team work effort. They must be able to get along well with their supervisors, coworkers, and originators who use the center.

Organizational skills. An important part of correspondence work is being able to properly log and file storage media and locate recorded material. While keyboarding on magnetic disks, employees in correspondence positions need to index or identify the material on the disk properly to be able to locate documents quickly when they are needed (Figure 10.6). Employees in correspondence positions, therefore, need organizational skills. Correspondence employees are also often called upon to help develop new filing and indexing methods for media. For correspondence employees to work efficiently, their workstations also must be well-organized (Figure 10.9).

Equipment skills. Correspondence employees need excellent typing skills. They also need to know how to operate a variety of different automated typing equipment and transcription equipment. In organizations that are integrating

Figure 10.8 A correspondence secretary needs excellent typing skills. *(Courtesy of WP/AS Concepts Company.)*

Figure 10.9 Correspondence secretaries need organized workstations. *(Courtesy of Steelcase, Incorporated.)*

Changing Roles of Office Workers

some of the new technologies, correspondence employees may need to know such things as how to insert OCR or phototypesetting codes as they keyboard, operate phototypesetting equipment or equipment with communications options, or enter data as well as text into terminals. Correspondence employees may also be required to have some knowledge of data processing as well as word processing concepts (Figure 10.7).

Special qualities. Employers look for people who are self-motivated and machine- and production-oriented to fill correspondence positions. The term "production-oriented" means that people must enjoy doing large volumes of work. People in correspondence positions must also enjoy new challenges and be willing to try new ideas and train on advanced equipment. They must be able to work amid distractions and enjoy working under the pressure of meeting deadlines. Moreover, they must be willing to support the teamwork concept and work for the good of the department. Employers often look for correspondence employees who have some understanding of word and data processing concepts.

Management Positions

Employees in management positions such as supervisors or managers of administrative support or correspondence support services (Figures 10.10 and 10.11) are responsible for managing people. They need skills in oral and written communications, human relations, supervision and decision making, organization, coordination, and equipment operation.

Oral and written communication skills. Employees in managerial positions need oral and written communications skills because they often write procedures manuals; prepare reports on production, equipment, operational costs, and problem areas; give presentations and demonstrations; conduct meetings; and communicate with people of various educational backgrounds. They also provide orientation sessions for originators and new operators and in-service training programs. They also often conduct tours of their centers and relate their successes to the public.

Human relations skills. Employees in managerial positions need human relations skills because they have to interact with originators and the center staff. They serve as a liaison between management and administrative and correspondence support. They are often called upon to use tact in dealing with unreasonable demands made by originators and to maintain a calm atmosphere in the center during rush periods. Keeping their staff members and originators happy often requires that they know how to deal with individual personalities. They also have to encourage originators to use the center and handle the public who comes to visit the center.

Supervision and decision-making skills. Managers need supervision and decision-making skills because they have to supervise a number of people, establish standards of work performance and measure production, hire and fire

Figure 10.10 A manager of administrative support services talking with administrative secretary who is using the Alden 400 Signa Fax System. *(Courtesy of Alden Electronic and Impulse Recording Equipment Company, Incorporated.)*

Figure 10.11 A supervisor of correspondence support services talking with a records processing manager. *(Courtesy of Wang Laboratories, Incorporated.)*

people, plan and control the budget, establish chargeback systems, and make salary and purchasing decisions. They must also work with management to set priorities, develop efficient workflow procedures, and control turnaround time.

Coordination skills. Managers act as coordinators. They coordinate the work of their center with several other departments. For example, if they are correspondence supervisors, they might have to coordinate word processing activities with those of the reprographics department. They might also have to act as coordinators between the center and the depertments from which work comes. Moreover, they act as coordinators within the center to foster the teamwork spirit among employees.

Equipment skills. Employees in managerial positions do not necessarily need to operate the equipment in their centers, but they need some knowledge of the equipment. They may, however, have to know how to operate such equipment as supervisory control monitors that control the flow of dictation into the centers (Figure 10.12), replenish media in automatic media changers located in the center, and use various types of calculating equipment.

Special qualities. Employers look for people to fill management positions who are flexible, self-motivated, decisive, broad-minded and objective. People in managerial positions must be willing to delegate responsibility and have an outgoing personality. They need to conceptualize how the center can handle new applications from other departments and visualize how different types of equipment might handle the existing and future workload. In addition to understanding the organization, its products, services, philosophy, and personnel policies, they must have an enthusiasm for word processing and the new technologies, an understanding of the workload, the ability to evaluate projects, anticipate problems, cope with shifts in the workload, and work under pressure. They also need to be fair in dealing with their subordinates, able to foster the teamwork spirit, and sensitive to the needs and problems of originators and subordinates.

Providing Career Paths

Employees will be more motivated if those who want to advance can see their jobs as stepping stones to advancement within the organization. Such stepping stones form what is referred to as a career path. An atmosphere in which secretaries can grow in their careers is created by rewriting job descriptions to offer growth within the organization.

How should career paths be designed?

Career paths should be made up of jobs which require few skills to jobs which require a great deal of skill. The jobs should be placed on the career path according to the value of the job to the organization. For example, jobs such as copying, some filing, mail handling, or answering phones that require one level of skill may be assigned to a lower paid employee on the bottom of a career path. Jobs that contain typing require a special skill and should have a higher value. These jobs should be given to more experienced employees at higher levels along a career path. Keeping track of budgets, supervising work loads,

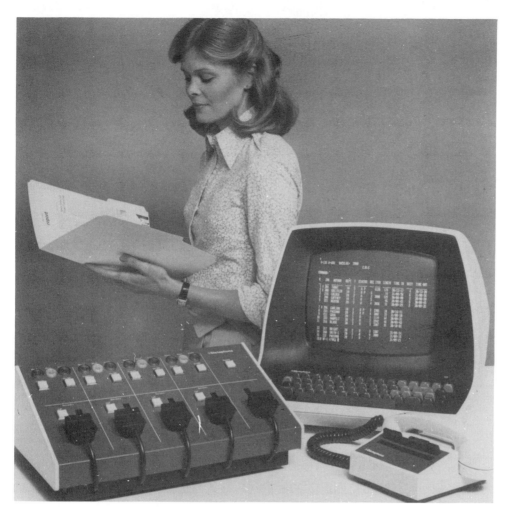

Figure 10.12 A supervisor often has to know how to operate supervisory control monitors that control the flow of dictation into centers. *(Courtesy of Dictaphone Corporation.)*

handling some tasks delegated by management have higher value because they require a greater level of responsibility. These jobs appear at the top of a career path.

Career Paths in Word Processing

Within an organization, two types of career paths are possible: lateral (horizontal) or vertical career paths. **Lateral career paths** are paths in a horizontal position. Lateral career paths allow employees who either do not have managerial qualifications or who do not wish to work in managerial positions to move to jobs that are on the same level as the position they hold.

An example of a lateral career path within a medical office might be allowing a correspondence secretary who handles medical records related only to laboratory work to transfer to another correspondence secretarial position that

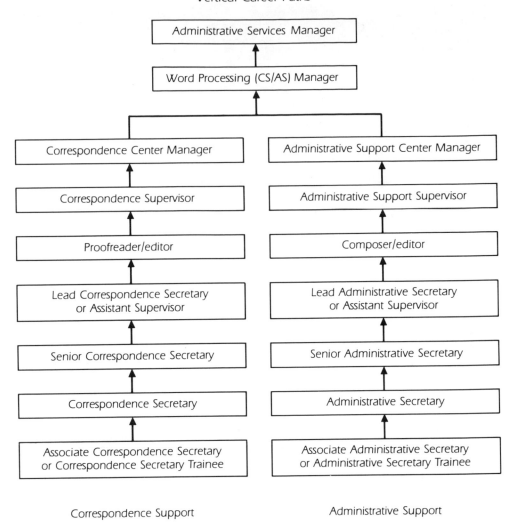

Figure 10.13 Vertical and lateral career paths.

handles all other medical reports, correspondence, and claims. The lateral career path will broaden the secretary's background in the medical field and provide new challenges for that secretary.

Another type of lateral career path may be created for the correspondence secretary who wants to get into an equal level administrative position or for an administrative secretary who wants to learn the word processing or information processing equipment and move into an equal level correspondence position.

Vertical career paths are career paths that lead upward to managerial positions. A vertical career path within an organization may be similar to the one shown in Figure 10.13, where the administrative and correspondence managerial functions are broken down into several different positions. The titles, of course, vary from organization to organization. The extent to which an organization might choose to break down these functions into separate positions would, of course, depend upon several different factors including the size of the organization. For example, some organizations may choose to have separate proofreader/editors, others feel that a proofreading job is monotonous and people become inefficient when they proofread for several hours.

Opportunities can be made to allow people to advance vertically within these three job functions or beyond these individual categories.

For example, one organization has four separate levels of administrative secretaries: associate administrative secretary, administrative secretary, senior administrative secretary, and administrative support supervisor. The associate administrative secretary does routine, repetitive, simple office work. The administrative secretary does varied and moderately complex assignments. The administrative secretary is expected to work independently and follow proper procedures. The senior administrative secretary handles more complex tasks than the administrative secretary. The senior administrative secretary works independently and the tasks require a degree of decision-making ability concerning the content and substance of documents. The administrative support supervisor has more significant responsibilities and works independently. The work requires analytical ability and the administrative support supervisor is also held responsible for error.

Provide job levels

Similar levels can also be set up for the correspondence secretaries. For example, repetitive applications that are easy to learn might be assigned to a level 1 correspondence secretary; while assignments that require decision making, complex formatting, highly technical vocabulary, and interaction with originators can be assigned to higher level correspondence secretaries.

As shown in Figure 10.13, people in all three categories can be given an opportunity to advance beyond their job category into management positions. For example, administrative secretaries can become involved in the operation of a department and experience enough of the types of activities that a manager performs to prepare them for future supervisory positions of administrative functions. An administrative position requires certain skills and duties. Applying these skills provides valuable training for supervisory positions. Employees, moreover, can be promoted into these positions from within the organization.

Opportunities to advance into management positions

Employees in correspondence positions, too, can advance toward management positions. For example, the correspondence secretary who develops the skills for that position, can become the supervisor of a word processing center or work group.

Managers are in a position to advance to other positions within the organization. They maintain direct ongoing contact with many originators throughout the organization. Since they deal with information, they are in a good position to learn more about their organization, their staff, their customers, and their competitors. They are systems-oriented, yet they are also people-oriented. They are in a unique position. The experience they gain should put them in a position to assume jobs of greater scope. Managers meet with other managers throughout the organization. Word processing supervisors, for example, meet with heads of administrative services departments such as the microfilm, mail handling, reprographics departments. In this way they are able to increase their knowledge of the organization and gain experience that will prepare them for other managerial positions within the organization.

Advancement beyond present managerial positions

Secretarial experience an asset

In the organizations where the new technologies are used, people are often promoted quickly from administrative or correspondence positions to an operative level of management. Secretaries are often chosen for management positions because they have an understanding of the organization and company policy, have good communication skills, and know how to plan and organize. Managers who have worked as secretaries often feel that their past secretarial experience helps them in their present positions. For example, Barbara Rochette, Word Processing Manager of Kwasha Lipton, a consulting actuarial and employee benefit service organization, in Englewood Cliffs, New Jersey says:

> *I have been Manager of Word Processing for 3 years and find it invaluable having come up in the ranks. I feel I can help with the operators' problems and understand them better, having been there myself. I think it's also extremely important for me to have a basic knowledge of any equipment used in the center so I know its capabilities as well as its liabilities. When I ask an operator to do something and give instructions as to when I need it, I know it's not an unreasonable request because I'm aware of what the operator can do with the particular piece of equipment. If I didn't know the equipment, I might easily request something almost impossible as many of our authors do. It's not the author's job to know what the center is capable of handling, but it certainly is mine.*
>
> *Knowing the equipment is helpful when there is an overload of work or when an operator is on vacation or out ill. There have been many occasions when I helped with the typing crunch, and I found that the operators really appreciated the help. They also thought it was great that I would take the time to help get the typing work out. I think it shows them that it really is a team effort working in a center. It helps to achieve the feeling of oneness that is necessary in any group effort.[1]*

Prepare for the Change

Moving up from secretary to manager

Many people question the ability of secretaries to move from secretarial positions to managerial positions (Figure 10.13). The reason that they give is that the two roles are in conflict. The traditional secretarial role is supportive (assisting others). The managerial role is to direct (motivating, leading, and evaluating others).

The person who wants to make this transition into management must be prepared. Some ways of preparing for a managerial position include the following.

1. Take classes on the job or at an educational institution. Classes that are helpful include accounting, statistics, human relations in business, psychology, office management, word processing management, data processing, and records management.

2. Obtain a position in the word processing center. This position may be

[1] Barbara Rochette to Marly Bergerud, September 5, 1979.

lead correspondence secretary, word processing coordinator, or center supervisor. These positions are sometimes referred to as "staff" positions.

3. Request special counseling, extra assignments, or project work from management that will assist in preparing you for the move into management.

4. Finally, be aware of the need for acceptance of yourself as a manager, approval by other managers as an equal, and approval by the people you are supervising.

Job Titles and Descriptions

Although job titles and descriptions vary from organization to organization, they provide an understanding of the scope of opportunities in word processing and related technologies.

International Word Processing Association Job Descriptions

The International Word Processing Association (IWPA) provides the job description and job titles shown in Figure 10.14 as guidelines for administrative, correspondence, and management job functions. These job duties and descriptions, however, cannot be expected to be the same for all organizations. In some organizations, for example, only word processing exists; in others, some of the new technologies have been integrated with word processing, creating additional jobs with varying job titles and descriptions.

Director of Information Support Systems (salaried). May be vice president or assistant to the vice president in some organizations. Has total responsibility for all aspects of an organization's office system, including word processing, administrative support, and other information processing. Insures the collaboration of all support functions. Reports to a chief executive officer.

Administrative Support Manager (salaried). Has full responsibilities for developing, maintaining, and evaluating all services structures under administrative support within an organization, such as filing, telephone, mail, and paraprofessional support. Monitors the success of the administrative support group and is familiar with the company's goals and objectives. Works closely with the word processing manager to insure cooperation of the two functions. May manage other major administrative duties such as records and retention, microfilm, print shop, purchasing, etc. Reports to director of information support systems in large organizations.

Staff Analyst (salaried). Responsible for consulting and assisting word processing and administrative support supervisors and managers. Conducts studies, reviews operations, and determines and recommends appropriate staffing, procedures, and equipment. Reports to director of information support systems or word processing manager or administrative support manager.

Director of Information Support Systems

Administrative Support Services	Correspondence Support Services
Administrative Support Manager	Word Processing Manager
Staff Analyst	Word Processing Supervisor
Administrative Support Supervisor	Proofreader
Senior Administrative Secretary	Word Processing Trainer
Administrative Secretary	Phototypesetting Specialist
	Word Processing Specialist II/
	Assistant Supervisor
	Word Processing Specialist I
	Word Processing Operator
	Word Processing Trainee

Figure 10.14 Job titles provided by the International Word Processing Association.
From "Job Titles and Descriptions," *Sixth Salary Survey Results, 1980* (Willow Grove, Penn.: International Word Processing Association, 1980), pp. 5–6, by permission.

Administrative Support Supervisor. May have the responsibilities of the senior administrative secretarial position in addition to scheduling and administering work flow to a team of administrative secretaries. Responsible for liaison with and training of users who benefit from administrative support. Evaluates staffing requirements, prepares management reports, recommends new methods of handling administrative secretaries. Reports to administrative support manager.

Senior Administrative Secretary. Has a record of exceptional performance. At times may act as assistant to supervisor of an administrative team, and is qualified to compose and edit documents for principals, provide research support, and perform other paraprofessional duties. Handles special projects and is fully aware of company standards and practices.

Administrative Secretary. Someone who works for a group of principals as part of a team under the direction of an administrative support supervisor or manager. Responsibilities include support functions such as filing; photocopying; maintaining calendars, records, and lists; providing special secretarial services; etc.

Word Processing Manager (salaried). Responsible for the overall operation of a word processing center, including the guidance of supervisors, personnel administration, staff requirements, user liaison and evaluation, design and implementation of future word processing systems. Also responsible for budgets, overall production reports, and coordination of services with administrative support. May also manage the operation of photocopying, printing, mailing, or graphics services. In larger organizations, the word processing manager reports to the director of secretarial support systems.

Word Processing Supervisor. With all the competencies of a word processing specialist II, a supervisor is responsible for the operation of a center (or section within a large center). Schedules and coordinates work flow and assists word processing personnel in document production and in establishing and maintaining quality standards. Also analyzes production data and procedures, identifies potential improvements and may be partially responsible for budgets and equipment recommendations. Reports to word processing manager.

Proofreader. Proofreads typed copy for text content, spelling, punctuation, grammar and typographical errors. May be responsible for setting grammar and format standards and guidance and/or training of secretaries and principals.

Word Processing Trainer. Someone with a minimum of 24 months' experience operating word processing systems who spends the majority of time training new operators. May also be responsible for instructing users in dictation methods and other procedures to insure maximum utilization of a word processing center. Should make recommendations to management with regards to new equipment purchases from the standpoint of ease of use.

Phototypesetting Specialist. A word processing operator who enters special codes while keyboarding and revising text that is to be the output on a photo-composition system. Has knowledge of points, picas, typefaces, leading, and other aspects of typesetting and printing.

Word Processing Specialist II/Assistant Supervisor. A person at this level exercises all of the competencies of word processing specialist I and may act as assistant supervisor. A word processing specialist II is able to operate all the information processing functions within the installation. Responsibilities include coordinating and assigning work, analyzing requirements for specific projects, communicating with users, compiling production statistics, and recommending changes in center procedures. May also assist in training personnel.

Word Processing Specialist I. A word processing operator with a minimum of 18 months' experience who can format, produce, and revise complicated documents such as lengthy technical and statistical reports from complex source information, including the retrieval of text and data from electronic files. Exercises independent action when interpreting instructions to produce a quality document, understands proofreader marks, and assumes full responsibility for document accuracy and completeness. Has a thorough knowledge of center procedures and maintenance of records. May operate word processing equipment in the telecommunications mode.

Word Processing Operator. The next level up from word processing trainee for those having 6 to 24 months' word processing experience. In addition to having all the qualifications and functions of word processing trainee, a word processing operator handles special documents, meets established quality standards, uses all of a machine's text editing functions and is familiar with department terminology and company practices.

Word Processing Trainee. Entry level position for those having up to 12 months' word processing experience. Must have adequate typing skills, good knowledge of grammar, punctuation, spelling, and formatting; the ability to use dictionaries, handbooks, and other reference materials; and be oriented toward teamwork and the use of machines. A trainee's functions include routine transcription and manipulation of text from various types of source information (dictation, handwritten, etc.). Maintains own production records and may be required to proofread own work.

Similar Job Categories in Data Processing and Word Processing

Separate technologies

Data processing and word processing began as separate technologies (Figure 10.15). In the early stages of the data processing industry, management assumed that computers were so sophisticated that ordinary employees could not be trained to operate them efficiently. Industrial engineers, systems analysts, and highly skilled people were hired as operators of these systems.

Initially, the person handling all of the computer-related work may have been called a data processor. This person designed systems for handling information, wrote programs, and operated the equipment. Gradually, specialties developed in data processing, with some people designing the system, others writing programs, and still others operating the equipment.

Early word processing

In the early stages of the word processing industry, a phenomenon different than that of the data processing industry occurred. Management saw the equipment as primarily a secretarial tool or a sophisticated typewriter. It was realized that word processing equipment was relatively easy to operate and employees such as typists and secretaries were encouraged to learn to use it. Word processing required no operator programming; operators used code keys located at the keyboard to manipulate the text. The codes were easy to learn and no special languages were necessary to operate the equipment. Initially, the person handling the word processing-related work may have been called a typist or a word processing secretary. Specialties developed rapidly in word processing and equipment capabilities became very sophisticated. Now some people operate word processing equipment, others design the systems, and still others manage various types of word processing systems.

Integrated technologies

Many similarities between the data and word processing industries exist. The technologies have integrated to the point that it is difficult to visually distinguish word processing from data processing equipment. Word processing equipment can have data processing capabilities, and some data processing equipment has word processing capabilities. Some careers in the two industries are also very similar. For example, the systems analyst for data processing may be involved in specifying or selecting particular pieces of data processing hardware to be used in operating a system. This person gathers data about the nature and amount of work and suggests programs to handle it. In word processing, the systems analyst is responsible for consulting and assisting correspondence and administrative support supervisors and managers. This person conducts studies, reviews operations, and determines and recommends appropriate staffing, procedures, and equipment. When word processing is implemented, the analyst periodically reviews the work the organization has and

Systems analyst

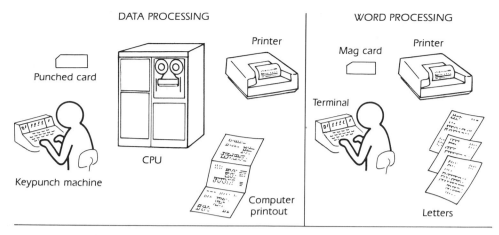

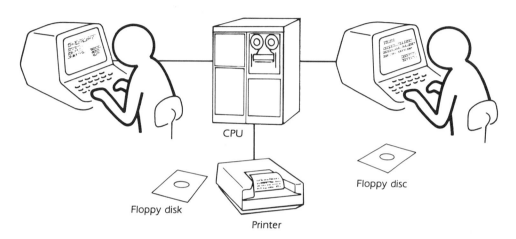

Figure 10.15 Word and data processing merge.

suggests how word processing can handle it.

Andrea Dermott, a systems analyst at Parotto Institute in Honolulu, Hawaii, is heavily committed to and involved with many aspects of the total word processing concept. Her duties involve specific application programming, writing procedural and user manuals, presenting information and training sessions, design and ongoing modification of the work measurement system, setting operator standards, providing productivity reports to senior management on the effectiveness and efficiency of the word processing operation, justifying equipment selection, and preparing and analyzing statistical reports. Communication experiments and data processing entry and retrieval systems/applications also consume a great deal of her time.

A second category of data processing jobs is the programmer whose role is in implementing a previously designed system by converting certain parts of the system into a set of instructions known as a program for the equipment.

DP/Programmer

Some specialized programmer jobs have appeared in word processing as well. A word processing programmer uses knowledge of computer science to write new programs for word processing equipment when the need arises. Two examples of the kinds of programs a programmer writes are given below.

Word processing programmer

In many organizations, work measurement is often done manually. To handle work measurement, a word processing programmer at Vandermeyden Engineering, Inc. in Duluth, Minnesota, wrote a program to afford more meaningful work measurement for each word processing operator. Although some word processing equipment can record the time or number of keystrokes or the number of lines an operator produces, this information is often meaningless for measuring the amount of effort on the part of an operator because some documents are much more complex and require much more effort than others. Heavy revisions or tabular typing, for example, require much more effort than merged letters. The work measurement program written by the programmer at Vandermeyden Engineering, Inc. allows the work to be categorized according to complexity, and each category is assigned a weighted factor. In this program, the amount of work done is multiplied by its complexity factor, and the equipment figures out how much the operator actually produced. The measurement is shown in number of pages. Each operator simply answers prompts on the screen to enter the needed data. This program can also be integrated with a chargeback system.

Another new program, also written by a programmer/operator, advances the word processing center into information management.

One law firm provides its attorneys with a dining room where attorneys can either have luncheons with clients or hold meetings. Each attorney, when using this facility, signs a slip for himself and his clients and is "charged" for their meals. Previously, the bookkeeping department manually counted these slips, wrote up daily reports for the dining room, tabulated monthly reports for each attorney, and combined all that into a monthly report for the firm. Now, these slips are sent to the word processing center. As the word processing operator accesses the program, an alphabetical list of all the attorneys in the firm appears on the screen. The operator scrolls to an attorney's name and types asterisks to signal which attorneys used the dining room that day and indicates how many clients, if any. The rest is automatic. Those names marked with an asterisk are selectively sorted out, and a daily report for the dining room is created. From that point, the program compiles the monthly report of each attorney's dining expenses. From this information, a cumulative monthly report is compiled for bookkeeping.

Data processing operator

Another computer-related job is that of the operator. Some of the jobs in this group (such as operating a keypunch or data entry terminal) draw on work routine and performance measures. Although these jobs do not demand possession of carefully developed skills or special training, they do require conscientious attention to details relating to operating the hardware. Also, satisfactory performance of such jobs requires that the person involved have sufficient capabilities to act quickly in correcting a problem.

Word processing operator

"Word processing operator" is one of the most widely used job titles in this industry. As a trainee, this person handles routine transcription and manipulation of text from various sources (dictation, handwritten, etc.), maintains production records, and proofreads work. The operator may also handle special documents, meet established quality standards, and use all of a machine's text-editing functions.

A person at the next level is often called a "word processing specialist." This person exercises all of the competencies of an operator, but also may act as an assistant supervisor. A word processing specialist is able to operate all the information processing equipment within the installation. Responsibilities include coordinating and assigning work, analyzing requirements for specific projects, communicating with users, compiling production statistics, and recommending changes in center procedures. This person may also assist in training personnel.

As the two technologies merge, the administrative, correspondence, and management positions are likely to be enhanced. The administrative position is likely to become a paraprofessional role. The administrative position will handle more of the manager's responsibilities. Using the computer, the administrative employee will do such things as compile reports and gather information for management decision making. A top administrative position probably will require a college degree and computer training.

Data processing and word processing roles merge

The correspondence employees will handle higher level word processing and data processing assignments. The higher level correspondence positions will require people with typing skills and some computer knowledge.

The word processing manager could become a vital person in coordinating word and data processing support for an organization. This employee is a prime candidate for such a coordination role because a person in this position has experience with people and equipment.

Opportunities for Special Employment Groups

Modern technology has also created new career paths for paraplegics, quadriplegics, and people with **auditory** or **visual impairments**. (Figure 10.16).

Auditory Impairment

Word processing and other related technologies have created tasks that can be done by persons with impaired hearing. Some of these tasks are:

Hearing impairment no barrier

1. Copy typing.

2. Using photocomposition or other copy processing equipment.

3. Proofreading (especially with word processing teams which have remote CRTs. The person with impaired hearing can proofread at a remote CRT while the transcriptionist is transcribing).

4. Opening, screening, and routing incoming mail.

5. Establishing and maintaining files.

6. Compiling reports for managers in analysis and decision-making activities.

7. Inventorying word processing center supplies and equipment.

8. Doing reference work.

9. Receiving, logging, and distributing incoming work.

10. Doing final editing and proofreading of work leaving center.

Visual Impairment

For some time, visually impaired people have had opportunities to perform in word processing positions. They could transcribe straight copy onto automated typewriters from equipment; however, proofreaders were needed. They could also maintain records when there is a coding system such as Braille used in addition to the regular file notations. However, the development of new equipment has opened up new job opportunities.

A company called Triformation Systems, for example, has developed **braille devices**. They are devices that **emboss** or raise information on a page. The visually handicapped then have available the same information as is supplied for sighted people in normal print or on video terminals. Using brailling devices such as the one shown in Figure 10.17, blind operators can send information to teletypes, other printers, computers, and some other data processing equipment. The continuous strip of paper tape allows blind operators to read what they have typed as well as receive incoming messages. Some brailling devices can receive information and then emboss the paper at speeds up to 120 words a minute.

Brailling devices make proofreading possible

One brailling device can operate at speeds up to 120 characters per second and can produce computerized page readouts of Braille in 10 seconds. With this device, the visually-impaired person is able to proofread (Figure 10.18). The inability to proofread was once one of the greatest disadvantages for the visually impaired.

IBM has developed a Braille electric typewriter (Figure 10.19) that enables both blind and sighted typists to use their skills in a new, meaningful way. This typewriter does not require typists to learn new systems; they simply type on a familiar keyboard. As they type, the letters are embossed on the page. The embossed copy provides raised characters for ease of proofreading and correcting while the paper is still in the machine.

Audible instructions for the blind

Another development is the **Audio Typing Unit** (ATU) introduced by IBM in 1979 to assist the visually impaired in operating IBM word processing equipment (Figure 10.20). One piece of equipment that the ATU attaches to is the IBM Mag Card II (MC/ST II). The function of the ATU is to assist operators in revision work by audibly giving the specialist instructions. The ATU tells operators what line they are on, reads the last character, word, or line that was just played out, phonetically pronounces characters or words, and announces whether the material has been recorded, read, or scanned. It also tells the operator if a card needs to be placed in the console for recording. The speaking unit on the ATU is a voice synthesizer which speaks in a monotone, computer-like voice audible to the operator through a headset or from a speaker. This device gives visually-impaired people opportunities for independently recording work on word processing equipment.

Before this device was invented, visually-impaired operators needed the assistance of a tutor, a brailling device, or an **Opticon**. An opticon is a sensing device that transfers a coded signal to the visually-impaired person's fingertips.

Figure 10.16 Quadraplegic operating dictation equipment. By using a magnetic mouth wand, a quadraplegic can gain a high level of self-sufficiency with the new dictation system (Sony VR-35). *(Courtesy of Sony Corporation of America, Business Products Division.)*

Figure 10.17 A brailling device. The keyboard of the ISE-1 is similar to that used by thousands of teletype operators throughout the world. The keys are set out in character positions in a manner similar to most typewriter keyboards, and trained touch typists are able to readily adapt to this keyboard. A built-in electronic device permits the operator to employ high-speed typing of familiar words without entering an erroneous code or losing a stroke. *(Courtesy of Triformation Systems, Incorporated.)*

Figure 10.18 A braille embosser. LED 120 is a stand-alone computer terminal printer that outputs a 40 character braille line on fan-fold continuous form paper at 180 lines per minute. *(Courtesy of Triformation Systems, Incorporated.)*

Figure 10.19 A braille typewriter. The typebars on this typewriter function in the same way as those on a conventional machine. Instead of printing out characters on the surface of a sheet of paper, however, they emboss Braille cells. A Braille character is called a "cell," and is an arrangement of raised dots indicating a letter or other symbol. The typebars on this typewriter form an entire Braille cell in a single keystroke, at the touch of a keybutton. *(Courtesy of International Business Machines Corporation.)*

Figure 10.20 The Audio Typing Unit (ATU). *(Courtesy of Corporation.)*

ATV opens new careers and expands opportunities for the visually impaired. For example, Mary Wimberly, who earned a master's degree in Russian from the University of California at Los Angeles and taught Hebrew and Braille to the blind, learned the IBM Mag Card II and became the first blind word processing operator in Orange County, California.

Mary uses the Opticon in her job at the University of California at Irvine. With the Opticon, she can proofread her own work. The Opticon in Figure 10.21 consists of a removable camera that attaches to the top of the Mag Card II frame. After words or lines are typed, the camera is moved along a rod with the right hand. The left end of the camera is attached to the retina portion of the Opticon. To proofread, the operator inserts the left hand into the retina portion of the Opticon (Figure 10.22). The left first finger reads letters and words from electronic vibrations. Mary explains, "It raises print letters so you can read them with your fingers."

Figure 10.21 Opticon. *(Courtesy of North Orange County Regional Occupation Program.)*

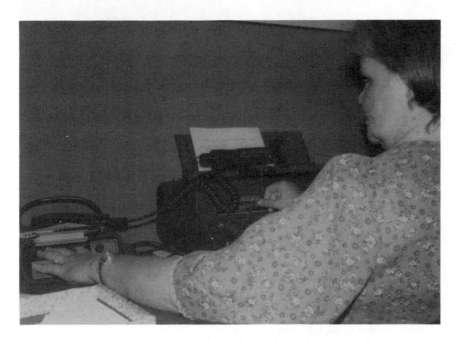

Figure 10.22 Mary Wimberly operating the Opticon. *(Courtesy of North Orange County Regional Occupation Program.)*

Opportunities for Special Employment Groups

Figure 10.23 A voice data entry system. The Voice Data Entry System is a user-programmable speech recognition terminal that operates alone or with a host computer. *(Courtesy of Interstate Electronics, a subsidiary of A-T-O.)*

The area of voice processing could open up many new opportunities for people with visual or auditory impairments. For example, as voice recognition modules are added to word processing systems, formatting of documents and global search and replace can be done with voice commands. As these systems become more popular, the visually impaired will be able to use voice commands to tell how the material is to be set up and have information such as numbers verified by vocal machine response. An example of voice recognition equipment already in existence that holds great promise for people with visual or auditory impairments is the voice data system in Figure 10.23 that verifies input data with vocal machine responses. The same equipment can verify voice input with responses printed on the visual screen.

The **Large Print Video Terminal** (LPVT) is another product developed by a blind person for the visually impaired. It is manufactured by a company called Arts Associates, Inc. of Boston, Massachusetts. The LPVT displays characters in three sizes: standard (3/16"), double height (3/8"), and giant (1-1/2").

As these new technologies emerge, visually-impaired students, employees, and professionals will find new areas of achievement in a wide range of job opportunities.

The following sections describe people at work in information processing careers.

An Information Processing Sales Representative

Leo Orye is a sales representative for Wang Laboratories, Inc., in Maryland. There is no "average" day for Leo Orye. Every day is different. But Leo loves the variety, the people, and the pace of his job. As a sales representative, he markets word processing/data processing systems.

When he first joined Wang, an equipment manufacturer, Leo had no previous sales experience; his background was in data processing. He had worked for another company in their data processing operations; later he took a position as operations manager with a new firm. During that time he gained experience and knowledge in business, especially data processing, and supplemented his experience with job-related courses at John Hopkins, Essex Community College, and through vendor courses related to the profession.

Although Leo had never before been involved in sales, he had been involved in purchasing, so he knew about sales from the other side of the fence. When he applied for a position at Wang Laboratories, the interviewer said she recognized qualities in Leo that she believed could make him a successful salesperson, and she promptly offered him the opportunity to prove it. He has been with Wang for three years and his territory now extends from part of Baltimore to as far away as Frederick, Maryland.[2]

A Word Processing Supervisor

Jan Smith is a word processing supervisor at Occidental Research in Irvine, California.

When Jan joined the word processing center as supervisor two years ago, their five word processors were uncomfortably situated in an 8′ by 35′ office. Crowding created an impersonal environment where people and machines seemed to mesh together. With the reconfiguration of the center to include five word processors, an OCR reader, and a stand-alone printer, expanding and rearranging the center became imperative.

Now the expanded Occidental word processing center covers 800 square feet and is functionally and aesthetically superb. Jan viewed privacy for the operators as the number one consideration. "Individuals need to have their own space," Jan commented, feeling that providing such space reduces distractions and allows each individual to function independently. Another of Jan's primary objectives was to provide a bright, cheerful atmosphere for the operators to work in. This objective has been accomplished beautifully with an open office plan using brightly colored panels, many plants, and plenty of light. The center

---

[2]*Inside Word Processing* (Baltimore Chapter, International Word Processing Association) 5, no. 6 (January 1980): 2.

is surrounded by large windows that increase the spacious appearance of the center.

Jan also wanted to provide easy access to the supplies and tools such as files and forms that the operators frequently use. These resources are housed within the center and are readily available. Each operator also has a telephone to use in contacting authors when questions arise about their work. Jan feels that these discussions have helped to establish an exceptional rapport which benefits both operators and authors alike.

Large wooden table tops were designed and constructed by the building staff of Occidental to fit over the file cabinets of the word processors. The installation of these counters has provided each operator with a smooth and attractive work surface.

Now, approximately eight months since the center was relocated, what results does Jan see? "Morale is up, productivity is up, and we all have a greater sense of pride in our surroundings."[3]

A Word Processing and Microfilm Supervisor

Jeanne M. Perkins is employed at the national headquarters of Toyota Motor Sales, U.S.A., Inc. in Torrance, California, and has worked at Toyota's regional offices as well. She started there 11 years ago as an executive secretary and has a broad background in administrative services (purchasing, personnel, accounting, regional operations). Three years ago, when Toyota decided to implement a centralized word processing center, Jeanne was promoted to word processing and microfilm supervisor.

Jeanne recently completed an in-depth equipment evaluation study (which she plans to publish), resulting in Toyota's requisition for a shared-logic system. After the new system is installed and she has completed the rewriting of operator and user manuals and instituted implementation, Jeanne will be involved in a feasibility study to determine Toyota's future needs with respect to coordinating microfilm, facsimile machines, telex, and communications, and keeping in tune with the needs of the office of the future.[4]

A Consultant

Mr. Reg Little is President of Reg Little & Associates, Inc., with offices in Washington, D.C., as well as a Canadian branch, Reg Little & Associates Limited with offices in Winnipeg and Montreal. He also acts as word processing consultant to all Air Canada system offices. At the present time, he has ongoing activities in Washington, Vancouver, Pittsburgh, Toronto, and Halifax.

Mr. Little's firm has been active in small business consulting as well as consulting for major accounts like the Federal Trade Commission and the Interstate Commerce Commission. Although most of his consulting business is generated in the U.S.A., where he employs a staff of 16, Reg now has two consul-

---

[3]*The Orange Crate* (Orange County Chapter, International Word Processing Association) 1, no. 4 (January 1980).

[4]*South Bay Chapter Newsletter* (International Word Processing Association), January 23, 1980, p. 3.

tants working out of his Montreal office and is considering expansion into Toronto and Vancouver.

Mr. Little, often referred to as "Mr. Word Processing", was a founder and first elected national President of the International Word Processing Association (IWPA). He was instrumental in chartering the Ottawa, Toronto, and Vancouver Chapters of IWPA and has given many talks to each of those organizations. He was a catalyst for the beginning of the word processing industry in Montreal, which now employs hundreds of Canadians. He was instrumental in having the first endless loop, centralized dictation system installed in a Canadian business office. He was also the first in Canada to introduce the decentralized word processing concept.[5]

A Sales Support Specialist

Carol Schamberger is a sales support specialist with OCS (Office Communications Specialist, Inc.), the vendor for CPT Corporation and Hendrix Corporation. OCS is headquartered in Buffalo, New York, and has a branch office in Rochester, New York. In her new position, Carol will have responsibility for doing in-house customer word processing surveys, programming customer applications, and acting as a word processing consultant for OCS. Carol will advise customers on how to set up a word processing center and also follow through with implementation of methods and procedures after installation.[6]

An Information Processing Senior Planning Analyst

Bill Owens is a senior planning analyst for Southern Company Services. He develops, conducts, and participates in long-range feasibility studies. Southern Company Services provides technical support and other specialized services to the Southern Company, parent of the Southern Electric System. This "family" includes Alabama Power Company, Georgia Power Company, Gulf Power Company (Pensacola, Florida), Mississippi Power Company, and Southern Company Services (Atlanta, Georgia; Birmingham, Alabama; and New York).

When a company or department of the Southern Electric System requests a study involving information processing, that request goes to Bill in the data center. Sometimes Bill acts as project leader when a study requires the development of a project team. He conducts the study, makes recommendations based on his findings, and includes any potential savings. If the company or department that originated the request accepts the recommendations, it then requests implementation. Bill's assignment normally ends once implementation has been completed.

That's precisely how Bill became involved in word/text processing. In 1974 the engineering division of Southern Company Services designed a nuclear facility for Alabama Power Company. Reports for the project contain thousands of pages with approximately 300 copies needed for distribution.

[5]"About our Speaker," *Synopsis* (Ottawa Chapter, International Word Processing Association) February 1980, p. 1.

[6]"New Position," *Everything That's Current* (Western New York Chapter, International Word Processing Association) 2, no. 6 (December 1979): 3.

"It was a big paper problem that they (engineering division) were dealing with, and at the time they were using some of the earliest word processing equipment available," Bill said. So the data center was asked to find a more effective, efficient means of publishing the reports. The Southern Company eventually purchased a word processing software package as a result of the data center's evaluation.

Bill is also a project leader for a similar assignment for the Vogtle nuclear facility of Georgia Power Company. Bill coordinates the team responsible for setting up an information network. The Bechtel Corporation in Los Angeles, Westinghouse in Pittsburgh, the Vogtle plant site, along with SCS's Birmingham, Alabama office form the network. The network will consist of support terminals in Los Angeles, communications from Pittsburgh, on-line access at the plant site, and compilation and publication responsibility in Birmingham.

Bill's professional activities relating to word/text processing have grown since his initial experience in 1974. A company vice president has given Bill the special opportunity of preparing a paper explaining the specific steps the Southern Electric System must take to prepare for the electronic office.

His current responsibilities have also taken him to the purchasing department of Gulf Power Company. A "text processing methodology," as Bill labels computer-aided word processing systems, will produce savings in the purchasing department by keyboarding all the information utilized on the purchasing, requisition, and expediting forms. An eventual interface with certain inventory control data processing systems will minimize wasted time (from a couple of weeks to a few days) and inconvenience by automatically identifying an item to be reordered and supplying a descriptive text for that item.

Bill recently completed an assignment to implement special word processing capabilities in the public relations department of Georgia Power Company and SCS. With the new system, publication abstracts, speeches, and photographs can be stored on a computer at Georgia Power Company. Along with supplying the inquirer with a brief abstract, the system also furnishes a physical file location where the complete document can be found. At SCS, responses to media questions can be obtained by entering certain key words.

For example, suppose a reporter had to know the definition of a term relating to nuclear energy. An employee of the public relations department would keyboard the term, and within seconds the reporter would be provided with the definition. This system enables the company to give rapid and consistent answers to media inquiries.[7]

A Unique Word Processing Operator

Carol Ashland is testimony to the fact that not only can someone who is blind function as a word processing operator, but can excel in the position as well.

Carol went to Olympia Vocational-Technical Institute in Olympia, Washington to train as a medical transcriber. She recalls that she quite incidentally took training on a Mag Card II "just for the fun of it." When she moved to Oregon, the

---

[7]"Meet Bill Owens, Our Shining Star," *Words* (International Word Processing Association), February/March 1980, p. 45.

Commission for the Blind put her in touch with the Willamette National Forest Service Districts. Since she knew how to operate a nondisplay mag card (IBM MC/ST) terminal, she got a position as an operator in the word processing center in 1976.

Carol is now training officer/transcriber, training all the new word processing operators for the entire forest service. They switched to a display terminal (3M's Linolex information processor) in 1977 and plan to install them in all seven service districts of the Willamette National Forest, the largest forest in the United States.

"I admit that I was rather worried when it became apparent that we were going to switch to a machine with a CRT," states Carol. "However, I have had no more problems adapting to it than anyone else in the office."

How does a blind person read a CRT screen? Telesensory Systems Inc. in Palo Alto, California developed a device called the Opticon, which stands for "optical to tactile converter." The user holds a small camera in the right hand and moves it over a page, or with the proper lens, over a CRT screen. The camera picks up the print image, and the opticon converts the letters, via tiny vibrating rods, into Braille (read by the index finger of the left hand). Technology is already under development to make verbal instead of tactile readout a reality, either through the hand-held camera or with automatic scanning. This will solve some of the worst problems for the blind operator and will open up new opportunities.

Carol says that reading with the Opticon is slow at best, but is still far better than not reading at all.

"As a blind operator myself, I know that the Opticon makes work in a word processing center possible, with a little effort, for any blind person with the aptitude and desire for it — provided he can find an employer willing to give him the chance to prove himself." Carol feels that the last is often the biggest problem blind people face.

One might assume that complex equipment makes it impossible for a blind person to function in a word processing environment. Carol points out that such is not the case at all: "Some of the equipment seems almost to have been designed with a blind person in mind, since some of the features allow a blind operator to efficiently perform the complex tasks which were not previously possible."

Until recently, Carol felt that tabular material was probably the most difficult work for a blind word processing operator to process.

"A multicolumn printer makes tables easier, however. The machine decides if a heading or entry is going to need more than one line, and automatically adjusts everything else." Much of the work at the Forest Service is, in fact, in tabular format.

"I believe that a blind person can handle most of the jobs we do in word processing," she says. "The problem is not in running the equipment, but the manner in which jobs are sent to the center. Dictation is the most efficient way for a blind person to receive material. Almost everything can be dictated, including tables, revisions, contract clause numbers, and fill-ins.

"Though my situation may be somewhat unique now, the most important point I can make is that it need not be. I am no genius and have no special abilities. There are many other blind people who have the ability to do the things I am doing. It takes basic secretarial skills, an affinity for machines, and the patience to work through the inevitable problems.

"But these requirements are no different than those for sighted operators. Not every blind person can learn to successfully operate word processing equipment. However, the same is true for sighted people."

Carol admits that it hasn't been easy. There are certain considerations and problems that she feels any blind operator is going to have.

"Because I cannot go look something up in a book with any degree of efficiency, and wish to avoid bothering the other operators to find it out, I have had to be more thoroughly trained than the average operator. This takes understanding on the part of my supervisors, as it costs more in terms of both time and money for this extra training."

Another problem she has encountered is that most people have not worked with a blind person before, and some have fears and doubts as to how to handle the situation.

"It takes a particularly willing and able teacher to embark on such a project with openness and a willingness to ask questions and not to prejudge.

"No one knows better what a blind person can do than the person himself, and it is a mistake to prematurely decide that a person cannot do a given thing. It is the blind person who is more likely to know the different alternative techniques available to him, or whom to contact if he himself does not know them."

Carol sees her own future as holding some interesting opportunities. She feels she might like to eventually get involved in computer programming, though she very much enjoys her position as training officer for the forest service.[8]

A Records Supervisor

Robert Jackson is a former commercial fashion designer, who walked into word processing purely by accident. He is now records supervisor for a consulting firm that is designing a new public transportation system for Atlanta.

It all started about four years ago. Tired of the hectic pace of designing junior sportswear for various manufacturers, Robert took a state civil service exam in accounting. (He had previously attended Georgia State University and studied finance.) This led to an opening for a personnel clerk with Parsons, Brinckerhoff, Quade & Douglas, Inc., and Tudor Engineering Co. This company had just been commissioned as a joint venture by the Metropolitan Atlanta Rapid Transit Authority (MARTA) to design a rapid transit system for the city. He decided to apply for the opening, and found out that the personnel clerk position actually entailed the maintenance of a sophisticated records system for over 550 personnel, using a time-sharing system (Bowne). At the time, the firm had completed the conceptual stage of the project and was in the process of hiring and transferring employees at a dizzying rate; hence the need for a computerized records system.

As Robert became familiar with the operation of the time-sharing system, he and Bowne set it up to handle all of the firm's information processing needs.

[8]"Carol Ashland: Willamette National Forest's Unique Operator," *Words* (International Word Processing Association), Summer 1978, p. 56.

Now, as records supervisor, Robert oversees the records operations of the joint venture, which include thousands of pages of specifications reports, drawings, documents and indexes. This operation is handled by nine operators using seven time-sharing terminals with two mag card typewriters. With such information being constantly updated, the firm averages over 1,000,000 lines of printing a month.

Robert also oversees the firm's microfilming operations. In addition to about 600 cubic feet of paper records, the firm microfilms all specifications, drawings, etc. after they are no longer needed, as well as more complex reports and confidential documents.

Robert and his staff are setting up an index of all pieces of equipment in the transportation system. He estimates this index will be about 50,000 pages long.

In addition, two operators are using the system to set up an index of the microfilmed records of thousands of specifications drawings. "Without our word processing system, it would be virtually impossible to index all these records and drawings," he says emphatically.[9]

A Management Support Manager

Since the inception of word processing operations at Montgomery Ward in Chicago in 1971, Camille Grejczyk has been working her way up the career ladder. Now serving as management support manager, she has turned her sights on making word processing a more recognized professional operation.

Camille entered Montgomery Ward over 14 years ago as a high school senior participating in Wardettes, the company's office occupations program. In 1971 she was transferred from the legal department, where she was initially placed, to become a keyboard operator in Ward's pioneering word processing center.

Demonstrating a flair for working with staff personnel and management alike, she was soon given added responsibilities. By 1975 she had worked her way from coordinator and supervisor positions to manager of 17 mini-centers and a master center.

"After being in word processing so long," Camille declares, "we have proven the concept works for various applications. Now we're starting to work on our professional image by developing a group of thinking employees who can determine the most efficient way to perform an application. This gives authors confidence in what we are doing."

Taking a professional approach, she finds, demands a great deal of flexibility and balance in establishing employee requirements and incentives. "I'm designing stringent employment application tests," she remarks, "to obtain the cream of the crop."

"Once accepted, they will be put through a training program where they will acquire necessary skills and learn company standards and procedures. Operators will start out in the mini-centers and move to the master center. Those who show outstanding performance will be advanced to new job positions to handle special applications beyond regular text-editing functions."

The whole idea, conceived by Camille, is to pay attention to quality control. Making this one of her next chief objectives, she wants to make authors aware

[9] "Close Up," *Words* (International Word Processing Association), Winter 1977–1978, p. 48.

that their work is being handled in a professional manner.

Camille's extensive experience has taught her the necessity for maintaining control over centralized and decentralized word proce sing operations. She emphasizes, "When control is lax, each mini-center (placed near the principals it serves, to generate short, one- to four-page correspondence) takes a different approach to every job. In the master center (where lengthy documents and special applications are handled), the production environment causes quality and dedication to suffer."

Her plan is to have mini-center word processing operators supervised by a team of professionals. She reports, "I am currently developing such positions as quality controller (proofreads, makes sure formats and procedures are followed, and analyzes problems in the center), coordination controller (oversees workflow in the word processing environment), analyst (designs special applications), and librarian (keeps track of documents stored on shared-logic systems)."

As operators' skills improve, they will progress to the master center, Camille explains. "There they can advance to applications specialist, handling applications beyond text-editing functions. These functions will include maintaining the corporate telephone directory, preparing a monthly report of customer complaints, and keeping track of all grades people earn while attending Ward's training courses. Application specialists, in turn, will be groomed for the job of analyst."

Camille would also like to create an administrative support organization and have it work closely with the word processing support group as a total management support organization. In addition, she would like to help Montgomery Ward use its word processing gear for electronic mail purposes and to mechanize the filing system.

But even more important, she realizes, is the people. She comments, "I think there is a lot of talent going to waste. I'd like to harness that talent and get people to think about how to perform applications better. With a professional team, we'll be on our way to the office of the future."[10]

Training

Training is necessary for success

Training people for jobs in the area of information processing is vital to the success of the operation. Training also improves the performance of employees on their existing jobs. Consequently, ongoing training programs are also vital for success.

Training helps employees feel that they are important. As a result, their attitudes towards the organization may improve. After training, employees are better capable of doing their jobs. The result is often improved morale and reduced turnover.

Training employees also makes them more valuable to their employer. Training increases employee job opportunities because a greater number of employers will be interested in their skills.

[10]*Word Processing Systems*, Profile. Geyer-McAllister Publications, Inc. February 1980, p. 36.

People in managerial positions need courses in areas such as human relations, grievance handling, and leadership. Training managers to do a better job of supervising frequently eliminates the cause of many employee complaints. People in administrative and correspondence positions need to be trained in center procedures and on any equipment that they will use in their work.

Everyone needs training

Types of Training

Several different methods of training are used to prepare people for positions in information processing. On-the-job training is training that is done at the work place. Either a manger or employee appointed by the manager does the training. On-the-job training is most often used to teach knowledge and skills that can be learned in a short time and where few employees are involved. Simple machine operations and work procedures are examples of skills that can be learned on the job.

On-the-job training

Simulations are training sessions that duplicate work conditions. Often the simulations only duplicate certain conditions and are not true simulations. For example, in industry, employees may be given some typical kinds of work applications to do on certain types of equipment. In high schools, colleges, and other training institutions outside the industry, people are often only trained to operate equipment.

Simulations

Simulations are used when large numbers of people such as typists need to be trained. The simulations are generally conducted by instructors who are usually formally educated and have had classes in teaching methods.

Although simulations are one form of classroom training, another form is most frequently used where problem solving, theories, and new concepts need to be learned. The classroom lends itself to several techniques, such as lectures, case studies, and role playing. Classroom training for information processing exists both in industry and outside industry in public and private educational institutions.

Classroom training

Sources for Finding Employees and Employment

Finding employees for the right jobs and knowing where to go to find a position is important. Employers and potential employees use the following sources: advertising within the organization itself, classified advertisements, employment agencies, contacts, professional associations, and training institutions.

One of the best sources for finding employees is the organization itself. Employers advertise new positions within the organization. Employees who volunteer for the jobs often work out better than those who are put into the jobs without being given any choice.

Advertising within the organization

Another source of employment information is classified advertisements in newspapers. Classified advertisements such as the ones in Figure 10.1 often attract employees who are already trained and have good skills. They are helpful places to look when seeking positions in information processing.

Classified advertisements

Employment agencies

Employment agencies are good sources for finding employees because they match the jobs with the people. In recruiting employees, employers can use both public and private agencies. Many agencies specialize in finding people with machine skills; others, in finding people for managerial positions. Employment agencies are also good places to start when looking for positions in information processing.

Contacts

Former employees, customers, and contacts in other companies often are sources for finding employees. Former employees often return to a company because they have left for some personal reason or because they are unhappy working in a new organization. Customers and contacts in other companies often provide good leads for finding people with special skills. Meeting people in information processing often helps prospective employees to locate jobs in that area.

Professional associations

Professional associations and conventions are places where many organizations recruit employees. Some associations provide a job placement service for members. People can make good contacts at these organizations, that often lead to finding future employees and employers. The International Word Processing Association and the Word Processing Society are two associations that have chapters throughout the United States.

Training institutions

Schools and colleges are rapidly becoming a source of employees. Some colleges are providing courses in word/information processing concepts, and management. Many schools provide job placement services to help students get their initial jobs in information processing.

Summary

The role of the office worker has changed. The traditional secretary has become a specialist instead of a generalist; secretaries can assume either administrative or correspondence positions in the environments created by the new technologies. A new management position has also been added to supervise the new work environments.

The new positions created by the new technologies require highly skilled employees. Many new opportunities also exist for employees who learn new skills and who keep up with the developments in office technology. Employees, moreover, have to be motivated to increase their level of skills by knowing that their new skills will lead to higher level positions and advancement within the organization. Career paths, therefore, are provided. Career paths do not always have to be vertical or leading upward. They may be horizontal or lateral. Lateral career paths are necessary for employees who wish to try different areas of information processing. Lateral career paths enable employees to move into jobs that require the same level of skill and are at the same salary level.

The secretary who wants to move into management now has a greater opportunity because the secretarial position provides a good training ground for an information management position. Secretaries often have an understanding of the organization and company policy, have good communication skills, know how to plan and organize, and are familiar with equipment. Secretaries, however, have to be able to change from a supportive role to a managerial role. Since the two roles are in conflict, the secretary needs to prepare for the change.

Word and data processing began as separate technologies, but their technologies have begun to merge. Many of the jobs in data processing have corresponding jobs in word processing. Moreover, people in administrative, correspondence, and managerial roles in word processing are also finding themselves involved in data processing.

Key Terms

Generalist
Specialist
Cross-training
Lateral career paths
Vertical career paths
Auditory impairment
Visual impairment
Brailling devices
Embossing devices
ATU
Opticon
LPVT

Study Guide

This study guide provides you with feedback to find out how well you are doing. Use a separate sheet of paper to record your answers. When you have finished check your responses with the answers at the back of the book.

Matching: Choose the answer that best defines the word in the left column.

1. Lateral career path	a. a person whose job description contains one type of duty such as typing.
2. Generalist	b. moving from a particular job with certain responsibilities and salary to another with equal responsibilities and salary.
3. Specialist	c. A person whose job description contains several different types of duties.
4. Auditory impairment	d. Preparing people to rotate jobs.
5. Embossing device	e. A hearing loss or impaired hearing.
6. Cross-training	f. Equipment that produces raised letters on a typewriter.

Multiple choice: Select the letter or letters that best answer each question.

7. Until the embossing device was developed, one of the most difficult problems for the visually-impaired person was:
   a. proofreading
   b. keyboarding
   c. formatting

8. Specializing means:
   a. Secretaries do either typing or nontyping work.
   b. Secretaries do one type of typing.
   c. Secretaries do only one type of administrative work.

9. Secretaries might choose to specialize for the following reasons:
   a. The work is easier.
   b. Secretaries can move upward based on their ability.
   c. Secretaries can select a career path that best suits their personality and preferences.

10. Which of the following are lateral career paths?
    a. A correspondence secretary who handles medical records relating to laboratory work transfers to another correspondence position that handles all other medical reports, correspondence, and claims.
    b. A correspondence secretary moves to an administrative secretarial position that has equal responsibilities and pay.
    c. An administrative secretary moves into a word processing management position.
    d. An administrative trainee moves into an administrative secretarial position.

11. Jobs that make up a vertical career path should be designed:
    a. By the secretaries.
    b. According to the value of the job.
    c. For executive secretaries only.
    d. Should progress from jobs which require little skills to jobs which require a great deal of skill.

12. Career paths should never:
    a. Advance people beyond word processing managerial positions.
    b. Be horizontal.
    c. Be designed for administrative secretaries, but not for correspondence secretaries.
    d. None of the above.

Completion: Write the correct answer(s) on a separate sheet of paper.

13. LPVT stands for _____.

14. Opticon is _____.

15. The word processing position that requires that people enjoy training on different types of equipment is _____.

16. The name of the device that gives audible instructions to the blind is _____.

True/False: Write + for True, 0 for False for each question.

17. At present, only a few employment opportunities exist for people in word processing.

18. A correspondence position requires a person with good English skills.

19. An example of a lateral career path would be an advancement from correspondence trainee to correspondence secretary.

20. Word processing job titles and descriptions are consistent in all organizations.

21. The tasks performed in a correspondence position are very similar to the tasks performed in administrative positions.

22. Word processing managers should enjoy working more with equipment than with people.

23. Secretaries are often chosen for management jobs in word processing.

24. Shorthand is a requirement for correspondence positions.

Questions on Concepts

1. Explain three job positions in word processing.
2. Describe the criteria used for determining job titles and descriptions.
3. Compare the responsibilities or tasks of a correspondence position with the tasks of an administrative position.
4. Compare the attitudes required for a correspondence position with those needed for an administrative position.
5. Describe the duties of a manager.
6. Describe the characteristics needed for the job of manager in a word or information processing center.

7. Contrast the traditional office role of generalist with that of a specialist in a word processing center.
8. Explain why some people question the ability of secretaries to move from secretarial to managerial positions.
9. Explain what a lateral career path is and give an example.
10. Explain what is meant by vertical career paths.
11. Describe the kinds of equipment that help special employment groups, such as people with visual or auditory impairments.
12. Describe several types of training used in preparing people for positions in information processing.
13. Describe several sources of employment information in information processing.

Case and Activities

Brian Young and Associates employed six clerk/typists, four secretaries to department managers, and one secretary to the president of the firm before implementing word processing. In staffing its new word processing center, it transferred all four clerk/typists who passed a typing test of 40 wpm to the correspondence center and gave them all the same job title and classification of correspondence secretary. The two clerk/typists who did not meet this requirement were let go. They held B.A. degrees in English, but were not competent typists. The others did not hold degrees.

The center had two different types of automated typing equipment. The remaining clerk typists were given two weeks to learn each piece of equipment. They were to learn how to operate the equipment by using the equipment manuals.

The secretaries to the department heads and the secretary to the president of the organization were all given the job title and classification of administrative secretary. They were centralized in an administrative support center. Since these secretaries had all worked in various departments, the organization decided not to conduct any training session for them.

1. Do you agree with the organization's method of selecting the administrative and correspondence secretaries? Explain why or why not.
2. Discuss the organization's approach to providing training for personnel. Do you agree or disagree with it?
3. What problems might exist regarding motivation in this environment? How would you remedy these problems?

Activities

1. Interview a personnel manager of a large organization and inquire about new career paths in information processing.
2. Read an article in any of the new information technology trade journals and report on careers in information processing.
3. Interview a manager of a word or information processing center and ask what preparation the person had for the job and trace that person's career path.

CHAPTER 11

Directing the Staff

The objectives of this chapter are to:

1. Identify some problems organizations have with employee effectiveness.

2. List the need levels that motivate people.

3. Identify what motivates employees today.

4. Summarize the way in which satisfied and unsatisfied needs interact.

5. Contrast Maslow's need hierarchy with Herzberg's maintenance-motivation model.

6. Relate specific reasons why money does not motivate.

7. Explain three factors that shape employee morale.

8. Describe the characteristics of an enriched job.

9. Contrast traditional leadership with situational leadership.

10. Describe boss-centered, participative, and employee-centered leadership.

11. List some reasons why people resist change.

12. List ways of applying the principles of decreasing resistance to change to information processing.

13. Explain the idea of management assumptions about people.

14. Describe "Theory X" and "Theory Y" assumptions.

Every organization that has tasks to accomplish must use equipment, supplies, and people. It is often how these resources are used, rather than the amounts of them available, that determines the successful accomplishment of organization objectives.

This chapter will deal specifically with human resources and the ways that people can be effectively stimulated to work toward the objectives of an organization.

Creating an Effective Workplace: The Manager's Responsibility

We hear comments from managers of information processing that the kinds of employees in organizations today leave much to be desired. One manager recently made this remark, "I pay my employees a top wage. They have good fringe benefits and they have the best working conditions in the industry, but

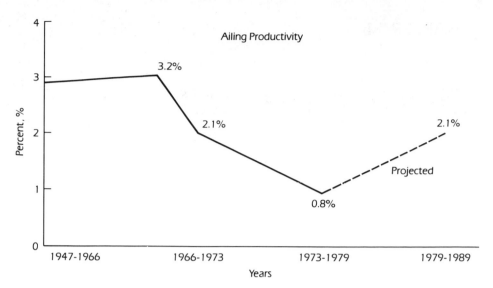

Figure 11.1 Ailing productivity.

just ask them to work a little overtime or come in a little early, and you discover that they won't help in a pinch." This statement illustrates the dilemma of some organizations. They spend a lot of money recruiting, selecting, training, and placing people in jobs but still experience poor attendance, high turnover rates, low productivity, and poor work quality.

Statistics suggest that absenteeism costs employees and the economy $20 billion a year from lost pay alone. In addition, industry spends $10 billion a year in such pay and $5 billion on fringe benefits that continue whether or not an employee comes to work. In May 1976, according to the Federal Bureau of Statistics, work hours lost through absenteeism came to 3.5%. A major manufacturer showed that a 1% rise in absenteeism could reduce profits by 4%. Absenteeism

has also increased among some state employees; the State of Maine reports that its absentee rate has increased by 6% in two years.

A recent poll conducted by the Gallup organization showed that a majority (52%) of U.S. employees do not work up to their potential. When asked how much more these employees could accomplish if they really wanted to, the response by 58% of those interviewed was 20% more each day. These statistics may explain, in part at least, the apparent slowdown in productivity of people and machines in the U.S. in recent years. The Conference Board, a nonprofit business research group, found that productivity peaked at 3.2% in the mid 1960s and has declined to an 0.8% rate today (Figure 11.1).

The automobile industry in the U.S. reports labor turnover among assembly line employees to be close to 30 percent a year with the costs of repairing new automobiles because of poor work quality up almost 50 percent in the last ten years. A survey done of word processing offices in Texas showed that the turn-

over rate among correspondence secretaries ranges from 26% to 36% a year.[1]

These problems in today's organizations all concern people—the human

[1]Robert B. Mitchell, "An Investigation of Job Satisfaction Among Correspondence Secretaries and the Impact of Supervision," *Delta Pi Epsilon Journal* 22, no. 1 (January 1980): 36.

Figure 11.2 People—the most important resource in information processing. *(Lanier "No Problem" courtesy of Lanier Business Products.)*

resources in the organizations (Figure 11.2). The following sections look at what effect managers have on these serious problems.

Motivation

Managers are responsible for building the kind of work environment that allows their employees to accomplish their own personal goals. But what are those goals? What is it that employees are seeking in today's organizations? Abraham Maslow, a prominent writer in the field of human motivation, helps us understand the forces that stimulate people to behave in one way or another. People behave as they do to satisfy certain basic needs. All actions, according to Maslow, can be explained by understanding the needs that people are striving to satisfy. These needs are arranged in a **hierarchy,** as shown in Figure 11.3, from the physiological, safety, and social needs in the **lower orders** through esteem and self-actualization in the **higher orders.**[2]

What do employees want?

The Need Hierarchy

Physiological Needs. The needs for food, water, shelter, and sex are considered physiological needs. Until these needs are met, people put all of their energies into satisfying them. For the person who is hungry, nothing else is important except getting food. The key concept to remember is that, according to Maslow, only an **unsatisfied need** will cause a person to act. For example, if you have

Food, water, shelter, sex

[2]Abraham Maslow, *Motivation and Personality*, 2nd ed., (New York: Harper and Row, 1970), pp. 35–58.

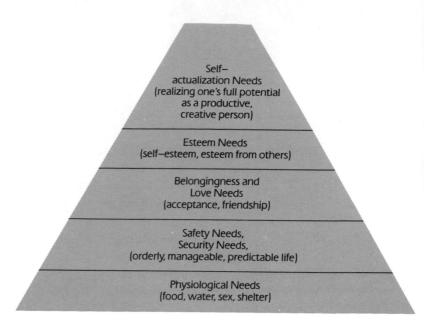

Figure 11.3 Maslow's need hierarchy.

just finished a large meal, offering you more food probably will not be the way to stimulate you to perform any work.

Predictable, manageable life

Safety Need. When a lower order need is satisfied, a higher order need emerges to stimulate the person. For example, when the physiological need is fulfilled, the safety need will become the motivator. The safety need is more than just the need to feel secure. You do need to feel secure in your life, to be sure, but beyond that you must feel that your life is orderly, predictable, manageable, and pretty much within your control. Adults do not often demonstrate their safety needs; but children do exhibit these needs. For example, children cling to parents when bright lights flash, loud noises occur, and when a parent's grasp on the child may loosen for an instant.[3]

Some offices are very insecure places to work. For example, managers' judgements are often biased when determining employees' competence. Rewards are given based on favoritism. The use of favoritism leads to feelings of insecurity. To help avoid favoritism in the office, organizations should develop employee appraisal plans for their employees. These employee appraisal plans should be based on whether employees accomplish mutually determined objectives. An employee's raises or promotions should not rely on a manager's personal judgements about the person, but rather on whether the employee met the objectives. The use of an objective appraisal plan goes a long way toward reducing favoritism.

A place in the group

Social Need. When safety needs are satisfied, the social need, sometimes referred to as the love need, becomes the motivator. The social need is the need to

[3]Erich Fromm, *The Art of Loving* (New York: Harper and Bros., 1956), p. 133.

Figure 11.4 Friendly work relationships provide employees with job satisfaction. *(Universal Text Editor 400 courtesy of Sperry Univac.)*

belong, or to be part of something. In today's society, people often do not have a chance to satisfy these social needs. Erich Fromm, in his book "The Art of Loving," writes of our alienation in today's society. People, he says, relate to one another for what they get rather than because they care. People need close, warm, personal contact with other people.[4] This need can be seen in the office in two parts. First, employees need to have good cooperative relationships with other employees (Figure 11.4). One way managers can satisfy this need is by providing a work environment where people can function as part of a team. Having a place in the group provides the employee with support and is much more satisfying than a "dog-eat-dog" work environment. For example, when asked what they liked about their word processing jobs, a group of correspondence secretaries in several word processing offices listed a friendly personal environment (Figure 11.5). Second, people need to have managers who show concern for them and who treat them as people, not objects to use or numbers to tabulate on index cards. Secretaries, for example, frequently have rather lonely jobs because they report to one principal who may be in an isolated location. Managers can make secretaries feel part of the team by including them in staff meetings and seminars and having them share assignments. Managers can also make new employees feel at home. Moreover, managers can make

[4]Ibid.

Figure 11.5 Cooperative team effort leads to more highly motivated workers. *(Courtesy of Four Phase Systems, Inc.)*

employees feel comfortable about coming to them with problems such as un-reasonable deadlines, hard-to-read copy, or equipment problems.

Ego Need. When their social needs are fulfilled, the ego need or esteem need becomes the motivator. Employees need to feel valuable; to have a firmly based, high opinion of themselves. Remember how you felt the last time an important decision you were capable of making was made by someone else and imperson-ally announced to you. This kind of decision making disregarded your talents and implied that your abilities and opinions were unimportant. You probably felt left out and not very valuable. Managers can help provide employees with a high opinion of themselves. For example, the manager of one word processing center uses the expertise of the employees when updating the procedures manual. Some senior word processing employees also assist in coordinating lengthy technical documents to assure that consistency and quality standards are met. In this way, concern for people is shown in the office. A recent study of word processing also shows that when office employees have freedom on the job and the responsibility to direct their own work, they are more apt to like their job.

Self-fulfillment Need. When ego needs are satisfied, self-fulfillment or self-actual-ization, the highest order need, then stimulates behavior. People are growing, learning organisms who must feel that their full potential will be allowed to

Feelings of value

Personal growth

Figure 11.6 Providing challenging work satisfies the need to grow and learn. *(Courtesy of 3M Graphic Division.)*

develop (Figure 11.6). To put it simply, "people must be more and more of whatever they are." An artist must create art, a musician must play music, a sculptor must create sculpture. And in the office, the kind of work that is done must be challenging. Too often people are asked to perform work that is mind-numbing; that bores them with its routine, monotonous tasks. Jobs have gotten too small for people. One organization reports that when it is feasible to allow a word processing employee to coordinate the work of others on a large project, there is a significant increase in motivation. One employee takes complete charge of the project and becomes "the expert" on that job. Sometimes the organization assigns "executive type" work, such as financial reports and subcontracts, to interested and qualified office employees to provide them with more challenge from their work. Some organizations have found that by allowing secretaries in their word processing centers to use slack time for self-improvement activities like cross-training or grammar skill development, job satisfaction is increased.

Our actions, therefore, in the work place can be explained by a hierarchy of needs. When need arises, we take action to satisfy it. If there is indeed satisfaction, the need is reduced and our behavior most likely will be positive. However, when a manager keeps employees' needs from being satisfied, as when people are required to work on a boring job, frustration develops and they are likely to behave negatively. That negative behavior in the work force shows up as high absenteeism and job turnover. Good managers are able to create work environments that remove barriers to need satisfaction. When these barriers are removed, the result is positive behavior. *Barriers cause negative behavior*

Where are today's employees on the hierarchy of needs? We hear managers talk mostly of economic rewards when referring to motivating employees. To *Do economic rewards motivate?*

(Motivation) Factors[1]	(Maintenance) Factors[2]
Achievement	Company policy and Administration
Recognition	Salary and fringe benefits
Advancement	Job security
The work itself	Working conditions
Challenging job	Technical supervision
Growth opportunities	Interpersonal relationships with peers, supervisors, and subordinates
Responsibility	Status
	Personal life

[1]Motivation factors are sources of satisfaction.
[2]Maintenance factors are sources of dissatisfaction.

Figure 11.7 Herzberg's motivation and maintenance factors.

stimulate an employee to produce more, for example, the organization pays more money in wages and salaries, bonuses, fringe benefits, and better working conditions. And when employees do not seem to respond much more energetically than before the rewards were given, they are often labeled lazy or uninterested. But are economic rewards really as important to motivate people today compared with a few decades ago, or are other needs more ready to be satisfied? The answer to this question can be seen in a motivation model developed by Frederick Herzberg (Figure 11.7). His model explores the possibility that many of our needs are no longer motivators. Some of our needs have been satisfied through life in an affluent society. A study done in Texas, for example, found that correspondence secretaries in word processing offices were more satisfied with their jobs if their salaries were fair rather than high.[5] Also, correspondence secretaries satisfied with their work were the ones least likely to leave the word processing field for higher paying jobs. The message for managers is that it does not make much sense to focus on satisfied needs to get employees to contribute more (Figure 11.8).

Maintenance-Motivation Model

Maintenance motivation model

Herzberg's model is called **maintenance-motivation**. Herzberg categorizes our needs into those which are motivators (**satisfiers**) and those which are **dissatisfiers** (maintenance). The maintenance factors are those things we have learned to expect from organizations. They simply maintain us at an existing level of activity but do not motivate us to higher levels of productivity. The maintenance factors are mostly lower order needs (physiological, safety, social) like wages, vacations, health insurance, retirement plans, and cooperative work groups. Although these are important to employees, they do not have the motivational effect that organizations expect.

Before discussing the motivators in the model, some comments are necessary about wages and motivation. Money as a motivator should not be disre-

[5]Mitchell, "An Investigation of Job Satisfaction," p. 36.

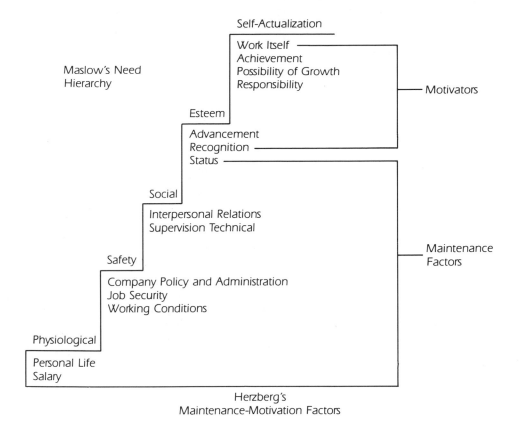

Comparison of Maslow and Herzberg Models (See also Keith Davis, *Human Behavior at Work*, 5th edition, New York, McGraw-Hill Book Company, 1977, p. 53.)

Figure 11.8 Comparison of Maslow and Herzberg models.

garded. It is true that the value of money as a motivator has declined in the last several decades. Whatever motivation money provides has very short term effects, but under certain conditions money can be quite an incentive. The importance of money varies among people as does the perception an employee has of whether money earned was tied to work effort. Money will only be a motivator if an employee has a high interest in money and is able to see that extra effort produces additional money. If it appears that every employee will receive more money, even when the effort of some is lower, the money ceases to motivate.

When is money a motivator?

The **motivators** (satisfiers) relate to higher order needs (esteem and self-actualization). These are factors that cause employees to be more productive, and they generally have positive effects on absenteeism, job turnover, and morale. The five motivators are: advancement, responsibility, work itself, recognition, and achievement.

The motivators

Advancement. People need to know what career paths are available. In offices, dead-end jobs occur all too frequently and cause frustration, especially for younger employees. But too often in the past, an employee's advancement was limited to a boss's promotion. Evidence about word processing operators shows

No dead-end jobs

Figure 11.9 Manipulation of text and data in the Xerox 800 and Xerox 850 word/information processors creates challenging work. *(Courtesy of Xerox Corporation.)*

that promotional opportunity is related to higher job satisfaction. Since many word processing offices now have administrative tasks, it is possible to develop specialized administrative skills and progress through the administrative area to supervision, or some other professional position.

Responsibility. Decision making should be delegated to the lowest possible level where people are closest to the problem and have the most information. In one word processing office, administrative secretaries now have more responsibilities. Since a great deal of the manager's work and decision making are delegated to them, their former more routine duties are given to other work groups. In another organization, secretaries have responsibility for their own work quality in tasks like proper keyboarding, storing of documents, and correct grammar and spelling. Regular training meetings are conducted where ideas are discussed and problems resolved.

The work itself. Jobs must be created that have some challenge (Figure 11.9). Routine, monotonous, boring jobs create apathy and frustration. To avoid routine, boring jobs, attempts are made by one aerospace organization to vary the work of its word processing center. Since the word processing center does work for many different departments, it has a wide variety of work from which to choose. If an employee spends a couple of hours playing out repetitive personal letters, the next assigned job might be statistical or technical. Another example of how this organization creates jobs with more challenge is by avoid-

Challenge and variety

ing splitting up jobs if possible. It makes employees in the word processing center responsible for completing a job from beginning to end. They are responsible for the quality, format, and filing of media.

Taking charge

Recognition. People need to have credit for their contributions to the organization. Moreover, office employees who feel they receive recognition on the job are generally more satisfied. A fair and objective appraisal program should indicate the employees who deserve commendation. An organization recently encouraged word originators to give compliments to operators when jobs were well done. Verbal commendations are passed on to employees and notes are routed to all center personnel and posted on the center bulletin board.

Getting credit

Achievement. People are motivated when their work can be performed from beginning to end. Seeing a job through to completion gives people a feeling of achievement. A recent study done with correspondence secretaries indicated that personal contact with word originators also significantly increased job satisfaction.[6] Instead of a fragmented job, they could see where their work tied into others' to make up a whole job.

Finishing what you start

The manager's job is to understand what motivates employees today and to provide the kind of work place which provides motivation rather than maintenance.

Morale

The last section showed how employee frustration arises when needs are not fulfilled; often this frustration causes negative attitudes about the organization. The feeling or attitude a person has toward an organization is called **morale** (Figure 11.10). It is often assumed that an organization either has or does not have morale; this is incorrect. The question is what kind of morale is present — good or bad.

Employee attitudes

Bad morale shows up in a number of areas: high labor turnover, excess waste and scrap, high absenteeism and tardiness, increasing numbers of grievances, and poor safety records (Figure 11.11).

A morale survey can be conducted that can show many areas of weakness and strength. The results of a survey can then be shown graphically in a **morale profile** (Figure 11.12). Important categories like pay, supervision, recognition, and chances for growth measurement can be easily seen. The results provide management with information to make changes.

The amount of wages that an employee receives has a strong effect on attitudes. People have ideas of how valuable their work is to the organization. If they receive less money for the work they do than they feel is equitable, their attitudes may become negative. One office study showed that where 69% of a group of employees were satisfied with their present wages, they had an average absentee rate of one time in six months. Another group of employees where only 44% were satisfied with their present wages had an absence rate of four times in six months. The employees' attitudes were affected strongly by their

The effect of wages

---

[6]Ibid, p. 37.

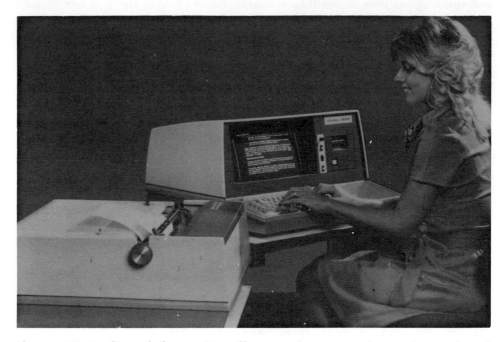

Figure 11.10 Good morale has positive effects on job turnover, absenteeism, and productivity. *(Lexitron Videotype 1000 courtesy of Lexitron Corporation.)*

perceptions of how fair the wages were.

The kind of work performed

The kind of work that people are required to perform is one of the strongest morale factors. Managers continue to break work down into increasingly fine specialties that are routine, boring, and offer little challenge to most employees. What enhances morale is to put split-up jobs back together again. By using employees' own knowledge and insights to design work so that they can begin to participate in the management of their jobs, good feelings about the organization develop. The strategy of putting jobs back together again is called **job enrichment.**

Job Enrichment

Work that has meaning

Job enrichment creates a job that has meaning. An employee will feel good about the job if it is perceived to be a worthwhile activity or important by some acceptable standard. Enriching jobs increases responsibility and people feel personally accountable for their effort. Employees must be able to determine if the outcome of their work is satisfactory. When this is accomplished, employees feel good personally and attitudes about the job become positive. There will be a high degree of "**internal motivation**" (self-direction) rather than reliance on external motivations like salary, fringe benefits, or working conditions.

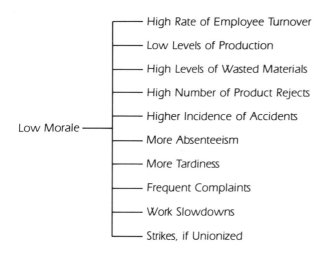

Low Morale
- High Rate of Employee Turnover
- Low Levels of Production
- High Levels of Wasted Materials
- High Number of Product Rejects
- Higher Incidence of Accidents
- More Absenteeism
- More Tardiness
- Frequent Complaints
- Work Slowdowns
- Strikes, if Unionized

Figure 11.11 Indications of low morale.

What Makes a Job Enriched?

Task Variety. What must be done to a job to change it from its simplified form to one which is said to be "enriched"? There are at least five changes which should be made in traditional work design to accomplish enrichment. First, the job must include in its design some task variety. The job must require the employee to perform activities that challenge skills and abilities. Task variety avoids the boredom of performing the same task repetitively for long periods. When a group of operators were asked what job activity factors they liked most about their word processing jobs, they named the variety of work and work that has challenging and creative content. An employee's description of work variety in a major automobile organization is typical. "There's a lot of variety in the paint shop. You clip on the color hose, bleed out the old color, and squirt; clip, bleed, squirt, yawn; clip, bleed, squirt, scratch your nose." What managers have done in traditional job design is the same as what has happened to how bread is produced. Flour is bleached to make white bread and many nutrients are removed, so we enrich it by adding vitamins and minerals to replace what is gone. Management is responsible for putting challenge back into the job.

Challenge skills and abilities

Whole Tasks. Second, there must be completion of a whole and identifiable task. Doing a job from beginning to end, with results that are easily observed, is important to develop good attitudes. Often jobs are designed in a fragmented way so that people perform specialized tasks that do not appear related to the completed project. In Europe, two automobile organizations have designed whole plants around the concept of "work teams." Two or more employees are given responsibility for whole tasks like assembling an entire automobile engine from beginning to end. A study done at AT&T with equipment operators shows similar changes in job design. Fourteen operators each keyboarded an equal amount of whatever work was distributed each day by an assignment clerk.

Put jobs back together

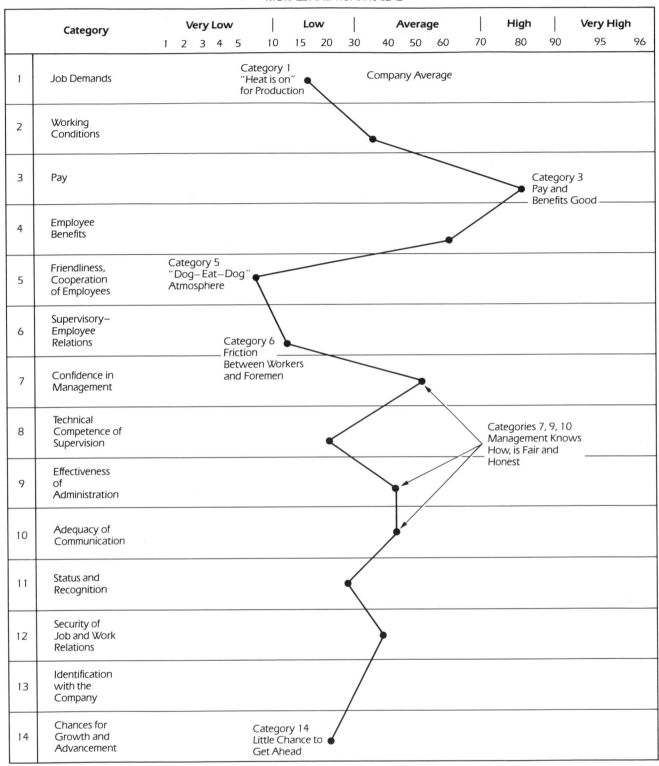

Figure 11.12 Morale and its appraisal.

Each operator was expected to comply with standards for quality and quantity set by the supervisor. After the enrichment, each operator was given a regular amount of keyboarding responsibilities. Each task involved completing an entire service for a department. For example, one operator handled the entire payroll for one department plus a monthly inventory for another department; the operator had whole tasks to complete. Compared to a control group, in ten months absenteeism and turnover dropped significantly and productivity increased. Another organization has found success when word originators come into the center and work directly with the operator. Many times the originator will request that the operator work overtime with the originator to complete a specific deadline. This direct contact between the originator and operator enforces the "whole task" idea.

Task Importance. Third, the task must be perceived to be important. Employees must see the impact of their work on the lives of other people. The assembly of pollution control equipment, for example, may be more enriching than a welding operation on an automobile assembly line. In word processing, keyboarding reports from a radiologist may be perceived to be more important than keyboarding collection letters for delinquent accounts.

Impact of your job on others

Job Autonomy. Fourth, employee freedom, independence, and judgment in scheduling and performing work is necessary for an enriched job. Employees ask for more decision-making responsibility to determine their own success or failure on the job. This concept is called job autonomy and is illustrated by a policy of some organizations known as **"flex time."** Not all employees desire the same hours of work; some are early risers and prefer starting early, others may want to begin a couple of hours later and work later in the afternoon, while still others may want to take two hours off in the middle of the day to do shopping or conduct personal business. With flex time, the employee has some control over hours worked and the flexibility has become successful where the organization's type of work makes it practical.

Freedom to make decisions

Knowledge of Results. Finally, employees must have knowledge of the results of their labor. They need to know how effective they are on the job. There must be some kind of objective performance appraisal program. The traditional program emphasizes "no news is good news." If the employee is not told something is wrong, the assumption is made that everything is all right. Or, if an appraisal program is used, it usually includes many subjective factors like cooperation, dependability, appearance, and attitude. Very little information is provided about actual performance. The effective appraisal program should focus on performance objectives that are mutually agreed upon by managers and employees.

Measuring your performance

Leadership

The amount of money an employee earns and the kind of work that is required have been shown to have a strong effect on attitudes about an organization. There is yet another major morale factor which should be discussed because of the impact it has on people in the workplace and the accomplishment of goals:

Figure 11.13 A manager at Stanford Research Institute uses information processing technology to assist in communication and decision making. *(Courtesy of SRI International.)*

Leaders create the desire to produce

leadership. Managers must be the kind of leaders who are able to create desire in employees to accomplish the objectives of the organization. A study that investigated the impact of supervision on job satisfaction in a word processing office is helpful to illustrate this point. In order to achieve higher job satisfaction and performance, operators chose an employee-centered supervisor over a boss-centered supervisor. But what do these two terms mean? The answers to this question lie in an understanding of changes which have occurred over the last few decades in our notion of how people really lead.

Traditional Leadership

Trait theory

Traditional leadership concepts focused mostly on what a leader is rather than what a leader does. The **trait theory** of leadership is typical and illustrates this point of view. Leaders were believed to have a set of personality characteristics (traits) which made them more qualified, in most situations, to motivate employees towards goals. A leader, according to this theory, is more intelligent than followers, has an orientation to the future rather than dealing only with present issues, is better able to communicate (better verbal skills), and generally has an internal decision-making process which is free of strong influence of other people or groups (Figure 11.13). These are probably valid characteristics of successful leaders, but they don't tell very much about how to lead people. So

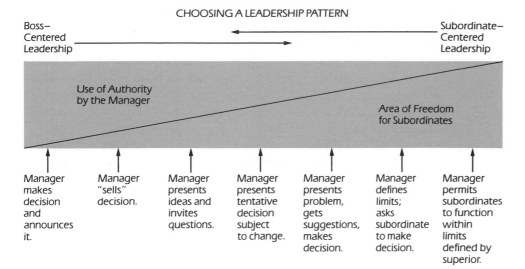

Figure 11.14 Choosing a leadership pattern.

most studies of leadership today try to deal with what a leader does, not what a leader is.

Viewing leadership more in terms of what should be done by the leader brings us to the interrelationships of three variables: the value system of the leader, the kinds of employees in the organization, and the situation in the workplace. Given these three variables, leadership becomes an influence process. This means that the leader must influence employees to accomplish goals, realizing that different leaders, employees, and situations may require very different kinds of leadership approaches.

Leadership as an influence process

Situational Leadership

The ideas expressed in the preceding paragraph represent the current leadership theory, **situational leadership.** A model by Tannenbaum and Schmidt (Figure 11.14) can be used to illustrate the responsibility of managers in this area. **Boss-centered** (autocratic) leadership appears on the left of the example and represents all decisions that are made solely by the manager. Moving to the right on the scale, the area of authority by the boss decreases while the area of freedom for the employee (subordinate) increases. On the right of the model, **employee-centered** (laissez faire) leadership is shown. This represents decisions made primarily by employees with little involvement by the manager. Midway between boss-centered and employee-centered leadership is a region where freedom and authority are equal. Here the manager consults with employees, asks for their opinions and judgments, but is still responsible for making the decision. This leadership style is called **participative** or democratic. For every decision that must be made, managers can choose the style of leadership which is most effective considering the leader's values, the kind of employee involved, and the situation. In one situation it may be necessary to use an autocratic style of leadership, while in others a participative or laissez faire style

What kind of leadership to use?

would work best. For example, a manager may not feel comfortable allowing employees the freedom to make decisions. Because of that manager's value system, personality, or general feeling of insecurity, a boss-centered style of leadership may be used. The real problem arises when employees prefer more freedom in decision making and the manager continues with an autocratic style. This idea was illustrated earlier in the study on the impact of supervision on job satisfaction. The kind of employees in the organization will also determine the kind of leadership style chosen by the manager. Some employees may not be interested in decision making because they are not skilled enough or they may lack the maturity to accept responsibility for making important decisions. If the manager has this kind of information about the organization's employees, boss-centered decisions may be necessary. For example, entry-level employees should not be held responsible for making the decision to replace all machines with sophisticated information processing equipment.

The situation a manager encounters will affect the style of leadership that is most effective. For example, time is an essential part of the decision-making process. Involving more people takes added time and when time is of the essence, a manager may need to use an autocratic style of leadership. If the task to be performed is highly technical, or when employees do not for some reason have enough information to make a good decision, the leader may have to make the decision.

The need for flexibility

The challenge, then, is for the manager to recognize the flexibility available in leadership styles. The leader should assess accurately the leader's own values, the employees' abilities, interests, and level of maturity, and the situation they all find themselves in, and choose the leadership style which will be most effective.

Pressures for Change

Because the pressures for change in our society have accelerated greatly in the last few decades, leaders must make decisions in a very difficult environment. Technological change represents one of the most significant pressures for change. Eighty percent of all scientists who ever lived are still alive today. The commercial jet transport, body organ transplants, space vehicles, and birth control pills did not even exist prior to World War II.

What changes have we undergone?

Societal changes in our country also must be considered important. Close to 50% of the work force is now made up of women. The problem of male/female roles is a real issue in many families across the country. We have "instant" communication of ideas, conditions, and events, creating a smaller world that forces us to deal with pressures unknown in the past. The rapid movement of people and goods has developed an interdependence among people not known a few decades ago, and is seen in our dependence on foreign oil producers.

Resistance to Change

People in organizations tend to develop a particular set of relations with their work environment. They may not particularly like the situation that has developed, but at least they are secure in knowing what to expect. They work to maintain a steady level of need satisfaction such as wage and working conditions, feelings of value, status, contact with friends, and self-expression, and will attempt to protect themselves from a loss of any of those needs. Any behavior designed to protect us from real or imagined change is called **resistance behavior.** Examples of this behavior may be employee hostility, employees performing their tasks in a sloppy manner, evidences of employee apathy, and often unhappy work groups.

Resistance behavior

Different people see different meanings in a change. Some may see it resulting from a job that was done poorly, some may fear a job will be eliminated, while others sense a loss of power and prestige. Resistance is encountered because management represents a force pushing for change, which, if not introduced properly, will be met by strong deterrent forces.

How do people view change?

To an organization, the processing of information using new technologies may mean a change in procedures, equipment, reporting relationships, required skills, and physical work environments. Before an organization introduces any of the information processing technologies, it is important to apply what is known about decreasing resistance to change.

Communicating Change

Resistance can be expected if the nature of the change is not made clear to the people who will be affected. People fear situations when they have incomplete information. Considerable planning is needed to prepare those affected by the change for the change itself.

Decreasing resistance to change

Employees need to know why the information processing technology is being considered. Employees need to be aware of the costs of producing documents and the problems associated with the traditional office. Employees should also be aware of what changes to expect. They should not have to wait to see walls being removed and equipment appearing to know that the change to information processing is taking place, but should be informed of the entire implementation schedule.

Employees need to know what is happening

A good reason for telling employees from the beginning about information processing is to gain their cooperation and support in the studies that have to be made concerning the work they do. Employees will be more ready to cooperate if they understand the reasons for the studies. When employees are asked questions about their jobs and are asked to keep records about their work, they should be informed about what information processing is. This procedure will prevent many misunderstandings about the change that is taking place.

To gain full cooperation, it is necessary to achieve accurate information from the studies. It would help if employees knew that information processing was endorsed by top management, information processing benefits everyone concerned, and the intent of information processing is not to do away with employees' jobs, but rather to eliminate repetitive work and provide them with more enriched jobs.

Employees need to be oriented at the beginning in a series of meetings and then kept informed throughout the implementation of information processing.

At first, employees may have objections to information processing, but these meetings should dispel their doubts by providing answers to any objections they may have.

Selling the Concept

Employees need to feel that information processing will benefit them. Part of the success of selling information processing to management and to the secretaries is in overcoming the fears of both groups. Managers often see information processing as an attempt to take away their personal secretaries. They often feel that taking away their personal secretaries reduces their status and diminishes the control they have of their own work. Managers often resent the introduction of information processing because it represents a new and drastic change to their routine. Secretaries have the same fears of losing status and losing control and the same opposition to changing their routines and learning new things. Both managers and secretaries also might feel that information processing will reveal any inadequacies they possess. Often in the manager/ secretary relationship, one of the two covers for the other's inadequacies. A change to information processing might reveal that a manager has poor grammar skills or that a secretary might not be a very fast typist. An important part of information processing is getting people to overcome these fears (Figure 11.15).

Provide little disruption to habits and routines

Changes need to be made slowly. Changing all procedures and routines overnight creates chaos. Introducing information processing in stages helps people learn new procedures and adjust gradually to new routines. It also ensures a smoother transition toward total information processing.

If working relationships such as the manager/secretary relationship have to be changed, both the managers and secretaries should recognize advantages that make the change more acceptable. For example, if managers can see that the new arrangement will allow them to get more work done, and if secretaries can see that they will have new career alternatives and better opportunities for advancement, they will be less reluctant to make the change.

Have employees participate

The more employees participate in change, the more that they will accept it. Employees need a chance to participate not only in the initial studies that are necessary to make decisions about information processing, but in revising existing procedures, writing new procedures where none existed, selecting color schemes for the new environment, and anywhere else their suggestions can be used. When information processing is introduced gradually in a department, employees who become experts on information processing equipment become excellent resource people. Their expertise can be used when planning for future information processing installations in other departments or when it comes time to upgrade and select new equipment. After employees know the equipment, they also can improve procedures by determining better and more efficient ways of producing documents. The manager of information processing needs to look upon employees as a creative resource and be willing to share some managerial authority with those who are directly affected by the change.

1. Employees can list what they dislike about their jobs. They can discuss how information processing will benefit them by eliminating distasteful parts of their jobs.
2. Employees must be informed about how information processing will:
   a. Distribute the workload.
   b. Remove the tedium of repetitive work.
   c. Make the office a more efficient unit.
   d. Produce higher quality work.
   e. Increase production.
   f. Cut office costs.
3. Employees can be shown how information processing handles actual applications from their own organization and makes their work easier.
4. Films from vendors can be shown that demonstrate how equipment can save employees' time and provide them with added convenience.
5. Statistics can be gathered from local organizations that saved money and decreased the amount of time necessary to produce the document after installing information processing.
6. Employees can be informed of new career paths created by information processing and how information processing has improved employee positions in other organizations.
7. Employees can visit similar organizations where information processing has been successfully installed or attend vendor equipment demonstrations, business convention displays, or open houses.
8. Information processing magazines and trade journals can be made available to employees.
9. Employees can be encouraged to become involved in information processing and to attend meetings of organizations such as the International Word Processing Association.
10. Employees can attend information processing seminars or classes at local colleges and universities.

Figure 11.15 Positive ways to sell the concept.

The Effect of Management Behavior on Organization Relationships

It is important to understand why some managers treat you differently than do other managers. Because you are an administrative support person who reports to an office manager, you bring to that manager your ideas for a new flex time policy. The new policy would meet the needs of the employees better and would have a positive effect on morale. Your idea is rejected and you begin to question your competence, value, and opportunity for personal growth in the organization. But the reason for the manager's behavior may be the assumptions your manager has about what people are like.

Douglas McGregor developed some ideas about this managerial behavior after many years of observing managers in organizations. McGregor believed

Theory X Assumptions	Theory Y Assumptions
People:	**People:**
1. Inherently dislike work and when possible, will avoid it.	1. Feel work is a natural phenomena that can be enjoyed.
2. Have little ambition, tend to shun responsibility and prefer to be directed.	2. Not only accept responsibility but actually seek it.
3. Above all, want security.	3. Will exercise self-direction toward organization goals.
4. Will only achieve organization goals if they are coerced, controlled and punished.	4. Have the capacity for solving organization problems.
5. Will take advantage if given the opportunity.	5. Have intellectual potential which is only partially used.
Managers who have this philosophy will:	Managers who have this philosophy will:
1. Exercise tight controls over employees.	1. Offer individual freedom.
2. Use close supervision (watch people closely).	2. Allow opportunity for using initiative.
3. Offer little freedom to make decisions.	3. Use general supervision.
4. Impose many rules and regulations.	4. Consult with employees to solve problems.

Figure 11.16 McGregor's Theory X and Theory Y.

that managers have different views concerning the nature of people and he called them Theory X and Theory Y.

Assumptions About People

Negative assumptions

Theory X (Figure 11.16) takes the view of people that is quite cynical and negative. Theory X managers make the following assumptions about people with whom they work: people by nature are lazy and work as little as possible, they lack ambition and will avoid responsibility, they are gullible and not very bright, and they like to be directed and controlled.

Positive assumptions

Theory Y, on the other hand, takes a very different position with respect to what people are like. Theory Y managers assume that work can be as satisfying as work or play, people are not inherently passive but rather become that way through experiences in the organization, people want more responsibility, not less, and intellectual potential is only partially used and is widely distributed throughout the population. The importance of these two theories lies in the effect they have on employee behavior. People in organizations will often behave

Effect of assumptions on behavior

as managers expect them to behave. It is almost as if a self-fulfilling prophecy is in operation. When a person is assumed to be lazy, irresponsible, not very bright, resistant to change, or burdened with other Theory X assumptions, it is not unlikely that a person will begin to behave that way. On the other hand, if Theory Y assumptions are followed by a manager, the employee will rise to meet those expectations. Some information processing managers treat their employees in a way that leads to superior performance. Other managers unintentionally treat their employees in a way that leads to a lower performance than they are capable of achieving.[7]

[7]Douglas McGregor, *Leadership and Motivation*, ed. Warren G. Bennis and Edgar H. Schein (Cambridge, Mass.: The M.I.T. Press, 1966), pp. 5–15.

The kinds of assumptions managers have about people will create the **organization climate.** It will show up in organizations much like the weather in different geographical areas in the United States. Some regions are cloudy and stormy for many months of the year, others have more sunshine and less ominous conditions. Organizations follow the same pattern; some are cold, hard, cynical, and use threats and fear to motivate employees. The kind of climate where these conditions exist is **autocratic.** It can be caused by managers with Theory X assumptions about people. Usually the organization uses penalties and rewards (carrot-and-stick style of managing) to motivate employees. The employees follow orders and use very little of their own creativity because managers believe they, in most cases, know how to do it better. The Ford Motor Company of the early 1900s is an example of how leadership can affect the climate of the organization. In 1925, of every ten automobiles sold in the United States, six of them were Fords. But 15 years later, Ford's share of the market had declined to only 20%. What caused this severe decline in the success of Ford? The owner and key executive was Henry Ford, who was a production genius. However, he ran the organization as if he were the only person who knew how to make correct decisions. His management staff was there only to carry out his decisions. They were not allowed to make many important decisions themselves. Henry Ford tried to run a billion-dollar organization with himself as the person almost solely responsible for it. People executed orders but seldom were allowed to create them. The result of Ford's Theory X management was to create an autocratic organization climate that restricted employee growth and enthusiasm.

An example of theory X

In contrast, other organizations may have an easy-going, relaxed, and satisfying climate. This kind of organization climate is called **supportive** and is usually created by Theory Y managers. The supportive climate allows for employee learning and growth. It supports the employee's performance on the job and appeals to higher-order need satisfaction.

An example of theory Y

One large organization allows employees a larger voice in how they do their jobs and makes sure that management does not treat employees as interchangeable cogs in a machine. It is an ongoing process for that organization, where management fosters an open expression of attitudes. A major United States airline has found that managers of high-performing work groups have a pattern of management practices that creates and maintains a favorable group climate. This management practice differs dramatically from the practices of managers of low-performance groups. In all high-performing groups, they discovered that subordinates feel responsible for performance. In low-performing groups, subordinates did not feel the same high level of responsibility for performance. It is apparent that management practices that instill a feeling of responsibility are critical to effective performance, and Theory Y practices will do this more successfully than Theory X ideas.

Management practices and effective performance

Summary

There are many organizations using information processing today that show less than desirable employee performance. Managers are responsible for motivating employees to accomplish results; but goals should be met with the least cost, time, and effort. Employees in today's organizations are demanding a different kind of management than in the past. Because the average employee is more educated and affluent, managers must provide them with a workplace that focuses on learning and growth. Economic rewards are not sufficient any longer to stimulate people to accomplish organization objectives. Managers need the ability to be flexible and to use different leadership styles as situations and people change.

Key Terms

Need hierarchy	Trait theory
Lower order needs	Boss-centered leadership
Higher order needs	Participative leadership
Maintenance-motivation model	Employee-centered leadership
Dissatisfiers	Situational leadership
Satisfiers	Resistance behavior
Motivation factors	Organization climate
Morale	Theory X
Morale profile	Theory Y
Job enrichment	Self-fulfilling prophecy
Traditional leadership	Autocratic climate
Flex time	Supportive climate

Study Guide

This study guide provides you with feedback to find out how well you are doing. Use a separate sheet of paper to record your answers. When you have finished check your responses with the answers at the back of the book.

Matching: Choose the answer that best defines the word in the left column.

1. Supportive climate
   a. hierarchy of needs

2. Autocratic climate
   b. to have feelings of value

3. Self-fulfilling prophecy
   c. maintenance-motivation model

4. Theory Y
   d. an important part of job enrichment

5. Situational leadership
   e. a traditional approach to leadership

6. Trait theory
   f. takes into account the employee, the leader, and the situation

7. Task variety
   g. leads to a relaxed and more productive organization climate

8. Frederic Herzberg
   h. a leader's attitude will affect the way employees behave

9. Ego need
   i. Ford Motor Company in the 1920s

10. Abraham Maslow
    j. usually associated with Theory Y.

Multiple choice: Select the letter or letters that best answer each question.

11. Maslow's need hierarchy includes all but one of the following needs:
    a. Physiological
    b. Self-fulfillment
    c. Advancement
    d. Ego
    e. All of these

12. The need to feel our lives are orderly and predictable is:
    a. Physiological
    b. Social
    c. Ego
    d. Self-fulfillment
    e. None of the above

13. All but one of these have a strong effect on organization morale:
    a. Amount of wages
    b. Morale surveys
    c. Kind of work
    d. All of the above

14. For a job to be enriched, it should have which of the following elements?
    a. Whole tasks
    b. Simplified tasks
    c. Task importance
    d. A and C
    e. B and C

15. Traditional leadership includes all but one of the following:
    a. Personality traits
    b. What a leader "is"
    c. Leader is more intelligent than followers
    d. Leadership is an influence process
    e. None of these

Completion: Write the correct answer(s) on a separate sheet of paper.

16. A _____ climate appeals to higher order need satisfaction.

17. Only an _____ need will cause us to act or be motivated.

18. If we have a boring job, our _____ need will probably not be satisfied.

19. The satisfiers in Herzberg's model relate to _____ order needs.

20. A _____ can be conducted in an organization to show areas of morale strength and weakness.

21. The assumption that people are lazy and not very bright is a Theory _____ assumption.

22. Freedom, independence, and judgment in scheduling work is called _____ .

True/False: Write + for True, 0 for False for each question.

23. The first need in Maslow's need hierarchy is the safety need.

24. The social need is the need to belong or be part of something.

25. A satisfied need is a strong motivator.

26. Wages and fringe benefits are the strongest motivators for employees today.

27. Recognition is considered a maintenance factor.

28. Most organizations have very little morale.

29. Autocratic leadership is less effective than democratic leadership in getting employees to accomplish more.

30. Theory Y leaders have a positive view of employees in an organization.

Questions on Concepts

1. Discuss some problems in employee effectiveness experienced by organizations.
2. Describe the theory of motivation developed by Abraham Maslow.
3. Discuss the needs which are motivators today.
4. Explain Herzberg's Maintenance-Motivation Model.
5. Discuss the conditions in which money is a motivator.
6. Describe the major factors that affect employee morale.

7. Explain what can be done to enrich a job.
8. Discuss the differences between traditional leadership and situational leadership.
9. Contrast the different styles of leadership called boss-centered, participative, and employee-centered.
10. Explain what is meant by management assumptions about people.
11. Discuss how management assumptions relate to Theory X and Theory Y.

Case and Activities

The Timeco Company was established in 1900 as a full-line insurance company handling life, casualty, and marine contracts. A few years ago, Timeco leased a computer to process the documents that have increased in number because of an increase in sales volume.

One group of office employees represented a particular problem for management. Their rate of output was inadequate, error rates were high, due dates and schedules were missed, and absenteeism was very high (especially before weekends and holidays). The group consisted of 98 operators, 7 assignment clerks, and a supervisor. Their job was to transfer information from printed or written documents into information processors for computer input. The size of the keyboarding requests varied from a few documents to 2,500.

Assignment clerks received jobs from originators. The work was parceled out in batches and was expected to take about one hour per operator. Operators were told, "Keyboard only what you see. Don't correct any originator errors." The documents were then proofread by other employees and sent to a supervisor. The supervisor screened them for formatting errors and due dates before sending them to the computer.

1. What problem do you see in this case?
2. Why are the indicators of morale negative?
3. How many job enrichment factors do the office employee's jobs have?
4. What could be done to solve the problem?

Activities

1. Interview the supervisor of an information processing center and find out what job enrichment factors were included when office jobs were designed.
2. Read an article on leadership or motivation in one of the following periodicals: Fortune, Harvard Business Review, Journal of Business. Give a five-minute oral report.
3. Visit an information processing center, talk with office employees, and then prepare a report on employee attitudes about the organization. Based on employee comments, make some conclusions about the type of organization climate that exists.

CHAPTER 12

Industry Case Studies

The objectives of this chapter are to:

1. Discuss some reasons why word processing has been implemented in various organizations.
2. Describe how several organizations have implemented word processing.
3. Compare the procedures and work handled in any two organizations.
4. Describe administrative support in one organization.
5. Describe how word processing expanded in one organization.

6. Discuss career paths in several organizations.
7. Discuss how environmental factors were handled in several organizations.
8. Discuss work measurement and how it benefited one organization.
9. Explain flexible scheduling and why it is used in one organization.
10. Discuss production increases in any organization as a result of word processing.
11. Describe the future plans of one organization.

All the studies in this chapter involve actual organizations where word processing has been implemented. In some of the organizations, word processing was implemented first, then information processing. In others, information processing will be implemented in the future. This chapter describes the background of the organization and gives information such as why the organization decided to implement word processing, how word processing was implemented, why word processing is successful in that particular organization, procedures and work processed in the center, the environment created for word processing, and future plans for the integration of technologies.

Law Firm

Word processing is often implemented in law firms. One law firm using word processing is Arent, Fox, Kintner, Plotkin, and Kahn in Washington, D. C. (Figure 12.1)

Figure 12.1 Word processing center at Arent, Fox, Kinnter, Plotkin, and Kahn, Federal Building, Washington, D.C. *(Courtesy of the law firm of Arent, Fox, Kinnter, Plotkin, and Kahn.)*

Background

Arent, Fox, Kintner, Plotkin, and Kahn is located in the Federal Bar Building in Washington, D. C. It currently employs 115 attorneys and a support staff of 170. Legal departments include federal communications, international, maritime/aviation, tax, real estate, government contracts, antitrust, litigation, securities and labor.

The Introduction of Word Processing

The law firm of Arent, Fox, Kintner, Plotkin and Kahn introduced word processing to their attorneys in order to reduce increasing office costs. Management decided to focus on methods for increasing attorney billable hours by eliminating time-consuming and repetitious proofreading, increasing document turnaround for text editing, reducing support staff where one secretary to each attorney had been traditional and workloads were often uneven, and decreasing costly overtime.

How Word Processing Was Implemented

Jane Hruska, former word processing manager writes: "Jack Palmer, the office manager, conducted a survey of automatic typing equipment and found the introduction of IBM's Magnetic Tape Selectric Typewriters in the 1960s to be a viable solution for his cost-reduction plan. Mr. Palmer, along with the management committee, decided to purchase an MT/ST during the late 1960s and decided to expand to three units by 1971. This decision was based on the relative success of the firm with boilerplating form letters.

"The MT/ST was replaced by IBM's Mag Card II stand-alone text editor during the early 1970s due to increased speed and versatility of the new equipment. Due to the decentralization of eight mag card units, operators began to give priority to favorite attorneys. This practice resulted in user dissatisfaction and service to less than 25% of the firm. Playback of lengthy documents (15 characters a second) was clearly inefficient since operators were idle during that time. These problems prompted the office manager to search for a more sophisticated word processing system.

"During the latter portion of 1974, Arent, Fox purchased the LCS Computext minicomputer, which is a shared logic, in-house computer. This system was installed and operators were trained in a centralized center in February of 1975.

"The minicomputer in the LCS Computext system was originally programmed by a lawyer for legal use. This minicomputer coordinates five electronic typing stations (ETS), one cathode ray tube (CRT), one electronic printing station (EPS) character printer for final copies, and one line printer for draft copies. Instead of magnetic cards, the system uses magnetic disks for storage of text; each disk holds about 1,000 pages of text. Computer-based equipment is incredibly versatile and fast. The EPS mentioned above plays out final copy at 55 characters a second (about 3½ times faster than the Mag Card machines) and, unlike the mag card equipment, the operator is free to start a second document while the printer is running. The storage capacity is much greater and extensive revisions are no problem. The equipment stops when the machine runs out of ribbon; it stores mailing lists and weekly dockets.

"The office manager allocated space and recruited a word processing supervisor who in turn developed systems for training operators, organizing workflow, and introducing attorneys to the potential of the equipment and the rules of its use."

Success of Word Processing

"The results at Arent, Fox are impressive. The eight Mag Card II units and eight operators have been replaced with five Computext terminals and support equipment operated by eleven operators (supporting three shifts). Whereas less than 24% of the lawyers in their firms used the Mag Card service, today 98% are using the Computext. Production figures indicate that the new WP center produced 60 pages for each operator during a 7½-hour day in January 1967, and 179.2 pages for each operator during the same length day in 1977. This latter figure is four times the national average for WP systems."

"These statistics reflect sound management decisions at several levels. The firm's senior lawyers not only examined their needs closely, learned from the lessons of the MT/ST and Mag Card systems, and made a choice of new equipment based on thorough research, but they also openly endorsed the system to all the attorneys in the firm and invested the system supervisor with the authority over as well as the responsibility for the WP center.

"The supervisor herself was hired into the position from outside the firm;

unlike her counterparts at other firms, her authority has not been undercut by top management. Her control over the unit is enhanced by the fact that she believes strongly that her operators should work as a team. Every operator is trained to perform all tasks—input, revision, and proofreading—and everyone rotates through these tasks. Boredom is reduced and the general atmosphere is one of cooperation and interdependence rather than competition. Although personality problems have arisen, largely centered on irritating personal habits, they have been largely resolved through group sensitivity sessions. Since she also handles all hiring for the unit, the supervisor also has immediate control over the personalities and skills being introduced into the group. She seeks recent high school graduates who are fresh, enthusiastic, and with above-average typing speed and a firm grounding in grammar. Besides its production figures, another aspect reflecting favorably on the WP center has been its low turnover rate: only three operators have left, one to be married, one to relocate to another city, and one to become a customer service representative for Automation Development, Inc. which now owns Computext.

"The supervisor also has some control over the use to which the attorneys in the firm put the WP center. In this respect, she may be unique among supervisors in comparable positions. In introducing the new system, only one small group of attorneys was at first granted access to the Computext. Once their work was routinely running through the unit with efficiency, some of the Mag Card Typewriters were phased out and another group of attorneys was invited to use the Computext. Group after group was added until virtually all of the WP production in the firm was centered in the computer facility. Attorneys are still not allowed to seek the keyboarding of a particular operator. This practice allows control of the workflow to remain with the supervisor. No documents under ten pages in length are accepted by the unit. The system, therefore, is used for work it accomplishes with maximum efficiency."

Career Paths

"When the center originated, the staff included a word processing supervisor and operators. Today career paths have been established to include a word processing manager, supervisors, and assistant supervisors for each of three shifts. The new titles have increased salary benefits and job enrichment, as well as provided an opportunity for operators to advance."

Procedures

"The WP center guarantees a finished document by the next morning, or earlier if pressed. To help fulfill this guarantee, the supervisor at Arent, Fox has had a system for logging in work since the facility was introduced. The group at Arent, Fox feels part of its efficiency results from their having developed 32 standard and 50 nonstandard forms for the computer."[1]

---

[1]Jean Hruska, 1979: personal communication.

The field of word processing is growing so rapidly that many temporary and permanent personnel agencies are specializing in word processing and training people for word processing positions. An example is CoverGirl, Temporary Office Personnel, Inc., in White Plains, New York.

Background

CoverGirl, Temporary Office Personnel, Inc. is a temporary and permanent placement agency. It is the largest in Westchester County. It has 35 staff employees. It places 700 temporaries in the field each week.

Why Word Processing Was Implemented

Dorothy Swegal, president, writes: "CoverGirl/Gateway decided to use word processing for a very simple reason: the need to supply our client companies with qualified operators, both temporary and permanent. In 1972, we were using an MC/ST I as a computer time-sharing terminal, and trained our own staff on the terminal in-house. As the need for operators arose among our client companies, we started an informal training program for temps who qualified. The sessions were usually held in the evening and on Saturdays and were very successful. A student could return to practice on his own at any time when the MC/ST was free. As we began to find more and more uses for the terminal — mailing lists, letters to clients, procedure manuals, etc. — we expanded and got a second MC/ST I."

"Today we have 2 MC/ST I's, 2 MC/ST II's, 1 MC/ST A, and a Vydec. The Wang is on order and scheduled to be delivered in four weeks. For the past five years, we have had a formal, scheduled training program, which we offered free to qualified applicants. We have trained approximately 250 applicants a year, using two full-time instructors. The demand has been so great that just recently we decided to offer the training program to our client companies for a modest charge."[2]

Food Services

Word processing is often implemented in the offices of food service organizations. An example of one food service organization using word processing is Sambo's Restaurants, Inc. in Santa Barbara, California. (Figure 12.2)

Background

In an amazingly short time, Sambo's Restaurants, Inc. (SRT) has grown from one small pancake shop to the nation's largest chain of 24-hour, full-service

[2]Dorothy Swegal, 1979: personal communication.

Figure 12.2 Word processing center at Sambo's Restaurants, Incorporated, Santa Barbara, California. *(Courtesy of Sambo's Restaurants, Incorporated.)*

family restaurants. As of August 31, 1979, there were 1,088 restuarants in operation in 47 states.

There are approximately 750 corporate employees and 50,000 restaurant employees nationwide. The word processing center is presently serving the Corporate Headquarters and the Pacific Regional Office, both in Santa Barbara and Carpinteria, California. The other four Sambo's regional offices handle their needs locally.

Why Word Processing Was Implemented

Sally Lyons, word processing manager writes: "Electric typewriters were distributed throughout the company and typing, along with administrative functions, were handled by administrative secretaries.

"Due to rapid growth of the company and a lack of space to accommodate personnel, the administration department consolidated the traditional typing pool into a centralized word processing center to more efficiently handle the typing needs of the company.

Food Services

"Sambo's Restaurants, Inc., considered the following advantages of word processing over the conventional typing pool when making the decision to use word processing in its corporate headquarters."

1. *Increased Productivity.* Initial keyboarding is quicker because typists do not have to be concerned with making errors. Errors can easily be corrected after copy is proofed. Equipment automatically plays out final copy three to six times faster than typists can type it on electric typewriters. Since the information is captured on various media such as magnetic cards and diskettes, rekeyboarding is unnecessary. Moreover, it is simple to add, delete, or move around material once the material is on media. Constant material (stored material that does not change) need not be reproofread. Therefore, proofreading time is saved.

2. *Confidentiality.* With word processing, control can be maintained over who has access to confidential company information.

3. *Consistency.* With word processing, standard procedures can be set up to provide consistency in the way the documents were formatted. Individual typists would not be able to type documents different from what the company desired.

4. *Quality.* Work done on automated equipment can be produced error-free; therefore, there is no need for cutting, taping, or using correction fluid. Proofreading procedures can be set up to assure that work is error-free.

5. *Turnaround.* Turnaround time increases from three to six times on updated or revised materials.

6. *Permanent File Library.* Files of stored media can be retained indefinitely for weekly or monthly updates or revisions. Standard letters can be stored and selected, with variables being incorporated as needed.

7. *Cost.* Personnel costs can be saved because one automated typewriter can produce the work of two or three typists. The employee's time is more productive because the same information need not be rekeyboarded nor does standard or constant material have to be reproofread.

How Word Processing Was Implemented

"An area was designed for the new word processing staff and equipment in a work-station setting. It began with five operators (previously typists) and five mag card machines. Procedures were implemented with the help of the vendor and center operator input. The center concept became operational in April 1976."

Procedures and Work Processed in the Word Processing Center

"Work comes into the Center by interoffice mail or facsimile from the various locations of Sambo's users within Santa Barbara and Carpinteria. Work may also be dictated through a central dictation system in the center via telephone.

"Work is logged daily by originator, date, type of work, line count, and estimated completion time. It is then assigned by the supervisor to an operator for completion. All work comes in with a word processing job request indicating special instructions, i.e. line spacing, paper, or format. The operator processes and proofs. It then is briefly proofed by the supervisor and mailed out in the interoffice mail.

"The center produces an average of 200,000 typed lines per month and services approximately one hundred users.

"The work done by the center is varied and includes manuals up to 200 pages, statistical work, text and technical reports, letters, memos, forms, and address and employee lists."

Staff Is Better Used

"A word processing operator can concentrate all effort and time on the typing function. The administrative functions can be handled by an administrative secretary. With no interruptions for filing, phone answering, or making appointments, production and accuracy are increased. Moreover, more time is available to administrative secretaries to assume more nontyping responsibilities."

Future Plans

"Sambo's intends to improve the communications between regions and corporate headquarters by initiating electronic message sending devices, to expand its word processing capabilities to its five regional offices, and to communicate between centers and the mainframe computer located in the management information services (MIS) department.

"Sambo's long-term plan is to integrate word processing and data processing. Word processing and data processing are realizing the likeness of their service functions and the need for each: data processing's sophisticated numeric manipulation and high-speed printing capability and word processing's text manipulation and high quality printing capability. With each working in conjunction with the other, they can together provide a total information processing service to the user in a cost-effective and expedient manner."[3]

Electronics Research

Word processing is often implemented in organizations that do electronics research. An example of one electronics research organization using word processing is Sierra Research Corporation in Buffalo, New York.

Background

Sierra Research Corporation is a research organization whose primary business is electronic development and manufacturing of radar and telemetry

---

[3]Sally Lyons, 1979: personal communication.

systems. Another division designs and manufactures computer-based data collection systems for specialized industrial applications. They do not have offices overseas, but do have international representatives and numerous overseas contracts. They employ approximately 650 people.

How Work Was Handled Prior to Word Processing

Doreen Nolan, administrative services manager, writes: "Prior to implementing word processing, technical typing was done by three typists in the technical publications department. Overloads were distributed to other departmental secretaries who may not have been familiar with the particular type of work. No measurement techniques were employed and most overloads and peaks were "last-minute-reactive" situations. Salaries for typists were lower than the secretarial group, with little incentive for improvement. Subcontract (temporary help) typists were also used."

Why Sierra Research Investigated Word Processing

"After investigating the workload, it became apparent that most technical documents were generated by revising previous documents. New text was constantly revised. Many departments also generated boilerplate-like correspondence. Therefore, Sierra Research decided to implement word processing."

How Sierra Implemented Word Processing

"The office was not physically reorganized; increased document requirements were taken to word processing as a gradual changeover. Technical typists were transferred to word processing with general typists replacing them in the technical publication department. A shared-logic word processing system was selected for the word processing center. No particular piece of equipment or operator is dedicated to one particular task."

Procedures and Work Processed in the Word Processing Center

"All formal company documents are sent to the center where they are permanently stored on disk. Eventually, they will be transferred to micrographics as part of a permanent company library.

Most documentation is technical and consists of 100 to 1000 pages per document, with the average being about 400 pages. Some standard correspondence is also handled. The word processing center also envelops telecommunications (i.e., telefax and teletype as well as regular mail, intracompany mail, and telephones)."

"Word processing operators are rated on a comparative level to computer operators and in a direct line with the secretarial structure. The progression is: word processing trainee, operator, senior operator, specialist, and assistant supervisor. The salary structure has also been adjusted accordingly."

Future Plans

"Our center does not, as yet, interface with data processing although it is a very likely future step. Communications will probably be the first step in integrating with data processing. Immediate expansion includes acquiring OCR (Optical Character Recognition) devices. Current data processing equipment consists of a CPU with two disk drives, a 430-line printer (chain driven), and three Diablo 1620 terminals."[4]

Federal Government

Word processing has been implemented by many government agencies. One government agency using word processing is the U. S. Nuclear Regulatory Commission in Washington, D.C.

Background

The U. S. Nuclear Regulatory Commission was created by the Energy Reorganization Act of 1974. Previously the U. S. Nuclear Regulatory Commission was called the U. S. Atomic Energy Commission. It was the U. S. Atomic Energy Commission that implemented word processing because paperwork was increasing and in 1969 all government agencies were restricted to replacing only 75% of the people the agency lost.

The Nuclear Regulatory Commission is an independent regulatory agency. Most of the work involves review and licensing of nuclear power reactors and radioisotopes for medicine and industry. The agency employs close to 3,000 people. It has five regional offices throughout the U. S.

Equipment and Procedures at the U. S. Nuclear Regulatory Commission

Frank Malone, Director of Administrative Services, writes: "We started with MT/STs, went over to Mag Cards, and our centers are now utilizing IBM System 6s with ink jet printers. In some program offices, we have CRT word processing equipment in walk-up locations for secretaries to use on an as-needed basis. So far, there have been very few scheduling conflicts. We are also beginning to use optical character recognition scanners in some of the program offices to facili-

[4]Doreen Nolan, 1979: personal communication.

tate the processing of revision typing work. All work done on word processing equipment in the program offices is recorded on operating log sheets. In this way, we can determine whether the equipment is being utilized for revision-type work and hours used per day. Most of the heavy-revision documents consisting of 6 to 200 pages are done in the centers. The centers use a simple page count measurement and code of difficulty for determining center productivity."

The Growth of Word Processing at the U. S. Nuclear Regulatory Commission

"When word processing was first installed, it was done on a pilot basis. We installed three machines, hired three operators, and a working supervisor. Prior to starting the center, a thorough review was made of some of the agency's reading files to determine the extent and kind of revision and redundant typing done by the secretaries. The Director of Administration made the decision to implement word processing with full support of top management. Within one year after operation, the chairman of the AEC participated in an awards ceremony for the entire central word processing staff. This award was the largest group award made in AEC. In 1970, the person responsible for implementing word processing in the agency received the Presidential Management Improvement Award for his work with word processing. From its fledgling inception in 1969, CRESS, the name of the word processing operation, is now staffed with twenty word processing operators, one manager, three supervisiors, and three proofreaders. The three units produce about 20,000 pages a month. The assistant to the Director of Administration is the principal agency consultant for determining the need for new word processing equipment or upgrading of existing equipment."

The Environment for Word Processing

"When word processing was implemented, no major reorganization of the office was made. We did, however, centralize the operation and made the necessary environmental changes by carpeting the floors and installing acoustical draperies. Since we expected the operators to be working in a production environment as contrasted to the social environment of the business office, we wanted to make the center as comfortable as possible. As more equipment and people were added to the center, we found it necessary to add air conditioning units."

Future Plans

"Our future plans are to continue operating on a centralized and decentralized basis of word processing. We expect optical character recognition will play a prominent part in our word processing operations. We will also increase our photocomposition capabilities. Our future plans are to make word processing part of the agency information technology management plan. Our plans are to have an agency information technology manager who will be responsible for coordinating the generation of information technology to improve the level and quality of services delivered to the public and to increase the productivity of the agency workforce.

"Word processing has been doing its job for NRC, allowing personnel with sharp typing skills to pursue a word processing career, and freeing secretaries for more administrative work.

"In NRC we're convinced that our move into the office of tomorrow will change our ordinary functioning from being reactive to productive. We are now developing goals to improve the management of technology in our agency, and word processing will be one of the predominant tools. Also, we fully recognize that human engineering requires making all of our new office tools to fit people, not the other way around. The priority in the 1980s will be the same as in the 1960s — people, procedures, and equipment."[5]

Foreign Government

Word processing is often implemented in many different levels of government. One example of where word processing is used in local government of a foreign country is in Warringah Shire Council in Sydney, Australia.

Background

Warringah Shire Council is a local government of Warringah Shire. The Council is made up of several departments among them the Department of Administration, Town Planning, Health and Building, and Engineering.

Why Warringah Shire Council Introduced Word Processing

"As part of its policy to continually review its operations and costs, the Council, in mid 1977, accepted the proposition that steps should be taken to utilise the latest technology and most up-to-date methods in streamlining administration and management techniques. As part of this proposal, it gave authority for tenders (bids) to be called for word processing and centralised dictation equipment.

"During its original consideration of the proposal, the Council appreciated that it was difficult to estimate precise savings which would arise but experience had shown elsewhere that there was considerable potential for savings even if only to arrest staff growth which goes hand in hand with the constantly increasing workload occurring in local government areas of the size of Warringah Shire. The Council concluded that as a containment of future growth of administrative staff and associated costs was an important objective, this was the direction in which it should be moving. It was, however, emphasised that there would be no prospect of the installation of the equipment causing retrenchment of any employee."

[5]Frank Malone, 1979: personal communication.

"As far as word processing is concerned tenders were called, closing on 7th October, 1978. Seven tenders were received. A very comprehensive study was undertaken in respect of all the equipment offered by the tenderers (vendors). All equipment was looked at in the offices of the various companies, generally on more than one occasion and, as well, actual working installations were visited where possible. The investigation team visited Randwick, Campbelltown and Wyong Councils where word processing equipment was already installed.

"The types of equipment offered were largely in three groups: stand-alone units that used "floppy disk" storage media, magnetic card storage media, and "shared logic" systems with visual display screens.

"From the outset, the objective of this Council was for word processing units to do as much typing as possible for all Council departments. It was, therefore, intended to include a lot of "on-off" one-time work. While appreciating the advantages of the shared logic systems, it was felt, for this Council's particular purposes, it would be preferable to acquire stand-alone units rather than separate input and printing machines. As far as magnetic card storage was concerned, it was considered that the volume of Council work was such that considerable cataloguing and storage would be involved. Therefore, the conclusion was reached that the Olivetti TES 501 units would be most suitable for the Council's needs. Another important consideration was the price and in this regard the Olivetti equipment (bearing in mind the number of units likely to suit the Council's needs) compared favourably.

"In the light of all the circumstances, having regard to this Council's particular aims and objectives, the Council decided to acquire 6 Olivetti TES 501s. Appropriate arrangements were made to organise a word processing centre staffed by a supervisor, machine operators, and administrative assistants. The assistants, as well as being trained as operators to ensure maximum use of the machines during the absence of regular operators, carry out secretarial duties. The emphasis is on maximum use of the machines with as little interruption as possible.

"The typing work of the Council Departments has been transferred to the centre on a staged basis, beginning with the Administration Department, followed by the Town Planning, Health and Building, and Engineering Departments."

Procedures and Work Done

"During the transfer of work to the Centre, the opportunity was taken to standardise some letters and revise the comprehensive lists of standard conditions applicable in some town planning, subdivision, and building applications. Manuals were compiled comprising the standard letters and conditions and issued to authors and operators. This practice has resulted in considerable time savings in work preparation."

"The system has now been in operation for about nine months and authors and operators alike are now quite familiar with the new methods. During the initial stages, there were some problems as departments had to get used to the centralised system. There was also, to some extent the expected problem of 'resistance to change.' However as the advantages of the new equipment and associated procedures became apparent the problems and complaints have been overcome.

"In fact, it can be concluded that typing staff growth has, at least, been arrested and overall efficiency has increased. The installation is considered to be very successful."[6]

Employee Benefit Services

Word processing is often implemented in organizations that handle employee benefits. One such employee benefit service organization is Kwasha Lipton Consulting Actuaries and Employee Benefit Services in Englewood Cliffs, New Jersey.

Background

Kwasha Lipton is one of the nation's foremost consulting firms specializing in employee benefits. It provides a full range of services to clients on domestic and international programs which include retirement plans, pension plans, benefit booklets, and the like. It does not sell a product so the image its clients receive of KL is through the typed material sent to them. Quality is of the utmost importance in its typed work.

Why Kwasha Lipton Introduced Word Processing

Barbara Rochette, manager of word processing writes: "Our center presently services 140 people as compared to under 100 ten years ago. Besides the growth of our own company staff, the number of clients we service has increased tremendously. There is no doubt that we would have had to at least triple our typing staff and equipment to keep up with this growth if it were not for automated typing equipment and the overall approach of word processing."

[6]Information provided through the courtesy of John Preston, Sales and Marketing Manager, Olivetti Corporation, Sydney, Australia.

"Kwasha Lipton did not enter into word processing deliberately. We just happened to work ourselves into it slowly. At the time, we thought we were merely upgrading equipment and methods to improve productivity and produce high-quality typewritten material at reasonable cost.

"We avoided many of the pressures placed on people trying to implement a new office setup for word processing. We had the advantage of always having had a typing pool so there was little restructuring that needed to be done.

"We began in 1965 by adding an IBM Composer System to our typing pool, which at that time consisted of Executive typewriters. The Composer system proved to be very time-consuming in terms of training and revision capabilities. In many instances it was more feasible to use the old cut-and-paste method for masters as we had used for typed work from the Executive typewriters. Whenever we did this, our Composer tapes were not updated properly and by the time we decided to end the use of the Composer we had well over 300 tapes that were incorrect. What a waste of time and money. I must admit though, at the time, the finished printed product was beautiful and seemed worth the time and money, but what a long road to take to get that printed product.

"Over the years, equipment was periodically updated to keep pace with new efficiencies available. We introduced mag cards to our still-existent typing pool in 1968 and we found their revision capabilities superior to the composer. Switching from a typing pool to a word processing center was a gradual process which took about three years to complete. It was sometime during these three years that we realized we had entered the world of word processing. We could not operate a word processing center the same way we operated our typing pool. Methods and procedures had to be developed in order to maintain the efficiency of the equipment. No longer could a typist just take a job and type it. Determinations had to be made as to how the job should be handled, should it be stored, and for what period of time. A filing system had to be initiated for items now being stored and retrieval of these items had to be simple as most things were updated frequently. Work load had increased also and more stringent priority requirements had to be set and most important, all of this led to the need of full-time management of the Center.

"Kwasha Lipton switched to Vydec word processing units in 1976 and gradually replaced all mag card units in the Center. We are presently working closely with our data processing department so we can eventually make use of our mainframe computer for our word processing storage needs.

"The standards at KL are extremely high since the typewritten copy sent from our offices is the only tangible material the client has of our work. We make little use of form letters or boilerplate information. Kwasha Lipton has always prided itself on individual attention to a client's needs, and this is reflected in any typing done for a particular client. What one client receives from us you can be sure will not be duplicated in work done for another client."

Center Staff at Kwasha Lipton

"Our present staff in the Center consists of one manager, one working supervisor, seven operators full-time days, one administrative secretary at a set-up desk to log work in and out and keep records of work being processed, five administrative secretaries for filing, message desk coverage, switchboard relief, proofreading, photocopying, stocking supply cabinets, etc., and five parttime operators evenings (there is no evening supervisor)."

Word Processing Management Position at Kwasha Lipton

"Ten years ago when we were still a typing pool, the supervisor handled many details of the office that were not directly related to typing. The supervisor was in charge of all incoming and outgoing typing, the messenger who brought and delivered such typing, input to the print shop, completed work from the print shop, supplies for typing and printing, first aid supplies, office boys for mail delivery, interviews, and many other details. Many times you might say the typing pool was the great melting pot. If someone in the company was not directly responsible for something it suddenly became the responsibility of the typing supervisor. As you can imagine, there was little time for the supervisor to manage anything but her own workload. Even managing her workload was a feat in itself. She truly had to be a "jack of all trades" but, unfortunately, master of none because she had no time to master anything. Fortunately, word processing changed all this. The duties of a manager of word processing, in most cases, are more clearly defined. To function in this position, the manager of word processing must have the ability and willingness to delegate those responsibilities which do not demand the manager's overall personal attention. Good delegation is beneficial to both the manager and the people working with the manager. The manager must also be attuned to all aspects of the work of the principals (originators) the center serves, must like people and be able to work comfortably under pressure. Upper management, moreover, must give the managers responsibility and the manager must know how to assume it."

Career Paths at Kwasha Lipton

"Our operators are trained to handle all assignments in the center. Within the center, there are varying levels in the salary structure. These variations exist because of the level of work the operator performs. Naturally, we have a couple of operators who can handle any job, while others may be capable of doing it, but it would take them twice as long and require a lot of assistance. Career paths, however, are not formally set up. We allow our operators to be interviewed for any position that opens up in the company if they are interested in it and feel they have the necessary qualifications. In the past four years, six center employees have moved into other departments in positions unrelated to word processing and have done very well and are happy with their new positions."

Recordkeeping and Work Measurement at Kwasha Lipton

"When we had fully implemented the center with mag cards and the composer system, we knew word processing was a growing area that we did not want to lose sight of. In search for new and better equipment for our needs and new management techniques, we attended workshops, seminars, equipment shows, and subscribed to word processing magazines. The value of attendance at these functions proved a necessary part of our growth. One of the most valuable lessons we learned during these early years was the importance of work measurement. The information provided us by work measurement helped us determine what the equipment could do for us, couldn't do, and how much document production cost us. It also helped us to determine the types of equipment we would need to look for in the future. It did not take us very long to determine that revision was the major portion of our work. By the time we were fully immersed in word processing, these work measurement records proved to be the most important tool in selling new ideas and concepts to upper management. I would not like to give the impression that this recordkeeping was simple—it took us many tries before we came up with a system that was workable for us. Fortunately, we have an in-house computer and by sitting down with our systems analyst and telling him what we were looking for in the form of records, we finally came up with a very workable solution. I feel it is a definite aid to have a computer working in this area, but it is by no means necessary. It would take longer, but much of the information we receive from the computer could also be accomplished without it."[7]

Medical Research

Word processing is often implemented in organizations that conduct medical research. One research organization using word processing is the Institute for Medical Research, a nonprofit research corporation located in Santa Clara, California.

Background

The Institute for Medical Research (IMR) is a nonprofit research corporation located in the Santa Clara Valley, with approximately 150 employees. Facilities and administrative services are provided for investigators from Stanford University and the Santa Clara Valley Medical Center, as well as for IMR's own core of researchers. Additional clerical services are also available to local physicians and scientists.

Why IMR Investigated Word Processing

Stephanie Ferguson, grants officer for the Institute for Medical Research (IMR), writes: "The past three years have shown a tremendous growth pattern. The size of the Institute doubled twice. Growing pains resulted in all areas of endeavor, but especially in providing clerical services for investigators. We fell into two modes of operation, 'extremely heavy' and 'crisis', even with the addi-

---

[7]Barbara Rochette, 1979: hersonal communication.

tion of two new secretaries and correcting selectrics at our disposal. Coordinating grants and contract applications, mass mailings, and manuscripts became increasingly difficult, and deadlines were being met dangerously close. Lack of time for revisions necessitated the paste-and-cut method, with duplicated copies serving as originals — definitely not professional output. Standard administrative tasks were permanently relegated to the 'pending' file."

Why IMR Needed Information Processing Capabilities

"The problems we were facing were not hard to evaluate. IMR was in the beginning stages of a membership drive, as well as building campaign. Also, regulations regarding conducting and reviewing research were becoming increasingly complex and current filing and monitoring methods were not proving adequate. In addition to our urgent text processing needs, file data access and manipulation was becoming imperative, and use of our in-house computer for this purpose was logistically out of the question. We felt that an information processor would be able to handle both of these applications, and proceeded with a systems and cost/benefit analysis. Fortunately, the administrative director, a progressive individual, had indeed given word processing much thought. She was extremely supportive, and readily backed the purchase of the equipment at this time. Since, as the grants officer, I was directly responsible for the majority of items that would be routed through the processing center, evaluation and choice of equipment was left to me; however, our director made the final purchase decision."

How IMR Handled Environmental Factors

"Upon selecting IBM's Office System 6 processor, with ink jet printer and automatic paper handling, we felt that a quiet location would be important in minimizing distractions and increasing production. The Grants Office was moved to a suite across the hall, and an entire room designated as the Information Processing Center. A "dedicated" circuit was installed to accommodate the equipment. Shortly thereafter we ordered another processor, this time one with an impact printer. The noise factor, which was already a problem in an enclosed room, was expected to increase substantially so we installed Soundsoak wall panelling."

Procedures and Work Processed in the Information Center

"Currently, our information processing center serves over 50 principals in both text and file management processing. All requests are routed through the supervisor, logged in, and assigned a priority rating. Requests are then processed according to that rating and, once they begin a project, the information processing operators communicate directly with the principals if there are any questions. We serve research investigators in processing technical documents of 20 to 300 pages in length. For our own administrative offices we process standard 2 to 3 page letters and documents (some of which are prerecorded paragraphs); print and revise lengthy manuals; are implementing a personnel records system; and are coordinating a membership drive and building fund, which involve mass mailings and file systems of approximately 7,000 records. In addition, we are implementing a document flow system for our research review committee, which will store approximately 300 pieces of information on each research application, play out monthly committee agendas, letters to applicants and research review committee members, store minutes and reports of the proceedings, and act as a tickler file to assure review again in one year's time."

Who Uses Word Processors

"Some of our project investigators themselves use word processors. One study employs an Apple II as part of a national medical information network. While it is a computer capable of evaluating complex medical variables, it also serves word processing functions, storing and revising questionnaires, consent forms, and related documents."

Benefits and Future Plans

"Data is not yet available with regard to the savings word processing is accomplishing at IMR, but from a subjective viewpoint, each operator is now able to handle the work of approximately 1.75 full time equivalents. We expect this to increase in the future. Training, organization, and initial input of files have proved to be more lengthy than we originally anticipated, but even so we are increasing production capabilities. Eventually we plan to add communications capabilities. Who knows, within the next few years we may even see a CRT on each desk here at IMR. What we do know for sure is that the capability of information processing systems is increasing rapidly. We hope to use these changes to our advantage."[8]

Health Care

Word processing has been implemented in many hospitals. One hospital using word processing is Lincoln General Hospital in Lincoln, Nebraska (Figure 12.3).

Background

Lincoln General Hospital is a 286-bed acute care facility located in Lincoln, Nebraska.

Why Lincoln General Hospital Introduced Word Processing

Marlene Riggs, Director of the word processing center, writes: "Lincoln General Hospital first instituted its word processing center in 1971 in an attempt

[8]Stephanie Ferguson, 1979: personal communication.

Figure 12.3 Word processing center at Lincoln General Hospital, Lincoln, Nebraska. *(Courtesy of Lincoln General Hospital.)*

to centralize and coordinate many of the common secretarial activities of all hospital departments."

How Word Processing Was First Implemented at Lincoln General Hospital

"The word processing department was created as an independent unit, in addition to the already established function of medical dictation and transcription, which was, and remains, a part of the hospital's Medical Records Department.

"The word processing center, when it was created, was equipped with the industry standard of IBM Magnetic Card Selectric Typewriters and was staffed with approximately three full-time employees. By June, 1977 the center had grown to a total of 8.2 full time equivalents with operation on two shifts, five days a week and had experienced upgrades in terms of equipment utilized through several levels of IBM Magnetic Card equipment, each time benefiting from a higher level of technology. Because of its heavy involvement in the areas of policy and procedure manual maintenance and permanent storage of records which had evolved to a very high level by 1978, the center was maintaining a library of over 5,000 magnetic cards."

Why Was a Feasibility Study Conducted

"The inherent inefficiencies of handling individual pieces of the recording media prompted the director of the word processing center, in May, 1978, to initiate a study to determine the feasibility of upgrading the center's equipment to utilize the new generation of word processing systems, which include the capability for storage and retrieval of large volumes of recorded material on random access disks."

What the Feasibility Study Was To Do

"The Management Engineering Department was contacted and a project request was drafted to initiate a study to research the productivity improvement potential of the higher technology word processing systems currently available on the market. The following tasks were identified in terms of accurately defining and mapping out the role that the word processing center would take for the next several years:

1. Analyze tasks and growth and forecast future demand for service.

2. Analyze labor requirements for existing workload mix and determine potential errors for productivity improvements through utilization of new technology and see if adequate justification can be found to upgrade the equipment to the new generation of word processing systems.

3. Analyze and compare competitive word processing systems vendors' equipment and recommend an alternative to management, considering functionality (features) costs, compatibility, and vendor (service) profile."

How the Data Was Analyzed

"Unit production data was analyzed several different ways and the 'closest fit' regression line was selected as a mathematical representation to forecast future demand. It was found that the center is averaging a growth of approximately 27,000 units per year (one unit equals 25 lines of reproduced information). It was also noted that if the current growth was sustained through the next several years, the current unit volume will increase from approximately 330,000 units in 1978, to almost 440,000 units by 1982. As was noted previously, the staffing level for the center had increased from 3 FTEs in 1971, to approximately 8.2 FTEs in 1978. Productivity figures were used in terms of standard units of production per worked person day for a 30-month period beginning in January, 1976. It was found that gross productivity had increased from 123 units per day in 1976, to 152 units per day in 1977. This rate of increase, however, did not carry into 1978, as the figure for the first six months of 1978 was 156 units per day. An extensive analysis was done to determine the underlying reasons for the large increase which occurred between 1976 and 1977, and the leveling off which occured between 1977 and 1978. It was noted that in 1973, when the standard unit measurement system was instituted, that 120 units per day was considered a benchmark for expected production by an experienced operator. This 120 unit per day figure was understood to include factors such as variation in demand for service, variation in complexity of workload, and level of skill for an "experienced" operator. By analyzing the turnover and relative longevity of employees in the center and also considering the periodic upgrading of equipment which occurs from time to time, there is indication to suggest that the productivity increase experienced in 1977 was due to primarily three factors: an extreme increase in workload over the previous year (which had remained relatively constant from the year preceding), along with a push by hospital management to maintain the staff at a relatively constant level; the staff experienced relatively little turnover in this period, with the average longevity being somewhere between three and four years each; some new equipment was added in this period which did result in an increased ability to process certain types of work. Conversely in 1978, we see a leveling off of the gross productivity of the word processing center. We attribute this to a saturation effect. The work force, although highly skilled and well-supervised, had reached the practical limit in terms of the existing technology offered in the equipment utilized. This conclusion was backed up by hard observation in that large amounts of time were being consumed by the operators being required to manually load and unload mag cards into the readers. In addition, record keeping was consuming ever more amounts of time. The overall conclusion in regard to this productivity analysis was that if the center desired to continue to reach higher levels of productivity, a major switch in equipment would be necessary in order to better utilize the talents of the operators.

"Unit costs were analyzed over this same period and it was found that although costs for labor and equipment had increased from $77,000 to $88,000 from 1976 to 1977, the increase in productivity experienced enabled the unit cost for the center to drop from 30.7¢ to 28.98¢. Unit cost projections were made for the years 1978 through 1982, using the future demand forecast developed in the initial part of the study tied with the 155 units per person day productivity level for 1978, and considering an 8% inflation factor for equipment and labor. The result is that the cost per unit is shown to increase from approximately 30¢ per unit in 1978, to 46¢ per unit in 1983, with a six year total for equipment and labor costs in excess of $900,000."

Conclusions of the Study

"The existing workload mix was broken down into eleven categories and was analyzed as to each area's productivity improvement potential through the utilization of a higher technology word processing system offering such capabilities as high powered text editing, large volume storage on disk media, and high speed printer. It was estimated that productivity gains were anywhere from 5% to 73% and could be accomplished by upgrading the word processing center equipment. The overall productivity improvement potential for a fully equipped "new generation" word processing system is estimated to be in excess of 32%."

How Vendors Were Selected

"Considering that over 100 vendors are currently marketing various types of text editing and word processing equipment, it was extremely difficult to perform a comprehensive survey and include all available vendors. Because of this, a prescreening was performed and approximately seven to eight vendor candidates were selected as having the most potential for implementation. These seven or eight vendors were then narrowed down to three finalists on the basis of their capabilities and compatibility with the existing system (considering that a phased implementation over a period of time had been specified by administration). These three vendor finalists were then evaluated independently and compared to criteria which was established to compare those aspects of a potential system which would be most beneficial to our institution. These features included things such as editing, input ability, output display, disk capacity, compatibility with the existing system, diagnostic ability, and expandability. The total composite for all the features was given a weighting of 55% in the final evaluation. Cost was also considered very heavily and was given a weighting of 30%. The final 15% was based on a vendor profile, which included such things as the company's dedication and involvement with the word processing field, the availability of service, and the training offered by the vendor during the implementation period.

"A selection was made and was recommended to, and approved by, the administration of the hospital for implementation in March, 1979. It was the consensus that this move will enable our institution to continue to provide a high level of word processing support to all levels and departments of the organization, and will enable us to respond to the everchanging and increasing needs of a dynamic health care institution.

"Considering the possibility of a phased implementation of a text-editing system over a five year period, there is sufficient indication that the current staffing level of 8.1 FTEs will be more than sufficient to accommodate the increased workload projected for this period. Analyzing the project unit costs for the period of 1978 through 1983, based upon the same projected demand and again considering an 8% inflation factor for equipment and labor, we see our units costs rising slightly from approximately 30¢ again in 1978, to the slightly over 36¢ per unit in 1983, when the text-editing system would be fully implemented. The six year total for projected equipment and labor costs is approximately $780,000. The total accumulated cost avoidance over a six year period through 1983, is projected to be $127,000."[9]

An Insurance Company

Insurance companies have huge volumes of paperwork and are one of the major users of word processing. An example of one insurance company that uses word processing is MONY, The Mutual Life Insurance Company of New York.

Background

"The first mutual life insurance company to begin operations in the United States was Mutual of New York (MONY), which issued its first policy in February, 1843. We employ 5,000 people throughout the United States and Europe. The

---

[9]Marlene Riggs, 1979: personal communication.

home office is in Manhattan. Several functions including files, archives, data processing systems, and policyowner services are located in the service center complex in Syracuse, New York. The center of which I am supervisor is the largest of its kind in MONY with a staff of 16 supporting approximately 400 users."

Why MONY Implemented Word Processing

Sally L. Kwasigroch, word processing center supervisor, writes: "The 'typing pool', which I was hired to supervise, was, for me, somewhat of a humiliation initially. Equipment was run down or archaic, staff was often ignored and disorganized, and we were taken for granted. There were few procedures, constant demands for rush work complicated our operation's efficiency, and heavy volumes necessitated overtime. Overtime was rule of thumb. Turnover was inordinately high as was our level of frustration. A primitive form of work measurement was in force although I must confess that I never understood what it was meant to accomplish. My negative feelings as supervisor of the area were such that I felt compelled to reverse our image in any way that I could. My boss supported my efforts and encouraged me whenever I wished to make changes, however insignificant. It was an uphill struggle which took nearly four years to accomplish."

How MONY Handled Environmental Factors

"In 1974, we relocated our staff and equipment to an area within the department which afforded us a degree of privacy. We did some decibel level readings and added carpets, drapes, and wall acoustical treatment to absorb some of the equipment noise and experienced immediate improvements in productivity. We changed our name to word processing center and created an identity for our staff."

New Career Paths and Flexible Scheduling

"Within two years, we shaped up a promotional program for the center's employees, published and circulated a service schedule, organized our staff into small work groups, cut three days off our service schedule, and jumped headlong into a massive cross-training effort to ensure efficient machine utilization and greater job satisfaction. Turnover diminished noticeably, skill levels improved, and a sense of pride became apparent within the center.

"In 1976, we installed a shared-logic text-editing system which approximately half of our staff operates and we reevaluated our promotional program, dropping one level off at the base and adding two at the top. There are four grade levels in the center, not including my own, beginning with a typist trainee/control clerk and progressing to senior typist, CRT operator, trainer/project specialist. Generally, job openings at the various levels are filled from within. It is not my practice to fill a vacancy in a higher level by bringing in

Year	Salaries	Total budget	Volumes	Staff
1980	$168,000	$187,000		17[a]
1979	144,344	174,032	437,214[b]	16
1978	140,232	172,395	405,447	16
1977	126,409	153,042	374,832	15
1976	127,625	181,551	355,621	18

a. New position being requested
b. Estimate based on first six month's volumes

Figure 12.4 Productivity increases at Mony, The Mutual Life Insurance Company of New York, Syracuse, New York. (*Courtesy of Mony, The Mutual Life Insurance Company of New York.*)

someone from off the street or from another area within the company. We have variable hours which allow the staff to select work hours convenient to their lifestyle. They may begin as early as 7:30 a.m. and leave as late as 6:00 p.m. In 1979, we initiated a work measurement study, the results of which included a staffing formula and performance standards for our CRT operators. Also, during 1979 we experienced something which we never experienced before—turnover due to promotions of four of our typists to other service areas in nontyping jobs. We had achieved something which was heretofore unthinkable—our typists were competing with other personnel for higher-level positions at MONY and were succeeding!

"At the personal level, word processing has given me tremendous exposure and enjoyment as well as the career I never planned. I have become active locally as the president of the Central New York Chapter of IWP and have had the opportunity at MONY of creating more of a job than I had when I was hired. In 1976, I was selected from a field of three dozen of my peers to participate in a workshop for supervisors with management potential. It was the first bit of tangible evidence that I had to suggest that my contribution to my operation and to MONY as a whole was worthy of note."

Production at MONY

"Our volumes are shown in the graph in Figure 12.4. I wouldn't be surprised if they totalled 40,000 pieces a month during 1980. The senior typists prepare a daily line count and average 900 lines per day. CRT operators' standard of performance is expected to measure at least 26 hours weekly (36-1/4 hours/week worked)."[10]

[10]Sally L. Kwasigroch, 1979: personal communication.

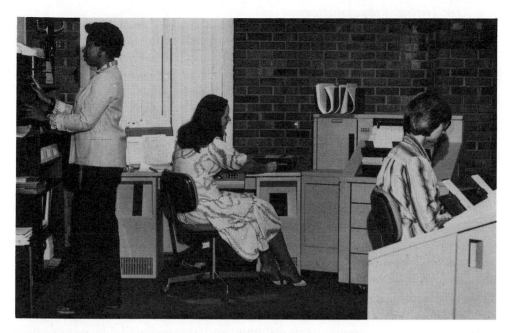

Figure 12.5 Main word processing center in sales and marketing at Hanes Knitwear, Winston-Salem, North Carolina. *(Courtesy of Hanes Knitwear.)*

Textile Manufacturing

Word processing is often implemented in organizations that handle textile manufacturing. An example of one textile manufacturing firm is Hanes Knitwear in North Carolina (Figure 12.5).

Background

Hanes Knitwear is a division of Hanes Corporation, a subsidiary of Consolidated Foods. A textile manufacturing firm, Hanes Knitwear employs more than 5,000 people, of which approximately 250 are located in the main office in Winston-Salem, North Carolina. The others work in manufacturing facilities in the U.S. and Puerto Rico.

Why Hanes Knitwear Introduced Word Processing

Dana R. Oliver, Manager of Office Services, writes: "The secretarial support system in the headquarter's offices was traditional; that is, secretaries performed combined functions of typing and administrative support. This system exhibited many of the shortcomings often found in a traditional office: uneven secretarial workloads, difficulty in handling peak typing or administrative requirements, little or no backup training among the secretaries, and a very low level of principal support in the area of delegated responsibilites. In addition, career path advancement for secretaries was possible only if they changed jobs to work for higher principals."

The Initial Presentation

"After an executive presentation of word processing was made by IBM to the president and vice presidents of the division, the decision was made to select one area of the company where word processing could be implemented and evaluated. The vice president of sales and marketing agreed for his departments to serve as the trial area. These departments included 34 principals and 21 secretaries."

Getting Top Management's Support

"At this point it should be stressed that having the backing and support of top management is essential from the very beginning of any investigation into word processing. At Hanes Knitwear the support was present from the start, and top management set division objectives for word processing before any studies were begun. Those objectives included increasing efficiency of support personnel and effectiveness of principals by reducing principal time spent on routine administrative duties, providing a sound nonexempt word processing structure to ensure greater responsibility and upward mobility, establishing office systems and procedures to achieve logical and evenly distributed work load and effective handling of peak work requirements, improving intracompany communications, and providing cost avoidance in hiring over a two-year period from date of implementation."

The Feasibility Study

"The first study was a typing benchmark study conducted by IBM. This study measured all typing done for a one-week period, both as to quantity and kind of typing. Based on the results of this study, the correspondence (typing) equipment was ordered, which included two IBM Office System 6/450 Information Processors (with ink jet printers) and three IBM Mag Card II Typewriters, together with five IBM 6:5 tone recorders for central dictation capabilities. The three Mag Card II typewriters were to be used by combination secretaries who would spend their time providing both typing and administrative support. This configuration would provide the buffer to handle peak typing loads as they occurred. This capability was determined to be necessary because of the custom nature of the Sales and Marketing work—extensive rush requirements during peak periods each month and numerous complex revisions to long documents.

"After completion of the correspondence study, a study team (consisting of two secretaries and two principals) was selected from the sales and marketing departments and went through a two-day training program at IBM to learn how to conduct an administrative study. This study was conducted to collect information regarding administrative (nontyping) work being performed by the secretaries and qualitative and quantitative support needs of the principals. Utilizing this information, a staffing configuration was developed which would meet these support needs."

"At the same time, several other decisions were made. First, the floor layout and staffing configuration lent themselves to dividing the administrative secretaries into four logical and distinct work groups (although secretarial work stations would not be moved). Each secretary within a work group would serve as primary support to assigned principals but would also be trained to serve as a backup for other secretaries in the group.

"Second, it was decided that all typewriters would be picked up. This move would accomplish three purposes: cause a true administrative assistant role to be assumed by the secretaries and recognized by the principals; permit the hiring of high-level candidates who, in some cases, lacked some of the traditional secretarial skills; and channel all typing to the correspondence specialists on the highly productive word processing equipment. One typewriter was left on a typing stand in each work group to facilitate typing of file folder labels, preprinted forms, and other small typing jobs best suited to an electric typewriter."

Career Paths at Hanes

"A new career path structure was also developed for correspondence and administrative secretaries, and the grade and salary levels were kept exactly the same for both. Unlike the former system, the new system provided the secretaries with the ability to obtain promotions without changing jobs. The primary criteria for promotion became the taking of increased initiative and responsibility and the assumption of more complex delegated tasks from the principals. This structure has been well received (having already resulted in several promotions) and serves as a significant motivational tool."

Management of the Administrative and Correspondence Functions at Hanes

"Two secretaries within the company were promoted to exempt supervisory positions, one correspondence (supervising 5 people) and one administrative (supervising 16 people). These supervisors coordinate all support work to ensure even workload distribution, work closely with principals to see that their support needs are met, and develop motivational and training programs for the secretaries in the system. The supervisors are also responsible for secretarial performance evaluation (with input from principals) and managing their individual parts of the word processing budget. The role of the supervisor is a critical one, and it appears that implementation of a word processing system would be most difficult and probably less successful without someone in that position."

"The correspondence system in sales and marketing was designed to produce approximately 67,000 typed lines per month. Seven months after implementation, the word processing center produced 208,000 lines. This increase appears to be due to increased departmental workloads, the addition of several new principals, and the increase in work submitted for typing because of the improved results in appearance and speed from the center. Consequently, it became necessary to reconfigure the correspondence system and to upgrade some of the equipment. The three combination secretaries became full-time typists, and all three Mag Card II typewriters were upgraded, two to IBM Office System 6/430 Information Processors (without printers) and one to an IBM 6240 Mag Card Typewriter (for those documents requiring impact printing). In addition, an IBM 6640 Standalone Ink Jet Printer was added to provide heavy playout capability. With this upgraded system, the work is being handled efficiently and quickly, with an average turnaround time for all work of approximately 3.5 hours. The ability and willingness to upgrade equipment as the complexion of the workload changes is critical to the continuing success of any word processing system."

Further Implementation

"Studies are soon to be done in other areas of the division so that implementation of Phase II can begin, since it takes approximately four months from the date of the typing study until the system can be implemented. In addition, studies into the feasibility of using the word processing equipment to communicate point-to-point with other Knitwear locations, such as zone sales offices and manufacturing facilities, are to begin within the next year. Word processing, as it spreads throughout the division, provides Hanes Knitwear with the capability to move toward the office of the future in an organized, logical manner with less disruption and fewer problems because of having already taken the first step in that direction."[11]

Diversified Manufacturing

Word processing is one of the technologies used in manufacturing organizations that are moving toward total information processing. An example of one of these organizations is Sundstrand Corporation in Rockford, Illinois.

Background

Sundstrand Corporation is involved in the design, manufacture, and sale of a variety of products requiring significant research, development engineering, and processing expertise. What began as a small machine tool shop in 1905 is today a worldwide corporation with diverse product lines. Sundstrand employs

---

[11]Dana R. Oliver, 1979: personal communication.

over 15,000 people, and has an annual sales exceeding $600,000,000. There are 24 Sundstrand manufacturing plants, as well as numerous field service offices located throughout the world. The corporate offices are located in Rockford, Illinois.

How Sundstrand Implemented Information Processing

Sundstrand created a special department called office services to implement the new technologies. Phillip Russell, administrative analyst, writes: "The purpose and goal of the office services department is to promote office efficiency through word processing, micrographics, convenience copiers, efficient filing systems, and other emerging office technologies."

"The mission of office services is to assist both management and office personnel with tools and services to do their job effectively, efficiently, and productively. Expertise must be brought to bear in a meaningful way if full advantage of the technological aids available to management and office personnel are to be realized. Technology must be adapted to fit the individual or individual need rather than making the individual/user bend to fit the available technology."

Staff in Office Services

"The staff of the office services department consists of seven people: the office services manager, an analyst, an administrative secretary, a micrographics supervisor, two micrographics technicians, and a micrographics camera operator. All personnel attempt to be responsive to the office needs of the entire corporate structure of Sundstrand."

What Office Services Does At Sundstrand

"The department of the Office provides other departments with the following services:

1. *Office copier services.* Office services analyzes and selects equipment to meet the users' requirements. It then places equipment where the capabilities of the equipment can best be used and where it can be convenient to the user. It selects appropriate price plans. It selects and evaluates consumable copier supplies. It monitors the maintenance of the copier equipment. It takes appropriate action when a piece of equipment has an excessive amount of downtime. It identifies people to fill key operator positions from the areas adjacent to copier equipment and makes provisions for their training.

2. *Record system analysis.* It analyzes departmental records; includes suggestions on how better to store records, file and retrieval techniques, code and index; and coordinates retention periods with the corporate legal department.

3. *Record filing and retrieval consulting.* It provides consulting services for department principals who require assistance in formulating file and/or retrieval methods and procedures. It may offer indexing and coding suggestions or suggestions concerning file equipment.

4. *Microfilming and microfilm system analysis.* It conducts an analysis of a record system. The analysis may indicate a need for microfilm. The microfilm analysis will consider the form or mode the microfilm will take. Consideration will be given to such things as how the microfilm will be indexed, retrieved, updated; long or short term storage, government or contractual requirements, and compatibility with existing systems. The user's requirements are major considerations.

5. *Microfilm equipment selection consulting.* The purchase, rental, or lease of user microfilm equipment is the budget responsibility of the using department. Office services plays a vital role in assisting the user in the selection of equipment. Office services personnel are aware of various types of equipment that satisfy specific needs. Office services provides information to the user which will result in making the proper decision in terms of the right equipment for user ease and convenience. Getting the best dollar value, standardizing equipment for compatibility with other systems whenever possible, providing assistance in preparing procurement authorizations, and coordinating deliveries and installations are other services.

6. *Word processing systems analysis.* Office services will conduct an analysis of an office word flow to assist the requesting department in determining if they have a word processing application. If a department determines that it has a word processing application, office services will assist the principals in integrating the new system into the existing systems. Office services will provide the principals (originators) with written procedures and assist in revising forms to adapt to the new word processing system.

7. *Word processing equipment selection consulting.* Office services will provide assistance in selecting equipment once it has been determined that a word processing system is the route to go to satisfy a need. Information will be provided the user concerning equipment to meet the system needs. Office services will coordinate vendor demonstrations and bring the equipment in-house whenever possible. Demonstrations on existing in-house word processing equipment will be arranged. Office services will, whenever possible, standardize equipment installation to promote compatibility. Standardization and compatibility provides backup in the event one system goes down."

Word Processing at Sundstrand

"Currently six departments in Sundstrand (Rockford) enjoy the benefits of word processing.

"The Legal Department has a Wang 25 Model II word processing system. The shared-logic system has five work stations, two printers, and a 2.5 megabyte hard disk. All current software is geared to text editing only.

"The proposal department has two AM 425 systems. One 425 has telecommunications to a Mergenthaler phototypesetter in the graphics arts department. Graphics arts also has a programmable Shaffstall interface that provides a flexible input to the phototypesetter. The third and final AM 425 unit is shared by personnel and public relations.

"Technical publications uses an IBM 6/452 for the production of service manuals to aviation companies. A mag card A and the 452 keyboards are the input. The output is a 55 cps Qume daisy wheel printer.

"At the conclusion of a word processing study, the test support department has chosen an NBI 3000. Although not yet implemented, the desired configuration is two NBI 3000 work stations (one with dual floppy disks, the other with one). Both stations would have telecommunications. The main unit would have statistical math and equation mode software and a Qume wide track printer with 2 daisy wheels for math printout."

Micrographics at Sundstrand

"A central micrographics lab was established for retaining the engineering drawings on an active aperture card filing system. After this was established, many other departments in Sundstrand took advantage of microfilm storage systems. The departments include personnel, technical publications, purchasing, field service, quality assurance, and many others. All microfilm produced by office services meets the standards required by the federal government for commercial and military documentation."

Future Goals for Sundstrand in Information Processing

Further goals by office services for Sundstrand are to provide:

1. Word processing using mainframe computer storage.

2. Word processing communicating via satellite through mainframe computer communications equipment.

3. Optical character recognition input to take the most advantage of word processing editing capabilities and to centralize word processing communications.

4. Standardized communications for office technology corporate-wide.

5. Electronic mail.

... and someday the total integration of all office technologies to greater serve the user at Sundstrand.[12]

---

[12]Phillip Russell, 1979: personal communication.

Questions on Concepts

1. List the reasons why word processing was implemented in the following organizations: Sierra Research, Kwasha Lipton, Lincoln General Hospital, Hanes Knitwear, CoverGirl Temporary Office Personnel, and Warringah Shire Council.

2. Compare the way word processing was implemented at Kwasha Lipton with the way it was implemented at Lincoln General Hospital.

3. Compare the procedures and work handled at Arent, Fox, Kinter, Plotkin, and Kahn to those at Sierra Research, Institute for Medical Research, Sambo's, and the Nuclear Regulatory Commission.

4. Describe administrative support at Hanes Knitwear.

5. Describe how production increased at MONY because of word processing.

6. Compare career paths at Kwasha Lipton with career paths at MONY and Hanes Knitwear.

7. Describe how environmental factors were handled at the Institute for Medical Research, MONY, and the U. S. Nuclear Regulatory Commission.

8. Discuss flexible scheduling and why it is used at MONY.

9. Describe the future plans for information processing at Sundstrand, Sambo's, Sierra Research, and the U. S. Nuclear Regulatory Commission.

10. Describe how vendors were selected at Lincoln General Hospital.

11. Explain why the Institute for Medical Research needed to have information processing capabilities.

12. Describe the benefits of work measurement at Kwasha Lipton.

13. Discuss management's support of word processing and the objectives set by top management for word processing at Hanes Knitwear.

14. List the reasons why word processing is successful at Arent, Fox, Kinter, Plotkin and Kahn.

Glossary

Access time. The time taken by a computer to locate data or an instruction word in its memory or storage selection and transfer it. Also, the time taken to transfer information from the input device to the location in the memory where it will be stored.

Action paper. Carbonless tissue or carbon set.

Activity survey. A data collection method used in a feasibility study.

Address. 1. (n.) Name given to a specific location of material on a recording medium. An address could be designated by a line number. 2. (v.) The act of finding such a location, usually through machine instruction.

Administrative secretary. Someone who performs nontyping duties for a group or principals as part of a team or functions as an assistant to executives.

Administrative support. One of the two broad areas of specialization under word processing. In general, it comprises all the nontyping tasks associated with traditional secretarial work carried out under administrative supervision.

Administrative support manager. A person who has full responsibility for developing, maintaining, and evaluating all service structures under administrative support within an organization.

Administrative support supervisor. A person who schedules and administers work flow to a team of administrative secretaries.

Ambient lighting. Lighting that is used in the background to complement task lighting.

Aperture cards. A card that has an opening in which a strip or frame of microfilm is mounted.

Application center. A center that specializes in one type of document or application.

Appraisal plan. A plan to identify the most competent employees; it identifies employees who are eligible for raises and promotions. The criteria for the appraisal should be based on objectives that are mutually determined by managers and workers.

Archive storage. An area commonly used to store documents away from the computer.

ASCII. American Standard Code for Information Interchange. Pronounced "ask'ee", this is an eight-level code for data developed by the American National Standards Institute. It was developed to ensure compatibility between data devices.

Asynchronous transmission. Transmission in which each single information character or "byte" is synchronized, usually by the addition of start and stop bits; a string of individual characters with a "stop" and "start" signal on either side of each single character, which move one at a time along a line. Asynchronous transmission is sometimes called StartStop transmission.

Attended operation For communication job operations, an operator is required at both the sending and receiving stations. The operator manually sets up the line connection and transfers the modem from talk (voice) mode to data mode.

Auto-Typist. Automated letter writer that uses a paper roll similar to the old piano rolls for its medium.

Autocratic climate. Use of threats and fear to motivate workers. Decisions are made mostly by the boss.

Automated typewriter. A general term covering all types of word processing keyboard equipment designed for repetitive and revision work.

Automatic carrier return. The carriage or a movable element returns to the left margin when you reach a certain point.

Automatic center. The capability to center words on a line.

Automatic media changers. Automatically eject the individual discs or cassettes after they become filled or at some predetermined time.

Automatic speech recognition. A system of equipment that understands or recognizes the human voice.

Automatic tab grid. A device that sets up tabs at frequent intervals, such as every five spaces.

Automatic typewriter. The simplest of the automated typewriters; used mainly for straight, repetitive output.

Automation. Using equipment to increase productivity.

Auxiliary storage. External medium on which information is electronically stored.

Bandwidth. The range of frequencies available for signalling; the difference, expressed in cycles per second (hertz), between the highest and lowest frequencies of a band.

Batch. A collection of similar work that could be produced during one operation.

Baud rate. The speed in bauds is the number of discrete conditions or signal changes that electronic media can handle per second. Signal transmission rate. If each signal is equal to only one bit, the baud rate is the same as the bit rate per second. When each signal determines more than one bit, the baud rate is not equal to bits per second.

Belt. A form of discrete media.

Bidirectionality. The printing device moves not only from left to right on the page but continues printing from right to left for increased speed.

Bisynch. A block or group of many characters that move together or are sent along the transmission line with a single "stop" and "start" signal bracketing the entire block of characters. Also known as binary synchronous.

Bit rate. The number of data bits per second, transmitted or received, between terminals. The amount of on-line data sent in the period of time is correctly specified in bits per second (BPS).

Bits per second (bps). The rate at which the information moves.

Black box. Slang for a central processor unit.

Blind terminals. Terminals that do not allow the entire page of material to be seen.

Blocking. A processing feature that takes information that has been keyboarded and saves it for when it is needed.

Boilerplate. A number of standard paragraphs that can be arranged in a specified order as needed; the stored paragraphs.

Boss-centered leadership. All decisions are made solely by the boss.

Bubble memory. Magnetic memory with a greater storage capacity than any other form of memory.

Buffer. A short-time electronic storage device that adjusts for a difference in the rate information flows when transmitting information from one device to another.

Buffer storage. A device into which information is assembled and stored ready for transfer.

Byte. A sequence of binary digits (bits) directly following one another, that are operated on as a single unit. Usually shorter than a word (made up of more than one byte), a byte is sometimes loosely called a "character."

Cablegram. An international telegram.

Carbon. A tissuelike paper treated with ink, wax, oil, and lampblack, or a film called Mylar.

Carbon pack. A commercially prepared set containing the original, carbons, and copy sheets.

Carbon process. A method of producing a limited number of copies.

Career path. A line of progression from one position to another, established by management to provide opportunity for advancement to higher level jobs.

Cathode ray tube. See *CRT*.

Central processing unit. A computer; see *CPU*.

Central recording systems. A system that consists of central recorders that are permanently installed and wired to either handsets or telephones.

Centralization. All word/information processing equipment is placed in a central location.

Centralized services. Administrative secretaries and correspondence secretaries grouped together in one area.

Chains. A device on a line printer which looks like letters embedded on a continuous loop of metal.

Change bars. Vertical bars that are inserted next to the text to show where changes will occur.

Channel. A path for electrical transmission between two or more points. A channel is sometimes referred to as a circuit, line, link, path, or facility. A communication channel can be open-wire, cable, microwave, or a combination of these. The function of a communications channel is to carry data.

Character. The coded symbol of a digit, letter, special symbol, or control function. The term "byte" is sometimes loosely used instead of the term "character."

Character impact printers. Devices that transfer characters by the striking of a piece of paper through an inked or carbon ribbon against a platen.

Chip technology. See computer-on-a-chip.

Clipping. Omitting of words because the mechanism does not engage fast enough.

Closed system. A system in which dictation media is never handled.

Cluster. A work group.

Cluster/shared-logic. Operators share the same power of the CPU and printer but they each have their own disk drives.

Columnar interchange. The ability to switch around whole columns of numbers automatically.

COM. Computer output microfilm; a method of storing information from a computer directly onto film in a miniaturized form.

Common carrier. A government-regulated company that provides public communications facilities, such as a telephone or telegraph company.

Communicating word/information processors. A machine that allows equipment to "talk" or documents to be transferred electronically between two points.

Communications. Moving or distributing the words and data from one location to another. Often referred to as distribution.

Computer-aided transcription (CAT). Transcription of machine shorthand notes automatically in a computer from words recorded on magnetic tape.

Computer-on-a-chip. A small chip of silicon that contains a central processing unit and a storage area memory; also called a microcomputer.

Continuous speech recognition. A system that recognizes speech as each word is spoken.

Control. Standardization of work and measurement of results.

Convert, conversion, converter. To change over into another form. In modems, the process of changing a business machine signal into a form that can be carried or transmitted through a telephone line facility. The signal may be changed in timing, shape, level, etc. Normally the business machine signal, digital in form, is converted to a voice compatible (analog) type system.

Copier/printers. Machines that combine both photocopying features and printing ability.

Copy sets. Another name for a carbon pack.

Core memory. Magnetized doughnut-like iron circles, each smaller than the head of a pin, strung together like beads on a wire, that hold bits of information.

Correspondence secretary. Persons trained to use word/information processing equipment; performs typing functions.

Correspondence support. One of the two broad areas of specialization under word processing that comprises most of the typing tasks associated with traditional secretarial work, carried out under correspondence support supervision.

CPI. Characters per horizontal inch.

CPS. Cycles per second or characters per second.

CPU. Central processing unit. Components of word processing and data processing systems which contain the arithmetic, logic, and control circuits for the basic system. In some systems, it may also include the memory storage unit and operator's console.

Cross-training. Secretaries are periodically rotated to different positions so they know all parts of each job.

CRT. Cathode ray tube. A screen that makes it possible to produce a document in the document cycle without the use of paper.

Custom environment. The environment in which nonroutine tasks are performed.

Daisy print wheel. An inexpensive plastic printing device.

Data communications. The transmission or receiving of data by means of data communication equipment, a data terminal, and a channel.

Data link. An established connection between two points over a communications channel.

Data processing. The use of electronic computers to gather, manipulate, summarize, and report on the numbers, statistics, and other information that flow through an organization.

Data set. A device that performs control functions to provide compatibility between business machines and communication lines for transmission over these lines. Also referred to as "line adapters" and "modems."

Decentralization. Equipment is placed in mini-centers close to a particular department.

Decentralized administrative support. The traditional boss/secretary relationship is not disrupted and managers retain their secretaries near their offices.

Dedicated. Used specifically by one user or for one type of work.

Dedicated line. A communications channel that is permanently connected between two or more data stations. Also called a "leased" or "private" line.

Desk-top unit. Word processing equipment that is generally small enough to be located on the originator's desk.

Diablo. Trade name of a typing mechanism employing a high-speed interchangeable print wheel.

Dictation equipment. A unit that contains a microphone or handset and a recorder.

Dictation/transcription unit. Combination units that can be used for dictating or transcribing dictation.

Dictionary. The capability to check the spelling of words against a number of frequently used or technical words.

Digital. Information that has been changed into signals which can be recognized, stored, and used by automated equipment.

Direct impression. Term applied to text-production techniques in which each character is struck onto the paper, as in conventional typing.

Director of secretarial support systems. A person who has total responsibility for all aspects of an organization's office system, including word processing, administrative support, and other information processing.

Discrete media. Small, movable, external media that are inserted into a dictation unit and used for recording dictation.

Discrete word recognition. The operator must pause between speaking each vocabulary item.

Disk. A form of discrete media.

Diskette/disk. A plastic-like disk coated with a chemical compound (oxide coated mylar film) that is enclosed in a protective folder and resembles a 45 rpm record in size and shape, on which information may be stored.

Display systems. Terminals that have a visual screen that show whatever is typed on the keyboard or is retrieved from storage.

Distributed systems. When word or data processing may be connected to a computer but can function independent of computer.

Distributed-logic. The logic or computer intelligence has been dispersed (sent) to the terminals, the printers, the storage centers, or other peripherals rather than concentrating all intelligence in one computer.

Distribution. Moving words and data (information) from one location to another. Also called communications. If done electronically over telephone lines, it is referred to as telecommunications.

Document analysis. A data collection method used in a feasibility study.

Document assembly. Stored paragraphs are assembled in any sequence desired to create a new document.

Document cycle. The workflow steps of a document, including origination, production, reproduction, filing, storage and retrieval, and distribution of a document.

Documents. Reports, letters, forms, proposals, and invoices.

Dot matrix. A group of closely spaced dots with a printed pattern that looks like the shape of the desired character.

Dual display. A CRT that displays two pages at one time; a thin-window display and a partial or full page display combined into one system.

Dual function equipment. Able to handle both the document requirements of clerical support as well as arithmetic requirements of basic data processing.

Dual pitch. Allows switching from one type size and style to other type sizes and styles on the same piece of equipment.

Dual-track tape system. When a correction or instruction is required on dictation equipment, the originator switches to another track. Also called "writing in the margin."

Dumb terminal. A terminal cannot function or is unable to work if the central computer ceases to work because it is dependent on the processing power of the central computer.

Dump. Taking the magnetic media recorded on the media of one word/information processor and inserting it into a media converter of another word/information processor to convert the information to another type of media.

EBCD (Extended Binary Coded Decimal). Requires six bits to make up a character.

EBCDIC (Extended Binary Coded Decimal Internal Code). Requires eight bits to make up a character.

Edit check. A feature that prevents you from making errors when filling in a form.

Ego need. A need to feel valuable; to have a firmly based, high opinion of yourself.

Electronic Computer Originated Messages (ECOM). Magnetic media must be keyboarded into one of the 25 post offices in the ECOM message system of the U. S. Postal System. Then, a facsimile of the original message is printed at a receiving post office and delivered with the regular mail.

Electronic cueing device. Indexing signals that are stored on the recording media of dictation equipment for the transcriptionist to use when transcribing.

Electronic mail. Modern electronic technology is used to send computerized information over satellites, cables, or telephone wires.

Electronic stencil maker. Electronic scanning reproduces an original document on a special stencil. As the stencil rotates on a cylinder, images are electronically burned into the new stencil as the scanning device electronically reads the information from the original stencil.

Electronic typewriter. Similar to other stand-alone systems. A typewriter that has some limited revision capabilities.

Electrophotography. A system that uses light to shape a character on a photosensitive surface.

Element. A printing device that transfers the image of characters onto paper.

Elite. A typeface that is equal to 12 characters per inch.

Employee-centered leadership. Also called laissez faire. Decisions made primarily by workers with little involvement by the manager.

Endless loop media. A medium where the two ends of the tape have been spliced together to form a continuous loop.

Ergonomics. A term used to describe the planning of workspace and environmental design that considers human factors.

Esteem need. A need to feel valuable; to have a firmly based, high opinion of oneself.

Ethernet. An intra-office communication network developed by Xerox Corporation to transmit information between connected workstations and support devices at high speeds.

External media. Media that is external, or outside, the machine on which information is electronically stored.

Facsimile (FAX). A system of telecommunication for the transmission of images for reproduction on a permanent form; a type of copier that electronically sends an original document from one location to a remote location where it is reproduced as a copy of the original document.

FCC (Federal Communications Commission). A board of several commissioners appointed by the President of the U.S. under the Communications Act of 1934, having the power to regulate all interstate and foreign electrical communications systems originating in the United States.

Feasibility study. A thorough study of the organization to determine the document needs of the employees.

Federal Express. A private service that offers guaranteed delivery of mail to a destination by a certain time.

Feedback. Information that tells whether expected results are obtained.

Fiber optics. Smooth glass-like thin tubes as fine as human hair that send a light source generated from electric power.

Files capability. Creates and updates lists and prints them out according to any of the categories in the list.

Firmware. Specific instructions that have been permanently placed or wired into the control memory of a piece of equipment.

First-in, first-out. Whatever dictation goes into an endless loop machine first gets transcribed first.

Flex time. Each employee schedules his or her own working hours.

Floppy. A term for a type of diskette/disk that is not rigid.

Fluorescent lighting. A type of lighting that uses less electricity, produces less glare, and generates less heat.

Fluid process. A method of reproducing material; also known as the spirit, liquid, direct, or Ditto process.

Font. A group of characters in a certain typestyle and having one of three type sizes (10 pitch, 12 pitch, or proportional spacing); for output, "font" refers to the electronics that produce the characters on the ink jet printer, another name for a typing element. Also, a name for phototypesetting elements.

Footnoting capability. Sets the bottom margin to allow space for footnoting.

Foreign exchange (FX). A service providing a line outside the local area. A company located in one area might wish to have a line in another area if they have a branch there or if they do a great deal of phoning to that area.

Form documents. Documents composed of information that is standard and does not change; that is used repetitively.

Form letter. The body of the letter is printed; the names and addresses are typed in.

Forms package. Features found on equipment that enable you to prepare invoices, purchase requisitions, and other types of forms.

Full page display. A display screen that shows 57 to 66 lines of text at one time.

Generalist. A person whose job description contains many varied duties.

Global search and replace. Searches through a document for words or sets of characters and replaces them with new ones.

Graphic communications. A method of sending charts, maps, and diagrams electronically.

Graphic forms. Charts, maps, and diagrams.

Hard copy. A document on paper (written, typed, or printed matter).

Hardware. The physical devices, mechanisms, parts, or assemblies that make up a business machine. (Software is a term sometimes used to describe the programs that control machine operation and functions. Software is sometimes "hard wired" when it is contained in electronic circuits; when it is hard wired it is also called "firmware", since it too now is a form of "hardware.")

Headers and footers. Places uniform information on each page such as section numbers and title names.

Heavy revision documents. Long textual material as found in reports and proposals.

Herzberg, Frederick. Developer of the maintenance-motivation model of worker motivation.

Holography. A photographic method of storing one trillion bits of information in a 3-dimensional arrangement internally in word/information processing equipment.

Horizontal career path. Allows employees who either do not have managerial qualifications or who do not wish to work in managerial positions to move to jobs that are on the same level as the position they hold. Also called lateral career path.

Hot lead printing. A method of typesetting that uses lead or brass plates in the printing process.

Hybrid system. A mixture of a centralized word processing center with a decentralized word processing center.

Implementing word processing. The process of replacing the traditional office with a word/information processing system.

In-house. Done within an organization rather than being sent out.

Information. Words, symbols, or numbers in written or unwritten form used to express an idea.

Information carrier. A pathway that handles information as it travels through space, over cables or telephone wires.

Information network. The way in which managers run the organization by communicating ideas to the appropriate people and places; systems tied together for moving information.

Information processing. The movement of words, symbols, or numbers from the origination of an idea to its final destination.

Information processing center. As equipment becomes more sophisticated and can do more than the production work of word processing centers, the term information processing center is used.

Ink jet printing. Characters are shaped by electrostatically spraying a very fine hairlike stream of ink onto paper.

Ink process. A method of reproducing material using ink; same as stencil duplicating.

Input. Source of information; getting information into an information processing system, primarily by keyboarding.

Input/output terminal. Keyboarding and printing capabilities combined into one piece of equipment.

Inscribed media. Media that cannot be erased or reused.

Integrated. Built into; internally a part of; a combination of.

Intelligence. Permits equipment to process certain parts of document information in special ways.

Intelligent printers. Printers combining laser, computer, fiber optics, and some copying technology.

Intelligent terminal. A terminal with its own computing power.

Interface. A connecting device; a point that connects yet separates the responsibilities of any two connected equipments. An interface may be a connecting cable between two pieces of equipment.

Internal media. Media that is inside the machine. It usually cannot be touched or handled.

Internal motivation. Self-direction rather than reliance on external motivations.

Internal storage. The recording of information inside automated equipment not usually touched or handled.

IWPA. International Word Processing Association.

Job analysis. Forms that allow employees to indicate their work categories and estimate the amount of time spent on each task.

Job autonomy. Decision-making responsibility given to employees so they can plan their own work.

Job enrichment.   The strategy of putting jobs back together again. Providing a job with variety, challenge, autonomy, achievement, and feedback.

Justified right margin.   Forming a straight rather than ragged right margin.

Laissez faire.   Employee-centered leadership.

Large central recording system.   A system meant for a large group of originators, anywhere from 25 to 1,000.

Laser.   A beam of pure red light that is capable of carrying millions of messages simultaneously.

Lateral career path.   See *Horizontal career path*.

LED (light emitting diode).   A device to let originators using dictation equipment see at a glance their location on a cassette; a lighted display on an automated keyboard.

Line printer.   A high-speed printer used as an output device.

Lists.   Documents composed of lists of information.

Lithography.   An offset printing process.

LPM.   Lines per minute.

Mag.   Short form of the word *magnetic*.

Magnetic card.   A plastic-like card coated with a chemical compound (oxide coated mylar film) on which information may be stored.

Magnetic media.   Media on which information may be stored and which can be reused.

Magnetic tape.   Plastic-like tape coated with a chemical compound (oxide coated mylar film) on which information may be stored.

Magnetic Tape Selectric Typewriter (MT/ST).   An IBM typewriter that uses magnetic tape to allow for revision of documents.

Mailgram.   A service offered by Western Union that combines the telephone service and the U.S. Postal Service.

Maintenance factors.   Factors that maintain a person at an existing level of activity but do not provide motivation to achieve higher levels of productivity.

Management.   People who are formally educated or trained to manage and who are responsible for decision making. The organization levels that plan, organize, direct, staff and control.

Management-oriented.   The manager has administrative or correspondence support.

Manager.   Responsible for managing human resources within an organization; plans, organizes, directs, staffs, and controls the organization.

Managerial workstation.   Same as a multifunction workstation; a CRT and keyboard that allows a manager to accomplish a variety of tasks through a terminal.

Marketing support representative (MSR).   A liaison between the organization and the user of automated equipment.

Maslow, Abraham. A prominent writer in the field of human motivation.

Master set. A three-sheet pack of paper used with a fluid duplicator. The top sheet is glossy white paper connected to a bottom sheet of carbon coated with a purple dye.

Math pack and math edits. A device that adds, subtracts, multiplies, and divides columns of figures or simply verifies the accuracy of column totals.

Matrix printer. A group of closely spaced dots with a printed pattern that looks like the shape of the desired character.

Media. The material on which information is recorded.

Media conversion. The method of changing or switching existing magnetic media files to the media of another word/information processor that uses another kind of magnetic media.

Media incompatibility. One type of media will not work on another word/information processor that requires another type of media.

Medium. Singular form of the plural word media. A paper or magnetic entity for recording used with information processing devices.

Megabyte. One million bytes.

Memory. Storage of information inside the automated equipment that is not usually touched or handled.

Merge. To combine together.

Merging capability. The ability to combine stored text such as a list of names and addresses with a stored letter.

Message switching. The technique of receiving a message, storing it until the proper outside circuit is available, and then retransmitting it. Also called "store and forward switching".

Microcassette. Media that holds up to 60 minutes of dicatation; 30 minutes on each side.

Microfiche. A sheet of film that may contain several hundred exposures in a grid pattern.

Microfilm jacket. A folder consisting of clear material sealed together on two sides that may contain strips of film.

Micrographics. The method of filing information on film using miniaturized images.

Microimages. Miniaturized images stored on film.

Microprocessor. A tiny chip smaller than the tip of your finger containing the equivalent of 15,000 transistors; a CPU with no memory.

Mimeographing. A trade name used for the reproduction process that uses ink and is also known as stencil duplicating.

Minicassette. Media that hold up to 60 minutes of dictation; 30 minutes on each side. See *microcassettes*.

Minicomputer mail forwarding system. A system designed to reduce the cost and delivery time associated with mail that is addressed to locations from which people have moved.

Mode of transmission. The method by which pulses or signals are moved along a telephone line.

Modem. A combining of *MO*dulator-*DEM*odulator. A device used for converting or changing signals (digital to analog and the reverse) and for transmitting or receiving a signal through common carrier channels. A modem is sometimes called a "data set" or a "signal converter device".

Morale. The feeling or attitude a person has toward an organization.

Motivator factors. Factors that cause workers to work toward objectives.

Movable type. A traditional method of setting type whereby each letter of type is moved or set into place by hand.

Multifunction workstation. Equipment that looks like a small television set with a keyboard and has several different functions. It may be placed on a manager's desk. See *Managerial workstation*.

Mylar. A form of carbon paper.

Narrowband carriers. Cables or telephone lines (private or leased) that have slow transmission rates and are used primarily for TWX.

Network. A series of points connected by communications channels. The switched telephone network is the network of telephone lines normally used for dialed telephone calls. A private network is a network of communications channels only for the use of one customer.

Nondisplay system. A system in which only the portion of the text that is changed appears on the printed page unless the entire text is played out on paper.

Nonimpact printer. A printer that has no printing device hitting a platen.

Nonproductive time. The time the secretary spends doing such things as walking to the copying machine or waiting for work.

Nonroutine work. Work that requires a great deal of skill; also known as custom work.

OCR. Optical character recognition.

OCR reader. A machine that scans pages of documents using optical character recognition.

Odometer. A counter on a dictation unit.

Off-line. Terminal equipment not at this time connected to a transmission line or not in direct communication over the transmission line; not connected to a computer.

Off-line operation. Operation in a noncommunicating or "home" mode.

Office landscaping. Open office planning to provide people with a feeling of open space.

Office of the future. A work environment that uses ergonomics in planning and computer systems with powerful capabilities for handling information.

Offset. A method of printing using a raised or depressed surface on the master in which the printing surface is level with the nonprinting surface.

On-line. Terminal equipment connected to a transmission line and in direct communication over telephone line; connected to a computer.

On-line operation. Operation over the telephone line, or in an "on-line" mode. Not an off-line or home mode operation; connected to a computer.

One-to-one relationship. One boss to one secretary.

Operator. A person who keyboards information or handles equipment operating functions.

Opinion survey. A data collection method used in a feasibility study.

Opticon. A sensing device that transfers a coded signal to a visually-impaired person's fingertips.

Oral interviews. An excellent way of collecting information to determine the attitudes of employees toward word processing, work, coworkers, management, and secretarial support.

Organization climate. The way in which people relate to each other. The tone of an organization caused by styles of leadership.

Origination. Handwritten, dictation to a secretary, or machine dictation of a document.

Originator. The person who uses handwriting, dictation to a secretary, or machine dictation to generate information.

Originator's questionnaire. Questions that reveal the work habits of originators, how they feel about the type of secretarial or administrative support they receive, and ask for suggestions.

Output. What the system produces—the final product or end result; the final printing of information after it has been keyboarded, stored, and edited; hard copy (paper).

Output equipment. Equipment that is used solely for printing and may be physically separate from a keyboard.

PABX. Private automatic branch exchange; machinery that switches calls between the public telephone network and inside extensions.

Pagination. The ability to number or renumber all of the pages of text.

Paper index strips. A way to give the transcriptionist special instructions.

Paper survey. A form of document analysis.

Paper tape. A strip of paper on which characters are represented by combinations of holes punched across the strip.

Partial display. Visual display screen with less than a full page of text being shown at one time.

Participative leadership. The manager consults with workers, asks for their opinions and judgments, but is still responsible for making the decisions.

PBX. Private branch exchange. Loosely, a manned switchboard.

Peripherals. Units that work in conjunction with, but are not a part of a unit, such as printers, phototypesetters, and scanners.

Phototypesetting. A printing process that uses photographic principles to produce an image. The master letter design is usually a film negative but may be stored as digital information in a computer.

Phototypesetting specialist. A word processing operator who enters special codes while keyboarding and revising text that is to be output on a phototypesetting system.

Phrase storage. The storage of certain phrases that are frequently used, such as "Yours truly," a return address, and greetings.

Physiological needs. Food, water, shelter, and sex.

Pica. A typeface that is equal to 10 characters per inch.

Pie chart. A circular chart in which data from surveys can be organized, analyzed, and sorted.

Pitch. The number of units or spaces per horizontal inch. The operation is selectable for 10 or 12 pitch or proportional spacing. May be referred to as dual or triple pitch.

Point. One location; a terminal or a workstation.

Point size. Type size.

Point-to-computer communications. A method of communication between equipment that requires two pieces or models of equipment of the same or two different manufacturers with identical format codes, protocols, Baud rates, and coding sets in order for communications to be possible.

Point-to-point communication. A method of communication between two pieces of equipment with modems required, with a communications controller/processor connecting them over telephone lines or a hard wire.

Poll satellite. Unattended units are ready to send documents automatically via satellite, if called upon by another remote machine.

Polling. A centrally controlled way (usually a host CPU) of calling or asking a number of terminals to allow any one of them to transmit information to the central location.

Portable dictation units. Usually battery-operated units intended to be used by originators for notetaking when they are away from the office.

Power keyboard. An early name used for power typewriters or text editors.

Power typewriter. Name of the first text editors.

Principal. See *Originator*.

Print wheel. A device that transfers the image of characters onto paper.

Printing device. The part of a word/information processor which transfers information to paper.

Private automatic branch exchange (PABX). Any PBX that operates without requiring operator assistance for outgoing and intraoffice calls.

Private branch exchange (PBX). Any manually-switched telephone system interconnected to incoming, outgoing, and intraoffice calls.

Private line. A channel or circuit provided to a subscriber for his or her use only. Also called a leased line.

Procedures. The proper methods of moving documents through the various stages of workflow; processing the document as efficiently as possible.

Procedures manual. A book containing all the procedures for users and administrative and correspondence secretaries.

Processing. Changes the input undergoes resulting in the final product; the ability of the equipment to change information into some other form.

Processing unit (CPU).   The controlling unit of a computer system, containing circuitry for logical decisions and arithmetic calculations, and a fixed amount of main storage.

Production environment.   The environment in which routine tasks are performed.

Production-oriented.   An atmosphere where large volumes of routine work are produced.

Productive time.   The time the secretary spends doing actual work such as typing, filing, and answering phones.

Program.   A set of machine instructions for the operation of automated equipment such as computers and word processing systems.

Programmer.   A person who designs programs or a set of instructions for equipment.

Proofmarks.   Special marks used in proofreading text that indicate needed revisions.

Proofreader.   A person who proofreads typed copy for text content, spelling, punctuation, grammar, and typographical errors.

Proportional.   A typeface where the alpha-numerical characters are given horizontal spacing related to their natural size.

Protocol.   A sequence of signals that controls the transmission between different devices. A controlled set of rules or codes used to communicate a machine language (may consist of specific sequences). Binary synchronous communications is a binary coded set of control characters put together in specific sequences.

Qume print wheel.   A refinement of the original daisy print wheel.

RAM.   Random access memory. A type of internal storage used in information processors; a chip that stores information and has no central processing unit.

Random access.   A method of storage on external media in which information is stored in any desired order.

Random sampling.   Observing the work habits of employees at various unannounced times.

Records management.   A method of handling the storage and retrieval of information through better control of people, procedures, and equipment.

Records processing.   A method of handling, storing, and retrieving information that may never need to be recorded on paper. Information may be entered via a keyboard into a computer and only retrieved if needed.

Reference documents.   Longer documents produced by the word processing center or reprographics departments.

Remote.   A distant, far-away, or "other end" location.

Remote location.   A station at the remote "other end" of a communications line.

Remote site. The location of the remote station at the other end of a communications line or channel.

Remote station. The machine site or location at the other end of a communications line or channel.

Remote terminal. A communicating machine other than a host CPU at the other end.

Repagination. The capability of renumbering all the pages of text.

Reprographics. A method of achieving a traditional form of hard copy output by duplication or reproduction; a term that is associated with newer methods of reproducing or duplicating information that may involve a computer and reproducing records on film.

Reverberation. The ability of sound to bounce off walls.

Roll film. A roll of microfilm that may or may not be housed in a cartridge or cassette.

Routine work. Work that takes little skill to learn and offers very little variation.

Safety need. The need to feel that your life is orderly, predictable, manageable, and pretty much within your control.

Satellite reflectors. Large dish-like objects used for bouncing radio signals back to earth.

Satellites. Mini-centers that consist of only one person.

Scanner. A device that reads typed characters from hard copy and automatically copies it onto something else.

Search. The ability to find priority work.

Secretarial log. A record of daily typing activities; a form of document analysis.

Security. Something that gives or ensures safety or protection.

Self-actualization. The highest order need. The need to grow and learn; to use all of your abilities.

Self-fulfillment need. See *Self-actualization*.

Sequential access. A method of storage on external media in which information is stored one item after another.

Service representative. A person trained in the electronics of the equipment who goes into the organization to repair equipment when and if it breaks down.

Shared resource. Any piece of word/information processing equipment that may tie into another related piece of equipment and is necessary for that equipment to perform functions in addition to its original design.

Shared systems. Equipment that contains CRTs, keyboards, printers, CPUs, and disk drives which can be shared by compatible pieces of equipment.

Shared logic. The sharing of combined pieces of equipment using common data bases.

Shared-media system. A stand-alone system that is connected to a separate printer that prints out the information from the media on the stand-alone.

Short one-time documents. Short documents such as letters and memos that are produced for one-time use.

Single element. A printing device; a device that contains all the letters, numbers, and symbols to be printed.

Situational leadership. The leader must influence workers to accomplish goals, realizing that different leaders, workers, and situations may require very different kinds of leadership approaches.

Small central recording system. A system meant for a small group of originators, anywhere from 2 to 25.

SNA. Systems network architecture. A communications method developed to eliminate the need for machines to be identical to communicate.

Social need. Sometimes referred to as the love need. It is the need to belong or to be part of something.

Software. A program that instructs the operations of word and data processing equipment; all nonhardware elements of a computer system, such as computer programs, procedures for training and operating, support documentation, design and test documentation, etc.

Sort capability. The capacity to rearrange information so that it appears in a different order.

Speaker dependent system. An automatic speech recognition system that requires a sample of how a person says each vocabulary item before it can recognize that person speaking the item.

Speaker independent system. An automatic speech recognition system that recognizes what is being said without ever having been previously supplied a sample of how that speaker says each vocabulary item.

Specialists. Secretaries who perform either correspondence or administrative duties.

Split keyboarding. A production technique in which material is keyboarded and edited on one word processing unit and played out on another.

Staff analyst. A person who is responsible for consulting and assisting word processing and administrative support supervisors and managers.

Stand-alone system. A system that consists of a single station (used by one person at a time); that is, it is not hooked up or connected to other systems or a computer.

Standard cassettes. Media that holds up to 120 minutes of dictation, or 60 minutes on each side.

Standard procedures. Guidelines and forms for all operators to follow to create uniformity in their work.

Station. One of the input or output points (terminal or host CPU) in a communications system.

Stencil duplicating. Often referred to as ink process or Mimeographing.

Stencil pack. A duplicating master consisting of a transparent film (optional), a stencil sheet (a porous sheet of tissue coated with a waxlike substance), a wax-coated cushion sheet, and a backing sheet.

Stored mailgram. A method that allows the user to store material for repeated use in units called a Telepost.

Subscribers. Organizations that have bought time on another organization's computer.

Superscripts and subscripts. The capability to place numbers slightly above or below the regular line of type where necessary.

Supportive climate. An atmosphere that allows for worker learning and growth. Managers listen to worker ideas and support their performance.

Switching. Pathways over which messages are sent.

Synchronous. Having a constant spacing of time between serial bits, characters or bytes, or events.

Synchronous communications. A group or block of many characters move together or are sent along the line with a single "stop" and "start" signal bracketing the front and back of the entire block of characters.

System. The operations, procedures, personnel, and equipment through which a business activity is carried on.

Systems analyst. Person who recommends to the organization the equipment to acquire to handle its needs and suggests ways existing equipment can be used to greater advantage.

Systems approach. Interaction of the document cycle with people, information, equipment, and procedures.

Table of contents update. The ability to update the table of contents of a report as new sections are added or as the section numbers and titles change.

Tank. A case consisting of a record head and a transcribe head in which the endless loop is contained.

Tapes. A form of discrete media.

Task lighting. Lighting that is provided for the worker to perform a specific task. It is usually built into the furniture.

Task lists. Forms that allow the secretaries to indicate their work categories and estimate the amount of time spent on each task.

Telecommunications. The electronic method of moving information. Information is communicated or sent over telephone lines.

Teleconferencing. See *Video communications*.

Telecopier. Same as a facsimile unit.

Teletypewriter. A unit with a keyboard, printer, and a paper tape punch/reader that records information onto storage media. The information can be sent over telephone lines to another teletype in another location.

Teletypewriter exchange service. A public, switched service of Western Union in which suitable arranged teletypewriter stations are provided with lines to a central office for access to other such stations throughout the United States, Canada, and Mexico. Abbreviated: TWX.

Telex. A dial-up teleprinter service of Western Union comparable to TWX, but with separate rates and certain operating differences, that enables subscribers to communicate directly and temporarily among themselves, and also with TWX users throughout the United States, Canada, and Mexico.

Terminal. A keyboard and visual display screen, sometimes called a workstation; a point at which information can enter or leave a communication network. Also term used to describe an input/output device to send or receive source data to another terminal device over communications lines. A host CPU can be considered a terminal also at times, but usually terminals are considered as devices which communicate to a host CPU.

Text-editing typewriter. Plays back documents repetitively; allows documents to be edited by adding or deleting paragraphs and rearranging margins.

Text editor. A machine with the ability to store typewritten material; designed primarily for heavy revision work.

Text/data entry. The initial keyboarding of information.

Theory X. The assumption by managers that people are by nature lazy and work as little as possible, they lack ambition and will avoid responsibility, they are gullible and not very bright, and they like to be directed and controlled.

Theory Y. Assumptions by managers that work can be satisfying as work or play, people are not inherently passive but rather become that way through experiences in the organization, people want more responsibility, not less, and intellectual potential is only partially used and is widely distributed throughout the population.

Thin windows. One-line, partial-line CRT or gas plasma displays, giving the operator a window into memory.

Time ladder. A chart recording the exact time it takes to perform each activity.

Time line. A schedule of data collection activities that are to take place during the feasibility study.

Time-shared system. An organization that has sold a portion of its computer power to another organization to use.

Time-sharing. Many users may simultaneously gain direct access to a computer from a remote location for the purposes of word or data processing.

Traditional filing system. Records housed in a variety of storage equipment such as cabinets, suspension folder equipment, rotary files, and open shelf files.

Traditional leadership concept. Focuses on what a leader is rather than what a leader does; emphasis is on leader characteristics. See *Trait theory*.

Traditional secretary. A pre-word-processing secretary; one employed as a general-purpose servant to an executive, to handle his or her correspondence, phone calls, errands and other random tasks, in contrast with an administrative or correspondence secretary.

Traffic. In communications, the flow of data and controls over a telephone line or network.

Trait theory of leadership. Leaders were believed to have a set of personality characteristics (traits) which made them more qualified to motivate workers toward goals.

Transaction documents. Active correspondence with customers and suppliers.

Transcribe or transcription. Making a written copy of dictated or recorded matter in longhand or on a typewriter.

Transcription equipment. The equipment the transcriptionist uses when listening to the originator's dictation.

Transcriptionist. A person who types at a keyboard from dictated material.

Triple pitch. Allows switching from one type size and style to other type sizes and styles on the same piece of equipment.

TTY. Teletypewriter equipment.

Turnaround time. The time it takes to complete work on a document and return it to the originator.

Twin track printer. Two print wheels on the same printer that can simultaneously print two of the same or different type fonts.

TWX. A teletypewriter service provided by Western Union. Generally used to transmit brief messages; Western Union Teleprinter Exchange Service.

Type size. Point size.

Typebar. A device that transfers the image of characters onto paper; a conventional typewriter mechanism.

Typist's questionnaire. Questions that relate to actual typing that is done. It asks a typist for details such as the number of carbon copies requested, the correction techniques used, and the use of copiers in the process of keyboarding.

Unattended operation. The automatic feature of a station's operation that allows the transmission and receiving of data with no machine operator being at the machine.

Upgradeable. New features can be added to the equipment as they are developed instead of having to replace the old model with a new one.

User. A person who uses word processing or some type of information processing.

User's manual. The procedures that apply to the originator are included in the manual and the administrative and correspondence secretaries have their own.

Vertical career path. Paths that lead upward to managerial positions.

Video. To see people on a screen from a remote location by electronically communicating a picture.

Video communications. Sending pictures of people involved in telephone conversations electronically that appear on a screen in another location.

Video conferencing. A visual connect via telephone lines between two or more parties through a screen with audio capabilities.

Video display. See *Cathode ray tube.*

Visual display screen. Similar to a television screen.

Voice-actuated. Machines that can recognize and respond to spoken words.

Voiceband carriers. A channel used for transmission of voice or data; upgraded telephone lines which cannot send information faster than 10,000 bits per second.

Voice clipping. A problem that occurs in some recorders because it takes time for the recorder to speed up when it is initially activated. Some of the words might be omitted or clipped.

Voice data entry. Another term for entering information into a machine using the human voice.

Voice interaction system. The system responds to the caller's voice.

Voice line. A telephone line used primarily for sending and receiving voice; also called a voice carrier.

Voice message system. A way to provide callers with an alternative to speaking directly with the person they call.

Voice processing. A method of originating information using the human voice for an information processing system.

Voice recognition system. A system that recognizes and responds to a limited vocabulary of human speech.

Voice reminder system. A system that allows someone to make a recorded message that will serve as a reminder of appointments, meetings, and other scheduled activities.

VOR (Voice-operated relay). Prevents the tape from running when the originator is not speaking.

WATS. Wide area telephone service; a U.S. telephone company service that permits a customer to dial an unlimited number of calls in specific areas for a flat monthly charge.

White sound. Putting a degree of sound back into an area devoid of sound.

White-space skipping. A method of compressing information in order to speed up the transmission.

Whole task. Doing a job from beginning to end.

Wide area telecommunication service (WATS). Telephone service that permits toll-free service throughout the United States or in a designated area for one flat fee.

Wideband carriers. Cables, microwave frequencies, or satellites that transmit information (primarily data).

Winchester disk. A hard disk usually contained in a box-like unit that rotates or drives the disk on which millions of characters of information may be stored.

Windows. A visual display screen divided into one or more sections.

Word originator. See *Originator*.

Word processing. People making better use of a managed system of information through improved procedures and modern equipment.

Word/information processing. A term used to define an industry during the period of transition from word processing to information processing.

Word processing center. The centralized location in which word processing functions take place.

Word processing manager. Someone who is responsible for the overall operation of a word processing center.

Word processing operator. Someone having 6 to 24 months' word processing experience operating equipment.

Word processing specialist II/assistant supervisor. Someone who exercises all of the competencies of a word processing specialist I and may act as assistant supervisor.

Word processing specialist I. A word processing operator with a minimum amount of experience who can format, produce, and revise complicated documents.

Word processing supervisor. Someone who is responsible for the operation of a center (or section within a large center).

Word processing system. A managed system of handling equipment, procedures, and people.

Word processing trainee. Someone having little or no word processing experience who is trained on the job.

Word processing trainer. Someone with experience operating word processing systems who spends the majority of time training new operators.

Work group. A unit of personnel engaged in a specific function useful to, or necessary for, organizational operation. A work group may consist of an entire establishment, a department, or a section within a department, but it is always an entity unto itself. It may provide both decentralized administrative and correspondence support.

Work measurement. A process of determining how much time is required to do a given amount of work.

Work sampling. Observing the work habits of employees at various unannounced times.

Work specialization. The division of secretarial tasks.

Work station. A terminal that consists of a keyboard and a visual display screen.

Work-oriented. Emphasis is on producing great volumes of clerical kinds of work.

Workflow. The steps in the flow of information in the document cycle including origination, production, reproduction, filing, storage and retrieval, and distribution.

WP. Word processing.

WPM. Words per minute.

Writing in the margin. As corrections or instructions need to be made, the originator switches to another track for dictation.

Answers to Chapter Study Guide Questions

Chapter 1
Matching
 1. f
 2. c
 3. e
 4. d
 5. a
 6. b
 7. h
 8. g
Multiple choice
 9. c
10. b
11. a
12. b
13. d
Completion
14. people, procedures, equipment
15. input, processing, output, control, feedback
16. voice processing, word and data processing, reprographics, records processing, micrographics, telecommunications
17. origination, production, reproduction, filing and storage, distribution
18. administrative
True/False
19. +
20. +
21. +
22. +
23. 0
24. +

Chapter 2
Matching
 1. d
 2. f

 3. b
 4. e
 5. h
 6. c
 7. a
 8. i
 9. g
10. c
11. b
12. b
13. a
14. b
Completion
15. dedicated
16. media
17. discrete, endless loop
18. tank
19. odometer, index strip, electronic cueing device
20. inscribed
21. voice operated relay (VOR)
22. discrete
True/False
23. +
24. +
25. +
26. 0
27. 0

Chapter 3
Matching
 1. b
 2. d
 3. a
 4. c
 5. g
 6. i
 /. h
 8. f

9. e

Multiple choice

10. d
11. a
12. b
13. c
14. d

Completion

15. automatic tab grid
16. pagination and repagination
17. check the accuracy of a column of numbers
18. check the spelling of words
19. merging

True/False

20. 0
21. 0
22. +
23. 0
24. +

Chapter 4

Matching

1. g
2. a
3. h
4. f
5. d
6. e
7. i
8. c
9. b
10. b
11. b
12. c
13. b

True/False

14. 0
15. +
16. 0
17. +
18. 0
19. 0
20. +
21. +
22. 0
23. 0

Chapter 5

Matching

1. c
2. e
3. d
4. b
5. a
6. i
7. h
8. g
9. j
10. f
11. a
12. c
13. a
14. a,b,d
15. a

Completion

16. voice message systems, voice reminder systems, voice recognition systems, speech recognition systems
17. carbon, fluid, stencil, offset, phototypesetting
18. computer assisted transcription
19. moveable type, hot metal or linecasting, cold type/strike-on, phototypesetting
20. appearance, length of run, paper size, speed, copy cost

True/False

21. 0
22. 0
23. 0
24. 0
25. 0
26. 0
27. 0
28. +
29. 0
30. +

Chapter 6

Matching

1. e
2. g
3. i
4. j
5. a
6. f
7. d
8. c
9. h
10. b

Multiple choice

11. c
12. d
13. b
14. b
15. b

Completion

16. voice, data, graphic, video
17. voice band or voice lines
18. narrowband, voiceband, wideband
19. microprocessor or chip, laser, fiber optics, satellite
20. graphic communication

True/False

21. +
22. 0
23. +
24. +
25. +

Chapter 7

Matching

1. d
2. e
3. g
4. f
5. b
6. a
7. c

8. i
9. j
10. h
Multiple choice
11. c
12. c
13. d
14. b
15. a
Completion
16. mode of transmission, protocol, speed/baud rate, coding
17. enter, send, receive
18. carrier-based systems and public postal systems, private and public teletype, facsimile, communicating word/information processors, computer-based message systems
19. electronic distribution using telephone lines
20. Mailgrams and Stored Mailgrams
True/False
21. 0
22. 0
23. +
24. +
25. 0

Chapter 8
Matching
1. c
2. d
3. a
4. e
5. f
6. b
Multiple choice
7. c
8. b
9. c
10. d
11. c
12. a
13. a
True/False
14. +
15. +
16. 0
17. 0
18. 0
19. +
20. +
21. +
22. +
23. 0
24. 0
25. +
26. 0
27. 0

Chapter 9
Matching
1. b
2. a
3. d

4. e
5. c
6. f
Multiple choice
7. c
8. b
9. b
10. b.
11. b
12. d
Completion
13. routine, nonroutine
14. centralized, decentralized, hybrid
15. distributed
16. role, item, action
True/False
17. +
18. +
19. +
20. +
21. 0
22. 0
23. 0
24. 0
25. 0
26. +

Chapter 10
Matching
1. b
2. c
3. a
4. e
5. f
6. d
Multiple choice
7. a
8. a
9. b, c
10. a,b
11. b,d
12. d
Completion
13. large print video terminal
14. a sensing device
15. correspondence position
16. audio typing unit
True/False
17. 0
18. +
19. 0
20. 0
21. 0
22. 0
23. +
24. 0

Chapter 11
Matching
1. j
2. i
3. h
4. g
5. f
6. e

7. d
8. c
9. b
10. a
Multiple choice
11. c
12. e
13. b
14. d
15. d
Completion
16. supportive, theory Y
17. unsatisfied
18. self-fulfillment
19. higher
20. morale survey
21. X
22. flex time
True/False
23. 0
24. +
25. 0
26. 0
27. 0
28. 0
29. +
30. +

Index